Praise for *She Who Is*

"Elizabeth Johnson's study is simply superb. The clarity of her analyses and judicious yet imaginative use of language advance feminist theology to a new level of discussion. Every serious student of theology must read this brilliant work of scholarship and creativity."

—Anne Carr, Professor of Theology,
Divinity School, University of Chicago

"In this lucid, troubling, deeply consoling book, Elizabeth Johnson seeks a liberating language for women and men to use together in addressing the mystery of God. I cannot imagine a serious reader who will not learn here to think and act and, yes, pray in a new way."

—Leo J. O'Donovan, S.J., President,
Georgetown University

"*She Who Is* is a brilliant contribution to theology. With erudition, Elizabeth Johnson illumines a wide range of topics: the doctrine of God, trinitarian theology, Spirit Christology, women's experience, and feminist theology. Its clarity makes it an outstanding and indispensable introduction to many issues within contemporary theology and to the relation of feminist theology to classical theology."

—Francis Schüssler Fiorenza,
Stillman Professor of Catholic Theological Studies,
Divinity School, Harvard University

SHE
WHO
IS

SHE
WHO
IS

The
Mystery of
God in Feminist
Theological Discourse

Tenth Anniversary Edition

ELIZABETH A. JOHNSON

A Herder & Herder Book
The Crossroad Publishing Company
New York

This Printing: 2003

The Crossroad Publishing Company
481 Eighth Avenue, New York, NY 10001

Copyright © 1992, 2002 by Elizabeth A. Johnson

Printed in the United States of America

Library of Congress Cataloging-in-Publication Data

Johnson, Elizabeth A., 1941-
     She who is : the mystery of God in feminist theological
discourse / Elizabeth A. Johnson.
          p.   cm.
     Includes bibliographical references and index.
     ISBN 0-8245-1925-6
     1. Feminist theology.   2. Femininity of God.   3. Language and
languages — Religious aspects — Christianity.   I. Title.
BT83.55.J64   1992
231′.4 — dc20   92-4178

For my mother, Margaret V. Johnson
my grandmother, Agnes Donovan Reed
and my godmother, Barbara Curtis Reed
with love, delight, and gratitude

CONTENTS

Part I
BACKGROUND: SPEECH ABOUT GOD
AT THE INTERSECTION OF MIGHTY CONCERNS

ILLUSTRATIONS

PREFACE TO THE
TENTH ANNIVERSARY EDITION

The tenth anniversary of the original publication of *She Who Is: The Mystery of God in Feminist Theological Discourse* is cause for celebration as well as lament. On the positive side, this book with its case for speaking about the trinitarian God in female metaphors received a very warm welcome. Honored with the Grawemeyer Award in Religion among numerous other tributes, it has been translated into German, Portuguese (Brazil), Italian, French, and Korean, with publication in Spanish now in process. Its critical reception also includes dozens of favorable book reviews, discussion in seminars at professional theological meetings, student theses and dissertations, and ongoing citations in the work of other scholars. The book's popular reception is evident in the way a wide array of people took inspiration from its images to create musical songs and hymns, artistic paintings and drawings, and moving poetry and prayers honoring God in female metaphors. I have received and treasure sheaves of letters from people in the churches describing how reading it has changed their understanding of God and consequently increased their appreciation of the struggle for the human dignity of women.

On the negative side, the forces of reaction oppose these insights with an array of tools from ridicule and trivialization to patriarchal dictates about liturgical translations. This reaction bases its argument on a propositional notion of revelation that reads only certain male terms as proper language for God. Such a position does not float abstractly in the air. It criticizes the use of female imagery for the divine with an awareness that such enrichment of our language entails a political change in the status of women in church and society in the direction of equality and mutuality. The opposition makes clearer than ever the basic argument in *She Who Is* that the truth about God, the human dignity of women, and the transformation of institutional structures are profoundly interconnected. Regrettably, we still have a long way to go.

If we look at *She Who Is* in a global context, the past ten years give reason for hope. The Beijing Conference on Women, hosted by the United Nations in 1995 and attended by sponsored women's groups from every nation, placed the need for women's education, health care, and economic and political opportunity on the agenda of every government, although many honor their commitment in the breach. Facts on the ground, such as women in leadership positions in society and in ministries in the churches, join together with continued struggles in law, intellectual research, and other culture-shaping endeavors to inch women's equality forward. The voices of African American women resound nobly in literature; domestic violence becomes a public issue; the concept of the feminization of poverty becomes a tool of concerned analysis. The recent disastrous situation in Afghanistan shed an unexpected light when the UN insisted that women must be included in the post-civil war, post-Taliban government being created; all-male governance of the human world is no longer officially acceptable, even to men. At the same time, worldwide, the lives of the majority of women with their dependent children continue to be pressed down by poverty, violence, lack of voice, and patriarchal norms. We are so very far from God's will being done on earth as it is in heaven.

Hence my blessing on this tenth anniversary edition of *She Who Is*. Joining the work of so many other women and men who hunger and thirst for justice, let it go forth as part of the leaven that continues to raise spirits against the forces that crush life. Let its publication be a renewed opportunity for readers, their churches, and the societies they influence to slip off the burka of exclusively male language for the Holy One and revel in the fresh vision of the incomprehensible mystery of Love. Let its theological ideas and images inspire them to partner with Holy Wisdom herself in witnessing to women's dignity and resisting whatever thwarts its flourishing.

ELIZABETH JOHNSON

ACKNOWLEDGMENTS

It is a pleasure to thank the many people and institutions whose insights, criticism, and support helped me to write this book. The nucleus of this work took shape when the Atlantic School of Theology in Halifax, Canada, invited me to deliver the biannual Pollack Lectures on the subject of "Naming God"; I am grateful for this opportunity, and for the welcome response from faculty and students. Catholic University of America, Washington, District of Columbia, granted me the gift of time in the guise of a year's sabbatical leave, and monies from its Faculty Research Fund further supported my work. Much of the writing was done at Weston School of Theology, Cambridge, Massachusetts, where I resided as a Visiting Scholar; this was a hospitable place, and I am indebted to the faculty and staff for many personal and professional kindnesses.

Segments of this work in progress were presented to the Women's Theology Seminar of the Catholic Theological Society of America; to the Systematics Theology Group of the Washington Theological Consortium; and to several sessions of the Women's Theological Discussion Group in Washington, District of Columbia, a regularly meeting circle of scholarly friends including Jane Blewett, Cheryl Clemons, Mary Collins, Cynthia Crysdale, Catherine Dooley, Sarah Fahey, Rose Gorman, Mary Hines, Mary Irving, Helen John, Georgia Keightley, Margaret Kelleher, Jan Leibig, Patricia McDonald, Sally McReynolds, Patricia Parachini, Maria Reilly, and Catherine Vincie. Feedback on these occasions was invaluable and my thanks go to these colleagues who took the time to read and critique.

My special appreciation goes to Mary Catherine Hilkert for our neverending discussions on the issues at hand and her continuous intellectual probing; several chapters have benefitted from her careful reading. Similarly, I am deeply grateful to David Power, Sharon Parks, and Anthony Rubsys who read whole sections of this work in progress and gifted me with their telling questions and encouragement. William Hill, friend and colleague now seriously ill, enriched my thinking during many long conversations about Aquinas on God. Mary Ann Donovan and Walter Principe, scholars of early Christian theology, graciously offered pertinent suggestions from their field. I also benefitted from particular insights offered by my colleagues Charles Curran, Robin Darling, Robert Eno, and William Loewe. Outside the theological academy my sisters, Virginia Gerace, Margaret Bia, Kathleen Lombardo, Rosemary Johnson Hurzeler, and Susan Johnson, and my sister-in-law, Theresa Johnson, lent wisdom from their own experience to the chapter on God as Mother.

My research was greatly facilitated by Bruce Miller, librarian at Catholic University of America. Thanks also to Anders Tune, my graduate assistant at that university, for his careful work checking notes; and to Coleen Hoffman, my graduate assistant at Fordham University, for generous help in the final stages, especially preparing the index. With their expertise at the computer, Ron Brown in Washington and Roger Repohl in New York greatly assisted in producing the manuscript.

My great appreciation continues to my editor, Frank Oveis, whose sensitivity, good humor, and encouraging ways make the publishing process an excellent adventure in collaboration. Copy editor John Huckle gave the manuscript a reading marked by high critical intelligence, which I very much appreciate. My religious community, the Sisters of Saint Joseph of Brentwood, New York, has been a constant source of support and inspiration for my theological reflection and for this I am most grateful. Finally, this book is dedicated to my mother, godmother, and grandmother, three women whose different loves nurtured me as a human being and whose own goodness grounds my conviction that it is indeed right to speak about the mystery of God in female metaphor.

The lines from "Transcendental Etude" are reprinted from *The Fact of a Doorframe: Poems Selected and New, 1950–1984,* by Adrienne Rich, by permission of the author and W. W. Norton & Company, Inc. Copyright © 1984 by Adrienne Rich. Copyright © 1975, 1978 by W. W. Norton & Company, Inc. Copyright © 1981 by Adrienne Rich.

Grateful acknowledgement is given to the editors for permission to reprint material from my essays that originally appeared in these journals:

"The Incomprehensibility of God and the Image of God Male and Female," *Theological Studies* 45 (1984) 441–65.

"Jesus, The Wisdom of God: A Biblical Basis for Non-Androcentric Christology," *Ephemerides Theologicae Lovanienses* 61 (1985) 261–94.

PART I

BACKGROUND: SPEECH ABOUT GOD AT THE INTERSECTION OF MIGHTY CONCERNS

Chapter 1

INTRODUCTION:
TO SPEAK RIGHTLY OF GOD

Vision begins to happen in such a life
as if a woman quietly walked away
from the argument and jargon in a room
and sitting down in the kitchen, began turning in her lap
bits of yarn, calico and velvet scraps,
laying them out absently on the scrubbed boards
in the lamplight, with small rainbow-colored shells. . . .
Such a composition has nothing to do with eternity,
the striving for greatness, brilliance —
only with the musing of a mind
one with her body, experienced fingers quietly pushing
dark against bright, silk against roughness,
pulling the tenets of a life together
with no mere will to mastery,
only care. . . .

—Adrienne Rich[1]

A Crucial Question

A small vignette from the late fourth century reveals how fascinating the Christian people of that time found the question of right speech about God. In a culture imbued with Greek philosophical notions, debate raged over the question of whether Jesus Christ was truly divine or whether he was a creature subordinate to God the Father. Rather than being an esoteric issue confined to theologians or bishops, this discussion engaged the participation of a broad range of people. One famous remark by Gregory of Nyssa caught the situation precisely: "even the baker," he said, does not cease from discussing this, for if you ask the price of bread he will tell you that the Father is greater and the Son subject to him.[2]

What is the right way to speak about God? This is a question of unsurpassed importance, for speech to and about the mystery that surrounds

3

human lives and the universe itself is a key activity of a community of faith. In that speech the symbol of God functions as the primary symbol of the whole religious system, the ultimate point of reference for understanding experience, life, and the world. Hence the way in which a faith community shapes language about God implicitly represents what it takes to be the highest good, the profoundest truth, the most appealing beauty. Such speaking, in turn, powerfully molds the corporate identity of the community and directs its praxis. A religion, for example, that would speak about a warlike god and extol the way he smashes his enemies to bits would promote aggressive group behavior. A community that would acclaim God as an arbitrary tyrant would inspire its members to acts of impatience and disrespect toward their fellow creatures. On the other hand, speech about a beneficent and loving God who forgives offenses would turn the faith community toward care for the neighbor and mutual forgiveness.[3]

Speech about God shapes the life orientation not only of the corporate faith community but in this matrix guides its individual members as well. God is that on which you lean your heart, that on which your heart depends, "that to which your heart clings and entrusts itself," in Martin Luther's memorable phrase.[4] As the focus of absolute trust, one to whom you can give yourself without fear of betrayal, the holy mystery of God undergirds and implicitly gives direction to all of a believing person's enterprises, principles, choices, system of values, and relationships. The symbol of God functions. Neither abstract in content nor neutral in its effect, speaking about God sums up, unifies, and expresses a faith community's sense of ultimate mystery, the world view and expectation of order devolving from this, and the concomitant orientation of human life and devotion. No wonder that even the baker joined in the debate over the right way to speak about God.

In our day interest in right speech about God is exceptionally alive in a new way thanks to the discourse of a sizable company of bakers, women who historically have borne primary responsibility for lighting the cooking fires and feeding the world. The women's movement in civil society and the church has shed a bright light on the pervasive exclusion of women from the realm of public symbol formation and decision making, and women's consequent, strongly enforced subordination to the imagination and needs of a world designed chiefly by men. In the church this exclusion has been effective virtually everywhere: in ecclesial creeds, doctrines, prayers, theological systems, liturgical worship, patterns of spirituality, visions of mission, church order, leadership and discipline.[5] It has been stunningly effective in speech about God. While officially it is rightly and consistently said that God is spirit and so beyond identification with either male or female sex, yet the daily language of preaching, worship, catechesis, and instruction conveys a different message: God is male, or at least more like a man than a woman, or at least more fittingly addressed as male than as female. The symbol of God functions. Upon examination it becomes clear that this exclusive speech about God serves in manifold ways to support an imaginative and structural world that excludes or subordinates women. Wittingly or not, it undermines women's human dignity as equally created in the image of God.

Gradually or abruptly, peacefully or in anger, happily or with great anguish, quietly like the woman in Adrienne Rich's poem that heads this introduction or shouting from the city walls like Sophia in the Book of Proverbs (8:1–3), myriads of women and a number of men are turning from the restrictive inheritance of exclusive God-talk. For some, the journey involves a sojourn in darkness and silence, traversing a desert of the spirit created by the loss of accustomed symbols.[6] For others, new language is born as women gather together creatively in solidarity and prayer, and as sister scholars uncover alternative ways of speaking about divine mystery that have long been hidden in Scripture and tradition.[7] In this matrix feminist theologians, engaging in the traditional theological task of reflecting on God and all things in the light of God, are shaping new speech about God that, in Rebecca Chopp's memorable phrase, are discourses of emancipatory transformation, pointing to new ways of living together with each other and the earth.[8] Respectful of their own equal human dignity, conscious of the harm being done by the manifold forms of sexism, and attentive to their own experiences of suffering, power, and agency, these women are engaged in creative "naming toward God," as Mary Daly so carefully calls it, from the matrix of their own experience.[9] This is not an intellectual endeavor only, although it is certainly that, but a movement with roots deep in the human spirit. Women, long considered less than adequate as human persons, claim themselves as active subjects of history and name toward God out of this emerging identity, to practical and critical effect.

What is the right way to speak about God? The presenting issue in debates about inclusive language is ostensibly whether the reality of women can provide suitable metaphor for speech about God. The intensity with which the question is engaged from the local to the international level, however, makes clear that more is at stake than simply naming toward God with women-identified words such as mother. The symbol of God functions. Language about God in female images not only challenges the literal mindedness that has clung to male images in inherited God-talk; it not only questions their dominance in discourse about holy mystery. But insofar as "the symbol gives rise to thought,"[10] such speech calls into question prevailing structures of patriarchy. It gives rise to a different vision of community, one in which the last shall be first, the excluded shall be included, the mighty put down from their thrones and the humbled exalted — the words of Mary of Nazareth's song of praise (Lk 1:52), creating conditions for the formation of community characterized by relationships of mutuality and reciprocity, of love and justice. Introducing this mode of speech signals a shift, among those who use it, in their sense of the divine, a shift in total world view, in highest ideals and values, in personal and corporate identity. Such usage is urged upon the whole faith community in the conviction that it bears a fruitful and blessed promise. What is the right way to speak about God in the face of women's newly cherished human dignity and equality? This is a crucial theological question. What is at stake is the truth about God, inseparable from the situation of human beings, and the identity and mission of the faith community itself.

Context: Mystery Mediated in History

The unfathomable mystery of God is always mediated through shifting historical discourse. As the vignette about the baker from the fourth century makes clear, language about God has a history. Tracing these changes both in the scriptural period and throughout subsequent history makes clear that there has been no timeless speech about God in the Jewish or Christian tradition. Rather, words about God are cultural creatures, entwined with the mores and adventures of the faith community that uses them. As cultures shift, so too does the specificity of God-talk.

In one of those myriad interesting little discussions that Aquinas carries on in the formal framework of the *quaestio*, he deals luminously with the legitimacy of this historical development. The question at hand is whether it is proper to refer to God as "person." Some would object that this word is not used of God in the Scriptures, neither in the Old Testament nor in the New. But, goes his argument, what the word signifies such as intelligence is in fact frequently applied to God in Scripture, and so "person" can be used with confidence. Furthermore, he muses, if our speech about God were limited to the very terms of Scripture itself, then no one could speak about God except in the original languages of Hebrew and Greek! Broadening the argument, Aquinas defends the use of extra-biblical language about God on grounds of historical need: "The urgency of confuting heretics made it necessary to find new words to express the ancient faith about God." In conclusion he clinches the argument with an exhortation to appreciate this new language: "Nor is such a kind of novelty to be shunned; since it is by no means profane, for it does not lead us astray from the sense of scripture."[11]

The wisdom carried in this argument supports in striking fashion patterns of speaking about the mystery of God that are emerging from the perspective of women's experiences. It is not necessary to restrict speech about God to the exact names that Scripture uses, nor to terms coined by the later tradition. So long as the words signify something that does characterize the living God mediated through Scripture, tradition, and present faith experience, for example, divine liberating action or self-involving love for the world, then new language can be used with confidence. Moreover, the urgency of confuting sexism, so dangerous to women's lives in the concrete, makes it imperative to find more adequate ways of expressing the ancient good news that faith is to proclaim. Nor is such novelty to be shunned for it does not lead astray from the sense of Scripture — if, that is, the sense of Scripture means the promise of God's creative, compassionate, liberating care bent on the whole world, including women in all our historicity and difference. The present ferment about naming, imaging, and conceptualizing God from perspectives of women's experience repristinates the truth that the idea of God, incomprehensible mystery, implies an open-ended history of understanding that is not yet finished.

The historical open-endedness of talk about God is due not only to its location in time, place, and culture, which is the case with all human speech, but to the very nature of what we are talking about. The reality of God is mystery beyond all imagining. So transcendent, so immanent is the holy mystery of God that we can never wrap our minds completely around this mystery and exhaust divine reality in words or concepts. The history of theology is replete with this truth: recall Augustine's insight that if we have understood, then what we have understood is not God; Anselm's argument that God is that than which nothing greater can be conceived; Hildegaard's vision of God's glory as Living Light that blinded her sight; Aquinas's working rule that we can know that God is and what God is not, but not what God is; Luther's stress on the hiddenness of God's glory in the shame of the cross; Simone Weil's conviction that there is nothing that resembles what she can conceive of when she says the word God; Sallie McFague's insistence on imaginative leaps into metaphor since no language about God is adequate and all of it is improper.[12] It is a matter of the livingness of God. Given the inexhaustible mystery inherent in what the word God points to, historically new attempts at articulation are to be expected and even welcomed. If the concept of God confesses the infinity and the incomprehensibility of holy mystery, then, as Karl Rahner argues, "it actually postulates thereby a history of our own concept of God that can never be concluded."[13]

In what now reads like unwitting prophecy, the Second Vatican Council spoke of this dynamic of divine mystery mediated in history by using the organic metaphor of growth:

For there is a growth in the understanding of the realities and the words which have been handed down. This happens through the contemplation and study made by believers who treasure these things in their hearts (Lk 2:19, 51), through the intimate understanding of spiritual things they experience.[14]

What the council did not envision but what is clearly happening today is that this dynamism is operative among believers who are women. Women are newly contemplating and studying things they have treasured and, through the intimate understanding of spiritual things they experience, are effecting a growth in the understanding of the realities and words that have been handed down. In faith and struggle women are growing the church into a new moment of the living tradition. As Anne Carr has so eloquently put it, the women's movement comes as a transforming grace for the whole church although, terrifyingly, grace may always be refused.[15]

Purpose: Connecting Feminist and Classical Wisdom

My aim in what follows is to speak a good word about the mystery of God recognizable within the contours of Christian faith that will serve the emancipatory praxis of women and men, to the benefit of all creation, both human beings and the earth. In so doing I draw on the new language of Christian feminist theology as well as on the traditional language of Scripture and classical theology, all of which codify religious insights.

By Christian feminist theology I mean a reflection on God and all things in the light of God that stands consciously in the company of all the world's women, explicitly prizing their genuine humanity while uncovering and criticizing its persistent violation in sexism, itself an omnipresent paradigm of unjust relationships.[16] In terms of Christian doctrine, this perspective claims the fullness of the religious heritage for women precisely as human, in their own right and independent from personal identification with men. Women are equally created in the image and likeness of God, equally redeemed by Christ, equally sanctified by the Holy Spirit; women are equally involved in the ongoing tragedy of sin and the mystery of grace, equally called to mission in this world, equally destined for life with God in glory.

Feminist theology explicitly recognizes that the contradiction between this theological identity of women and the historical condition of women in theory and practice is glaring. This leads to the clear judgment that sexism is sinful, that it is contrary to God's intent, that it is a precise and pervasive breaking of the basic commandment "Thou shalt love thy neighbor as thyself" (Lv 19:18; Mt 22:39). It affronts God by defacing the beloved creature created in the image of God. Faced with this sinfulness, church and society are called to repent, to turn around, to sin no more, to be converted.[17] Corresponding to this theological stance, feminist theology advocates the reform of patriarchal civil and ecclesial structures and the intellectual systems that support them in order to release all human beings for more just designs of living with each other and the earth. Far from being a theology done for women alone, it calls to strengths in women and men alike who care for justice and truth, seeking a transformation of the whole community.

By classical theology I mean the body of thought that arose in early Christian centuries in partnership with the Greek philosophical tradition and continued through the medieval period, molding the discourse of the churches at the beginning of the modern era. This tradition continues to shape contemporary language about God, both explicitly and implicitly, whether accepted or rejected, in popular and intellectual circles, particularly in its language about the Supreme Being, divine attributes, and trinitarian persons.

The feminist perspective, which honors women's humanity, women as *imago Dei*, finds this classical tradition profoundly ambiguous in what it has meant for female well-being. It has aided and abetted the exclusion and subordination of women, but also sustained generations of foremothers and foresisters in the faith. Along with the need for criticism of classical thought, my own inclination leads me in addition to give it a hearing, listening for wisdom that may yet prove useful. My approach is somewhat analogous to interreligious dialogue: after centuries of suspicion the Second Vatican Council set free in the Catholic church a hospitable spirit toward the world religions, affirming that whatever is true and holy in them reflects a ray of divine light.[18] Formed in that spirit, I find it coming home to roost in the attempt to see that whatever is true and holy in classical theology may also reflect a ray of divine light.

Taking a cue from feminist methodologies in related fields, I ask whether, when read with a feminist hermeneutic, there is anything in the classical tradition in all of its vastness that could serve a discourse about divine mystery that would further the emancipation of women. The answer, I think to have found, is in the affirmative. Treatises on the

Spirit, on incarnation, on creation, on Trinity, and on the one God who is overflowing source of life can release fragments of wisdom and fruitful possibilities when read with an eye to this challenge. The project afoot here probes inherited discourse and seeks its scattered rays of truth, hoping to accomplish a critical retrieval in the light of women's coequal humanity. Of necessity the probe is highly selective, and makes no pretense of adequately surveying the wealth of classical positions. What is chosen, however, may be suggestive of further critical retrievals that are possible.

This project is fraught with complexity. Not only is the referent of the word God utterly incomprehensible, the fathomless mystery that surrounds the burning mystery of our own lives, so that it is impossible to do justice to the subject. Not only are Scripture and tradition historically ambiguous monuments to patriarchy's view of its own rightness, so that the contribution of the Christian heritage cannot be simply presumed or easily retrieved while at the same time it continues to be a source of life for millions. But women's interpreted experience is as diverse as concrete women themselves so that "the" perspective of women is not a unity nor immediately to hand. In fact, sensitivity to difference is an intellectual virtue being positively celebrated by feminist thought in resistance to centuries of univocal definition of "woman's nature." The diversity, cultural, interracial, and ecumenical, is consciously prized as a condition for connectedness, for women have the insight born in pain that a monolithic position inevitably works to the disadvantage of somebody, usually the most powerless. Hence new religious insights are being articulated by women on different continents, in North America and Europe obviously,[19] but also in Latin America, Asia, and Africa.[20] In the United States women of distinct racial and cultural identities expound religious wisdom in voices that criticize the dominance and racism of white liberal feminism while seeking constructive ways to theologize from Hispanic[21] or African American perspectives.[22] Even within North American feminist theology done by white, economically advantaged women, diversity abounds. Various typologies have been suggested to order the field, such as the distinction between revolutionary or goddess feminism, which seeks religious meaning beyond the dominant religious traditions of the West, and reformist feminism, which aims to correct these inherited traditions.[23] New readings of the tradition are offered by women belonging to different branches of the Jewish and Christian traditions.[24] Women of diverse sexual orientations and family relations clarify the meaning of faith from their own life vantage points.[25] Questions, clarifications, and new visions are heard from women of various economic and social classes.[26]

The ecumenical, interracial, and international spectrum of women's theological voices ensures that the ways of speaking about God are many. Within this symphony of voices, sharply discordant at times, my own stance is inevitably shaped by my social location as a white, middle-class, educated and hence privileged citizen of a wealthy North American country. It is further specified by my intellectual formation and participation in the Catholic community, augmented by vast instruction gained from the ecumenical conversation of present-day Christian theology and the even wider discourse of feminism. Concomitantly, my American provincial innocence has been lost due to travels and study in the Middle East and Asia, and as a result of teaching in Africa and Central America. It is especially the months of teaching in South Africa under the state of emergency, giving lectures that turned into sessions of mutual grappling with the meaning and praxis of faith in situations of massive suffering due to injustice, poverty, and violence, that have honed for me the feminist theological paradigm into liberation contours and given it a global intent.[27]

Hence, amid the diverse streams of feminist theology that currently offer live intellectual options, and valuing the contributions made by each, my own stance is within the liberation stream of Catholic Christian feminist theology.[28] In my judgment this way of thinking makes an incisive analysis of the problem, offers an inclusive vision, and holds out a practical promise for future advance within my religious tradition. References to feminist theology in what follows may be taken to refer to this particular approach. For me the goal of feminist religious discourse pivots in its fullness around the flourishing of poor women of color in violent situations. Not incidentally, securing the well-being of these socially least of women would entail a new configuration of theory and praxis and the genuine transformation of all societies, including the churches, to open up more humane ways of living for all people, with each other and the earth. The rising of the women is the rising of the race — precisely because women with their network of relationships are at the lowest ebb, marginalized, and yet sustaining every society. The incoming tide lifts all the boats in the harbor. Only when the poorest, black, raped, and brutalized women in a South African township — the epitome of victims of sexism, racism, and classism, and at the same time startling examples of women's resiliency, courage, love, and dignity — when such women with their dependent children and their sisters around the world may live peacefully in the enjoyment of their human dignity, only then will feminist theology arrive at its goal. At that point it can retire from its liberation mode with a good conscience, although other forms of religious discourse from the perspective of women will, I trust, continue to emerge.

From this position, this book explores one way of speaking about one core religious symbol, which itself is but one among many needed theological and thealogical labors. It is "one more county heard from," which at the same time delights in other ways and finds them variously valid and helpful.

Feminist artisans and poets have been designing evocative metaphors for the creative work women do. Spinning, weaving, and quilting, all taken from women's domestic chores, provide an evocative description of scholarship as it seeks to articulate new patterns from bits of contemporary experiences and ancient sources.[29] In the spirit of these metaphors, this exploration attempts to braid a footbridge between the ledges of classical and feminist Christian wisdom. Throwing a hermeneutical span from side to side may enable some to cross over to the paradigm of women's coequal humanity without leaving behind all the riches of the tradition that has been their intellectual and spiritual home. It may demonstrate how much we can pack and take with us on the journey. It may also feed the hunger of others, especially women, already crossed over for whom the tradition had become a land of famine instead of a land of plenty. In yet another metaphor depicted in Adrienne Rich's poem that opens this chapter, this study quietly pushes bits of insight from classical theology here and there in the effort to pull the tenets of a Christian feminist discourse together.

Rendering insights into systematic speech about God may be premature, for the experiences of women continue to grow, generating an ever-expanding naming. We are still at the stage of building, finding, forming, thinking, and feeling our way ahead. No doubt too, the design of theological systems and their contents will change with continued feminist discourse. The very concept of a system may be too restrictive. At this point, however, enough has broken through, been struggled with, prayed over, celebrated, and been articulated by astute thinkers and artists with and without academic credentials that this present schema may serve as one way of consolidating gains while preparing for further advance. Susan Sontag has said somewhere that there are ways of thinking we don't yet know about. There are ways of speaking about God that we don't yet know about. In both what it says and does not say this book is testimony to that truth. My hope is that the path ventured upon here will be suggestive of lines of thought and action that proceed deeper into justice toward women and right speaking about God, which are inseparable.

Plan

Given the relative newness of the horizon of understanding within which this study is working, Part I provides context and background for the speech about God which follows. This first chapter broadly introduces the issue; chapter two limns the standpoint and challenge of feminist theology; chapter three lays out specific options that I have taken regarding Christian feminist speech about God. The reader who is familiar with the ways of feminist theology may prefer to skip these chapters and go more directly to the heart of the matter. Part II gathers assets from women's articulated experiences, from Scripture, and from classical theology, which can serve as resources for an emancipatory pattern of speech about God. Using these resources, Part III explores a theology of God starting out from below, beginning with the vivifying and renewing Spirit as God's presence in the world and then exploring in succession speech about each of the "persons" of God's Trinity. Throughout this section we test the capacity of female images to bear and disclose what Christian truth testifies to as the blessed action of God in the world, and call upon the language of classical theology to give these images density. In Part IV female symbols, found to be indeed *capax Dei*, are traced as they give rise to thought. Discourses about God's Trinity, living being, and relation to the suffering world are searched for their emancipatory potential.

In the end this exploration points toward God with the coinage SHE WHO IS, a divine title signifying the creative, relational power of being who enlivens, suffers with, sustains, and enfolds the universe. SHE WHO IS points to holy mystery beyond all imagining who creates women as well as men to be *imago Dei*, the grammar of God's self-utterance and participants in her liberating care for this conflictual world and all its creatures.

Scotosis vs. the Glory of God

Speaking of the blessing that feminist theological discourse is for the church, Mary Collins notes, "One of the best gifts for the critical mind and for a living tradition is the gift of a new question."[30] Not everyone sees it this way, however. It is not uncommon for those whose certitudes and securities may be threatened by women's emerging theological speech to relegate it to the periphery of importance. Such a hardening of the mind against unwanted wisdom can be called a scotosis and the resulting blind spot a scotoma, in Bernard Lonergan's pointed terminology.[31] Scotosis results when the intellectual censorship function, which usually operates in a good and constructive manner to select elements to give us insight, goes awry. In aberrant fashion this censorship function works to repress new questions in order to prevent the emergence of unwanted insight. This happens not only to an individual in isolation but more especially to communities as a whole. Within a given community, different clusters of people are implicitly defined by patterns of relationship to each other. Any particular group is prone to have a blind spot for insight that would reveal its well-being to be excessive or founded on distorted assumptions. The powerful tendency of such group bias is to exclude some fruitful ideas and to mutilate others by compromise. Scotosis is present when group interest limits intelligence. Relegating the theological question of God-talk in relation to women's flourishing to the periphery of serious consideration in academy, church, and society is an instance of this phenomenon. It is the refusal of insight as a function of group bias. The only remedy is conversion.

The investigation undertaken here into inclusive discourse about God proceeds, by contrast, from the basic theological assumption that right speech about God is inseparable from solicitude for all creatures, and in particular for human beings in the rightness of their personal, interpersonal, social, and ecological relations. This insight is crystallized in Irenaeus's axiom *Gloria Dei vivens homo:* the glory of God is *homo*, the human being, the whole human race, every individual person, fully alive.[32] Because God is the creator, redeemer, lover of the world, God's own honor is at stake in human happiness. Wherever human beings are violated, diminished, or have their life drained away, God's glory is dimmed and dishonored. Wherever human beings are quickened to fuller and richer life, God's glory is enhanced. A community of justice and peace (thriving among human beings) and God's glory increase in direct and not inverse proportion.

Given the destructive power of evil and the anguish of radical suffering, both the mystery of God's glory and human flourishing are terrifyingly at risk in history. The truth about God is twisted to justify human oppression, and companion creatures are demeaned in the name of a distorted view of divine will. "By deforming God we protect our own egotism," Juan Luis Segundo contends. "Our falsified and inauthentic ways of dealing with our fellow men are allied to our falsification of the idea of God. Our unjust society and our perverted idea of God are in close and terrible alliance."[33] *Gloria Dei vivens homo:* the historically mutual jeopardy of divine honor and creaturely thriving gives to this well-loved aphorism the protesting character of hope against hope.

If the glory of God, by God's own free design, is at stake in human flourishing and the well-being of the whole world, then it is legitimate to press the ancient maxim to a critical, concrete focus, bringing to light the female reality included in the Latin *homo*. We can say, *Gloria Dei vivens mulier:* the glory of God is woman, all women, every woman everywhere, fully alive. Wherever women are violated, diminished, have their life drained away, God's glory is dimmed and put at historical risk: hence sexism is religiously unconscionable. Conversely, fragmentary experiences of women's flourishing anticipate that new heaven and new earth where the glory of God will be unfathomably justified. A community of justice and peace, including women's flourishing, and God's glory increase in direct and not inverse proportion.

Inherited Christian speech about God has developed within a framework that does not prize the unique and equal humanity of women, and bears the marks of this partiality and dominance. This language is now under fire both for its complicity in human oppression and its capacity to rob divine reality of goodness and profound mystery. Christian feminist emancipatory discourse aims at empowering women in their struggle to make their own humanity as *imago Dei* historically tangible, and thereby to secure a foothold for the glory of God in history. Given the interlocking of oppressions in the world, that is, the connivance of sexism with racism, classism, militarism, humanocentrism, and other forms of prejudice, this effort at renewed speech about God is vitally significant for the church and the world in all of their constitutive dimensions.

•

The intellectual vitality of the feminist theological agenda is matched and even outpaced by its existential importance. What is at stake is simultaneously the freeing of both women and men from debilitating reality models and social roles, the birthing of new forms of saving relationship to all of creation, and indeed the very viability of the Christian tradition for present and coming generations. Are the religions of the Book up to the challenge? According to Wolfhart Pannenberg's penetrating analysis of the dynamics of the history of religions, religions die when their light fails, that is, when they lose the power to interpret convincingly the full range of present experience in the light of their idea of God.[34] If God is worshiped as the guiding reality, the source and goal of all, then the truth is tested by the extent to which the idea of God currently available takes account of accessible reality and integrates the complexity of present experience into itself. If the idea of God does not keep pace with developing reality, the power of experience pulls people on and the god dies, fading from memory. Is the God of the Jewish and

Christian tradition so true as to be able to take account of, illumine, and integrate the currently accessible experience of women? This is an absolutely critical theological question. Borrowing a page from Gregory of Nyssa who did his own share of pondering the holy mystery, I think that "We must, therefore, make our reply at greater length, tracking down the truth as best we can, for the question is no ordinary one."[35]

Chapter 2

FEMINIST THEOLOGY
AND CRITICAL DISCOURSE
ABOUT GOD

I know that it feels a kind o' hissin and ticklin' like to see a colored woman get up and tell you about things, and Woman's Rights. We have all been thrown down so low that nobody thought we'd ever get up again; but we have been long enough trodden now; we will come up again, and now I am here.

— Sojourner Truth[1]

The Lens of Women's Flourishing

For at least a thousand years Christian theology has understood itself as the endeavor of *fides querens intellectum*, faith seeking understanding, or searching for a deeper discernment of the meaning of the gospel and its interpretive confessions, and concomitantly, looking for deeper understanding of human life and the whole universe in the light of the graciousness of divine mystery. Recent political and liberation theologies have emphasized that faith's quest for understanding must be rooted in the seed-bed of practice and must lead in turn to salvation in the concrete, a position summed up in the quip that we need to adopt that legendary Noah Principle: no more prizes for predicting rain; prizes only for building arks. In both classical and liberation instances, theology is commonly a discipline of speaking which moves back and forth, spiraling around life and faith within the cultural context of a given time and place.

Christian feminist liberation theology is reflection on religious mystery from a stance which makes an a priori option for the human flourishing of women. Making a fundamental option as such is not unique to feminist theology. Every theological reflection has a center of gravity that unifies, organizes, and directs its attention. Roger Haight describes it well:

A focus for a theology then is the dominant interest, passion and concern, the unifying theme, that holds the whole of it together as a coherent vision.... Like the lens that draws rays of light to a center, but without blocking any of their light, so too a centering concern of a theology should organize and unify theological data thematically, but without negating the legitimate concerns represented by other and lesser problems.[2]

The lens of women's flourishing focuses faith's search for understanding in feminist theology. It does so in the context of myriad sufferings resulting from women's being demeaned in theory and practice in contradiction to the creative power, dignity, and goodness that women appreciate to be intrinsic to their own human identity. When this suffering is brought to consciousness, when its causes are analyzed, when dangerous and therefore suppressed memories of women's agency are brought to light, and the praxis of resistance and hope are begun, then conditions exist for a new interpretation of the tradition. Feminist theology results when women's faith seeks understanding in the matrix of historical struggle for life in the face of oppressive and alienating forces.

Theology done from this perspective presses a strong critique against traditional speech about God. It judges it to be both humanly oppressive and religiously idolatrous. Oppressive: by drawing imagery and concepts for God almost exclusively from the world of ruling men, inherited speech functions effectively to legitimate structures and theories that grant a theomorphic character to men who rule but that relegate women, children, and other men to the deficient margins. Whether consciously or not, sexist God language undermines the human equality of women made in the divine image and likeness. The result is broken community, human beings shaped by patterns of dominance and subordination with attendant violence and suffering. Idolatrous: insofar as male-dominant language is honored as the only or the supremely fitting way of speaking about God, it absolutizes a single set of metaphors and obscures the height and depth and length and breadth of divine mystery. Thus it does damage to the very truth of God that theology is supposed to cherish and promote.

A superficial notion of this critique judges it to be narrowly concerned with what is bemusedly labeled "a women's issue." The issue of the right way to speak about God, however, is central to the whole faith tradition, nor does its pivotal role diminish because the speakers are coming anew into their own voice. The charges of oppression and idolatry cannot be so lightly dismissed. What is ultimately at stake in this question is profoundly substantive, being simultaneously the quest for a more just and peaceful order among human beings and the truth, however darkly glimpsed, of the holy mystery of God. Nor can the two be separated.

Feminist theology's critique of traditional God language enters the history of theology at a critical juncture. Under the impact of modernity and postmodernity for the last two centuries, Christian speech about God has suffered a series of shocks that have rendered it more and more problematic. In response, theology has been generating new language by a creative combination of hermeneutical retrieval of ancient texts and appropriation of contemporary experience. Women's search for less inadequate ways of speaking about God today intersects with other theological efforts to rethink the inherited doctrine of God, which itself has already been in a crisis of reformulation for some time.

Speech about God at the Intersection of Mighty Concerns

Classical Theism

It has not been just any concept of God that has come under particular and sustained fire since the beginning of the modern era, but that configuration of elements identified by the term philosophical or classical *theism*. In a general sense the term theism refers to the concept of God developed by medieval and early modern theology in close contact with classical metaphysics. It signifies the understanding that there is God (contrary to atheism), that God is one (contrary to polytheism), and that the one God is not to be identified with the world (contrary to pantheism). As it developed in the course of medieval reflection and especially as it was systematized in both Protestant and Catholic theology done in the rational spirit of the Enlightenment, theism takes on a precise coloring. It signifies the so-called natural knowledge of God arrived at primarily through philosophical inference, or that idea of God which separates the one God from knowledge of God's Trinity, places consideration of this one God first, and views this God alone in "himself" apart from any *kenōsis*, incarnation, self-communication in grace, or other self-involving activity with the world.

Theism in this specific sense views God as the Supreme Being who made all things and who rules all things. Although architect and governor of the world, it is essential to God's deity that "he" (the theistic God is always referred to in male terms) be essentially unrelated to this world and unaffected by what happens in it so as to remain independent from it. This view therefore excels at stressing divine transcendence, although divine immanence tends to slip from view. The perfections of the theistic God are developed in contrast to the finitude of creatures, leading to speech about God the creator who is "infinite, self-existent, incorporeal, eternal, immutable, impassible, simple, perfect, omniscient, and omnipotent," in the descriptive list drawn up by H. P. Owen.[3]

The theistic God is modeled on the pattern of an earthly absolute monarch, a metaphor so prevalent that most often it is simply taken for granted. As a king rules over his subjects, so God the Lord has dominion over his creatures, a view which, in Sallie McFague's analysis, is intrinsically hierarchical whether the divine reign be accomplished through dominance or benevolence.[4] Theoretically, theism adheres to the assertion that the mystery of God is beyond all images and conceptualizations. Yet the history of theology shows how in practice theism has reified God, reducing infinite mystery to an independently existing Supreme Being alongside other beings, a solitary, transcendent power who together with the world can be thought to form a larger whole. In Herbert Vorgrimler's summary, partially borrowed from the seventeenth-century thinker who first coined this word, theism is a "conviction of the existence of an absolute, world-transcendent, personal God, who made the world from nothing and permanently sustains it, and who enjoys all those attributes of infinity, almighty power, perfection and so on, about which there was unanimity in Judaism, Christendom and Islam from the Middle Ages onward."[5]

Theism's Demise

With the slow but inexorable breakup of the classical and neoclassical world, theism has found critics on many fronts. Nineteenth- and twentieth-century forms of atheism repudiate it as an alienating projection of human consciousness, an opium that deadens the pain of social and economic oppression, an illusion motivated by wish-fulfillment, or a hypothesis unnecessary for scientific investigation.[6] Protest against the occurrence of radical suffering in history, particularly of the innocent, also leads thinkers to reject the theistic God. A God who could put an end to such misery but instead "allows" it for whatever reason appears morally intolerable.[7] As the voices of the poor and violently suppressed come to speech, the theistic idea of God is criticized for its supposed neutrality, so easily weighted toward a divine mandate for passivity, obedience, and submission and so often co-opted to sustain unjust civil and ecclesiastical rule.[8] Interreligious dialogue with the living traditions of the East raises the question of the naive anthropomorphism associated with much of the language about the theistic God and, by making known the paths of Eastern mysticism, offers a profound corrective.[9]

Heidegger's judgment on the end product of classical theism now echoes from thinkers of diverse theological perspectives: "Man can neither pray nor sacrifice to this god. Before the *causa sui*, man can neither fall to his knees in awe nor can he play music and dance before this god."[10] Walter Kasper even speaks of "the heresy of theism," meaning the nontrinitarian notion of a unipersonal God who stands over against the world as imperial ruler and judge.[11] In response to the insufficiencies of classical theism, a goodly number of theologians have been seeking other ways of speaking about God. These theological efforts are leading to discourse about, in Anne Carr's felicitous summary, the liberating God, the incarnational God, the relational God, the suffering God, the God who is future, and the unknown, hidden God of mystery.[12] So profound are these changes and deviations from the classical approach that it is not uncommon for theologians engaged in their development to proclaim that a "revolution" in the idea of God is occurring in our day.[13]

Intersection

It is at this historical juncture where speech about God is being re-shaped to include intrinsic relatedness to the world, alliance with human flourishing, liberating care for the poor, and greater mystery that feminist theology joins the theological effort, intersecting with these other concerns at every point. At the same time, feminist theology's fresh language about the mystery of God from the perspective of women's lives and its specific critique of the sexism not only of the classical tradition but also of most reconstructive efforts to date bring a care into the conversation that has not been spoken until now.

Classical theism emphasizes in a one-sided way the absolute transcendence of God over the world, God's untouchability by human history and suffering, and the all-pervasiveness of God's dominating power to which human beings owe submission and awe. Is this idea of God not the reflection of patriarchal imagination, which prizes nothing more than unopposed power-over and unquestioned loyalty? Is not the transcendent, omnipotent, impassible symbol of God the quintessential embodiment of the solitary ruling male ego, above the fray, perfectly happy in himself, filled with power in the face of the obstreperousness of others? Is this not "man" according to the patriarchal ideal? Feminist thought sees a more intrinsic connection between those characteristics of the theistic God found problematic in nineteenth- and twentieth-century critiques and the fundamental sexism of the symbol of this God than is usually realized.

The same holds true for more contemporary discourse. There is not one religious tradition or theological school existing in the world today, nor one atheistic critique of religious tradition, nor one sociopolitical arrangement nor liberating critique of such structures, nor culture of East or West that yet does justice to the full humanity of women. Valuable as insights from contemporary theology may be, these are as yet only partial and even dangerous to the degree that they implicitly assume that men, ruling or otherwise, form a universal norm for defining humanity and for speaking about God. What has failed to come to expression in reinterpreted religious symbol systems and theological language is the human reality of vast numbers of women: women disbelieving or seeking meaning in the midst of secular culture; women and their dependent children as the majority of the poor, and consequently the lifting of their voices as the "irruption within the irruption" of liberation theology;[14] women as bearers of the wisdom of the East; women created in the image of God so truly that their concrete reality can provide suitable metaphor for the holy mystery of God. As theology begins to respond to its tradition of exclusivity in the light of the experience of the "other half" of the human race, the so-called revolution in the concept of God takes a turn into new and unsuspected depths.

Feminist Theology

To provide a framework for understanding feminist theological discourse about God in both its critical and constructive moments, it will be helpful to consider some salient features of this form of theology in itself.

However diverse their views, women doing feminist theology share one major aspect of a common social location: their speech sounds from the margins of the dominant androcentric tradition. "To be in the margin," as Bell Hooks writes, "is to be part of the whole but outside the main body."[15] It is not an unnecessary place, but a place of systematic devaluing. Being there signifies being less, being overlooked, not having as much importance. From this position feminist theology listens and speaks not just about women but about the whole social-symbolic order that it observes from this liminal vantage point, questioning the rules, terms, and practices of the center. The speech that it generates aims at resistance and transformation not only of the suffering of the margins but of the whole design.

Analysis of Sexism

From the margins feminist liberation theology sees clearly that society and the church are pervaded by sexism with its twin faces of patriarchy and androcentrism. This social sin has debilitating effects on women both socially and psychologically, and interlocks with other forms of oppression to shape a violent and dehumanized world.

Sexism, in Margaret Farley's generic description, is "belief that persons are superior or inferior to one another on the basis of their sex. It includes, however, attitudes, value systems, and social patterns which express or support this belief."[16] Historically, sexism has maintained that persons of the male sex are inherently superior to persons of the female sex by nature, that is, by the very order of things, and it has acted in discriminatory ways to enforce this order. In a pattern analogous to racism, this prejudice classifies a group of human beings as deficient, ordains certain subordinate roles for them, and denies them certain rights on the basis of personal physical and/or psychological characteristics alone. Just as racism assigns an inferior dignity to people on the basis of their skin color or ethnic heritage, so too on the basis of biological sex and its attendant functions sexism considers women essentially less valuable than men, and labors mightily to keep them in their "proper" social "place." In both *isms* bodily characteristics are made to count for the whole essence of the human being, so that the fundamental dignity of the person is violated. Sexism like racism betrays the fundamental inability of a dominant group to deal with otherness, to acknowledge equal humanity and kinship with those who are different from themselves.

Sexism expresses itself in social structures and personal attitudes and action, the two being intertwined in the public and private realm.

Patriarchy is the name commonly given to sexist social structures. Coined from the Greek *patēr/patros* (father) and *archē* (origin, ruling power, or authority), patriarchy is a form of social organization in which power is always in the hand of the dominant man or men, with others ranked below in a graded series of subordinations reaching down to the least powerful who form a large base. As classically defined by Aristotelian political philosophy, this system involves not simply the natural rule of men over women but very precisely the absolute rule of the freeborn male head of household over wives, children, male and female slaves, and nonhuman property as the cornerstone of the very structure of the state. The traditional pyramidal pattern of social relations in nondemocratic forms of state governance, families, the church, and the like has sedimented the dominance of ruling men to the point of making it seem indeed natural.[17] Religious patriarchy is one of the strongest forms of this structure, for it understands itself to be divinely established. Consequently, the power of the ruling men is said by them to be delegated by God (invariably spoken about in male terms) and exercised by divine mandate.

Androcentrism, from the Greek *anēr/andros* (male human being), is the name commonly given to the personal pattern of thinking and acting that takes the characteristics of ruling men to be normative for all humanity. The androcentric order lifts up especially the adult ruling man as the paradigm for the humanity of all others in the human race. Women, children, and those men who do not fit this standard are considered not fully human but secondarily so, in a way derivative from and dependent upon the normative man. In its language and theoretical framework, the androcentric world view self-affirms the ruling male as normal and standard, and alienates the female and nonruling males as deficient, auxiliary, "other."

In theology androcentrism ensures that ruling men will be the norm for language not only about human nature but also about God, sin and redemption, the church and its mission. One of the most influential androcentric syntheses in the Catholic tradition is that of Aquinas, which may serve as an illustration of how such a pattern of thinking works. Aquinas accepted, as part of the Aristotelian heritage that he was shaping into Christian language, the notion of ancient Greek biology that the male seed carried all the potency for new life. He furthermore figured that under optimum conditions men, who are the pinnacle of creation, would reproduce their own perfection and create sons. The fact is, however, that they do not, for at least half of the time they generate daughters who fall short of the perfection of the male sex. This indicates that the man was not up to par at the time of intercourse. Perhaps his seed was damaged, or he was short on energy due to hot, humid weather. In Aquinas's own words:

Only as regards nature in the individual is the female something defective and misbegotten. For the active power in the seed of the male tends to produce something like itself, perfect in masculinity; but the procreation of a female is the result either of the debility of the active power, of some unsuitability of the material, or of some change effected by external influences, like the south wind, for example, which is damp, as we are told by Aristotle.[18]

Woman's defective nature and the further fact that woman in the garden of paradise and elsewhere is an occasion of sin for man do not indicate, however, that it would have been better had God never created woman at all. Woman is created by God for a very definite purpose, namely, reproduction, which is the only thing that man cannot do better without her help. As for her being a temptress to man, Aquinas argues, the perfection of the universe depends on shadows as well as light, and in any event God can bring good out of any evil.

Since the soul informs the body, woman's defective physical state leads Aquinas to the conclusion that woman's soul is likewise deficient, her mind weak in reasoning and her will fragile in choosing the good. For her own good she needs to be governed by others wiser than herself: "by such a kind of subjection woman is naturally subject to man, because in man the discretion of reason predominates."[19] From woman's natural inferiority in the order of creation Aquinas reasonably deduces a host of consequences, such as that children should love their fathers more than their mothers since the father is more eminent; women may not be ordained priests since priesthood signifies the eminence of Christ and women do not signify what pertains to eminence; women should not preach since this is an exercise of wisdom and authority of which they are not capable; and so on. Some commentators have observed that there are elements in Aquinas's theology that could have led him to a more positive evaluation of women's nature, factors such as his argument that the first woman was directly created by God rather than by angels, as some thinkers were then arguing; or his belief that in one sense women were indeed created in the image of God.[20] But the patriarchy of his own culture coupled with the androcentrism of the Christian and philosophical heritages with which he was working led him to accept without question the subordination of women as the God-given order of the world.

The effective history of Aquinas's theology in the Catholic church illustrates how powerfully androcentric thought functions to legitimate patriarchy. As an intellectual model it constructs the world in language, mindset, imagery, and the distribution of value in such a way as to marginalize women and justify structures that exclude them from full and equal participation. Aquinas is but one example. Feminist analysis leads to the conclusion that whether consciously intended or unintended, bias against the genuine humanity of women is not superficial but is intrinsic to inherited religious structures and paradigms of thought that are firmly in place.

Women experience the effects of sexism both socially and psychologically; nor, as the feminist axiom "the personal is the political" insightfully acknowledges, can the two be divorced. The litany is long and painful.

In society women have for most of history been denied political, economic, legal, and educational rights — in no country in the world are these yet equal to men in practice. In situations where people suffer intolerably from poverty and racism, the dynamic of sexism burdens women with added and profound exploitation: they are the underclass that functions as "slaves of the slaves," subordinated to men who themselves are already oppressed. According to United Nations statistics, while forming more than one-half of the world's population women work two-thirds of the world's working hours, own one-tenth of the world's wealth and one-hundredth of the world's land, and form two-third's of the world's illiterate people. Over three-fourths of starving people are women with their dependent children.[21] To make a dark picture even bleaker, women are bodily and sexually exploited, physically abused, raped, battered, and murdered. The indisputable fact is that men do this to women in a way that women do not do to men. Sexism is rampant on a global scale.[22]

In the Christian community the prejudice of sexism shows itself in analogous ways.[23] For most of its history women have been subordinated in theological theory and ecclesial practice at every turn. Until very recently they have been consistently defined as mentally, morally, and physically inferior to men, created only partially in the image of God, even a degrading symbol of evil. Women's sexuality has been derided as unclean and its use governed by norms laid down by men. Conversely, they have been depersonalized as a romantic, unsexed ideal whose fulfilment lies mainly in motherhood. Even as I write, women in the Catholic community are excluded from full participation in the sacramental system, from ecclesial centers of significant decision making, law making, and symbol making, and from official public leadership roles whether in governance or the liturgical assembly. They are called to honor a male savior sent by a male God whose legitimate representatives can only be male, all of which places their persons precisely as female in a peripheral role. Their femaleness is judged to be not suitable as metaphor for speech about God. In a word, women occupy a marginal place in the official life of the church, that is, necessarily there but of restricted value.

Women's sense of themselves as active agents of history comes in for severe diminishment under sexist dictation. Subordination affects the imagination to the point where, in a dynamic similar to that suffered by other colonialized groups, women internalize the images and notions declared about them by the ruling group and come to believe it of themselves.[24] Being inculturated in a thousand subtle ways through familial socialization, education, the media, and religious practice to the idea that women are not as capable as men, nor are they expected to be, leads to an internalized sense of powerlessness. The internalization of secondary status then functions like a self-fulfilling prophecy, inculcating low self-esteem, passivity, and an assessment of oneself as inadequate even where that is patently untrue.

This process is strongly aided and abetted by male-centered language and symbol systems, key reflections of the dominant group's power to define reality in its own terms and a powerful tool of its rule. Women have been robbed of the power of naming, of naming themselves, the world, and ultimate holy mystery, having instead to receive the names given by those who rule over them. Since language not only expresses the world but helps to shape and create it, learning to speak a language where the female is subsumed grammatically under the male gives girl children from the beginning the experience of a world where the male is the norm from which her own self deviates: "Those of us who have grown up with a language that tells them they are at the same time men and not men are faced with ambivalence — not about their sex but about their status as human beings."[25] In sexist civil and religious society, women's basic human experience of uniqueness becomes an experience of otherness, of being alien and not fitting in, of being out of place and of little consequence.

Feminist assessment of sexism, expressed in patriarchal structures and androcentric thought and action, and issuing in political and psychological damage to women, interlocks with appraisals of racism, economic classism, militarism, and cultural imperialism produced by other liberation theologies, and to analyses of the destruction of the life-systems of the earth identified by ecological theory.[26] These are biases that derail intelligence and wreck the common good. The fundamental sin is exploitation, whether it be expressed in the domination of male over female, white over black, rich over poor, strong over weak, armed military over unarmed civilians, human beings over nature. These analogously abusive patterns interlock because they rest on the same base: a structure where an elite insists on its superiority and claims the right to exercise dominative power over all others considered subordinate, for its own benefit.

Gerda Lerner, among others, has put forward the thesis that the social subjugation of women is historically the original form of the oppressor-oppressed relationship, and thus the working paradigm for all others.[27] According to her study of the creation of patriarchy, this social system did not emerge with the original human ancestors. Rather it emerged over time for many reasons in connection with dominance by race and class. When after victory in war men killed the defeated males but forcibly took women of conquered groups into their own harems or households, they were simultaneously learning skills of domination that could eventually be applied to conquered men as well.

Making the same point from a qualitative rather than historical perspective, Rosemary Radford Ruether argues that suppression of the female is the paradigm for male power-over in other arenas. The self-image of ruling-class men is modeled on a certain ideal of true humanity or selfhood, allowing them to claim that they alone possess intrinsically the desirable qualities of spirit, initiative, reason, capacity for autonomy and higher virtue. Women are projected as the "other," the repository for qualities men cannot integrate into their self-image and therefore the antithesis over against which they define themselves. This repressive view of the alien female then serves as the basic model for project-ing views of inferiority onto other subjugated groups, lower classes, conquered races, nonhuman creatures:

Subjugated groups are perceived through similar stereotypes not because they are alike, but because the same dominant group (ruling-class males) are doing the perceiving. [As with women] all oppressed peoples tend then to be seen as lacking in rationality, volition, and capacity for autonomy. The characteristics of repressed bodiliness are attributed to them: passivity, sensuality, irrationality and dependency.[28]

Given such an assessment of the deficient humanity of others, the way is cleared for ruling men to exploit and suppress without a guilty conscience.

This analysis does not conclude that only men are capable of act-ing in a dominating fashion. Given the right opportunity, women too may sin this way. Historians, for example, show how, distorted by the corrosive acid of racism in the antebellum South, some white women, themselves cast in a strong hierarchical system, could and did act in an oppressive and violent manner toward their female slaves.[29] The point that feminist theorists press is that the structures and attitudes of sex-ism are a pervasive, powerful and often overlooked key to the creation of disastrous social inequity in many forms. In my judgment, anyone who would underestimate the wrongs occasioned by sexist prejudice deserves the classic rebuke that Anselm gave to his questioner Boso: *nondum considerasti quanti ponderis sit peccatum*, "you have not yet weighed the gravity of sin."[30]

Sexism, racism, classism, imperialism, militarism, humanocentrism: the interconnection of these patterns of domination deepens the fem-inist theological agenda. Addressing the question of the subordination of women brings into view the entire structure of what has com-monly been taken to be "reality." What is being looked for is not simply the solution to one problem, but an entire shift of world view away from patterns of dominance toward mutually enhancing relationships.

Methods, Criteria, Goal

In its methodology, criteria, and goal, feminist theology is deeply af-fected by the foregoing analysis of sexism. To resist the debilitating effects of patriarchy and to generate new understanding, it characteristically appeals to women's experience, a resource seldom considered in the history of theology. Just what precisely comprises women's experience is a matter of intense study and debate, for experience with its intrinsic interpretation differs as women differ according to their context of race, class, culture, and other historical particularities. There is urgency in the effort today to move away from an idea of women's experience derived solely from white, middle-class North Americans toward a multidimensional analysis respectful and celebratory of women's differences. But foundational to feminist liberation theology across the board is the specific experience of protest against the suffering caused by sexism and a turning to the flourishing of women in all their concrete femaleness. This may be articulated as a conversion experience with its twin aspects of contrast and confirmation: contrast between the suffering of sexism and the *humanum* of women, and confirmation of women's creative agency and power, both mediated through the same Christian tradition.[31]

Drawing energy and light from this social experience, feminist theology engages in at least three interrelated tasks: it critically analyzes inherited oppressions, searches for alternative wisdom and suppressed history, and risks new interpretations of the tradition in conversation with women's lives.

1. The work of deconstruction unmasks the hidden dynamic of domination in the Christian tradition's language, custom, memory, history, sacred texts, ethics, symbolism, theology, and ritual. Asking the question *cui bono?* — to whose advantage is this articulation or arrangement of reality? — feminist theology exposes the ruling-male-centered partiality of what has been taken as universal and the interests served by what has seemed disinterested. Nor has this sexist bias been accidental. It is like a buried continent whose subaqueous pull has shaped all currents of the theological enterprise, so that Christian theory and praxis have been massively distorted.

2. Negatives alone do not nourish. Feminist religious scholarship also searches for ignored, suppressed, or alternative wisdom both inside and outside of that mainstream, for bits and pieces that hint at the untold stories of the contributions of women and the possibility of different construals of reality. The hope is to discover dormant theological themes and neglected history that will contribute to a future of full personhood for women. Although women's words have been censored or eliminated from much of Christian heritage, in the midst of the pain of dehumanization women have nevertheless always been there, in fidelity and struggle, in loving and caring, in outlawed movements, in prophecy and vision. Tracking and retrieving fragments of this

lost wisdom and history, all in some way touchstones of what may yet be possible, enable them to be set free as resources for transforming thought and action.[32] A similar retrieval marks the more theoretical reflection of systematic theology. The creation of male and female in the divine image; the sacrament of baptism that recreates women and men in the image of Christ and initiates a new form of community; eschatological hope for a cosmos redeemed in all of its dimensions — these and other elements of belief are plumbed to release their liberating truth, which challenges the churches to become faithful to the best of their own tradition.

   3. In the light of its critique and glimpses of alternatives, feminist theology reconstructs. It attempts new articulations of the norms and methods of theology itself and newly envisions Christian symbols and practices that would do justice to the full humanity of women as a key to a new whole.[33] In addition to theology's classic companion, philosophy, itself being rethought in feminist categories, the human sciences and women's literature are partners in the building.[34] This is a creative moment, typical of all great advances in theology. Life and faith are thought in new ways that promote the equality of women and all the oppressed in a genuine community of mutuality with those who formerly dominated. A time to tear down, a time to build up; a time to throw stones away and a time to gather them together — the season of feminist theology involves all of these at once.

   Criterion. In the course of this program one criterion recurs as a touchstone for testing the truth and falsity, the adequacy and inadequacy, the coherence and incoherence of theological statements and religious structures. This criterion, variously enunciated, is the emancipation of women toward human flourishing. As a gauge it is applied in a practical way, the adequacy of a religious symbol or custom being assessed according to its effects, for if something consistently results in the denigration of human beings, in what sense can it be religiously true? One particularly clear articulation of this criterion is given by Rosemary Radford Ruether:

The critical principle of feminist theology is the promotion of the full humanity of women. Whatever denies, diminishes, or distorts the full humanity of women is, therefore, appraised as not redemptive. Theologically speaking, whatever diminishes or denies the full humanity of women must be presumed not to reflect the divine or an authentic relation to the divine, or reflect the authentic nature of things, or to be the message or work of an authentic redeemer or a community of redemption.

   This negative principle also implies the positive principle: what does promote the full humanity of women is of the Holy, it does reflect true relation to the divine, it is the true nature of things, the authentic message of redemption and the mission of redemptive community.[35]

The principle of the promotion of true humanity is not new nor unique to feminist theology. Classical theology's doctrine of the human being as *imago Dei*, fallen and redeemed, also utilizes it. What is different is that it is now claimed by women as applying equally also to themselves: "Women name themselves as subjects of authentic and full humanity."[36] Although this full humanity has not yet appeared in recorded history, given women's subordinate lot, it has perdured often in unrecognized ways, and can be glimpsed in an act of constructive imagination.

This gauge of women's flourishing is complex, given the multidimensional character of human existence. All persons are constituted by a number of essential relations, which may be called anthropological constants. These include relation to bodiliness as the medium of human spirit; relation through the body to the whole ecological network of the earth; relation to significant other persons as the matrix in which individuality arises, and to community as the context for identity; relation to social, political, and economic structures; conditioning by historical time and place; the play of theory in the praxis of one's culture as opposed to instinct alone; and orientation to hope and the pull of the future. These constants mutually condition one another, and are constitutive of the humanity of persons.[37] In choosing the lens of women's flourishing to focus its thinking, feminist theology takes the total personhood of women with utter seriousness, advocating women's well-being personally and corporately in all of these constitutive dimensions.

The criterion of the liberation of women toward human flourishing thus involves the whole of historical reality, reaching through the specific, multifaceted oppressions suffered by women to include every aspect of life on this planet.

Goal. The goal toward which this theological effort passionately journeys is transformation into new community. Feminist liberation theology hopes so to change unjust structures and distorted symbol systems that a new community in church and society becomes possible, a liberating community of all women and men characterized by mutuality with each other and harmony with the earth. Feminist theologians love the vision of wholeness, equality and freedom celebrated in an early baptismal hymn: in the oneness of Christ Jesus "there is neither Jew nor Greek, neither slave nor free, neither male nor female" (Gal 3:28). The stress on equality does not obviate differences either between women and men or among the vast diversity of women. Rather, it signifies an intrinsic valuation of women as human beings, created, sinful, redeemed, with all the dignity, rights, and responsibilities that accrue as a consequence. This vision of redeemed humanity, though never fully realized, becomes more actual in every partial move from situations of domination/subordination to a community where subservience is unknown thanks to relationships of mutual respect, reciprocal valuing, and sharing in solidarity with the dispossessed.

In the perspective I am delineating two options are ruled out: reverse sexism, which would place women in dominant positions to the diminishment of men, and a sameness, which would level out genuine variety and particularity, disrespecting uniqueness. Instead, the goal is the flourishing of all beings in their uniqueness and interrelation — both sexes, all races and social groups, all creatures in the universe. This calls for a new model of relationship, neither a hierarchical one that requires an over-under structure, nor a univocal one that reduces all to a given norm. The model is rather inclusive, celebratory of difference, circular, feminist — we reach for the words.

The goal of feminist theology, in other words, is not to make women equal partners in an oppressive system. It is to transform the system. The recipe, in Rebecca Chopp's homely metaphor, does not call for society and church to "add women and stir," for this simply subjects what has been excluded to the prevailing order.[38] Nor, in Rosemary Radford Ruether's image also taken from the kitchen, will it do simply to give women a larger piece of the pie, for women are designing a new way of baking the pie, even rewriting the recipe. She explains:

All of us, both men and women, oppressor and oppressed, need to be converted, in somewhat different ways, to that whole humanity which has been denied to us by systems of alienation and social oppression. This fuller humanity demands not only a conversion of the self into its fuller possibilities, but a conversion of society, a transformation of those social structures that set people in opposition to each other. We seek a new social order, a new order of human-nature relations, that both mandates and incarnates mutuality.[39]

Ultimately the eschatological dream of a new heaven and new earth where justice dwells takes hold here, with no group dominating and none being subordinated, but all participating according to their gifts and being equally, mutually valued in a movement of transcending liberation, peace, and joy. The genius of feminist theology has been to see that for the traditional eschatological dream to become historical reality at all, the liberation of women as genuine human persons in communities of mutuality is essential.

For theology as an academic discipline, it is clear that placing women's experience at the center of inquiry and pressing toward transformation of oppressive symbols and systems are occasioning an intellectual paradigm shift of great magnitude.[40] There is new data at hand, which prevailing theory cannot account for, making the search for a new configuration of the whole essential. This is not minor tinkering with the discipline but an effort toward major reshaping of theology and the religious tradition that gives rise to it. Journeying out of an andro-centric world into more inclusive conceptualization shifts the center of the theological universe, much as Copernicus's discovery of the earth's rotation around the sun changed forever the ancient geocentric view.[41] In the process of this major recentering virtually every inherited given comes under scrutiny and is subject to critique, revision, and renewal in the interest of greater liberation in faith and life. High on the agenda is discourse about God.

Critique of Speech about God

To even the casual observer it is obvious that the Christian community ordinarily speaks about God on the model of the ruling male human be-ing. Both the images that are used and the concepts accompanying them reflect the experience of men in charge within a patriarchal system. The difficulty does not lie in the fact that male metaphors are used, for men too are made in the image of God and may suitably serve as finite begin-ning points for reference to God. Rather, the problem consists in the fact that these male terms are used exclusively, literally, and patriarchally.

Exclusively. In spite of the multitude of designations for divine mys-tery in the Bible and later, lesser-known sources, prevailing Christian language names God solely with male designations, causing the rest to be forgotten or marginalized. Thus speech about God in female meta-phors or in images taken from the natural world lies fallow, and can even appear deviant. To give one outstanding example, liturgical prayer is di-rected to the Father, through the Son, in the unity of the Holy Spirit, with even the latter being masculinized through the use of grammatically male pronouns.

Literally. In spite of ample testimony in the Scriptures and later tra-dition that the mystery of God is beyond all human comprehension, the exclusively male symbol of God is spoken in an uncritically literal way. Such speech signifies, if not in explicit theory at least effectively in the subliminal power of the imagination, that maleness is an essen-tial character of divine being. We have forgotten what was clear to early Christian thinkers, namely, that Father and Son are names that designate relationships rather than an essence in itself, and that as applied to God they, like all human finite names, are subject to the negation of the rule of analogy.[42] It is true that sophisticated thinkers deny that the maleness of the symbol of God is meant to be taken literally, for divine being transcends sexual bodiliness. Yet the literal association of God with maleness perdures even in highly abstract discussions, as exemplified in the statement, "God is not male; He is Spirit."[43] The assumption of divine maleness comes to light in the cognitive dissonance set up by marginalized speech such as Julian of Norwich's:

The mother can give her child to suck of her milk, but our precious Mother Jesus can feed us with himself, and does, most courteously and most tenderly, with the blessed sacrament, which is the precious food of true life.[44]

Such language provides an opportunity for divine mystery to be glimpsed when the noun *mother* and the pronoun *himself* grate against each other. By contrast, when words such as father, king, lord, bridegroom, husband, and God himself are used, there is usually no sense of inappropriateness. The incidental implication of maleness seems to have slipped in as essential. This is demonstrated empirically by the dismay often registered when and if God is referred to with female images or pronouns. If it is not meant that God is male when masculine imagery is used, why the objection when female images are introduced? But in fact an intrinsic, literal connection between God and maleness is usually intended, however implicitly.

Patriarchally. The precise ideal from the world of men that has provided the paradigm for the symbol of God is the ruling man within a patriarchal system. Divine mystery is cast in the role of a monarch, absolute ruler, King of Kings, Lord of Lords, one whose will none can escape, to whom is owed total and unquestioning obedience. This powerful monarch is sometimes spoken of as just and harsh, threatening hell fire to sinners who do not measure up. But even when he is presented as kindly, merciful, and forgiving, the fundamental problem remains. Benevolent patriarchy is still patriarchy.

The exclusive and literal patriarchy of the symbol of God goes forward in concrete metaphors and abstract concepts. In the history of Western art the most common depiction of deity is that of an old white man with a white beard: recall Michelangelo's image of God the Creator on the ceiling of the Sistine Chapel, calling into life a single younger man in his own image. Imagery of the trinitarian God most often consists of an older white-bearded man, a younger brown-bearded man, both Caucasian, and a dove.[45] The power of these and other images as they give rise to thought insures that metaphysical descriptions of the divine nature also betray an androcentric bias. Even the most abstract theological concepts begin with and are still attached at some point to concrete models. To wit: Greek philosophical tradition equates the male principle with spirit, with mind and reason, and most importantly with act, reserving for the female principle a contrasting identification with matter, with the inferior body and passion, and most importantly with potency. In this profoundly dualistic world view, male is to female as autonomy is to dependence, as strength is to weakness, as fullness is to emptiness, as dynamism is to stasis, as good is to evil. Since the divine principle is pure act and goodness, it necessarily must exclude all dependency, potency, passivity, and prime matter. The logic of this set-up leads inexorably to the conviction that the divine can properly be spoken of only on the model of the spiritually masculine to the exclusion of the passive, material feminine.

Accordingly, while Aquinas, for example, notes that the Scriptures attribute to God the Father what in our material world belongs to both father and mother, namely, the begetting of the Son, he nevertheless argues that God cannot be spoken of on the analogy of mother for God is pure act, whereas in the process of begetting, the mother represents the principle that receives passively.[46] This assumption and its attendant androcentric presuppositions permeate the classical philosophical doctrine of God as well as the specifically Christian doctrine of God's Trinity.

Although Christology done in the light of the gospel depiction of Jesus of Nazareth has the potential to critique the patriarchy of the God-symbol, the movement toward exclusive and literal masculinization of God has been dramatically intensified as a result of dogmatic development in Christology. According to the Chalcedonian formulation, one and the same Christ is made known in two natures, human and divine, concurring into one hypostasis. The close union between human and divine natures — a hypostatic union — coupled with confession of Jesus the Christ's personal identity as "God from God" has tended to allow the sex of the human being Jesus to be transferred to God's own being. Interestingly enough, this has not happened with other historical particularities of the human Jesus, such as his ethnic heritage, his nationality, his age, his socioeconomic status, and so on. But in spite of Chalcedon's strictures against mixing or confusing the two natures in Christ, the practical effect of this definition has been to promote the viability of male metaphors and the unsuitability of female ones in speech about God. As visible image of the invisible God, the human man Jesus is used to tie the knot between maleness and divinity very tightly.

Feminist theological analysis makes clear that exclusive, literal, patriarchal speech about God has a twofold negative effect. It fails both human beings and divine mystery. In stereotyping and then banning female reality as suitable metaphor for God, such speech justifies the dominance of men while denigrating the human dignity of women. Simultaneously this discourse so reduces divine mystery to the single, reified metaphor of the ruling man that the symbol itself loses its religious significance and ability to point to ultimate truth. It becomes, in a word, an idol. These two effects are inseparable for damage to the *imago Dei* in the creature inevitably shortchanges knowledge of the Creator in whose image she is made. Inauthentic ways of treating other human beings go hand-in-glove with falsifications of the idea of God.

Sociological and Psychological Effects

The symbol of God does not passively float in the air but functions in social and personal life to sustain or critique certain structures, values, and ways of acting. Sociologists of religion shed clear light on this power of religions to structure the world. Following Clifford Geertz's oft repeated formulation, there is an interdependent relation between a religion's symbol system, the moods and motivations it establishes, its concept of the general order of things, and the aura of factuality that surrounds both the moods and the concepts.[47] Since the symbol of God is the focal point of the whole religious system, an entire world order and world view are wrapped up with its character. Specific ideas of God support certain kinds of relationship and not others. Some views of the divine are perverted, so that devotion to this God leads to inhuman structures and behaviors. For example, God spoken of as a wrathful tyrant can be called upon to justify holy wars and inquisitional torture chambers. Language about God as universal creator, lover, and savior of all, on the other hand, moves believers toward forgiveness, care, and openness to inclusive community. The symbol of God *functions*, and its content is of the highest importance for personal and common weal or woe.[48]

Patriarchal God symbolism functions to legitimate and reinforce patriarchal social structures in family, society, and church. Language about the father in heaven who rules over the world justifies and even necessitates an order whereby the male religious leader rules over his flock, the civil ruler has domination over his subjects, the husband exercises headship over his wife. If there is an absolute heavenly patriarch, then social arrangements on earth must pivot around hierarchical rulers who of necessity must be male in order to represent him and rule in his name. This men do to the exclusion of women by a certain right, thanks to their greater similarity to the source of all being and power. The dissonance sounded by the fact that this supposed similarity lies in sexual likeness, while God is taken to be beyond all physical characteristics, is not noticed. Exclusive and literal imaging of the patriarchal God thus insures the continued subordination of women to men in all significant civic and religious structures.

This symbolism also justifies the androcentric world view of male superiority and female inferiority that accompanies such structures. When God is envisioned in the image of one sex rather than both sexes, and in the image of the ruling class of this sex, then this group of men is seen to possess the image of God in a primary way. As Paul Tillich saw, religious symbols are double-edged, directing attention both toward the infinite which they symbolize and toward the finite through which they symbolize it. Whenever a segment of reality is used as a symbol for God, the realm of reality from which it is taken is elevated into the realm of the holy, becoming "theonomous." For instance,

if God is symbolized as "Father," he is brought down to the human relationship of father and child. But at the same time this human relationship is consecrated into a pattern of the divine-human relationship. If "Father" is employed as a symbol for God, fatherhood is seen in its theonomous, sacramental depth.[49]

Again, "if God is called the 'king,' something is said not only about God but also about the holy character of kinghood."[50] The human reality used to point to God becomes by that very act consecrated, revealed in its own holy depths.

This is a worthwhile and fruitful insight. But what results when the human reality used to point to God is always and everywhere male? The sacred character of maleness is revealed, while femaleness is relegated to the unholy darkness without. Such silence is typical of theological discourse shaped by an androcentric notion of humanity. The patriarchal symbol of the divine sculpts men into the role of God, fully in "his" image and capable of representing "him," while women, thought to be only deficiently in the image of God and ultimately a symbol of evil, play the role of dependent and sinful humanity who when forgiven may then be recipients of grace or spiritual helpers. No one has yet summed up more pithily the total sociological and theological fallout of androcentric symbolism for the divine than Mary Daly with her apothegm "if God is male, then the male is God."[51]

This state of affairs has a profound impact on women's religious identity. The God-symbol is not only a visual phantasy but a focus of a whole complex of conscious and unconscious ideas, feelings, emotions, views, and associations, very deep and tenacious. For women, speech about God couched exclusively in male terms does not point to the equal participation of women and men in the divine ground. Male images allow men to participate fully in it, while women can do so only by abstracting themselves from their concrete, bodily identity as women. Thus is set up a largely unconscious dynamic that alienates women from their own goodness and power at the same time that it reinforces dependency upon men and male authority. Carol Christ has analyzed this in particularly acute fashion:

Religious symbol systems focused around exclusively male images of divinity create the impression that female power can never be fully legitimate or wholly beneficent. This message need never be explicitly stated ... for its effect to be felt. A woman completely ignorant of the myths of female evil in biblical religion nonetheless acknowledges the anomaly of female power when she prays exclusively to a male god. She may see herself as like God (created in the image of God) only by denying her own sexual identity and affirming God's transcendence of sexual identity. But she can never have the experience that is freely available to every man and boy in her culture, of having her full sexual identity affirmed as being in the image and likeness of God.... Her "mood" is one of trust in male power as salvific and distrust of female power in herself and other women as inferior and dangerous.[52]

Speech about God in the exclusive and literal terms of the patriarch is a tool of subtle conditioning that operates to debilitate women's sense of dignity, power, and self-esteem.

The symbol of God functions. When the root metaphor for the divine in Christian discourse is patriarchal, then as the orienting focus of devotion, as the paradigmatic notion that "sums up, unifies, and represents in a personification what are taken to be the highest and most indispensable human ideals and values in a community,"[53] it inevitably sustains men's dominance over women. Sociologically it reinforces the rule of the fathers by rooting such arrangements in the divine order of things, on the model of "God himself," and thus male rule is given a sacred backing. Psychologically, exclusive, patriarchal imagery for the divine functions as a tool of symbolic violence against the full self-identity of female persons, blocking their identity as images of God and curtailing their access to divine power. As long as ultimate mystery is spoken about in exclusive and literal patriarchal terms, then persons fitting that description will continue to relate to others in a superior way. Here the ambiguity in the inherited doctrine of God becomes clear insofar as speech about God in patriarchal metaphors, in a demonic twist, becomes an architect of injustice, a fountainhead of enslavement.

Theological Effects

The effective history of patriarchal speech about God also bears directly on the religious significance and truth of what is said about divine mystery. Feminist theological analysis makes clear that the tenacity with which the patriarchal symbol of God is upheld is nothing less than violation of the first commandment of the decalogue, the worship of an idol. An idol is not necessarily a god in the shape of an animal, a golden calf or little statue with no breath that needs to be carried, as described in the Hebrew Scriptures. Rather, any representation of the divine used in such a way that its symbolic and evocative character is lost from view partakes of the nature of an idol. Whenever one image or concept of God expands to the horizon thus shutting out others, and whenever this exclusive symbol becomes literalized so that the distance between it and divine reality is collapsed, there an idol comes into being. Then the comprehensible image, rather than disclosing mystery, is mistaken for the reality. Divine mystery is cramped into a fixed, petrified image. Simultaneously, the religious impulse is imprisoned, leading to inhibition of the growth of human beings by the prevention of further seeking and finding.

Throughout the Jewish and Christian traditions prophetic thinkers have challenged the propensity of the human heart to evade the living God by taming the wildness of divine mystery into a more domesticated deity. In his inimitable style Calvin describes the temptation:

the mind of man is, if I may be allowed the expression, a perpetual factory of idols . . . the mind of man, being full of pride and temerity, dares to conceive of God according to its own standard and, being sunk in stupidity and immersed in profound ignorance, imagines a vain and ridiculous phantom instead of God.[54]

Prophets and religious thinkers have long insisted on the need to break down false idols and escape out of their embrace toward the living God, speech about whom becomes in its own turn a candidate for critique whenever it is held too tightly. The process never ends, for divine mystery is fathomless. In the language of patriarchy C. S. Lewis grasps this with telling clarity:

My idea of God is not a divine idea. It has to be shattered time after time. He shatters it Himself. He is the great iconoclast. Could we not almost say that this shattering is one of the marks of His presence? . . . And most are offended by the iconoclasm; and blessed are those who are not.[55]

What needs to be shattered according to feminist theological critique is the stranglehold on religious language of God-He. Normative imaging and conceptualization of God on the model of ruling men alone is theologically the equivalent of the graven image, a finite representation set up and worshiped as if it were the whole of divine reality. What is violated is both the creature's limitation and the unknowable mystery of the living God. In spite of the tradition's insistence on the radical incomprehensibility of God; in spite of the teaching that all words for God, being finite, fall short of their intended goal; and in spite of the presence of many names, images, and concepts for the divine in the Scripture and later Christian tradition, this tradition has lifted up the patriarchal way of being human to functional equivalence with the divine. More solid than stone, more resistant to iconoclasm than bronze, seems to be the ruling male substratum of the idea of God cast in theological language and engraved in public and private prayer. But

it is idolatrous to make males more "like God" than females. It is blasphemous to use the image and name of the Holy to justify patriarchal domination.... The image of God as predominant male is fundamentally idolatrous.[56]

In sum, exclusive, literal patriarchal speech about God is both oppressive and idolatrous. It functions to justify social structures of dominance/subordination and an androcentric world view inimical to the genuine and equal human dignity of women, while it simultaneously restricts the mystery of God. Neither effect can be addressed in isolation, for both are part of a complex system. Criticism of unjust structures and exclusive world views necessarily entails criticism of the idea of the divine interwoven with them; conversely, questioning dominant religious imagery has potent consequences for reordering the body politic, which is either supported or challenged by prevailing speech about God. Structural change and linguistic change go hand-in-hand.

The above analysis does not necessarily lead to the conclusion that in a different context traditional male symbols of God, key among them the image of father, could not function beneficently to point to the mystery of God. All good symbols of God drive toward their own transcendence, and what is rejected as an idol may yet return as an icon, a vehicle of divine power and presence, in different circumstances. But in the concrete situation of patriarchy, such symbols in fact do not function to emancipate women, however much they may be adjusted toward kindness and other desirable characteristics. In such a situation the burden of proof lies with the position that holds that exclusive and literal language about God as father, king, and so forth does in fact help to realize women's flourishing. Pragmatically, the proof is not forthcoming.[57]

How might the symbol of God be spoken anew so that in conceptuality and praxis what has been suppressed to date may be realized? And how might this discourse contribute spiritually and politically to women's flourishing and theologically to advancing the idea of the mystery of God in dialogue with insights stemming from other mighty concerns? Contemporary theology presents multiple options from among which I have made three choices. To these we now turn.

Chapter 3

BASIC LINGUISTIC OPTIONS: GOD, WOMEN, EQUIVALENCE

I walked along the railroad tracks, smelling the rain coming in the wind. The rain came, falling heavily all along the land to my left, a sheet of rain which stopped precisely at the trestle embankment. It never crossed the rails. I walked the edge of the rain, a straight line between rainfall and no rainfall.... The gift was precise, measured. I told Grandpa about this. He said: "Everything has a place where it ends." I told Memaw. She said: "That was the edge of the rim."

— Meinrad Craighead[1]

Why the Word God?

A certain liability attends the very word God, given the history of its use in androcentric theology. Insofar as it almost invariably refers to a deity imaged and conceptualized in male form, this word is judged by some feminist thinkers to be a generically masculine form of naming divine reality, and thus not capable of expressing the fullness of feminist insight. In one creative solution, Rosemary Radford Ruether uses the experimental form of reference "God/ess." This is "a written symbol intended to combine both the masculine and feminine forms of the word for the divine while preserving the Judeo-Christian affirmation that divinity is one."[2] The difficulty with this coinage comes, however, when one turns to oral speech. While indeed pointing in its written form toward a truly inclusive understanding of the divine, the term according to Ruether's own description is unpronounceable and hence not usable as language for worship, preaching, or teaching. Rebecca Chopp's robust use of the term "Word," so central to the Reformation tradition, limns yet another option.[3] In classical theology the Word indeed denotes deity, and does so in its English translation without any immediately obvious connection to gender. This expression furthermore has the advantage of connoting the power to speak, which women are claiming and celebrating in the emancipatory discourses of feminist theology. In certain contexts speech about the Word will continue to be a fruitful usage. As soon as one introduces classic theological reflection on God's Trinity, however, or the christological questions entailed in the association of the historical man Jesus with the Word, this term too reaches a limit.

Appreciating the insights that are unleashed when the traditional mold is thus broken, my option here is for yet another path. Given the long history of the term God in Christian theology, and especially given its continued and public use virtually everywhere from the most heartfelt worship to secular swearing, the word is not so easily dropped. In this book it continues to be used, but is pointed in new directions through association with metaphors and values arising from women's experience. Keeping the term may well be an interim strategy, useful until that time when a new word emerges for the as yet unnameable understanding of holy mystery that includes the reality of women as well as all creation. On the way to that day, language of God/She is aimed at generating new content for references to deity in the hopes that this discourse will help to heal imaginations and liberate people for new forms of community.

The dilemma of the word God itself, however, is a real one and not easily resolved. Its effective history has been brutal as well as blessed. This is poignantly crystallized in Martin Buber's report of a passionate exchange he once had while a house guest of an old philosopher. One morning Buber arose before the sun to proofread galleys of a piece he had written about faith. His host, also an early riser, asked him to read the piece aloud. To Buber's chagrin, his old host reacted vehemently:

How can you bring yourself to say "God" time after time?... What word of human speech is so misused, so defiled, so desecrated as this! All the innocent blood that has been shed for it has robbed it of its radiance. All the injustice that it has been used to cover has effaced its features. When I hear the highest called "God," it sometimes seems almost blasphemous.[4]

The old philosopher spoke more truly than he knew. The innocent blood of women shed for this word, the burning of thousands of wise and independent women called witches, for example, and the continuing injustice of subordination done to women in God's name is only now coming to light, and it is grave. Perhaps we should have done with the word God altogether.

Buber's response has always interested me. Rather than offering a rebuttal he agrees with the old philosopher's critique, seeing however a different option:

Yes, it is the most heavy-laden of all human words. None has become so soiled, so mutilated. Just for this reason I may not abandon it. . . . The races of man with their religious factions have torn the word to pieces.... Certainly, they draw caricatures and write "God" underneath; they murder one another and say "in God's name." But when all madness and delusion fall to dust, when they stand over against Him in the loneliest darkness and no longer say "He, He" but rather sigh "Thou," shout "Thou," all of them the one word, and when they then add "God," is it not the real God whom they implore, the One Living God?...We must esteem those who interdict it because they rebel against the injustice and wrong which are so readily referred to "God" for authorization. But we may not give it up.... We cannot cleanse the word 'God' and we cannot make it whole; but defiled and mutilated as it is, we can raise it from the ground and set it over an hour of great care.[5]

Buber did not see that in the light of dominant androcentric discourse about God a problem remains even when people turn from "He" to "Thou," for it is still a male personage who is subliminally envisioned, still a "Thou" in the image of "He." Nevertheless, his basic hunch, that the term God covered with the dirt of past offenses may yet be redeemed if it connects with an hour of great care, may serve as a program. Acknowledging the poverty and idolatry connected with the term, it may yet be transformed in a different semantic context generated by women's experience. Ultimately this strategy may be superseded, for old wineskins cannot forever hold new wine. But the wager I am making is that at this point in time pouring the new wine of women's hope of flourishing into the old word God may enable it to serve in new ways. Using "God" in a new semantic field may restore the word to a sense more in line with its Greek etymology, which, according to ancient interpreters, meant to take care of and cherish all things, burning all malice like a consuming fire.[6]

Why Female Symbols of God?

Normative speech about God in metaphors that are exclusively, literally, and patriarchally male is the real life context for this study. As a remedy some scholars and liturgists today take the option of always addressing God simply as "God." This has the positive result of relieving the hard androcentrism of ruling male images and pronouns for the divine. Nevertheless, this practice, if it is the only corrective engaged in, is not ultimately satisfactory. Besides employing uncritically a term long associated with the patriarchal ordering of the world, its consistent use causes the personal or transpersonal character of holy mystery to recede. It prevents the insight into holy mystery that might occur were female symbols set free to give rise to thought. Most serious of all, it papers over the problem of the implied inadequacy of women's reality to represent God.[7]

The holy mystery of God is beyond all imagining. In his own epistemological categories Aquinas's words still sound with the ring of truth in this regard:

Since our mind is not proportionate to the divine substance, that which is the substance of God remains beyond our intellect and so is unknown to us. Hence the supreme knowledge which we have of God is to know that we do not know God, insofar as we know that what God is surpasses all that we can understand of him [the "him," so easily assumed, being the problem that this book is addressing].[8]

The incomprehensibility of God makes it entirely appropriate, at times even preferable, to speak about God in nonpersonal or suprapersonal terms. Symbols such as the ground of being (Paul Tillich), matrix surrounding and sustaining all life (Rosemary Ruether), power of the future (Wolfhart Pannenberg), holy mystery (Karl Rahner), all point to divine reality that cannot be captured in concepts or images. At the same time God is not less than personal, and many of the most prized characteristics of God's relationship to the world, such as fidelity, compassion, and liberating love, belong to the human rather than the nonhuman world. Thus it is also appropriate, at times even preferable, to speak about God in personal symbols.

Here is where the question of gender arises. Given the powerful ways the ruling male metaphor has expanded to become an entire metaphysical world view, and the way it perdures in imagination even when gender neutral God-language is used, correction of androcentric speech on the level of the concept alone is not sufficient. Since, as Marcia Falk notes, "Dead metaphors make strong idols,"[9] other images must be introduced which shatter the exclusivity of the male metaphor, subvert its dominance, and set free a greater sense of the mystery of God.

One effective way to stretch language and expand our repertoire of images is by uttering female symbols into speech about divine mystery. It is a complex exercise, not necessarily leading to emancipatory speech.[10] An old danger that accompanies this change is that such language may be taken literally; a new danger lies in the potential for stereotyping women's reality by characterizing God simply as nurturing, caring, and so forth. The benefits, however, in my judgment, outweigh the dangers. Reorienting the imagination at a basic level, this usage challenges the idolatry of maleness in classic language about God, thereby making possible the rediscovery of divine mystery, and points to recovery of the dignity of women created in the image of God.

The importance of the image can hardly be overstated. Far from being peripheral to human knowing, imaginative constructs mediate the world to us. As is clear from contemporary science, literature, and philosophy, this is not to be equated with things being imaginary but with the structure of human knowing, which essentially depends upon paradigms to assemble data and interpret the way things are. We think via the path of images; even the most abstract concepts at root bear traces of the original images which gave them birth. Just as we know the world only through the mediation of imaginative constructs, the same holds true for human knowledge of God. Without necessarily adopting Aquinas's epistemology, we can hear the truth in his observation:

We can acquire the knowledge of divine things by natural reason only through the imagination; and the same applies to the knowledge given by grace. As Dionysius says, "it is impossible for the divine ray to shine upon us except as screened round about by the many colored sacred veils."[11]

Images of God are not peripheral or dispensable to theological speech, nor as we have seen, to ecclesial and social praxis. They are crucially important among the many colored veils through which divine mystery is mediated and by means of which we express relationship in return.[12]

The nature of symbols for divine mystery is rather plastic, a characteristic that will serve this study well. According to Tillich's well-known analysis, symbols point beyond themselves to something else, something moreover in which they participate. They open up levels of reality, which otherwise are closed, for us, and concomitantly open up depths of our own being, which otherwise would remain untouched. They cannot be produced intentionally but grow from a deep level that Tillich identifies as the collective unconscious. Finally, they grow and die like living beings in relation to their power to bear the presence of the divine in changing cultural situations.[13] In the struggle against sexism for the genuine humanity of women we are today at a crossroads of the dying and rising of religious symbols. The symbol of the patriarchal idol is cracking, while a plethora of others emerge. Among these are female symbols for divine mystery that bear the six characteristics delineated above. Women realize that they participate in the image of the divine and so their own concrete reality can point toward this mystery. Use of these symbols discloses new depths of holy mystery as well as of the community that uses them. Women's religious experience is a generating force for these symbols, a clear instance of how great symbols of the divine always come into being not simply as a projection of the imagination, but as an awakening from the deep abyss of human existence in real encounter with divine being.

The symbol gives rise to thought. With this axiom Paul Ricoeur points to the dynamism inherent in a true symbol that participates in the reality it signifies. The symbol gives, and what it gives is an occasion for thinking. This thought has the character of interpretation, for the possibilities abiding in a symbol are multivalent. At the same time, through its own inner structure a symbol guides thought in certain directions and closes off others. It gives its gift of fullest meaning when a thinker risks critical interpretation in sympathy with the reality to which it points. So it is when the concrete, historical reality of women, affirmed as blessed by God, functions as symbol in speech about the mystery of God. Language is informed by the particularity of women's experience carried in the symbol. Women thereby become a new specific channel for speaking about God, and thought recovers certain fundamental aspects of the doctrine of God otherwise overlooked. To advance the truth of God's mystery and to redress imbalance so that the community of disciples may move toward a more liberating life, this study engages imagination to speak in female symbols for divine mystery, testing their capacity to bear divine presence and power.[14]

Why Not Feminine Traits or Dimensions of God?

Having opted to use the word God, and to do so in connection with female symbols, there is yet another decision to be made. At least three distinct approaches to the renewal of speech about God in the direction of greater inclusivity can be identified in current theology. One seeks to give "feminine" qualities to God who is still nevertheless imagined predominantly as a male person. Another purports to uncover a "feminine" dimension in God, often finding this realized in the third person of the Trinity, the Holy Spirit. A third seeks speech about God in which the fullness of female humanity as well as of male humanity and cosmic reality may serve as divine symbol, in equivalent ways. Searching the implications of each can show why the first two options lead into a blind alley and why only equivalent imaging of God male and female can in the end do greater justice to the dignity of women and the truth of holy mystery.

Feminine Traits

A minimal step toward the revision of patriarchal God language is the introduction of gentle, nurturing traits traditionally associated with the mothering role of women. The symbol of God the Father in particular benefits from this move. Too often this predominant symbol has been interpreted in association with unlovely traits associated with ruling men in a male-oriented society: aggressiveness, competitiveness, desire for absolute power and control, and demand for obedience. This certainly is not the Abba to whom Jesus prayed, and widespread rejection of such a symbol from Marx, Nietzsche, and Freud onward has created a crisis for Christian consciousness. But it is also possible to see God the Father displaying feminine, so-called maternal features that temper "his" over-whelmingness. William Visser't Hooft, for example, argues that while the fatherhood of God is and must remain the predominant Christian symbol, it is not a closed or exclusive symbol but is open to its own correction, enrichment, and completion from other symbols such as mother.[15] Thus gentleness and compassion, unconditional love, rever-ence and care for the weak, sensitivity, and desire not to dominate but to be an intimate companion and friend are predicated of the Father God and make "him" more attractive.[16] A clue to the use of this approach in an author is almost invariably the word *traits:* the Bible allows us to speak of maternal traits in God (Visser't Hooft); to transform our over-masculinized culture, we need to relate to the feminine traits of God (O'Hanlon); although we have forgotten this, the God of revelation has feminine traits such as tenderness (Congar); God is not simply male but has maternal traits (Küng).[17] In this way of speaking God remains Father but in a way tempered by the ideal feminine, so that believers need not fear or rebel against a crushing paternalism.

While this approach is appearing in the work of a fair number of men theologians trying to address the problem of sexism, and while it has the advantage of moving thought counter to the misogynism that has so afflicted Christian anthropology and the doctrine of God, women theologians are virtually unanimous in calling attention to its deficien-cies and in precluding it as a long-range option. The reasons for this are several. Even with the introduction of presumably feminine features, the androcentric pattern holds. Since God is still envisioned in the image of the ruling man only now possessing milder characteristics, the fem-inine is incorporated in a subordinate way into an overall symbol that remains masculine. This is clearly seen in statements such as: God is not exclusively masculine but the "feminine-maternal element must also be recognized in Him."[18] God persists as "him," but is now spoken about as a more wholistic male person who has integrated his feminine side. The patriarchy in this symbol of God is now benevolent, but it is nonethe-less still patriarchy. And while the image of God as ruling male as well as real male persons made in "his" image may benefit and grow from the development of nurturing and compassionate qualities in themselves, there is no equivalent attribution to a female symbol or to actual women of corresponding presumably masculine qualities of rationality, power, the authority of leadership, and so forth. Men gain their feminine side, but women do not gain their masculine side (if such categories are even valid). The feminine is there for the enhancement of the male, but not vice-versa: there is no mutual gain. Actual women are then seen as capable of representing only feminine traits of what is still the male-centered symbol of God, the fullness of which can therefore be represented only by a male person. The female can never appear as icon of God in all divine fullness equivalent to the male. Inequality is not redressed but subtly furthered as the androcentric image of God remains in place, made more appealing through the subordinate inclusion of feminine traits.

A critical issue underlying this approach is the legitimacy of the rigid binary system into which it forces thought about human beings and reality itself. Enormous diversity is reduced to two relatively opposed absolutes of masculine and feminine, and this is imposed on the infinite mystery of God. The move also involves dubious stereotyping of certain human characteristics as predominantly masculine or feminine. Even as debate waxes over the distinction between sex and gender, and about whether and to what extent typical characteristics of men and women exist by nature or cultural conditioning, simple critical observation reveals that the spectrum of traits is at least as broad among concrete, historical women as between women and men.[19] In the light of the gospel, by what right are compassionate love, reverence, and nurturing predicated as primordially feminine characteristics, rather than human ones? Why are strength, sovereignty, and rationality exclusively masculine properties? As Rosemary Ruether astutely formulates the fundamental question: Is it not the case that the very concept of the "feminine" is a patriarchal invention, an ideal projected onto women by men and vigorously defended because it functions so well to keep men in positions of power and women in positions of service to them?[20] Masculine and feminine are among the most culturally stereotyped terms in the language. This is not to say that there are no differences between women and men, but it is to question the justification of the present distribution of virtues and attributes and to find it less than compelling as a description of reality. Such stereotyping serves the genuine humanity of neither women nor men, and feeds an anthropological dualism almost impossible to overcome. Adding "feminine" traits to the male-imaged God furthers the subordination of women by making the patriarchal symbol less threatening, more attractive. This approach does not, then, serve well for speech about God in a more inclusive and liberating direction.

A *Feminine Dimension: Holy Spirit*

Rather than merely attribute stereotypical feminine qualities to a male-imaged God, a second approach seeks a more ontological footing for the existence of the feminine in God. Most frequently that inroad is found in the doctrine of the Holy Spirit, who in classical trinitarian theology is coequal in nature with the Father and the Son. In the Hebrew Scriptures the Spirit is allied with female reality as can be seen not only by the grammatical feminine gender of the term *ruah*, which in itself proves nothing, but also by the use of the female imagery of the mother bird hovering or brooding to bring forth life, imagery associated with the Spirit of God in creation (Gn 1:2) and at the conception and baptism of Jesus (Lk 1:35 and 3:22). Semitic and Syrian early Christians did construe the divine Spirit in female terms, attributing to the Spirit the motherly character which certain parts of the Scriptures had already found in Israel's God.[21] The Spirit is the creative, maternal God who brings about the incarnation of Christ, new members of the body of Christ in the waters of baptism, and the body of Christ through the epiclesis of the eucharist. In time the custom of speaking about the Spirit in female terms waned in the West along with the habit of speaking very extensively about the Spirit at all.

There have been various attempts in recent years to retrieve the full trinitarian tradition while overcoming its inherent patriarchy by speaking about the Spirit as the feminine person of the godhead. When the Spirit is considered *the* feminine aspect of the divine, however, a host of difficulties ensues. The endemic difficulty of Spirit theology in the West insures that this "person" remains rather unclear and invisible. A deeper theology of the Holy Spirit, notes Walter Kasper in another connection, stands before the difficulty that unlike the Father and Son, the Holy Spirit is "faceless."[22] While the Son has appeared in human form and while we can at least make a mental image of the Father, the Spirit is not graphic and remains theologically the most mysterious of the three divine persons. For all practical purposes, we end up with two clear masculine images and an amorphous feminine third. Furthermore, the overarching framework of this approach again remains androcentric, with the male principle still dominant and sovereign. The Spirit even as God remains the "third" person, easily subordinated to the other two since she proceeds from them and is sent by them to mediate their presence and bring to completion what they have initiated. The direction in which this leads may be seen in Franz Mayr's attempt to understand the Holy Spirit as mother on the analogy of family relationships: if we liberate motherhood from a naturalistic concept and see it in its existential-social reality, then we can indeed see how the mother comes from the father and the son, that is, how she receives her existential stamp and identity from them both within the family.[23] As even a passing feminist analysis makes clear, while intending to rehabilitate the feminine, Mayr has again accomplished its subordination in unequal relationships.

The problem of stereotyping also plagues this approach. More often than not those who use it associate the feminine with unconscious dreams and fantasies (Bachiega), or with nature, instinct, and bodiliness (Schrey), or with prime matter (Mayr), all of which is then predicated of God through the doctrine of the Holy Spirit.[24] The equation is thus set up: male is to female as transcendence is to immanence, with the feminine Spirit restricted to the role of bearing the presence of God to our interiority. This stereotyping appears even in a creative attempt by process theologian John B. Cobb to come to grips with the charge of idolatry of the male in worship and thought. While acknowledging that currently the received polarity of feminine and masculine is subject to redescription, he goes on to identify the Logos, the masculine aspect of God, with order, novelty, demand, agency, transformation; and the Spirit, the feminine aspect of God, with receptivity, empathy, suffering, preservation. The lines are drawn: the Logos provides ever-new initial aims and lures us always forward, while the feminine aspect of God responds tenderly to our failures and successes, assures us that whatever happens we are loved, and achieves in her totality a harmonious wholeness of all that is.[25] There is real danger that simply identifying the Spirit with "feminine" reality leaves the overall symbol of God fundamentally unreformed and boxes actual women into a stereotypical ideal.

Recent Catholic theologies of the Spirit on three continents bear this out. In Europe Yves Congar has synthesized the learning of a lifetime in his trilogy on the Holy Spirit which gives an excellent comprehensive overview of the history of the doctrine of the Spirit and its ecumenical thorniness in relation to Orthodox churches. With a view toward contemporary concerns, he also adduces historical precedent for casting the Spirit in a feminine mold, calling the Spirit the feminine person in God, or again, God's femininity. In developing this idea Congar warns against locking women into the "harem" of preconceived roles of charm and passivity, and seeks to avoid this pitfall by concentrating on the maternal functions of the Spirit, which are interpreted as substantive and active. Accordingly, he describes ways in which the Spirit brings forth, loves, and educates as a mother does, by daily presence and communication that operates more on an affective than intellectual level.[26] However, while acknowledging that women want to emerge from preconceived notions to be simply and authentically persons, this author effectively reduces women's identity to the one role of mothering, an utterly important one to be sure, but just as certainly not the only role women exercise in the course of a lifetime. Nor is its execution devoid of the exercise of intellect.

In his essay on Mary as the maternal face of God, Latin American theologian Leonardo Boff holds that the Holy Spirit is the person in the Trinity who appropriates the feminine in a unique way and who can be said to have feminine, especially maternal, traits. What the feminine consists of is described philosophically and theologically under the primary rubric of the Jungian *anima*. Maternity, which Boff sees as constitutive of the personhood of women, accords primarily with love and self-giving, which are classical names for the Spirit. What is unique about this discussion is the novel hypothesis according to which the feminine dimension of the Spirit is worked out in affinity with the person of the Virgin Mary. In analogy with the incarnation of the Word in Jesus, the Spirit divinizes the feminine in the person of Mary, who in turn is to be regarded as hypostatically united to the third person of the blessed Trinity, for the benefit of all womankind:

The Spirit, the eternal feminine, is united to the created feminine in order that the latter may be totally and fully what it can be — virgin and mother. Mary, as Christian piety has always intuited, is the eschatological realization of the feminine in all of its dimensions.[27]

The simplest feminist analysis makes clear that in the case of actual women in all their historical concreteness, the categories of virgin and mother come nowhere near summing up the totality of what is possible for women's self-realization. Furthermore, even Boff's analysis of the feminine in relation to the Virgin Mary runs aground, finally, on the rocks of inconsistency. His moving depiction of Mary as a prophetic woman of liberation announcing God's justice in her *Magnificat* runs counter to his other descriptions of her participating in salvation "silently and unassumingly" according to the norm of the feminine.[28]

In developing his thesis Boff is self-critically aware that his is a male view of femininity, and he issues warnings against the male tendency either to consider women infantile characters or to overidealize them. He is trying to give women direct access to the divine, as Christian men have always enjoyed with their physical similarity to Jesus. In spite of this, however, his option for uncritical Jungian ground where the feminine is equated with darkness, death, depth, and receptivity and the masculine with light, transcendence, outgoingness, and reason, even while allowing that neither set of qualities is limited to men or women alone, coupled with his limitation of this feminine dimension to the Spirit alone within the godhead, insures an outcome that is not liberating for women.

Working out of a primarily Lonerganian context liberally salted with North American philosophy, Donald Gelpi develops a foundational pneumatology by constructing a theology of "Holy Breath" from the perspective of human religious experience.[29] In the effort to find a suitably personal iconography for the divine Breath, usually portrayed as a bird or fire, he taps into the feminine image rooted in Scripture as developed by Jungian personality theory. Well aware of the objections to the sexist connotations of archetypal imagery and writing passionately against sexism, he shows how a transvalued archetype of the feminine, that is, one divested of its shadow side, may appropriately organize feminine images of the Holy Breath and her functions of birth, enlightenment, and the transformation of life.

Once again, however, a difficulty ensues with this correlation between the Spirit, the feminine archetype, and the situation of women. Jungian archetypes are open to the charge of sexism not necessarily in the sense of being misogynist, which notion Gelpi seeks to allay, but insofar as they shrink the identity of the vast range of concrete and different women into preset characteristics and limit their options to historically predetermined roles. These roles are culturally conditioned by the society in which Jung lived, and do not include intellectual, artistic, or public leadership. Furthermore, Gelpi's effort to remove the shadow side of the feminine in order to find suitable metaphor for God debilitates one powerful source of female energy. In the conflictual, suffering world, actual women need to tap into their own pride and anger as sources of empowerment rather than be stripped of these so-called shadows.

In a church rigorously structured by patriarchal hierarchy, a Dominican, a Franciscan, and a Jesuit have tried to alleviate the sexism of the central symbol for God by imaging the Holy Spirit as feminine. I for one appreciate their efforts even as I criticize their results. The goodwill of these men is palpable and their intent is positive. Yet their methodological options insure that they do not listen to women's own self-definitions but develop a one-sided view of "the feminine" structurally conducive to the public power and private well-being of men. Besides the very real question of whether nature or culture shapes these descriptions of "feminine" roles, their effect on the being and function of concrete, historical women is deleterious and restrictive. Nurturing and tenderness simply do not exhaust the capacities of women; nor do bodiliness and instinct define women's nature; nor is intelligence and creative transformative agency beyond the scope of women's power; nor can the feminine be equated exclusively with mothering, affectivity, darkness, virginity, the Virgin Mary, or the positive feminine archetype without suffocating women's potential. Rosemary Ruether's question returns again in force, as to whether the very concept of the "feminine" used to define the essence of actual historical women is not a creature of patriarchy, useful insofar as it relegates women to the realm of the private and the role of succoring the male. When used to describe the Holy Spirit as the feminine dimension of God, the result is not a view of God that may liberate, empower, or develop women as *imago Dei* in all their complex female dimensions.

Unexamined presuppositions about the doctrine of God itself raise a further theological question about this approach. In what sense can it be claimed that God has "dimensions," let alone the dualistically conceived dimensions of masculine and feminine? Such an idea extends human divisions to the godhead itself. It actually ontologizes sex in God, making sexuality a dimension of divine being, rather than respecting the symbolic nature of religious language.

We must be very clear about this. Speech about God in female metaphors does not mean that God has a feminine dimension, revealed by Mary or other women. Nor does the use of male metaphors mean that God has a masculine dimension, revealed by Jesus or other men; or an animal dimension, revealed by lions or great mother birds; or a mineral dimension, which corresponds with naming God a rock. Images and names of God do not aim to identify merely "part" of the divine mystery, were that even possible. Rather, they intend to evoke the whole. Female imagery by itself points to God as such and has the capacity to represent God not only as nurturing, although certainly that, but as powerful, initiating, creating-redeeming-saving, and victorious over the powers of this world. If women are created in the image of God, then God can be spoken of in female metaphors in as full and as limited a way as God is imaged in male ones, without talk of feminine dimensions reducing the impact of this imagery. Understanding the Holy Spirit as the feminine dimension of the divine within a patriarchal framework is no solution. Even at its best, it does not liberate.

Equivalent Images of God Male and Female

While both the "traits" and the "dimensions" approach are inadequate for language about God inasmuch as in both an androcentric focus remains dominant, a third strategy speaks about the divine in images taken equivalently from the experience of women, men, and the world of nature. This approach shares with the other two the fundamental assumption that language about God as personal has a special appropriateness. Behaviorism notwithstanding, human persons are the most mysterious and attractive reality that we experience and the only creatures who bear self-reflective consciousness. God is not personal like anyone else we know, but the language of person points in a unique way to the mysterious depths and freedom of action long associated with the divine.

Predicating personality of God, however, immediately involves us in questions of sex and gender, for all the persons we know are either male or female. The mystery of God is properly understood as neither male nor female but transcends both in an unimaginable way. But insofar as God creates both male and female in the divine image and is the source of the perfections of both, either can equally well be used as metaphor to point to divine mystery. Both in fact are needed for less inadequate speech about God, in whose image the human race is created. This "clue"[30] for speaking of God in the image of male and female has the advantage of making clear at the outset that women enjoy the dignity of being made in God's image and are therefore capable as women of representing God. Simultaneously, it relativizes undue emphasis on any one image, since pressing the multiplicity of imagery shows the partiality of images of one sex alone. The incomprehensible mystery of God is brought to light and deepened in our consciousness through imaging of male and female, beyond any person we know.[31]

Although drawing their predominant speech about God from the pool of male images, the biblical, early theological, and medieval mystical traditions also use female images of the divine without embarrassment or explanation. The images and personifications are not considered feminine aspects or features of the divine, to be interpreted in dualistic tension with masculine dimensions or traits, but rather they are representations of the fullness of God in creating, redeeming, and calling the world to eschatological shalom.

Ancient religions that spoke of deity in both male and female symbols may also be helpful in clarifying the thrust of this third approach. As evidenced in psalms and prayers, male and female deities were not stereotyped according to later ideas of what was properly masculine and feminine, but each represented a diversity of divine activities and attributes. In them "gender division is not yet the primary metaphor for imaging the dialectics of human existence,"[32] nor is the idea of gender complementarity present in the ancient myths. Rather, male and female enjoy broad and equivalent powers. A goddess such as Ishtar, for example, is addressed by devotees as a source of divine power and sovereignty embodied in female form, and praised as a deity who performs the divine works of dividing heaven from earth, setting captives free, waging war, establishing peace, administering justice, exercising judgment, and enlightening human beings with truth, along with presiding over birth, healing the sick, and nurturing the little ones.[33] When a god such as Horus is addressed, he is credited with similar functions. Both male and female are powerful in the private and public spheres.

The point for our interest is that the female deity is not the expression of the feminine dimension of the divine, but the expression of the fullness of divine power and care shown in a female image. A striking example of the same intuition is given in Luke's Gospel in the parallel parables of the shepherd looking for his lost sheep and the homemaker looking for her lost coin (15:4–10). In both stories someone vigorously seeks what is lost and rejoices with others when it is found. Neither story discloses anything about God that the other hides. Using traditional men's and women's work, both parables orient the hearer to God's redeeming action in images that are equivalently male and female. The woman with the coin image, while not frequently portrayed in Christian art due largely to the androcentric nature of the traditioning process, is essentially as legitimate a reference to God as is the shepherd with his sheep. Conversely, God spoken of in this way cannot be used to validate role stereotyping wherein the major redeeming work in the world is done by men to the exclusion or marginalization of women.

The mystery of God transcends all images but can be spoken about equally well and poorly in concepts taken from male or female reality. The approach advocated here proceeds with the insight that only if God is so named, only if the full reality of women as well as men enters into the symbolization of God along with symbols from the natural world, can the idolatrous fixation on one image be broken and the truth of the mystery of God, in tandem with the liberation of all human beings and the whole earth, emerge for our time.

Options

The linguistic options which guide this study, made with the judgment that they are appropriate and necessary, converge into speech about God using female metaphors that intend to designate the whole of divine mystery. Theoretically I endorse the ideal of language for God in male and female terms used equivalently, as well as the use of cosmic and metaphysical symbols. In actual fact, however, male and female images simply have not been nor are they even now equivalent. Female religious symbols of the divine are underdeveloped, peripheral, considered secondarily if at all in Christian language and the practice it continues to shape, much like women through whose image they point to God. In my judgment, extended theological speaking about God in female images, or long draughts of this new wine, are a condition for the very possibility of equivalent imaging of God in religious speech. This book's choice to use mainly female symbolism for God, let me state clearly, is not intended as a strategy of subtraction, still less of reversal. Rather, it is an investigation of a suppressed world directed ultimately toward the design of a new whole. Shaping this kind of speech is not an end in itself but must be received as an essential element in reordering an unjust and deficiently religious situation. Until a strong measure of undervalued female symbolism is introduced and used with ease, equivalent imaging of God male and female, which I myself have advocated and still hold to be a goal, remains an abstraction, expressive of an ideal but unrealizable in actual life.[34]

In the task of shaping new discourse about God this study draws on a number of key resources: women's interpreted experience, and critical retrieval of elements in Scripture and the classical tradition. Each of these in its own way contributes building blocks for a liberating naming toward God. To these resources we now turn.

The Creation of Adam, detail from Michelangelo, *Sistine Chapel Ceiling* (1508–12: Vatican City). Courtesy of Alinari/Art Resource, N.Y.

Lucas Cranach, the Elder, *The Holy Trinity above a Landscape and within a Gloriole of Angels* (c. 1516–18: Kunsthalle, Bremen). Oil on wood; 41 x 29 cm. Courtesy of the Kunsthalle, Bremen. (278–1904/22).

Meinrad Craighead, *Hagia Sophia*

"We are born remembering; we are born connected. The thread of personal myth winds through the matriarchal labyrinth, from womb to womb, to the faceless source, which is the place of origination."
— Meinrad Craighead, "Immanent Mother," in
The Feminist Mystic, edited by Mary Giles
(New York: Crossroad, 1982) 82–83.

William Blake, *Elohim Creating Adam* (1795: Tate Gallery, London). Courtesy of the Tate Gallery, London/Art Resource, N.Y. (N–05055).

Mary Lou Sleevi, *Spirit of Wisdom*

As it is written,
I call you my sister.
Come.
You are pure and simple Wisdom,
so young and so old.
Renewing all things, you never change. . . .

Painting and text from Mary Lou Sleevi, *Women of the Word* (Notre Dame, Ind.:
Ave Maria Press, 1989) 104–5. Used by permission of the artist.

Frontispiece, *Liber Chronicarum* (*Nuremberg Chronicles*), published 1493, Hartmann Schedel (1440–1514). National Gallery of Art, Washington, D.C. Gift of Paul Mellon, in Honor of the Fiftieth Anniversary of the National Gallery of Art. (03–77–7711).

Dina Cormick, *Creator God most beautiful*

In the beginning
the earth was dark and without sound,
and God arose and began to dance
— Creator God most beautiful —
and in the music of her song
She called forth all life into being.

"... This started out as an icon, using the traditional format of the Byzantine type, but then I felt that this had to be transformed into more of a feminist imaging, so instead of a rectangular mode I shifted into a circle — like a breast, source of nourishment, the circle of eternity, symbol of earth and mothering, of woman. I use a lot of simple daisy flowers because I love them, and I think a flower is a beautiful logo for a woman. ..."

— from a letter by Dina Cormick, Durban, South Africa.
Painting used by permission of the artist.

Unnamed Mexican woman:

"I am working in a little town on the Isthmus. We have about 40,000 people to encourage to form Basic Christian Communities. The bishop is excellent, a wild man determined to turn the church over to lay people. The poverty is horrible, grinding, demeaning; the people lively, warm, suffering. I will be here for at least two years and think I will learn a lot. This is a wonderful image of God, no? I think we are neither in the raw cotton or the thread, but in the twirling. . . ."

— from a postcard sent from Mexico by Michael Siefert, S.M.

PART II

FOREGROUND:
RESOURCES FOR
EMANCIPATORY SPEECH
ABOUT GOD

Chapter 4

WOMEN'S INTERPRETED
EXPERIENCE

Iron is strong, but fire tempers it.
Fire is awesome, but water extinguishes it.
Water is forceful, but the sun dries it.
The sun is mighty, but a storm cloud conceals it.
A storm cloud is explosive, but the earth subdues it.
The earth is majestic, but men master it.
Men are powerful, but grief overtakes them.
Grief is heavy, but wine assuages it.
Wine is powerful, but sleep renders it weak.
Yet woman is strongest of all.

—from a history of Ethiopia, 1681[1]

Consulting human experience is an identifying mark of virtually all contemporary theology, as indeed has been the case at least implicitly with
most of the major articulations in the history of Christian theology.[2] Listening to the questions and struggles of the people of an era, their value
systems and deepest hopes, gives theology of the most diverse kinds an
indispensable clue for shaping inquiry, drawing the hermeneutical circle, revising received interpretations, and arriving at new theological
insight. Feminist reflection is therefore not alone in its use of human
experience as a resource for doing theology. What is distinctive, however, is its specific identification of the lived experience of women, long
derided or neglected in androcentric tradition, as an essential element
in the theological task. Given the diversity of women in the concrete, the
precise shapes of women's experience along with the validity of naming
any particular characteristic or way of being in the world "female" are
matters of intense study and debate.[3] There is no stereotypical norm.
Yet living within patriarchal systems does forge among women recognizable experiences of suffering along with typical patterns of coping
and victoriously resisting, strategies that enable women to survive. Out
of a plethora of such experience, this chapter explores one strand that is

61

fundamental to emancipatory speech about God in feminist liberation theology, namely, the experience of conversion.

A central resource for naming toward God, the very matrix that energizes it, is the breakthrough of power occurring in women's struggle to reject the sexism of inherited constructions of female identity and risk new interpretations that affirm their own human worth. This foundational experience can be suitably described in the classic language of conversion, a turning around of heart and mind that sets life in a new direction. Its ramifications reach deeply into the creative process in which speech about God is forged, as it affects at a basic level interpretations of spirituality, moral values, and doctrine. Thus women's awakening to their own human worth can be interpreted at the same time as a new experience of God, so that what is arguably occurring is a new event in the religious history of humankind. This conversion, moreover, brings in its wake a concomitant judgment about the positive moral value of female bodiliness, love of connectedness, and other characteristics that mark the historical lives of women in a specific way, so that what is fitting for the mystery of God to be and to do receives new contours. These shifts in the religious and ethical realms are retrieved in the explicit language of doctrine: in all concreteness and difference women claim full ownership of their human identity as *imago Dei* and *imago Christi.* This theological interpretation of female identity is the center of gravity for feminist discourse about the mystery of God.

The Dynamism of the Conversion Experience

In myriad ways women are newly involved in experiencing and articulating themselves as subjects, as active subjects of history, and as *good* ones. Given the negative assessment of women's humanity under patriarchy, this self-naming has the character of a conversion process, a turning away from trivialization and defamation of oneself as a female person and a turning toward oneself as worthwhile, as in fact a gift, in community with many others similarly changing. This conversion amounts to nothing less than a rebirth and is accomplished in a dialectic of contrast and confirmation.

Contrast. There is an experience of lived oppression, interpreted precisely as oppressive and therefore wrong. As the many-faceted dehumanization into which women are cast comes to consciousness through struggle against it (praxis) and shared, frequently prayerful thought about it (reflection), a sense of indignation grows. The contradiction between the suffering caused by sexism and the *humanum* of women, between the crushing on the one hand and women's own dignity on the other, gives rise to a profound and irrevocable *no*. This should not be! The judgment arises: we are worth more than this. Indignation generates the energy for resistance, an act grounded on an equally deep and lasting *yes* to women's flourishing. The search commences then, both in action and theory, for new ways of living that will find what has been lost.

In a classic sense what transpires here is a negative contrast experience, giving rise through the violation of a good to a glimpse of its strong value in a new configuration.[4] It is the kind of fruitful experience that transpires when persons bump up against the stubborn resistance of historical reality to what they sense to be true, good, and beautiful. When reality is thus "dis-illusioning," the contrast challenges people to a decision: either close their minds and deny what they have experienced, or use it as a springboard to address and struggle with the causes of the suffering.

Confirmation. Through memory, narrative, and solidarity a positive acknowledgment of women's beauty and power as active subjects of history also begins to come to speech. While consistently subordinated in official practice women have in fact always been there, acting in myriad creative ways to live their own lives and bring about the good of others in the light of the gospel. The ambiguity of the Christian tradition lies precisely in this fact, that despite its sexism it has served as a strong source of life for countless women throughout the centuries and continues to do so today. Narrative remembrance of women's courage and power in their defeat and victory merges with new instances of women's creativity, leadership, and prophecy today to signal that, by the power of the Spirit of God, the history of women's empowerment has not ceased. The positive connection between women's wisdom and agency and the fragmentary but real coming of salvific moments in the Christian tradition opens a perspective on what might yet be.

Narrative remembrance functions to empower women not as individual monads but in a solidarity of sisters. While the particularities of poverty or plenty, racial and ethnic heritage, and so forth, chisel different contours of awareness, everywhere a modicum of the essential element of community is found in women's solidarity with each other, either face to face or in far-flung networks united by the spoken or written word and freely chosen action. By unleashing a positive type of history, that is, by forming communities of discourse, by engaging together in resistance to oppression and the creative praxis of liberation for all that they cherish, women come to an awareness that they are not nonpersons or half persons or deficient persons, but genuine subjects of history.[5]

Conversion. No to the disparagement of sexism in a yes to the goodness of being women accomplishes a basic conversion in attitude and practice. Given the insidious pervasiveness of sexism, this experience of turning has the fundamental character of hope, even hope against hope. Women bear the most ultimate trust, grounded in absolute mystery encountered as source and blessing of all that is female, that despite the present situation a more liberating and life-giving moment will arrive. Lament over women's suffering and celebration of women's creative agency couple with hope for a future that will be more beneficial. The energy released by this turning sustains practical efforts for change of structures and consciousness here and now. The pull of that future, promised but unknown, already realized in every small practical victory, directs the negative and positive energies in women's conversion experience toward transformation.

The category of conversion here receives a description somewhat different from that of classical theology where it typically connotes the process of disowning oneself or divesting oneself of ego in order to be filled with divine grace. Feminist analysis has long pointed out that this meaning is fruitful when it is uttered, as it originally was, from the perspective of the ruling male whose primordial temptation is likely to be the sin of pride or self-assertion over against others.[6] If pride be the primary block on the path to God, then indeed decentering the rapacious self is the work of grace. But the situation is quite different when this language is applied to persons already relegated to the margins of significance and excluded from the exercise of self-definition. For such persons, language of conversion as loss of self, turning from *amor sui*, functions in an ideological way to rob them of power, maintaining them in a subordinate position to the benefit of those who rule.

Analysis of women's experience is replete with the realization that within patriarchal systems women's primordial temptation is not to pride and self-assertion but rather to the lack of it, to diffuseness of personal center, overdependence on others for self-identity, drifting, and fear of recognizing one's own competence. According to cultural myth Sleeping Beauty lies in a hundred-year sleep waiting for the kiss of the prince to awaken her, while he is off maturing on the challenge of the quest.[7] In this situation grace comes to the sleeper not as the call to loss of self but as empowerment toward discovery of self and affirmation of one's strength, giftedness, and responsibility. Such is women's present experience of the perennial call to conversion. It involves a turning away from demeaning female identity toward new ownership of the female self as God's good gift. This is a deeply religious event, the coming into being of suppressed selves. Its significance in terms of spirituality, ethical values, and articulated doctrine has yet to be fully calculated, and yet is already bringing about new articulations of divine mystery.

Experience of Self, Experience of God

On the spectrum of historical mediations of encounter with God, the experience of oneself has a unique importance. One acute analysis of the intrinsic unity of the self and the symbol of God is offered by Karl Rahner, whose investigations in this area yield a way of appreciating the religious significance of what is going forward today in women's experience. According to Rahner's anthropological analysis, a human being is primordially 'spirit in the world,' that is, an embodied subject whose capacity for radical questioning and free and responsible action reveals that the person is structured toward an ever-receding horizon. This capacity shows that human beings are dynamically oriented toward fathomless mystery as the very condition for the possibility of acting in characteristic human ways. In other words, when caught in the act of being most personal, human beings disclose an openness toward infinite mystery as source, support, and goal of the operation of their very selves. Human beings are dynamically structured toward God. The Pantheon, an ancient shrine now a Christian church in Rome, offers an architectural analogy. We are not capped off, so to speak, but like that structure have a hole in the roof that admits rays of sun and rain and toward which our spirits, in the shadows, ascend.

Accordingly, the experience of God which is never directly available is mediated, among other ways but primordially so, through the changing history of oneself. Rather than being a distinct and separate experience, it transpires as the ultimate depth and radical essence of every personal experience such as love, fidelity, loneliness, and death. In the experience of oneself at these depths, at this prethematic level whence our own mystery arises, we also experience and are grasped by the holy mystery of God as the very context of our own self-presence. In fact the silent, nonverbal encounter with infinite mystery constitutes the enabling condition of any experience of self at all.

If the connection between the self and holy mystery be this intrinsic, then it follows that adjustments in the experience of one reality will of necessity affect experience of the other. Personal development of the self also constitutes development of the experience of God; loss of self-identity is also a loss of the experience of God. They are two aspects of one and the same history of experience. Writes Rahner, "The personal history of the experience of the self is the personal history of the experience of God"; "the personal history of the experience of God signifies, over and above itself, the personal history of the experience of the self."[8] Each mutually conditions the other.

Consequently, when a person claims the self in freedom, or finds a new way of loving others and thus oneself, or affirms oneself in trustful acceptance, then the changing history of this self-relation also entails living through a changing history of the experience of God. Conversely, when a person destroys a personally important idol, or glimpses new truth about God, or transcends all particular categories in reverence toward unfathomable mystery, these episodes in the history of one's experience of God are events directly belonging to the history of the self. To sum up a lifetime: "the personal history of the experience of the self is in its total extent the history of the ultimate experience of God also."[9]

Because of his concentration on the individual person in isolation from the constitutive relation to community, which provides the very tools of experience of self-including language, Rahner's method has been criticized by the next generation of theologians.[10] Rather than a transcendental approach, many critics opt for a fundamental theology in which the practical, communitarian structure of the logos of Christian theology becomes clear. Even here, however, the intrinsic link between historical experience and speech about God perdures. J. B. Metz, for example, shifts to a practical theology focused on the basic categories of memory, narrative, and solidarity. Those who have been nonpersons become active subjects of history through narrative memory of experiences of suffering and defeat as well as of resistance and victory, and through solidarity in the midst of historical struggle. At the same time this discourse and praxis accompany an idea of God who constitutes the identity of the subject, always under serious threat. A political theology of the subject goes hand in hand with dangerous speech about a God who frees slaves and raises up the crucified. Experience of self as an active subject in history and experience of God as liberator are a unity.[11]

It is in this deeply personal-and-religious dimension that women are caught up in new experiences, which when articulated move toward new speaking about God. The shock of the negative in traditional, internalized devaluations of women, known in the surge of self-affirmation against it, is at the same time new experience of God as beneficent toward the female and an ally of women's flourishing. In struggle, in connectedness, in particularity, in the everyday round of life's duties, in the love of self and other women, in the love of men in nonsubordinate ways, God is being experienced in new terms. Through women's encounter with the holy mystery of their own selves as blessed comes commensurate language about holy mystery in female metaphor and symbol, gracefully, powerfully, necessarily. The polyphony of discourses traditionally used to name God — narrative, prophecy, command, wise utterances, hymns of celebration and lament — sounds new notes as the stories, the prophetic criticisms, the imperatives, the wise insights, and the rising of women's spirits in praise and grief are articulated, for speaking about God and self-interpretation cannot be separated.[12] To give but one example, conversion experienced not as giving up oneself but as tapping into the power of oneself simultaneously releases understanding of divine power not as dominating power-over but as the passionate ability to empower oneself and others. And so forth. Mary Daly was astute in observing that women are not interested in fixing new static names upon God. Rather, in the ontological naming and affirming of ourselves we are engaged in a dynamic reaching out to the mystery of God in whose being we participate.[13]

The artist says it best. In a dramatic play about the metaphysical dilemma of being black, being female, and being alive, Ntozake Shange captures in one line the dynamism of new experience of women's selves in tandem with new language about God. After roiling adventures of prejudice, hurt, and survival, a tall black woman rises from despair to cry out, "i found god in myself and i loved her, i loved her fiercely."[14] It is this finding and fierce loving of the female self in relation to God and God in relation to self that is one root of feminist theological naming toward God.

Moral Values

The field of feminist ethics and moral development is rich with discoveries about the way women characteristically live and operate in the world.[15] These delineations of women's self-understanding are distinct from the debate over whether women are the way they are by nature or nurture, that is, by virtue of genes or the cultural construction of identity. Nor do they stereotype women or collapse the differences between them. What feminist ethics does, in the light of its fundamental principle that "women are fully human and are to be valued as such,"[16] as Margaret Farley articulates it, is to listen to women for clues as to how they experience and interpret reality, and to use these indicators as guides to construct a vision of a moral universe wherein women's well-being along with everything they cherish is promoted.

At the heart of feminist reconstruction of ethics, as I read it, is the affirmation that women are human persons with the capacity to exercise moral agency, with all the freedom and responsibility that this entails. Old, androcentric definitions of women as essentially passive are superseded in the move toward moral autonomy, accomplished in struggle and creative action. At the same time feminist ethics eschews the vision of the isolated moral agent so prized by the dominant view of man in Western culture and rejects the ideal of nonrelational autonomy as deficiently human. Out of women's self-understanding comes a different alternative from either dependency or detachment, namely, the coinherence of autonomy and mutuality as constitutive of the mature person.

Classic ethical formulations assume that the self is best defined over against the other. Students of personality formation now point out that this is primarily a male experience, springing from the pattern of the young boy with his mother. Needing to become himself, the boy becomes a self by separation, opposition, conquering his need for the significant other, his mother. When carried unnuanced into adulthood this stance quickly leads to the ideal of the solitary self, the *cogito, ergo sum* model of self-identity, which seeks strength in personal impermeability and defines power in adversarial relations over against others. The experience of the young girl with her mother yields an alternative paradigm whereby one becomes a true self not by total separation but by a dialectic of identification and differentiation, being and growing with the other in mutually enhancing relation.[17]

Drawing on this experience feminist ethics argues that the self is rightly structured not in dualistic opposition to the other but in intrinsic relationship with the other.[18] Rather than "we" meaning "not they," we and they are intertwined. Neither heteronomy (exclusive other-directedness) nor autonomy in a closed egocentric sense but a model of relational independence, freedom in relation, full related selfhood becomes the ideal. The vision is one of relational autonomy, which honors the inviolable personal mystery of the person who is constituted essentially by community with others.

The particular pattern of relationship consistently promoted in feminist ethical discourse is mutuality. This signifies a relation marked by equivalence between persons, a concomitant valuing of each other, a common regard marked by trust, respect, and affection in contrast to competition, domination, or assertions of superiority. It is a relationship on the analogy of friendship, an experience often used as metaphor to characterize the reciprocity/independence dialectic at the heart of all caring relationships. Women's moral development and psychology;[19] women's ways of knowing;[20] women's ways of loving;[21] women's ways of living bodily[22] – all are marked, upon reflection, by an intrinsic connectedness quite different from the male ideal in classic and contemporary culture. As Margaret Farley carefully notes in her influential essay on this subject, this revaluation of mutual relationship has within it the beginnings of a moral revolution.[23]

The centrality of relation ensures that feminist ethics presses ultimately toward the flourishing of all people, children as well as men, and the earth and all its creatures. In the realm of theory, if the self is not defined by opposition but by the dialectic of friendly, constitutive relation, then it begins to be possible to hold together in a rich synthesis all manner of previously dichotomous elements: not just self and other, but matter and spirit, passions and intellect, embodiedness and self-transcendence, nurturing and questing, altruism and self-affirmation, receptivity and activity, love and power, being and doing, private and public domains, humanity and the earth. Oppositional, either-or thinking, which is endemic to the androcentric construction of reality, dissolves in a new paradigm of both-and. Hence embodiment, sexuality, passion, the erotic are reclaimed as potential goods rather than the antithesis of spirit; social, economic, and political structures are matters of care as an intrinsic part of women's new blessing of themselves.

What this development in moral consciousness is bringing to the work of speaking about God is just beginning to be glimpsed. The traditional patriarchal notion of the divine follows closely the dualistic view of the self. Both the being of God, which stands over against the world, and the classical attributes of the divine with their implicit stress on solitariness, superiority, and dominating power-over, speak about holy mystery in an essentially unrelated way on the model of the male self typically constructed over against others. We have already seen that such an idea of God is deeply rooted in the ideal of ruling men within patriarchy, the ideal of being untouched by contingency and its pain, and able to best all comers. If, however, moral autonomy is grounded on relationship, if mutuality is a moral excellence, then language emerges that sees holy mystery as at once essentially free and richly related, the two being not opposites but correlatives. God's activity is discerned in divine, free, mutual relation rather than in divine distance, rule, and the search for submission. Changing the human ethical ideal has far-reaching ramifications for speech about God.[24]

Image of God, Image of Christ

Women's experience of self interpreted as experience of God, fleshed out with values characteristic of women's ways of being in the world, comes to a theological flashpoint when women begin to articulate and act in accord with their dignity as *imago Dei, imago Christi.* It is true that central to Christian anthropology has always been the doctrine that human beings, male and female, are created in the image of God, and that in the power of the Spirit members of the community, men and women, are transformed according to the image of Christ. However, a deep ambiguity has afflicted the *imago* doctrine throughout the Christian tradition. While affirming that human beings generically are created in the image and likeness of God, theology also adopted the hardy form of gender dualism found in Hellenistic thought. It was not a long step from the identification of men with mind, reason, and spirit and concomitantly of women with bodiliness and passion in a metaphorical sense, to a stance that cast actual men alone in the representative role of headship, the primary image of all superior qualities and therefore of God, while women were relegated to secondary status in nature and grace. This dichotomization of humanity proceeded to the point where women were even projected to be the symbol of evil, the anti-image of God, the representative of evil tendencies in the sin-prone part of the male self. Undergirded by a dualistic anthropology that sees human nature embodied in two essentially different and unequal ways, this view is the one that predominates throughout most of the history of Christian thought, although always in tension with texts that did grant full participation in the *imago Dei* to women.[25]

Interpreting women's conversion experience in theological terms presses feminist theology toward reclaiming the dignity of the image of God and Christ for women not only in general but in the concrete. To be precise, actual, historical women are created in the image of God and are bearers of the image of Christ. This affirmation of women's theological identity opens the door to critical retrieval of overlooked aspects of Scripture and tradition.

Imago Dei: Careful contemporary exegesis has shown that the two initial biblical creation stories include women equally in their purview of the human race. When the priestly author of Genesis 1 depicts God creating the human race in the divine image and likeness on the sixth day, the text makes clear that the compliment is intended for "male and female" together. All members of the species are equally favored with the theological identity of *imago Dei*, while the story introduces maleness and femaleness to flag the fact that human beings like other creatures are sexual and thus gifted with fertility.[26] Similarly, the Yahwist author of Genesis 2 constructs the narrative in such a way that the "earth creature" does not become sexually differentiated until the divine act radically alters *'adam* to create woman and man together as one flesh. "Their creation is simultaneous, not sequential."[27] Nor does Scripture polarize the human couple into a binary pattern of sexual complementarity with its hidden theme of domination. In both creation stories mutuality is the key to their relation.

The precise content of what it means for human beings to be created in the image of God has shifted in the course of theological history. In Genesis it is located in human stewardship of the earth and its creatures, ruling, using, and caring for the world as representatives of God. Patristic authors interpret the *imago* in a less functional, more essential way as the human race's kinship to divine reality, a relation interrupted by the factual separation of sin. Medieval theologians looked for the image's content in the human soul with its spiritual gift of rationality (*natura intellectualis*), while the Reformers translated it into functional terms and found it in original righteousness, the conformity of the human will with divine will. More recent interpretations have identified the image of God with human creativity, or with human community, or with the likeness of human beings to God in their whole person including bodily form. Some stress the incomplete character of the *imago Dei* since it is the eschatological destiny for which human beings are intended.[28]

As women's experience of their own worth is articulated today, ownership of the *imago Dei* doctrine is occurring at a foundational level. It is not necessary to choose among interpretations. After a long season of thirst all of the above, and more, are owned as matter for theological self-definition. Women are *imago Dei* in the exercise of stewardship over the earth and the capacity to rule as representatives of God, with ecological care; in their kinship by nature with holy mystery; in their rationality and intelligence and in their freedom capable of union with God; in their creativity, their sociality, their community with each other and with men, children, and the whole earth; in their bodiliness, their destiny. The wholeness of women's reality is affirmed as created by God and blessed with the identity of being in the divine image and likeness. Practically speaking, this leads to the moral imperative of respect for women, to the responsibility not to deface the living image of God but to promote it through transformative praxis. In linguistic terms it offers basic justification for speech about God in female symbols, since women themselves are theomorphic. If women are created in the image of God, without qualification, then their human reality offers suitable, even excellent metaphor for speaking about divine mystery, who remains always ever greater.

Imago Christi: Due to the androcentric nature of the traditioning process, the understanding that women are likewise christomorphic has been more difficult to grasp. A mentality centered on the priority of men has taken identification with Christ as its own exclusive prerogative, aided by a naive physicalism that collapses the totality of the

Christ into the bodily form of Jesus. From the earliest days Christians are indeed marked by the confession that Jesus is the Christ, the Messiah, the anointed, the blessed one. But this confession also witnesses to the insight that through the power of the Spirit the beloved community shares in this Christhood, participates in the living and dying and rising of Christ to such an extent that they can even be called the body of Christ. Identified with the redemptive acts of Christ's historical and risen life, women and men together form one body that lives through, into, with, and in Christ. Broken by sinfulness though they be, the members of the community are *en christō,* and their own lives assume a christic pattern.[29]

The baptismal and martyrdom traditions bear this out in ways that are being newly appreciated. An early Christian baptismal hymn cited by Paul sets the theme as it announces that the old barriers of race, class, and sex are transcended in a new form of identity: "As many of you as were baptized into Christ have clothed yourselves with Christ. There is no longer Jew or Greek, there is no longer slave or free, there is no longer male and female; for all of you are one in Christ Jesus" (Gal 3:27–28). Through baptism the Christian is ontologically identified with the death and resurrection of Christ, putting on Christ through the vitalizing power of the Spirit. This happens corporately, through becoming a member of the whole Christ. As a consequence, the baptized are recreated in every dimension of their existence: "If anyone is in Christ, that one is a new creature" (2 Cor 5:17). Destined for the fullness of participation in Christ in eschatological glory, the Jews, Greeks, slaves, free persons, males and females of the body of Christ are even now equally united with Christ in a union that connotes one flesh: "Don't you know that your bodies are members of Christ?" (1 Cor 6:15a).

If the model for sharing in the image of Christ be one of exact duplication, similar to the making of a xerox copy, and if Christ be reduced to the historical individual Jesus of Nazareth, and if the salient feature about Jesus as the Christ be his male sex, then women are obviously excluded from sharing that image in full. But every one of those suppositions falls short and twists the central testimony of biblical and doctrinal traditions. The guiding model for the *imago Christi* is not replication of sexual features but participation in the life of Christ, which is founded on communion in the Spirit: those who live the life of Christ are icons of Christ. Furthermore, the whole Christ is a corporate personality, a relational reality, redeemed humanity that finds its way by the light of the historical narrative of Jesus' compassionate, liberating love: Christ exists only pneumatologically. Finally, what is essential to the saving good news about Jesus is not his bodily sex but the solidarity of the Wisdom of God in and through this genuine human being with all those who suffer and are lost. To make of the maleness of Jesus Christ a christological principle is to deny the universality of salvation.[30]

One in Christ Jesus, baptized women precisely in their female bodily existence and not apart from it are *imago Christi*. Paul makes the meaning of this identification highly precise using the evocative idea of image/icon. Hope makes us act with great boldness, he writes, for we unveil our faces to gaze right at Christ. Then through the power of the Spirit "all of us are being transformed into that same image from one degree of glory to another" (2 Cor 3:18). The inclusive "all of us" makes clear that the whole community, women as well as men, are gifted with transformation "into the same image," in Greek the same *eikōn*, that is, the image of Christ. Another biblical example: in God's design the community is called "to be conformed to the image" of Christ (Rom 8:29). The Greek is instructive, for the members of the community are identified as *sym-morphos* to the *eikōn*, that is, sharing the form of the likeness, or formed according to the image of Christ. No distinction on the basis of sex is made, or needed; being christomorphic is not a sex-distinctive gift. Nor does it mean that women lose their femaleness or embodied sexuality. The image of Christ does not lie in sexual similarity to the human man Jesus, but in coherence with the narrative shape of his compassionate, liberating life in the world, through the power of the Spirit. Theologically, the capacity of women and men to be *sym-morphos* to the *eikōn* of Christ is identical.

A similar identification of women with Christ runs through discourse about those who suffer for the faith. In one stunning narrative Luke makes this christomorphism explicit: "But Saul, still breathing threats and murder against the disciples of the Lord, went to the high priest and asked him for letters to the synagogues at Damascus, so that if he found any belonging to the Way, men or women, he might bring them bound to Jerusalem." When the light from heaven flashes, when the voice from heaven asks "why do you persecute me?" when Saul wonders, "Who are you, Lord?" the momentous answer is profoundly instructive: "I am Jesus, whom you are persecuting" (Acts 9:1–5). Both men and women disciples are here identified with Jesus without distinction. The same theological assessment is given to both. Saul's murderous intent and tormenting actions against women disciples are rightly named actions against Christ, without qualification.

In the persecutions under the Roman emperors women martyrs continued to be seen in a christic way as graphic icons of the love and courage so central to the Christian story of salvation. Speaking about the torture of one Blandina, for example, Eusebius recounts that as she hung suspended on a sort of cross, her prayer and courage gave strength to her companions: "In this battle, they saw with their bodily eyes, in the form of their sister, the One who had been crucified for them."[31] Comments a French translator of this account, "Christians loved to discover, in their martyrs, the image of the suffering Christ."[32] The historical form of Christ may be male or female, *christa* or *christus*, but the underlying sacramentality between crucified persons and Jesus Christ is identical. The form of the sister is the form of Christ: in the free giving of their lives through participation in the Spirit women are recognized to be christomorphic in the most profound way.

Writing on the martyrs centuries later Vatican II continues this long-standing tradition of interpretation. Christ, writes the council, freely accepted death for the world's salvation. Martyrdom "transforms" a disciple into an intense image of Christ, for the martyr "perfects that image even to the shedding of blood."[33] The verbs actually used to describe the effect of martyrdom on a disciple are *assimilatur* and *conformatur*, connoting the closest possible relationship: the martyr is assimilated and conformed to Christ. In this text no distinctions are made on the basis of the martyrs' sex, nor should there be. The archbishop and the four North American churchwomen murdered in El Salvador in 1980, and the six university Jesuits with the two Salvadoran women killed a decade later all give a witness in the uniqueness of their own persons that is theologically identical. Jon Sobrino, also earmarked for death, got it exactly right when he wrote of the North American women:

I have stood by the bodies of Maura Clarke, Ita Ford, Dorothy Kazel, and Jean Donovan.... The murdered Christ is here in the person of four *women*.... Christ lies dead here among us. He is Maura, Ita, Dorothy, and Jean. But he is risen, too, in these same four women, and he keeps the hope of liberation alive. ... Salvation comes to us through all women and men who love truth more than lies, who are more eager to give than to receive, and whose love is that supreme love that gives life rather than keeping it for oneself. Yes, their dead bodies fill us with sorrow and indignation. And yet, our last word must be: Thank you. In Maura, Ita, Dorothy, and Jean, God has visited El Salvador.[34]

Martyrs join all those whose victory is celebrated on the feast of All Saints. As Vatican II writes of all the saints, they shared in our humanity and yet were transformed into especially successful "images of Christ." In them God vividly manifests the divine presence and "face," speaks to us, and gives us a sign of the coming kingdom, which powerfully draws us, surrounded as we are by so many witnesses and having such an argument for the truth of the gospel.[35] Once again in these texts there is no reservation about acknowledging the *imago Christi* to be the theological identity of women.

The fundamental egalitarianism of the baptismal and martyrdom traditions continues today in the baptismal and funeral liturgies, the latter building on the former. Both coming into and going out of the historical community are celebrated with the same texts and rituals whether the individual involved is woman or man; for the theological character of their being in Christ is identical. Created women, baptized women, persecuted women, martyred women, sinful and redeemed women of all varieties — all are genuinely *imago Dei, imago Christi.*

The fundamental capacity to be bearers of the image of God and Christ is a gift not restricted by sex. New religious experience of women's selves, coupled with feminist theological analysis, has resurrected this insight at the same time that it vigorously gives the lie to any views that shortchange women's theological identity. Such views are distortions of God's good creation in women. They do not derive from the egalitarian doctrines of the *imago Dei* or *imago Christi* central to Christian life, but from androcentric attitudes striving to protect patriarchal privilege. As such they are simply wrong, expressions of the sin of sexism. Women know from the experience of conversion that such views are also existentially ridiculous, as well as logically incoherent when set within the larger context of Christian belief. As women name themselves in power, responsibility, freedom, and mutual relatedness, and affirm themselves as embodied, self-transcending persons broken by sin and yet renewed by amazing grace, new ownership of the gift of the female self as *imago Dei, imago Christi* is transacted. Simultaneously, it becomes obvious that the *imago* is flexible and returns to its giver, so that women who are genuinely in God's image in turn become suitable metaphors for the divine.

Because the mystery of God is always and only mediated through an experience that is specifically historical, the changing history of women's self-appraisal and self-naming creates a new situation for language about divine mystery. Great images of the divine, as Martin Buber astutely describes, always come into being not simply as a projection of the imagination but as an awakening from the deep abyss of human existence in real encounter with divine power and glory. Images with the capacity to evoke the divine are in some way *given* in the encounter which at the same time brings persons to birth as persons, as Thou's, in reciprocal relation with the primary Thou.[36] In and through women's conversion experience and its many articulations new language about God is arising, one that takes female reality in all its concreteness as a legitimate finite starting point for speaking about the mystery of God.

Chapter 5

SCRIPTURE AND ITS TRAJECTORIES

A holy people and blameless race
Wisdom delivered from a nation of oppressors. . . .
she guided them along a marvelous way,
and became a shelter to them by day,
and a starry flame through the night.
She brought them over the Red Sea,
and led them through deep waters;
but she drowned their enemies,
and cast them up from the depth of the sea.

— Book of Wisdom 10:15–17

A Hermeneutic of Revelation

The search for emancipatory speech about God leads through the path of women's historical experience to the Bible, the literary precipitate of the founding religious experiences of the Jewish and Christian communities and a continuing resource for their life. Feminist interpretation makes piercingly clear that although egalitarian impulses are discernible in the Bible, the texts as such were written mostly by men and for men in a patriarchal cultural context and reflect this fact. The story of salvation is told from a male point of view, while the creative reflection and participation of women is neglected or marginalized, most often restricted to the one important function of bringing forth sons for the men who are bearers of the promise.

In keeping with the social location of biblical authors, although female and cosmic images of God are at times used, it is most often the world of patriarchy that provides the chief metaphors for discourse about the divine. Hence images of God as king, ruling lord, father, and master, along with linguistic references to God as "he" proliferate. When the belief that the biblical writings are the inspired word of God is added to this situation, and when the text is read in a literal manner, then the fact that these are also the words of historical, culture-bound human beings tends to slip from view. A certain cast of mind arises which holds that this male terminology for God is in a particular way "revealed" and must continue to predominate. "Revelation" then becomes a brake on the articulation of divine mystery in the light of women's dignity.

Undergirding this kind of appeal to Scripture is a certain idea of revelation, namely, that it is conceptual truth given by God to human beings in verbal form, either directly through the mind of the Evangelist or indirectly through founding historical events. This doctrinal model locates revelation in rational, linguistic statements communicated by God without error that give information about divine mystery and dealings with the world. In this view revelation is equated with the very words of the Bible, "with the meaning of the Bible," according to Avery Dulles, "taken as a set of propositional statements, each expressing a divine affirmation, valid always and everywhere."[1] Interpretation occurs as simple literal repetition, most often in the light of later dogmatic and theological tradition, in order to convey the conceptual knowledge thought to be carried in the biblical words or speech. The words and their literal meaning are written in stone. In this perspective, the church has no option in the light of women's pressing experience but to continue to repeat the pattern of language about God in the metaphor of ruling men.

In the course of history, however, theology has found other models of revelation viable, among them revelation as historical event, or as inner experience, or as dialectical presence, or as new awareness, or as symbolic mediation. Each has its own strengths and weaknesses and brings into play a particular style of interpretation. What is not under question is the fact that the text must be interpreted. As Dulles argues, "Since we are different, we understand the text in a different way, or we do not understand it at all. The lapse of time is not just a chasm to be overcome, but is the occasion for productive understanding."[2] The context for reinterpretation is a common life in faith, with the communities that produced the texts and the communities reading them today living in response to the covenanting God. In this perspective, when the interpreting community today is women themselves, or women and men together in the struggle for emancipation from sexism, then what ensues is interpretation guided by a liberating impulse. The healing, redeeming, liberating gestalt of the story of the God of Israel, the God of Jesus, in the midst of the disasters of history guides the reading of texts, becoming the principle by which some recede and others, long neglected, advance in importance. In the midst of emerging emancipatory discourse about the mystery of God from the history of women's experience, biblical language about God in female metaphors becomes a precious discovery.

For the Sake of Our Salvation

Although its attention was not focused on this precise issue, an instructive lesson in this regard is taught by Vatican II. At one point a burning question before the house was how to treat biblical texts that contain inaccurate historical or scientific information. The nineteenth-century's discovery of these factual mistakes in Scripture had occasioned fierce and still unresolved debates over biblical inerrancy. Either some of these empirically obvious errors were actually correct, in which case, in order to read them as the inspired word of God, one would have to disown modern history and science. Or else God who had inspired the texts was in error, a position even more unthinkable for believers. The felicitous conciliar solution, arrived at after heated debate and repeated drafts, was to endorse a quite different stance from either of those options. It names salvation as the lens through which to interpret the word of God. The Scriptures, writes the council, teach "firmly, faithfully, and without error that truth which God wanted put into the sacred writings for the sake of our salvation."[3] This wording was carefully chosen to avoid the impression that some biblical texts are inspired and inerrant while others are not. Rather, all of Scripture is affirmed to be inerrant in what matters "for the sake of our salvation," which then becomes the perspective through which the revealed truth of Scripture can emerge.

Here and in the paragraphs that follow the council insists that the Bible was not written to teach the natural sciences nor to give information about political history, but to witness to God's graciousness in the midst of a broken world. The footnote appended to this conciliar text points to the long tradition on which the council draws for this position. Augustine had written that although the sacred writers may have known astronomy, nevertheless the Holy Spirit did not intend to utter through them any truth apart from that which is profitable to salvation. Aquinas, too, had argued that things which do not pertain to salvation do not belong to inspiration. In sum, the veracity of God and the inerrancy of the biblical authors are engaged precisely where it is a matter of salvation. According to the Scripture's own intent it makes no other affirmations. All historical, geographic, chronological, and scientific details are to be seen within this total scriptural pattern and judged in terms of their service to the word of salvation.

This principle of interpretation can be fruitfully used not only for scriptural texts that today betray historical or scientific inaccuracies, but also for those that disclose political bias given their context in patriarchal society. Biblical authors are intrinsically historically conditioned and reflect the cultural assumptions of their own time and place. At the same time, the earthen vessel of their human language bears the treasure of saving truth *nostrae salutis causa*, "for the sake of our salvation."

After much anguish and debate in the nineteenth century, and with this implicit understanding, the slavery texts of the Bible were laid aside and no longer guide Christian discourse and behavior, for rather than contribute to the good news of salvation they long sustained a genuinely evil social institution. The same dynamic now directs the interpretation of sexist biblical texts that in an analogous way can be judged according to the norm of whether they release salvation for the most abused of women. It is most emphatically not salvific to diminish the image of God in women, to designate them as symbols of temptation and evil, to relegate them to the margins of significance, to suppress the memory of their suffering and creative power, and to legitimate their subordination. For the sake of our salvation: on the wings of this principle feminist hermeneutics lifts off from imprisoning discourse and flies around the Scriptures seeking what has been lost, to practical and critical effect.[4]

Jesus and Abba

This same principle is capable of guiding interpretation of Jesus' use of the paternal metaphor for God. For a literal-minded reader, the Christian community is not free to expand its repertoire of divine imagery due to the historically probable fact that Jesus spoke about and to God as father and taught his disciples to do likewise (Mt 6:9; Lk 11:2). The argument from this stance insists that Jesus' example and teaching make the paternal metaphor normative for the church in such a way that other names for God are excluded.

There are many difficulties with this line of reasoning, not the least being that it singles out for absolute emulation one particular motif from among the many things the Gospels depict Jesus saying and doing, ignoring many others. Jesus preached the coming reign of God, for example, a theme that is profoundly central to his ministry; the church no longer feels bound to speak about God in this way. He bid his disciples keep alive the memory of the woman who prophetically anointed his head, thereby commissioning him to his messianic destiny: "Truly I tell you, wherever the good news is proclaimed in the whole world, what she has done will be told in remembrance of her" (Mk 14:9). But even her name has been forgotten, nor has news of what she has done accompanied the missionary activity of the church. Examples could be multiplied. Why then must father become an absolute and exclusive nomenclature for divinity? Additional criteria are needed to discern the best road to take in the present, since there are many things that Jesus said and did that the church no longer follows.

Hermeneutical bridges are being built to Jesus' use of father from several directions at once that allow crossover to more flexible usage. It is not that any biblical scholar argues against the historically strong probability that Jesus did speak to and about God using the paternal metaphor,[5] but the exclusivity and frequency of such use is questionable.

Exclusivity. Jesus' language about God is not monolithic but is diverse and colorful, as can be seen in the imaginative parables he spun out. A woman searching for her lost money, a shepherd looking for his lost sheep, a bakerwoman kneading dough, a travelling businessman, the wind that blows where it wills, the birth experience that delivers persons into new life, an employer offending workers by his generosity — these and many other human and cosmic instances are freely taken as metaphors for divine mystery in addition to the good and loving things that fathers do. God's way of dealing with human beings is at once like and not like all of these. Later Christian talk about God is poor indeed compared with the riot of images spun out in the Gospels' depiction of Jesus' speech.

Moreover, the Jewish prayer tradition of thanksgiving, lament, longing, and praise was the religious matrix in which Jesus grew as a historical human being. His own prayer was shaped by the daily, weekly, and annual rituals of Jewish faith in home, synagogue, and temple. Matthew even depicts him wearing the prayer garment of the religiously observant Jewish male: "Then suddenly a woman who had been suffering from hemorrhages for twelve years came up behind him and touched the fringe of his cloak" (9:20). Comments the *New Jerome Biblical Commentary*, "fringe: This was part of the prayer shawl worn by the devout Jew."[6] As part of the community of Israel Jesus of Nazareth prayed like the Jew he was, communing with the mystery of God through the blessings, laments, psalms, and other prayer forms of his religious tradition. He died praying this way: "My God, My God, why have you forsaken me?" (Mk 15:34). In terms of appeal to the example of Jesus, insistence on father as the only term coherent with his praxis cannot be naively sustained.

Frequency. Critical biblical scholarship points out that, while it is historically most probable that Jesus sometimes addressed God with the Aramaic *'abbâ*, the paternal metaphor is not necessarily as frequent nor as central as a literal reading of the text might suggest. Word count shows that God is referred to as father in the Gospels with increasing frequency: 4 times in Mark, 15 in Luke, 49 in Matthew, and 109 in John.[7] More precisely, the frequency with which Jesus calls God Father breaks down even more dramatically: Mark 1, Q 1, special Luke 2, special Matthew 1, John 73. As James Dunn concludes, it is scarcely possible to dispute that "here we see straightforward evidence of a burgeoning tradition, of a manner of speaking about Jesus and his relation with God which became very popular in the last decades of the first century."[8] It is a matter of theological development in the early church rather than abundant use by the actual Jesus who lived.

Furthermore, appellations other than father carry as much if not more theological weight in the Gospels' depiction of Jesus' language. Elisabeth Schüssler Fiorenza's study of the synoptic Gospels shows that there Jesus' habitual term for God is *basileia tou theou*, a lively tensive symbol pointing to the reign of God, or God's own being actively establishing the community of shalom. The Sophia-God of inclusive compassion and care is evoked in every one of Jesus' parables and sayings that uses this symbol. Interestingly enough, *basileia* is a word of grammatically feminine gender, although this of itself does not establish the reign of God as a female image.[9] In John's Gospel where the use of father is so frequent, it is not the paternal image but the ineffable "I AM" that appears at the center of Jesus' self-revelation. Raymond Brown among others calls this appellation, in itself an important point of continuity with divine self-naming in the Hebrew Scriptures, the key to Johannine understanding of Jesus' experience of God.[10]

Taken as a whole, the gospel tradition demonstrates variety and plurality in Jesus' speech about God rather than the exclusive centrality of speech about God as father. To select this one metaphor and grant it sole rights does not follow the pattern of Jesus' speech but is governed by other considerations, most likely a subtle endorsement of the priority of the father in social arrangements.

However often Jesus may have used the father symbol in speaking of God, its meaning when he did use it is not in dispute. In context the Aramaic *'abbâ* connotes an intimacy of relation between Jesus and God, along with a sense of God's compassion over suffering, willing good in the midst of evil.[11] Made concrete in Jesus' preaching, life-style, and relationships with others, this idea of God is subversive of any form of domination. Jesus' Abba, in other words, is not a patriarchal figure who can be used to legitimate systems of oppression, including patriarchal rule, but a God of the oppressed, a God of community and celebration. Everyone related to the one Abba stands in a relation of mutuality with one another. In the words of the Matthean Jesus:

You are not to be called rabbi, for you have one teacher, and you are all brothers and sisters. Call no man father on earth, for you have one Father, who is in heaven. Neither be called masters, for you have one master, the Christ. Whoever is greatest among you shall be your servant; whoever exalts oneself will be humbled, and whoever humbles oneself will be exalted. (Mt 23:8–12)

The one gift of salvation coming from God through Jesus-Sophia in the Spirit upends power relationships, transforming all teachers, fathers, masters, great ones into servants of the little ones. By exalting the lowly and humbling the mighty it creates relationships that circle back and forth in a solidarity of sisters and brothers rather than up and down in graded ranks. Jesus' Abba signifies a compassionate, liberating God who is grossly distorted when made into a symbol and supporter of patriarchal rule.

The difficulty with the appeal to Jesus' use of father to restrict other options in naming toward God thus becomes apparent. It presses speech that was pluriform, subtle, and subversive into an exclusive, literal, and patriarchal mold, and simply does not do justice to the evidence at hand. It also does not take account of the effective history of the father symbol in Christianity, which grew hardened and fixed in alliance with patriarchal rule, thus imprisoning rather than releasing the good news it was originally intended to convey. Both the fluidity of Jesus' own language and the intent of the paternal metaphor itself in his hands allow and indeed call for other ways of Christian speaking about God in addition to the language of father.

Three biblical symbols in particular will enter into the discourse being explored in this book, namely, spirit, wisdom, and mother. In most of the texts where these symbols appear they are enmeshed in an androcentric framework, and so cannot be taken simply at face value. They need to be recovered within an egalitarian framework in order to release their emancipatory potential. Language born of women's historical experience can then interweave with these ancient symbols and discover, as material for new discourse, their hidden acknowledgment of women's creative power and goodness. Toward that end this chapter examines these symbols in their biblical appearance and later trajectories.

Spirit/Shekinah

When the Bible wants to speak about the transcendent God's creative presence and activity in the world, it turns to words that carry the connotation of divine outreach, terms such as spirit, angel, wisdom, and word. Spirit, literally meaning a blowing wind, a storm, a stream of air, breath in motion, or something dynamically in movement and impossible to pin down, points to the livingness of God who creates, sustains, and guides all things and cannot be confined.[12] Divine Spirit is not understood to be independently personal, as its symbolization in wind, fire, light, and water makes clear, but is the creative and freeing power of God let loose in the world. More than most terms for God's dynamism it evokes a universal perspective and signifies divine activity in its widest reaches.

The Hebrew word for spirit, *ruah*, is of grammatically feminine gender. This point in itself is inconclusive, for a word's grammatical gender does not necessarily indicate the maleness or femaleness of its object. Furthermore, the biblical Greek term for spirit, *pneuma*, is grammatically neuter, while the long-used Latin term, *spiritus*, is grammatically masculine. Noting these linguistic circumstances, the biblical translator and theologian Jerome figured they signified that God transcends all categories of sexuality and is indeed Spirit.[13]

Imagery that accrues around the Spirit, however, as well as the Spirit's functions hint at the appropriateness of speaking about Spirit in analogy with women's historical reality, not exclusively but legitimately. In the Hebrew Scriptures *ruah*'s activities include creating new life, working to sustain it in myriad ways, renewing what has been damaged, grieving over destruction, teaching people to be wise, and inspiring critique and enthusiasm, all of which have engaged the energies of generation after generation of women. Furthermore, Scripture at times uses a range of suggestive imagery to speak about these deeds, such as water that cleanses and refreshes, fire that warms and brightens, cloud that cools, wind that blows free. One such constellation of images for spirit centers around the symbol of the bird and her wings, long a symbol of female deity in ancient Near Eastern religions. Whether hovering like a nesting mother bird over the egg of primordial chaos in the beginning (Gn 1:2), or sheltering those in difficulty under the protective shadow of her wings (Ps 17:8; 36:7; 57:1; 61:4; 91:1, 4; Is 31:5), or bearing the enslaved up on her great wings toward freedom (Ex 19:4; Dt 32:11–12), divine Spirit's activity is evoked with allusion to femaleness. Other images taken explicitly from what has traditionally been women's work also signify the Spirit's work in the world. She is depicted as a woman knitting together the new life in a mother's womb (Ps 139:13), as a midwife, working deftly with those in pain to bring about the new creation (Ps 22:9–10), as a washerwoman scrubbing away at bloody stains till the people be like new (Is 4:4; Ps 51:7).

In the Christian Scriptures the Spirit is spoken of in connection with the ministry and resurrection of Jesus Christ and the growth of the community of disciples. Spirit designates the power of God at work in Jesus' preaching and healing, inspiring him to bring good news to the poor and to set free those who are oppressed (Lk 4:18). The term also points to the vitality and presence of the risen Christ and the spiritual power of new life experienced through faith. Here too female imagery of the bird along with wind, fire, and water point to the exuberance of the living God in female imagery. During Jesus' baptism as depicted by Luke, the Spirit descends upon him in the form of a dove (Lk 3:22). In Greek mythology, as Ann Belford Ulanov points out, the dove is the emblem of Aphrodite, goddess of love. Doves were even cultically protected, with towers erected for them and a steady supply of food provided. The figure of the dove in Christian art thus links the Holy Spirit with the broad pre-Christian tradition of divine female power: "Iconographically, the dove is a messenger of the goddess and of the Holy Spirit."[14]

Jesus' conversation with Nicodemus carries a clear maternal metaphor for the Spirit. A person must be born anew in order to enter the reign of God, Jesus insists, to which Nicodemus queries, "How can anyone be born after having grown old? Can one enter a second time into the mother's womb and be born?" (Jn 3:4). Jesus' reply keeps the metaphor of birth from the womb and amplifies it to speak of being born of God: "no one can enter the reign of God without being born of water and the Spirit. What is born of the flesh is flesh, and what is born of the Spirit is spirit" (3:5–6). God's Spirit is here likened to a woman bringing forth new life through childbirth, so that those who believe are truly "born of God." Unfortunately, as Sandra Schneiders comments, "the theological tradition which has controlled the reading of Scripture has insisted on its own male understanding of God to the extent that it has virtually obliterated from the religious imagination this clearly feminine presentation of God the Spirit as mother."[15]

In John's Gospel the Spirit is further identified as the paraclete, a figure who is seen to have vitally important postresurrection roles: to be the personal presence of Jesus after his historical absence due to death; to abide with the disciples, teaching, reminding, maintaining, and completing the work of Jesus and, as the "Spirit of Truth" (16:13), leading them into all truth; to serve as prosecuting attorney and judge convicting the world of sin for its hatred and unbelief (16:7–11).[16]

When these roles are reprised within the set of female metaphors that cluster around Spirit, a strong and useful language arises:

In the divine economy it is not the feminine person who remains hidden and at home. She is God in the world, moving, stirring up, revealing, interceding. It is she who calls out, sanctifies, and animates the church. Hers is the water of the one baptism. The debt of sin is wiped away by her. She is the life-giver who raises men [*sic*] from the dead with the life of the coming age. Jesus himself left the earth so that she, the intercessor, might come.[17]

The Spirit goes forth so that the hidden Christ can be made known; without her there is no church, no remembering, no salvation, no gracious future.

In the Jewish trajectory that developed after the close of the biblical canon, the Spirit of God typically came to be spoken of in the female symbol of the *shekinah*. This feminine grammatical term, derived from the Hebrew verb *shakhan*, "to dwell," which is used in numerous texts that speak of God's dwelling among the people (Ex 25:8; 29:45–46), quite literally means the "dwelling" or "the one who dwells." It is used in the targums and rabbinic writings as a synonym for divine presence among the people.[18] Rather than saying directly that God or God's Spirit descended on the Holy of Holies, for example, the rabbis say that the *shekinah* descended, with the same meaning intended. Rather than saying that God is present among those who are attentive to the divine word, they say "If two sit together and the words of the Law [are spoken] between them, the Shekinah rests between them."[19]

When the rabbis read Israel's history using this expression, God's elusive, powerful presence comes to light in the form of female presence. The *shekinah* is manifest in the symbols of cloud, fire, or radiant light that descend, overshadow, or lead the people. The form which comes to be associated most clearly with her is divine glory or *kabod*, the weighty radiance that flashes out in unexpected ways in the midst of the broken world. Most significant is her work of accompaniment, for "Wherever the righteous go, the Shekinah goes with them."[20] No place is too hostile. She accompanies the people through the post-slavery wilderness, and hundreds of years later into exile again, through all the byways of rough times. "Come and see how beloved are the Israelites before God, for withersoever they journeyed in their captivity the Shekinah journeyed with them."[21] In other words, God's indwelling Spirit was with them and her accompaniment gave rise to hope and encouragement in the darkness, a sense of divine fidelity to the promise of shalom.

Insofar as *shekinah* is a circumlocution for divine involvement with the tragic state of the world, it also points to divine compassion. When the people are brought low then the Shekinah lies in the dust, anguished by human suffering. To quote an example from the Mishnah, referring to capital punishment by hanging:

When a human being suffers what does the Shekinah say? My head is too heavy for Me; My arm is too heavy for Me. And if God is so grieved over the blood of the wicked that is shed, how much more so over the blood of the righteous.[22]

Made familiar by long use throughout medieval kabbalistic writings, *shekinah* is a term with female resonance that carries forward the biblical understanding of God's Spirit. It signifies no mere feminine dimension of God but God as She-Who-Dwells-Within, divine presence in compassionate engagement with the conflictual world, source of vitality and consolation in the struggle.[23]

In the early Christian centuries a similar trajectory developed, which made explicit use of female imagery to characterize God's Spirit. In Syriac Christianity the Spirit's image was consistently that of the brooding or hovering mother bird. Among other maternal activities, the Spirit mothers Jesus into life at his conception in Mary's womb, empowers him into mission at his baptism, and brings believers to birth out of the watery womb of the baptismal font. This doctrine of the motherhood of the Spirit fostered a spirituality characterized by warmth that expressed itself in private and public prayer. In one extant prayer the believer meditates:

> As the wings of doves over their nestlings,
> And the mouths of their nestlings toward their mouths,
> So also are the wings of the Spirit over my heart.[24]

In another prayer spoken in the context of liturgy the Spirit is praised and implored:

The world considers you a merciful mother. Bring with you calm and peace, and spread your wings over our sinful times.[25]

In time most of this maternal imagery migrated away from the Spirit and accrued to the church, called holy mother the church, and to Mary the mother of Jesus, venerated as mother of the faithful as well. The symbol of the maternity of the Spirit was virtually forgotten, along with Spirit/Shekinah's capacity as a term to evoke divine presence and activity in female form. But this resonance abides in the texts of Scripture and tradition, offering one resource for emancipatory speech about God.

Wisdom/Sophia

Another, even more explicit way of speaking about the mystery of God in female symbol is the biblical figure of Wisdom. This is the most developed personification of God's presence and activity in the Hebrew Scriptures, much more acutely limned than Spirit, torah, or word. The term itself is of feminine grammatical gender: *hokmah* in Hebrew, *sophia* in Greek, *sapientia* in Latin. While this does not in itself determine anything, the biblical depiction of Wisdom is itself consistently female, casting her as sister, mother, female beloved, chef and hostess, preacher, judge, liberator, establisher of justice, and a myriad of other female roles wherein she symbolizes transcendent power ordering and delighting in the world. She pervades the world, both nature and human beings, interacting with them all to lure them along the right path to life. Since this symbol is less well known than spirit, it will be well to linger in some detail over her description. Who is Sophia, what does she do, and what is the theological significance of this?[26]

Texts

After appearing briefly in the Book of Job at a preliminary stage of personification as a hidden treasure whose whereabouts are known only to God (Jb 28), Sophia strides into the Book of Proverbs with a noisy public appearance (1:20–33). She is a street preacher, a prophet who cries aloud in the market and at the city gates a message of reproach, punishment, and promise. On her own authority she proclaims that whoever refuses to listen will be struck with calamity and destroyed, whereas the one who does listen will dwell secure without fear of evil. Elsewhere in Proverbs this insight is generalized. Sophia is a giver of life, she is a tree of life, "she is your life" (4:13). So intimately is the divine blessing of life associated with her that she can proclaim "whoever finds me finds life" (8:35).

Sophia's second appearance as a street preacher (Prv 8) is more self-revelatory. After publicly raising her voice to demand attention to her words of truth, she slips into the first person singular form of speech to describe her own character and works. She has knowledge, insight, and strength that she wishes to impart; her words are truth. Worth more than finest gold or silver, she loves those who love her and promises that those who seek her will find her. She hates the way of arrogance and evil, being the one through whom just governance is established on the earth: "By me kings reign, and rulers decree what is just" (v.15). Indeed, the echoes of the prophetic promise of shalom sound in her self-description: "I walk in the way of righteousness, in the paths of justice" (v.20). This passionate self-description of Sophia who loves, hates, demands, promises, all in the interest of the ways of justice, truth, and life already evokes connotations of Israel's unnameable YHWH who speaks through the prophetic oracle. We note too that it is far from the stereotypical feminine so beloved by patriarchal anthropology.

The divine work of ordering and guiding does not exhaust the role of Sophia. More primordially she is related to the act of creation: "The Lord by wisdom founded the earth" (3:19). The great poem of Proverbs 8:22–31 unfolds this association in detail. Sophia existed before the beginning of the world as the first of God's works. Then she is beside God at the vital moments of creation as either a master craftsperson or God's darling child (the text is disputed). In either case, God takes delight in her. Conversely she always rejoices in God's presence, plays everywhere in the new world, and takes her own delight in human beings. The scriptural tradition of creation theology here receives another dimension with the idea that creation is not simply the act of a solitary male deity.

In Sophia's last appearance in Proverbs, the street preacher, life-giver, agent of justice, architect of creation, and God's darling, becomes simultaneously a construction worker, butcher, vintner, sender of prophets, and compelling hostess (9:1–6). Having built a house and prepared her table, she sends her maidservants out to the public cross-roads, themselves to become proclaimers of her word of invitation: "Come, eat of my bread, and drink of the wine I have mixed" (v.5). The call is to leave foolish ways and walk in the ways of Sophia, which are ways of insight, life, and peace. These three major wisdom poems of Proverbs (chap. 1, 8, 9) all present a personified figure who, while obviously transcendent, comes toward human beings, tests and challenges them. She is a beneficent, right-ordering power in whom God delights and by whom God creates; her constant effort is to lure human beings to life.

In the Book of Sirach the relation between Sophia and those who love her is described in ever greater detail. There is constant call to learn her ways, to put one's neck under the yoke of her instruction to gain immeasurable treasures (51:26). Her relation to the Creator of all also gains further definition. In a great song of self-praise uttered in the midst of a liturgical assembly she tells her own story: how she came forth from the mouth of the Most High and covered the earth like a mist; how her throne was in a pillar of cloud; how alone she made a grand proprietary tour of the heights and depths of the created world and its people; how she then searched the world for a resting place, and was told by the Creator to pitch her tent in Israel. Once there she flourished, and issued her compelling invitation:

> Come to me, you who desire me, and eat your fill . . .
> whoever obeys me will not be put to shame,
> and those who work with my help will not sin. (24:19, 22)

At the climax of Sophia's song, the author of Sirach breaks in to make a momentous identification. Sophia represents Torah, the book of the covenant of the Most High God (24:23).[27] Thus the universal and cosmic Sophia becomes particularly associated with the history of Israel and its precious covenant law. She, the intimate of God, pitches her tent and dwells among the people.

The figure of personified wisdom reaches its peak of development in the Wisdom of Solomon, a book most likely written in the first century B.C.E. in Alexandria, Egypt, and thus subject to broader cultural influence. Her identity, evoked in a fivefold metaphor, is intrinsically linked to the mystery of God: she is a breath of the power of God; a pure emanation of the glory of the Almighty; a radiance of eternal light; a flawless mirror of the working of God; an image of divine goodness (7:25–26).

Throughout this book the divine prerogative of omnipotence is ascribed to Sophia: "Though she is but one, she can do all things" (7:27). And what things she does! Creative agency is hers, for she is there before the beginning, being the "fashioner of all things" (7:12), the "mother" of all good things responsible for their existence and therefore knowing their inmost secrets (7:22). The power to arrange the universe harmoniously is also hers: "She reaches mightily from one end of the earth to the other, and she orders all things well" (8:1). Hers too the power to enlighten, for since she knows she can therefore teach skills and crafts, and knowledge of the structure of the world and the activity of its elements: the cycles of the seasons and the stars, the varieties of animals, plants and roots, the powers of spirits and the ways of human reasoning (7:17–22). Recreative agency, the power to make all things green again, is hers: "while remaining in herself, she renews all things" (7:27). And this renewing energy profoundly affects human beings in their relation to divine mystery, weaving them round with a web of kinship: "in every generation she passes into holy souls and makes them friends of God, and prophets" (7:27).

Redeeming agency belongs to her for throughout the course of history human beings "were saved by wisdom" (9:18). The extraordinary chapter 10 of this book retells Israel's salvation history from the first human being to the Exodus as the story of Sophia's redeeming power, attributing to her the saving deeds that are elsewhere recounted of YHWH. She protected Adam and delivered him from his sin. When Cain turned from her in anger, he perished. When the earth was flooded,

Sophia "again saved it, steering the righteous man by a paltry piece of wood" (10:4). She strengthened Abraham, rescued Lot, gave victory to Jacob, stayed in solidarity with Joseph when he went into the dungeon until she brought him to triumph and authority. Most dramatically, she worked through Moses to free the people from bondage, leading them over the waters and guiding them through the wilderness, as the verses at the head of this chapter narrate. Her saving power shows itself active in history as she brings about the decisive revelatory and liberating events of her people Israel. Finally, eschatological victory will be hers:

> For she is more beautiful than the sun,
> and excels every constellation of the stars.
> Compared with the light she is found to be superior,
> For it is succeeded by the night,
> but against wisdom evil does not prevail. (7:29–30)

The Book of Baruch adds one more element to the picture of Sophia. She appears upon earth and lives among human beings (3:37), this again being identified with Torah as in Sirach. The wise person is encouraged to walk toward the shining of her light. By contrast, the apocalyptic Book of Enoch tells a different story about Sophia's appearance on earth, a story of rejection. She goes forth to make her dwelling place among human beings, but finds none. Therefore she withdraws and returns to the heavens to take her seat among the angels (41:1–2).

In the light of all of these narrations, descriptions, and praises, reflection on Sophia's relation to the one God of Israel becomes crucial. Who is Sophia? At times she is depicted as a superior type of creature; but at other times she transcends created limitations and exercises divine power in creative and saving deeds. Community of life with her enables individuals to arrive at their destiny, and in the end enables the whole world and its history to be rightly ordered in justice and peace. Little wonder that the interpretation of her origin and meaning within the literature of monotheistic Jewish faith gives rise to diverse scholarly positions.

Interpretation

Debate on the interpretation of personified Wisdom remains unresolved, not least because the differences apparent in the various scriptural books written in diverse contexts make it impossible to apply any one interpretation to every text where Sophia appears. At least five solutions to the puzzle of her theological significance have been credibly argued. Some view Sophia as the personification of cosmic order, that is, of the meaning that God has implanted in creation. Others see her as the personification of the wisdom sought and learned in Israel's schools. Still others take the symbol to stand for a divine attribute, namely, God's discerning intelligence. A fourth opinion opts for the view that Sophia is a quasi-independent divine hypostasis who mediates between the world and the utterly transcendent God of Jewish monotheism.[28] While adequate in the light of certain wisdom texts, each of these ably argued positions runs aground if the breadth of Sophia's activity in the wisdom literature is taken stringently into account. There, her actions in creation and salvation are obviously divine ones.

This lends credence to yet a fifth option, which holds that Sophia is a female personification of God's own being in creative and saving involvement with the world. The chief reason for arriving at this interpretation is the functional equivalence between the deeds of Sophia and those of the biblical God. What she does is already portrayed elsewhere in the Scriptures as the field of action of Israel's God under the revered, unpronounceable name YHWH. She fashions all that exists and pervades it with her pure and people-loving spirit. She is all-knowing, all-powerful, and present everywhere, renewing all things. Active in creation, she also works in history to save her chosen people, guiding and protecting them through the vicissitudes of liberating struggle. Her powerful words have the mark of divine address, making the huge claim that listening to them will bring salvation while disobedience will bring destruction. She sends her servants to proclaim her invitation to communion. By her light kings govern justly and the unjust meet their punishment. She is involved in relationships of loving, seeking, and finding with human beings. Whoever loves her receives what in other scriptural texts is given by God alone.

Given the immediate religious context of the wisdom texts, namely, Jewish monotheism not amenable to the idea of more than one God, the idea that Sophia is Israel's God in female imagery is most reasonable. Rabbinic specialists themselves argue that neither wisdom nor word, neither God's name nor Spirit nor the *shekinah* were introduced into Judaism as secondary hypostases to offset the utter transcendence of the divine. Rather, these are ways of asserting the one, transcendent God's nearness to the world in such a way that divine transcendence is not compromised. Consequently, to say that Sophia is the fashioner of all things, that she delivered Israel from a nation of oppressors, or that her gifts are justice and life is to speak of the transcendent God's relation to the world, of *God's* nearness, activity, and summons. Accordingly, the Wisdom of God in Jewish thought is simply God, revealing and known.[29] The obvious conclusion to be drawn from the fact that Sophia's activity is none other than the activity of God, with the same effects and attributes being credited indiscriminately to either, is that Sophia personifies divine reality, in fact, is an expression of the most intense divine presence in the world. In the judgment of C. Larcher, the author of the Book of Wisdom in particular wanted to enrich the image of God through this personalization of divine influence in the world. The intention was to universalize the idea of the Jewish God under the impact of the wider culture of the time.[30]

Larcher's argument raises the point of the cultural context within which the figure of Sophia took shape. On this point scholarly opinion is virtually unanimous in pointing to the formative influence of an extrabiblical figure of a female deity. In the course of this century diverse candidates have been endorsed, including the Canaanite love goddess, Astarte, the Mesopotamian goddess Ishtar, the Egyptian goddess Maat, the Semitic mother goddess at Yahweh's side in Jewish worship at Elephantine, and the Hellenized form of the Egyptian goddess Isis.[31] Isis has been a particularly attractive candidate since in the first century B.C.E. this deity was widely venerated throughout the Hellenized world by ruler and slave alike. She was called *Kyria*, giver of life, inventor of language, agriculture, and navigation, protector of children and the union of man and woman, establisher of justice and peace, the many-named yet one power over the whole world, indeed "the holy and eternal savior of the human race."[32] The human love and devotion that this cult could inspire is evidenced in a hymn carved into an Egyptian temple around 85 B.C.E., which reads in part:

> Mighty One, I shall not cease to sing of your great Power,
> Deathless Savior, many-named, mightiest Isis,
> Saving from war cities and all their citizens. . . .
> As many as are bound fast in prison, in the power of death,
> As many as are in pain through long anguished sleepless nights,
> All who are wanderers in a foreign land,
> And as many as sail on the Great Sea in winter . . .
> All these are saved if they pray that you be present to help.
> Hear my prayers, O one whose name has great power;
> Prove yourself merciful to me, and free me from all distress.
> Isidorus wrote it.[33]

The Hellenized cult of Isis was experienced as a temptation to Jews of the diaspora to turn from the traditional faith of their ancestors, or at least to doubt it, especially as adherence to this quasi-official cult could bring political and sociological advantages such as career advancement. Personified Wisdom was the answer of Orthodox Judaism to this threat. There is very little doubt among scholars that Jewish authors both at home and abroad transferred characteristics of the mighty Isis to the figure of Sophia in a creative effort to counteract the religious and social attractiveness of this most popular deity. Not Isis but the Wisdom of God spoken of in her symbolism is the giver of life and salvation. Israel's God possesses the merits for which Isis is praised, and thus Jewish faith could be sustained in the face of this powerful challenge. In this regard, the very choice of saving deeds narrated in the Book of Wisdom is instructive for there the author chooses specific acts that stand in close parallel to the competencies of Isis. The saving of Noah (10:4), for example, while a biblical story, is never included in biblical lists of YHWH's saving actions, and yet coheres with the image of Isis as inventor of maritime trades and the protector of sailors. Such allusive retelling of Israel's saving history so that it resonates with the pattern of Isis worship had the potential to revitalize the biblical tradition in a new cultural context. It gave to Jews a means of self-definition over against paganism at the same time that it made their tradition similar enough symbolically to allow for enhanced social contact.[34]

Analyzing the dynamics at work in the wisdom tradition, Elisabeth Schüssler Fiorenza observes that the attempts of Jewish wisdom theology to defend monotheism were not characterized by fear of the goddess, unlike the attempts of the classical prophetic tradition. Rather, wisdom writers made a positive effort to use elements of the goddess cult, especially that of Isis, and to integrate these elements into their tradition in such a way that their own God could be presented in current categories. Goddess language was used to speak of the one God of Israel whose gracious and self-involving goodness was Sophia herself: "Divine Sophia is Israel's God in the language and *gestalt* of the goddess."[35] It was not an easy theological move, and the language of wisdom texts reveals the struggle that went on to describe Sophia as divine, and thus God, in female imagery without distorting the structure of Israel's faith and falling into the error of ditheism. The scholarly interpretation of Wisdom as a personification of God's own self holds that such an error was avoided. The controlling context of meaning remained the Jewish monotheistic faith with borrowings being assimilated to that faith. At the same time, through the use of new categories, Jewish beliefs about God and God's ways with the world were expressed in a way that matched the religious depth and style of the goddess literature and cult and counteracted its appeal. The wisdom literature, then, celebrates God's gracious goodness in creating and sustaining the world and in electing and saving Israel, and does so in imagery that presents the divine presence in the female gestalt of divine Sophia.

Christian Trajectory

Wisdom's later trajectory is quite complex, influencing Christian pneumatology, Christology, and Mariology.

Spirit-Sophia. The close affinity between *ruah* and *hokmah*, both symbols of God's energy involved in universal cosmic quickening, inspiring the prophetic word of justice, renewing the earth and the human heart, led to their being closely identified with each other in the Book of Wisdom. At the outset Sophia is presented as people-loving spirit, friendly to human beings: "wisdom is a kindly spirit" (1:6). Later in the book the metaphor shifts slightly so that Sophia, besides being spirit, herself possesses a spirit. This spirit is described in glorious vocabulary as having twenty-one attributes in all, or three times the perfect number seven:

intelligent, holy, unique, manifold, subtle, mobile, clear, unpolluted, distinct, invulnerable, loving the good, keen, irresistible, beneficent, humane, steadfast, sure, free from anxiety, all-powerful, overseeing all, and penetrating through all other intelligent spirits. (7:22–23)

Sophia's universal presence is analogous to God's Spirit insofar as she fills the world: "For wisdom is more mobile than any motion; because of her pureness she pervades and penetrates all things" (7:24), and sets people on the right path: "Who has learned thy counsel, unless you have given wisdom, and sent your holy spirit from on high?" (9:17). These and other allusive texts which bring Spirit and Sophia practically to the point of identity further strengthen the fittingness of speaking about the Spirit in female imagery, given Sophia's undoubted female symbolization.

Jesus-Sophia. First-century Christians, in their effort to express the experience of the saving significance of Jesus, ransacked the Jewish religious tradition and the surrounding Hellenistic culture for interpretive elements. Along with Son of God, Son of Man, Messiah, and Logos, the tradition of personified Wisdom was ready to hand. Divine Sophia had already been depicted in the Jewish tradition as sent by God to a specific place on earth, localized in Jerusalem, and particularized in the form of Torah. As Martin Hengel has noted, this particularization of the creating, saving power of God was of "decisive significance"[36] for the development of Christology, for in a further and more radical step of concretization, sometimes indirectly through identifying Jesus with Torah and sometimes in more direct fashion, the words, functions, and characteristics of Sophia were now associated with the human being Jesus.

What Judaism said of Sophia, Christian hymn makers and epistle writers now came to say of Jesus: he is the image of the invisible God (Col 1:15); the radiant light of God's glory (Heb 1:3); the firstborn of all creation (Col 1:15); the one through whom all things were made (1 Cor 8:6). Likewise, the way in which Judaism characterized Sophia in her dealings with human beings, Gospel writers now came to portray Jesus: he calls out to the heavy burdened to come to him and find rest (Mt 11:28–30); he makes people friends of God (Jn 15:15), and gifts those who love him with life (Jn 17:2). As the trajectory of wisdom Christology shows, Jesus was so closely associated with Sophia that by the end of the first century he is presented not only as a wisdom teacher, not only as a child and envoy of Sophia, but ultimately even as an embodiment of Sophia herself. In the words of Elisabeth Schüssler Fiorenza, "While the Jesus movement, like John, understood Jesus as the messenger and prophet of divine Sophia, the wisdom Christology of the Christian missionary movement sees him as divine Sophia herself."[37] James Dunn, too, judges that "Jesus is the exhaustive embodiment of divine wisdom"; M. Jack Suggs argues that for Matthew, "Jesus is Sophia incarnate"; according to Raymond Brown's analysis, "in John, Jesus is personified Wisdom."[38]

The tradition of personified Wisdom plays a foundational role in the development of Christology, and some of the most profound christological assertions in the New Testament are made in its categories. Paul is the first to write down the connection, noting "we preach Christ crucified, a stumbling block to the Jews and folly to the Gentiles, but to those who are called, both Jews and Greeks, Christ the power of God and the wisdom of God" (1 Cor 1:22–24). Christ crucified, the Sophia of God. Here is the transvaluation of values so connected with the ministry, death, and resurrection of Jesus: divine Sophia is here manifest not in glorious deeds or esoteric doctrine, but in God's solidarity with the one who suffers. While seeming to be weak and defeated, the personal Wisdom of God is in fact the source of life.

Among the synoptic Gospels Matthew's in particular depicts Jesus as Sophia's child who communicates her gracious goodness by befriending the outcast, who communicates her prophetic message, and who proves her right or justifies her though he is severely criticized by others. Jesus laments over Jerusalem, speaking a wisdom oracle that depicts him as a caring mother bird, before withdrawing like Sophia from the city that rejects him (23:37–39).[39] He utters Sophia's call to "Come to me," promising the weary her life-giving blessing of rest (11:28). Also like Sophia he urges the heavy-burdened to take his yoke upon them, promising that thereby they will find what they need (11:29–30). As von

Rad has pointed out, having Jesus speak of Sophia's yoke as "my yoke" is not an instance of casual borrowing; it is a paradigmatic Christian statement crafted by Matthew and meaning that Jesus is the fulfillment of Torah, is even himself Sophia-Torah.[40]

Not only Sophia's speech and deeds are appropriated in Matthew's Christology, but also Sophia's intimate relationship with the one who is God of all. What has been called the thunderbolt from the Johannine sky is actually Matthew's use of the wisdom tradition:

In that hour Jesus said, "I thank you, Father, Lord of heaven and earth, that you have hidden these things from the wise and understanding and revealed them to babes; even so, Father, for such was your gracious will. All things have been handed over to me by my Father; and no one knows the Son except the Father, and no one knows the Father except the Son and anyone to whom the Son chooses to reveal him." (11:25–27)

The exclusivity of mutual knowledge expressed in this text is biblically acknowledged elsewhere only of Sophia: only God knows Wisdom, and only Wisdom knows God.[41] On the one hand, the theme of the hiddenness of Wisdom provides the context for God's exclusive knowledge of her. Although human beings seek her high and low, only God knows the way to her, and finds her by his understanding (Bar 3:32). On the other hand, "the Lord of all loves her. For she is an initiate in the knowledge of God, and an associate in his works" (Wis 8:3–4). Being present from the beginning of God's works, she understands God's ways and the things that are pleasing to him (Wis 9:9). Furthermore, she shows these ways to her children who seek her and divine truth. Matthew adapts this tradition to present Jesus speaking as Sophia. Using the male imagery of Father and Son, the Gospel writer attributes to Jesus the exclusivity of mutual knowledge which the tradition up to that point had affirmed of God and Sophia. The point that becomes clear from Matthew's editing is that it is not the son tradition but the wisdom tradition that underlies the affirmation of revelatory intimacy between Jesus and his Abba. Given its roots in the style and content of the wisdom tradition, such an insight does not essentially need the male imagery for its christological affirmation.

Among the Gospel writers John is distinguished from the others primarily by the extent to which wisdom categories influence his portrait of Jesus as the Christ. The Prologue to his Gospel, which more than any other scriptural text influences the subsequent development of Christology, actually presents the prehistory of Jesus as the story of Sophia: present "in the beginning," an active agent in creation, descending from heaven to pitch a tent among the people, rejected by some, giving life to those who seek, a radiant light that darkness cannot overcome (Jn 1:1–18).

In addition to the Prologue, John's whole Gospel is simply suffused with wisdom themes. In fact, much of what distinguishes this Gospel so strikingly from the synoptics can be attributed to his adaptation of the wisdom tradition. Like Sophia, Jesus calls out in a loud voice in public places, uttering blessing and threat (7:28, 37). Like her he speaks in long discourses using the first person singular pronoun, proclaiming his elusive but attractive significance in the singular cadences of the "I am" statements (6:51; 10:14; 11:25). Both Jesus and Sophia are identified with Torah, which is light and life for human beings. The symbols of bread, wine and water, and the invitations to eat and drink relate Jesus to Sophia's nourishing activities.[42] The theme of seeking and finding, so constant in Sophia's interactions with people, resonates even in Jesus' first Johannine words, "What do you seek?" and the happy result for the disciples, "We have found the Messiah" (1:38, 41). Whoever seeks and finds him is promised the gift of life which he has come to give (10:10). More ominously Sophia's warnings about seeking and not finding ring out in Jesus' words to unbelieving hearts (7:34).[43] The idea of truth, of right instruction, of revelation of divine mysteries, and guidance in the paths pleasing to God all cast Jesus in Sophia's life-giving didactic role: he is the way, the truth, and the life (14:6). Disciples are encouraged to follow his path and are even called his children, while rejection of him spells death for the rejecters. Woven round with these elements is the theme of God's love and friendship. As with Sophia, whoever loves Jesus is beloved by God (14:23) and enters into a mutuality so profound that they may be called friends (15:15).

Given the influence of the wisdom tradition on John's depiction of Jesus, why does he substitute word/*logos* for wisdom/*sophia* in the Prologue? A plethora of scholarly answers is available. The Book of Wisdom had already equated *logos* and *sophia* in the act of creation (9:1–2); the Gospel *logos* would have had a valuable link with Hellenistic philosophy where it was a key concept; by the end of the first century, word was the term used to signify the apostolic kerygma; *sophia*'s use was increasingly problematic due to its adoption by budding gnostic groups.[44]

The thought of the Hellenistic Jewish philosopher Philo is also considered to have had a major influence, insofar as he affected the milieu in which late first-century theological reflection took place. In his work the relationship of *sophia* to *logos* is a complicated affair, but ends with *sophia* being disparaged because of her female character.[45] Adopting the dualistic pattern of Greek thinking, Philo held that the symbol of the female signified whatever was evil, tied to the world of the senses, irrational or passive; by contrast the symbol of the male represented the good, the world of the spirit, rationality and active initiative. Within this framework it would be inconceivable that divine *sophia* could remain female. Thus Philo argues:

For pre-eminence always pertains to the masculine, and the feminine always comes short of it and is lesser than it. Let us, then, pay no heed to the discrepancy in the gender of the words, and say that the daughter of God, even Sophia, is not only masculine but father, sowing and begetting in souls aptness to learn, discipline, knowledge, sound sense, and laudable actions.[46]

It is a short step from this attitude to the substitution of the male symbol for the female one, and a number of contemporary authors do adduce Wisdom's female character as a reason for what Joan Chamberlain Engelsman calls the "repression" of Sophia and her replacement by the Logos in John's Prologue.[47] Edward Schweizer proposes that it was in fact necessary for Christian thought to substitute the masculine designation for the feminine *sophia* because of the gender of Jesus. F. Braun argues that the masculine gender of *logos* is better adapted to the person of Jesus, while W. Knox comments that the fact that *logos* is masculine made it a convenient substitute for "the awkward feminine figure."[48]

The point is, however, that Christian reflection before John had not found it difficult to associate Jesus Christ with Sophia, including not only the risen and exalted Christ but even the historical Jesus of the ministry. Insofar as the gender of Sophia was a factor in her replacement by the Logos in the Prologue, it was coherent with the broader shift in the Christian community toward more patriarchal ecclesial structures and the blocking of women from ministries in which they had earlier participated. In other words, the suppression of Sophia is a function of the growth of sexism in the Christian communities.

The use of wisdom categories in the Christian Scriptures had profound theological consequences. It enabled the fledgling Christian communities to attribute cosmic significance to the crucified Jesus, relating him to the creation and governance of the world. It was also the vehicle for the developing insight into Jesus' ontological relationship with God, for none of the other Jewish scriptural symbols used — Son of Man, Messiah, Son of God — connotes divinity in its original gestalt, nor does the *logos*, which is barely personified in the Jewish Scriptures. To link the human being Jesus, however implicitly, with divine Sophia, God's gracious nearness and activity in the world, moves thought to see that Jesus is not simply a human being inspired by God but must be related in a special way to God. "Herein we see the origin of the doctrine of incarnation,"[49] writes Dunn, with consequent development in the Christian doctrine of God's Trinity.

What does it mean that one of the key origins of the doctrines of incarnation and Trinity lies in the identification of the crucified and risen Jesus with a female gestalt of God? Since Jesus the Christ is depicted as divine Sophia, then it is not unthinkable — it is not even unbiblical — to confess Jesus the Christ as the incarnation of God imaged in female symbol. Whoever espouses a wisdom Christology is asserting that Jesus is the human being Sophia became; that Sophia in all her fullness was in him so that he manifests the depth of divine mystery in creative and graciously saving involvement in the world. The fluidity of gender symbolism evidenced in biblical Christology breaks the stranglehold of androcentric thinking that circles around the maleness of Jesus. Wisdom Christology reflects the depths of the mystery of God and points the way to an inclusive Christology in female symbols.

Many times in the postbiblical period Sophia and Logos were seen as equivalent expressions of the one outreaching power and saving presence of God, as in this endearing statement of Origen:

We believe that the very Word of the Father, the Wisdom of God himself, was enclosed within the limits of that man who appeared in Judea; nay more, that God's Wisdom entered a woman's womb, was born as an infant, and wailed like crying children.[50]

During the fourth-century Arian controversy, subordinationist interpretations of Sophia were used by the Arian party to support their view that Jesus was merely a superior creature, while those fighting for the Nicene *homoousios* argued for the Son's divinity from Sophia's identification with divine presence and activity. With intended irony Joan Chamberlain Engelsman calls the whole uproar "Sophia's revenge": repressing Sophia's divine identity occasions denial of the divinity of Christ as well.[51]

In addition to theology and doctrine, wisdom Christology in the East was also expressed in stone in the succession of great churches built in the Eastern capital city of Constantinople and dedicated to Jesus the Christ under the title Hagia Sophia, Holy Wisdom. In the West theologians also continued to use Wisdom as a title for Christ. Writing of Christ being sent into the world, for example, Augustine does not hesitate to appeal to the story of Wisdom: "But she is sent in one way that she may be with human beings; she has been sent in another way that she herself might be a human being."[52] Jesus Christ is the human being Sophia became.

The wisdom reference continues to make an appearance in the liturgy during the season of Advent when in words taken from the Book of Wisdom (8:1) the first O Antiphon recited during the week before Christmas prays to Christ: "O Wisdom, who reaches from end to end, and orders all things sweetly and mightily, come and teach us the way of prudence." For the most part, however, christological reflection went forward using the idea of the Logos or Son, while most of this female wisdom imagery passed to the figure of Mary of Nazareth who, besides being addressed as the Throne or Seat of Wisdom, who is Christ, was herself fêted in the pre–Vatican II liturgy with texts taken from the wisdom tradition.[53] The figure of Sophia herself was quite forgotten, but remains in the biblical text as a startling female personification of the mystery of God in powerful and close engagement with the world.

Mother

By now it is clear that biblical female symbols for God range far and wide over the field of action and are not limited to the relationship and role of mothering. Yet this is a vitally important and uniquely female role, and another constellation of biblical symbols for God revolves around women's experience of bearing, birthing, and nursing new human beings. In texts widely scattered throughout the Hebrew Scriptures different aspects of being a mother — conceiving, being pregnant, going into labor, delivering, midwifing, nursing, carrying, rearing — become metaphors pointing to God's ways of relating to the world.[54] Several examples illustrate the power of this symbolism.

Pregnancy and delivery are coded in the Pentateuch's reprimand to the neglectful people of Israel: "You were unmindful of the Rock that bore you, and you forgot the God that gave you birth" (Dt 32:18), a theme that is carried forward in Moses' exasperated dialogue with God in Numbers 11:12–13. The "God that gave you birth" is graphically described by Second Isaiah, who uses the suffering of a woman grasped by labor pains to give words to divine anguish. Deep into the work of bringing about the new creation God speaks:

> For a long time I have held my peace,
> I have kept still and restrained myself;
> now I will cry out like a woman in labor,
> I will gasp and pant. (Is 42:14)

A mother's love symbolizes God's own care: "As one whom his mother comforts, so I will comfort you" (Is 63:13). And should tragedy strike and a mother's love fail, a dialectical metaphor arises as God is depicted as more reliable still:

> Can a woman forget her sucking child,
> that she should have no compassion on the child of her womb?
> Even if these may forget,
> yet I will not forget you. (Is 49:15)

A clear image of midwifery, women's historically characteristic role during the process of birth, emerges in the psalm of lament:

> My God, my God, why have you forsaken me?
> Why are you so far from helping me, from the words of my groaning?...
> Yet it was you who took me from the womb;
> you kept me safe on my mother's breast.
> On you I was cast from my birth,
> and since my mother bore me you have been my God. (Ps 22:1, 9–10).

These and other maternal symbols for divine mystery point in a certain direction when they begin to give rise to thought. In an illuminating study Phyllis Trible has shown how in Hebrew the word for woman's womb and the word for compassion are cognates, both further related to the verb *to show mercy* and the adjective *merciful:*

In its singular form the noun *rehem* means "womb" or "uterus." In the plural, *rahamîm*, this concrete meaning expands to the abstractions of compassion, mercy, and love.... Accordingly, our metaphor lies in the semantic movement from a physical organ of the female body to a psychic mode of being.[55]

This psychic mode of being, compassionate care, can be demonstrated by men as well as women, for example, by Joseph of the many-colored coat who yearns for his brother Benjamin (Gn 43:30), but it is a woman's love for the child of her womb that is the paradigmatic metaphor. Accordingly, when God is spoken of as merciful, the semantic tenor of the word indicates that the womb is trembling, yearning for the child, grieved at the pain. What is being showered upon the wayward is God's womb-love, divine love for the child of God's womb: "I will truly show motherly-compassion upon him" (Jer 31:20). The human experience of giving birth, with its physical and psychic relations, is an analogy that hints at the unfathomable depths of divine love. Trible summarizes her findings in a memorable way as the journey of a metaphor from the wombs of women to the compassion of God, by way of denial (even should she forget...). The allusion to the wombs of women carried in biblical words of divine mercy and compassion makes it clear that throughout the Bible references to God who loves as a mother are more numerous than the number of explicit maternal images would at first suggest.

Other images introduce yet further aspects of the experience of mothering, such as the fury women know when what they have created and nurtured is violated or destroyed. The prophet Hosea envisions the divine reaction to those who do injustice in terms of an angry mother bear:

> I will fall upon them like a bear robbed of her cubs,
> I will tear open their breast. (Hos 13:8)

Here is the great and terrible mother on the prowl for her own, a suitable metaphor for a feminist retrieval of the wrath of God.

In centuries following, biblical imagery of divine maternity reappear in discourse about God the Mother in various gnostic communities, some of whom describe the divine Mother as part of an original couple, others of whom write about her as prior to and creative of the male creator God.[56] It also leaves a trail in early Christian writings about the mercy of God the Father, whose loving activity in the eternal generation of the Son is likened to that of a mother; whose motive for the incarnation is maternal love; and who in the eucharist nurses us with the milk of forgiveness from the full breasts of his kindness.[57] As we have seen, it traces its way through devotion to the Christian Holy Spirit in the East. It surfaces again in christological piety where Christ is characterized in maternal terms; for example, Anselm of Canterbury prays to Jesus as the mother hen under whose wings we flee for protection, and Julian of Norwich centers her spirituality of friendship with our courteous Lord on the metaphor of his warm and hard-working motherhood.[58]

In Catholic Christianity by far the most influential conduit for this imagery has been veneration of Mary, whose presence is experienced as that of a caring mother at the heart of the church. Starting with the transfer to her of the iconography and devotional practices originally directed toward the Great Mother in the Mediterranean region, she is addressed as the mother par excellence, Mother of God, Mother of Mercy, Mother of Divine Consolation, our Mother. Those who are devoted to her experience first and foremost a relationship of trust to a powerful mother figure. In her symbolism the maternal birthing and caring metaphors that the Bible uses to describe God's unbreakable love for the people of the covenant find continuing, concrete expression. Thus, for innumerable believers this village woman, mother of Jesus, honored as Mother of God, functions as an icon of the maternal God, revealing divine love as merciful, close, interested in the poor and the weak, ready to hear human needs, related to the earth, trustworthy, and profoundly attractive. In devotion to her as a compassionate mother who will not let one of her children be lost, what is actually being mediated is a most appealing experience of God.[59]

•

In summary there are Jewish and Christian biblical texts that, with their trajectories, bear potent female images of the living God present and active throughout the world. When within a feminist perspective the clearly personified figure of Sophia is linked with the hints half-guessed in spirit and *shekinah* and the power of the mother symbol, both the aptness of speaking in female terms of the mystery of God and a modicum of material content for doing so come to light.

Discourse about holy mystery in the symbols of spirit, *sophia*, and mother provides glimpses of an alternative to dominant patriarchal language about God. Since these symbols as they stand are embedded within a text, a culture, and a tradition that are skewed by sexism, they cannot be taken and used without first passing through the fire of critical feminist principles. Otherwise what ordinarily results is a view of female symbols as "complementary" to those generated by male experience, which in effect results in the female symbols remaining supplementary, subordinate, and stereotyped within a dualistic framework. When the liberating vision of a community of equal and mutual disciples is endorsed and practiced, however, language generated by women's experience can interweave with these ancient symbols and their hidden recognition of women's creative power and goodness to shape new building blocks for emancipatory discourse about the mystery of God.

Chapter 6

CLASSICAL THEOLOGY

Beyond all conventions —
in the rejection of all untruth —
at the cost of security —
behind all negations —
when everything fails —
in the abandonment of everything:
the discovery of God.

—Henri de Lubac[1]

Throughout its history the Christian tradition has garnered some fascinating insights regarding the possibilities and limits of human knowing and speaking about God. This wisdom is codified with uncommon clarity in the theological *summas* of the medieval scholastics, among whom Aquinas's thinking is particularly rich owing to his intellectual conversation not only with ancient Greek and Christian sources but with Jewish and Arabic wisdom as well. At least three insights from this classical theology are helpful resources in the project of emancipatory speech about the mystery of God. These are the doctrine of God's hiddenness or incomprehensibility, the play of analogy in speech about the divine, and the consequent need for many names of God. Each of these classic insights can function to delimit patriarchal dominance in naming God, guiding speech in freer directions and supporting in a foundational way inclusive language about God as intellectually possible and religiously legitimate.

Divine Incomprehensibility

The holiness and utter transcendence of God present throughout all creation have always been an absolutely central affirmation of the Jewish tradition and its grafted branch, Christian faith. God as God, ground, support, and goal of all, is illimitable mystery who, while immanently present, cannot be measured, manipulated, or controlled. The doctrine of divine incomprehensibility or hiddenness is a corollary of this divine transcendence. In essence, God's unlikeness to the corporal and spiritual finite world is total. Hence human beings simply cannot understand God. No human concept, word, or image, all of which originate in experience of created reality, can circumscribe divine reality, nor can any human construct express with any measure of adequacy the mystery of God who is ineffable.

This situation is not due to some reluctance on the part of God to self-reveal in a full way, nor to the sinful condition of the human race, which makes reception of such revelation weak and limited, nor even to the contemporary mentality of skepticism about religious matters. Rather, it is proper to God as God to transcend all similarity to creatures, and thus never to be known comprehensively or essentially as God. In Augustine's unforgettable echo of the insight of earlier Greek theologians, *Si comprehendis, non est Deus:* if you have understood, then what you have understood is not God.[2] This sense of an unfathomable depth of mystery, of a vastness of God's glory too great for the human mind to grasp, undergirds the religious significance of speech about God. Such speech never definitively possesses or masters its subject but leads the speakers ever more profoundly into attitudes of awe and adoration.

It would be a serious mistake to think that what the Jewish and Christian traditions confess to be God's self-revelation through powerful acts and inspired words in history removes the ultimate unknowability of God. At times belief in such revelation has given rise to the dangerous situation in which the need to preach and interpret has resulted in words becoming too clear and ideas too distinct, almost as if they were direct transcripts of divine reality. At times theologians have forgotten the mystery they were dealing with and have created the impression that because of revelation the unknown God is now available for inspection, caught within narratives or metaphysical concepts. Revelation, however, no matter by what model it is interpreted, does not and cannot dissolve the mystery of God. In its light we see ever more clearly the incomprehensibility of God as a mystery of free and liberating love, love that draws near, chooses us without our deserving it, accompanies and bears us, walks the path of struggle, promises victory, dwells among us to gather us in. In a paradoxical way, as Karl Rahner puts it, "Revelation does not mean that the mystery is overcome by gnosis bestowed by God, even in the direct vision of God; on the contrary, it is the history of the deepening perception of God *as* the mystery."[3] Even and especially in revelation God remains the wholly other, blessedly present but conceptually inapprehensible, and so God.

The sweep of Jewish and Christian traditions bears this out, and a brief overview of some of their salient expressions shows just how strongly this conviction perdures. The Hebrew Scriptures contain no systematic development of the theme of divine hiddenness but disclose awareness of it through repeated stress on God's holiness, transcendent otherness, and freedom of action in history. At the head of the list of commandments, God's otherness comes to expression in the ban on the making and adoring of images:

I am the Lord your God who brought you out of the land of Egypt, out of the house of bondage. You shall have no other gods before me. You shall not make for yourself a graven image, or any likeness of anything that is in heaven above, or that is in the earth beneath, or that is in the water under the earth; you shall not bow down to them or serve them; for I the Lord your God am a jealous God. (Ex 20:2–5)

In view of the fact that despite this ban images of God at least in a verbal sense abound throughout the Scriptures, the intent of this command would seem to be that of preventing both polytheism and magic, while insuring that any image used of the holy and free God would remain cognizant of its own limitation.[4] There is but one God, comparable to no other individual or corporate created reality.

Abundant references throughout the Torah and the prophetic and wisdom writings spell out the implications of this insight. The holy name YHWH, signifying divine presence but not essence, is unfathomable (Ex 3:14). Even in the making of the covenant no one sees God's form (Dt 4:12, 15–16). Truly God is a hidden God, impossible to compare with anyone or anything else: "To whom then will you compare me, that I should be like him? says the Holy One" (Is 40:18, 25; 45:15). God the Holy One is God and not man (Nm 23:19; Hos 11:9). God is great, beyond what can ever be fathomed (Jb 36:26).

The idea of divine incomprehensibility in Scripture is not watered down with the advent of God in Jesus Christ. Rather, the mystery of the covenanting God remains the horizon within which early Christian believers interpret the life, death, and resurrection of Jesus Christ. The God who raised Jesus from the dead cannot be captured in silver, gold, stone, or any representation of the human imagination (Acts 17:29). God dwells in unapproachable light, whom no human being has ever seen or can see (1 Tm 6:16; Jn 1:18). God's knowledge is deep; divine judgments are unsearchable; divine ways are inscrutable (Rom 11:33-36). While present in the Spirit, God is greater than our heart (1 Jn 3:20). Even in Christ our knowledge is imperfect, so that we see now as though in a mirror, dimly, and know only in part (1 Cor 13:9, 12). Indeed, there is a sense in which the mysteriousness of God is brought to a more intense pitch in the experience of divine saving love poured out in Jesus Christ: "the mystery of divine incomprehensibility burns more brightly here than anywhere."[5] Thus, while the Scriptures are the inspired literary precipitate of communities involved in knowing and loving the one true God, biblical tradition itself bears witness to the strong and consistent belief that God cannot be exhaustively known but even in revelation remains the mystery surrounding the world.

When in the early Christian centuries biblical tradition encountered the Greek philosophical tradition, a certain congeniality was discovered on precisely this point.[6] The philosophical idea of God's inaccessibility to human conceptualization was rooted in the idea that the one ultimate origin of all things must be totally different from the everyday world of multiplicity and change. Finite and transitory structures cannot be traced back exactly to their distant origin, and thus the incomprehensibility of the one source of all is assured. This affirmation of the radical otherness of the world-ground in philosophical thought was attractive to early Christian theologians trying to express theologically the scriptural theme that God is unknown but present in the world and its history, and the two understandings became wedded in their thought.[7] While some, such as Justin, continued to appeal to the religious perspective, holding that God is nameless due to being unbegotten, there being no one prior to God to do the naming, more usual was the approach taken by Clement of Alexandria and Irenaeus, who worked with the philosophical idea of divine simplicity to arrive at the understanding that God is unknowable by any category. God is beyond place and time and description, and the divine essence cannot be adequately designated by any name.

The temptation in the apologetics of this period was to give the impression that revelation cleared up the provisional ignorance of the pre-Christian world, rather than to remember that God is *essentially* incomprehensible. Some theologians of this period can be read as having given in to this temptation. Tertullian, for example, had the insight that human beings comprehend God precisely in knowing God to be incomprehensible, but this did not shape his understanding of revelation, which he saw as providing a positive complement to divine mystery. Even the dogmatic formulations of the ecumenical councils of the first centuries, in which the Trinity and Christology were conceptualized, set up a dangerous situation in which the nature of God-talk could be forgotten. While they intended to protect the mystery of divine greatness, which acted compassionately for the world's salvation, they could nevertheless be construed as a wire fence that not only protected but also captured and tamed the unknown God.[8] However, precisely those thinkers who worked most vigorously to formulate the trinitarian and christological dogmas, Athanasius, Basil, Gregory of Nyssa, and Gregory of Nazianzus, also wrote strongly about the transcendence and incomprehensibility of God to offset the logical rationalism of Arian and Eunomian opponents. They above all were conscious of the inadequacy of the formulas and saw clearly that God's unlikeness to the world is total, so that we know best when we affirm that we do not know, which in itself is a religious kind of knowing.

In the West this consciousness is expressed cogently throughout the influential work of Augustine. All speaking of God, he insists, must be born out of silence and ignorance and return there, for God is ineffable. We give God many names but ultimately God is nameless, no name being able to express the divine nature. Since created perfections are a reflection of God, it is possible to predicate them of God; but none are said worthily. God *is* more truly than can be uttered, and exists more truly than can be thought.[9] In the end, it is easier to say what God is not than what God is:

If you have understood, then this is not God. If you were able to understand, then you understood something else instead of God. If you were able to understand even partially, then you have deceived yourself with your own thoughts.[10]

Lest we despair of ever knowing the divine in any way at all, however, Augustine consistently pushes the necessity of nescience to its genuine religious goal, the knowing of God through love. If we wish to savor something of God, then we should attend to our loving, for God is Love. "In loving, we already possess God as known better than we do the fellow human being whom we love. Much better, in fact, because God is nearer, more present, more certain."[11] The God who is utterly distinct from all creatures and hence better known intellectually by negating all symbols is nonetheless deeply known in human love, as love itself. By loving we embrace God. What we receive from early Christian theology is a pattern of positive affirmation coupled with agnosticism of definition, both essential to the truth of God. In the end, we are united to God as to an unknown, savoring God only through love.

The theological tradition of divine incomprehensibility began to find its way into official church teaching when, in response to a trinitarian controversy, the Fourth Lateran Council in 1215 taught how the meanings of words differ when they are applied to both God and creatures. When Jesus prays to his Father that his disciples "may be one in us as we also are one" (Jn 17:22), the word *one* applied to the disciples signifies a union of charity in grace while in reference to the divine persons *one* means a unity of identity in nature. So too when Jesus counsels that "you must be perfect as your heavenly Father is perfect" (Mt 5:48), this perfection is said of God and creatures differently. The council's understanding is summed up in a critically important axiom: between Creator and creature no similarity can be expressed without implying that the dissimilarity between them is ever greater.[12] The intent of this formula is not to allow a certain core of similarity to exist beyond which dissimilarity could begin, but to emphasize that wherever likeness of God and creature may be thought, it is forever undergirded by an even greater unlikeness. Despite the human creature's being made in the image and likeness of God, God is always ever greater.

Against this background the incomprehensibility of God received a new, paradoxical clarity when the university theologians of the thirteenth century made use of the idea that human speech about God is neither univocal nor equivocal in meaning, but analogical. This position, whose paradigmatic expression is found in Aquinas, is characterized by a powerful apophatic element, a theological agnosticism more pervasive than has usually been acknowledged. "Now we cannot know what God is, but only what God is not; we must therefore consider the ways in which God does not exist, rather than the ways in which God does."[13] Thus does Aquinas preface his mature discussion of the ways God is known and named. No created mind can comprehend the essence of God, that is, understand perfectly so that nothing is hidden from view. This Aquinas explains by means of an epistemology which requires that for knowledge of anything, some sort of mental image or species be formed of what is known, an image that is always necessarily definite and finite. There can be no such image of the infinite. God is positively misrepresented if any one image is thought to be adequate. Only in the union of heaven, when God's own self takes the place of such an image, will we be able to "see" God, and even then our created minds will not comprehend infinite actual being. God, then, is outside of all classes and categories and beyond the possibility of being imagined or conceived.

For Aquinas, the situation brought about by what is referred to as divine revelation does not change this character of human speech before the greatness of God. Neo-scholastic theology did not always recognize this. Using the outline of the *Summa Theologiae* as a paradigm of Aquinas's thought, its textbooks assume that first we deal with the nature of the one God in a natural theology derived from human reason with its limited ability to comprehend divine mystery, while next we consider the triune God who, while remaining mystery, gains a certainty and intelligibility in virtue of revelation.

Critical Thomistic scholarship today, however, points out that such a split between reason and faith in Aquinas's theology of God is not warranted. Even the so-called natural theology in the earlier questions of the *Summa Theologiae* is shaped and normed by the work's very first question on *sacra doctrina*. Here theology, all of it, is described as a subalternate science deriving its first principles not from the natural order but from revelation, the way music draws its principles from mathematics. Aquinas's so-called natural theology is already an exercise in faith seeking understanding and proceeds in the light of faith. Correlatively, the questions on the Trinity placed later in the *Summa* proceed under the sign of not-knowing already laid down by the earlier questions as true for all human knowing of divine mystery, whether that knowledge arises from traces of God in creation or from the revealed word.[14] Revelation gives certain key images of God not attainable through natural reason, as well as the gift of a clearer intellectual light by which to understand them. But it never gives human words precision or unwraps the divine nature for our knowledgeable grasp. Even in faith we remain united to God as to an unknown. With reference to Chrysostom, Augustine, Damascene, and Pseudo Dionysius, Aquinas systematically carries forward the tradition of divine incomprehensibility from the early Christian centuries:

The perfection of all our knowledge about God is said [by Dionysius] to be a knowing of the unknown, for then supremely is our mind found to know God when it most perfectly knows that the being of God transcends everything whatever that can be apprehended in this life.[15]

Ultimately, the highest human knowledge about God is to know that we do not know, a negative but entirely valid knowing pervaded by religious awareness.[16]

The truth of divine hiddenness receives insistent emphasis in that contemporary theology which seeks to retrieve the classical tradition for this age. The indifference of secular culture coupled with the ambiguity of history creates an ambience in which even for believers the experience of divine absence is often a characteristic of faith itself. "All that is divine is quickly passing by," and the fleetingness of divine presence thus strikingly expressed by Heidegger marks postmodern sensibility. According to Karl Rahner's analysis, this "burning experience of agnosticism" may be a positive thing, if human beings know that the meaning of their existence is shrouded in darkness but nevertheless trust the mystery surrounding it which is called God. It does, however, situate language about God in a new spiritual climate since for many people today the passing by of God is one key form in which faith transpires.[17]

Accordingly, with the sense that a renewed discovery of God for this age may well begin with a deepened experience of God's inconceivability, William Hill returns again and again to the "positive deepening of the darkness" in biblical revelation of God's trinitarian nature. God's unveiling is at the same time a veiling, always historically conditioned, never completely luminous. For both reason and faith the same problem perdures of how concepts and images generated from the world of creatures may point to the divine mystery and yield partial and inadequate, though authentic, knowledge of God.[18] Interpreting this theme in the framework of transcendental thought, Karl Rahner argues that the incomprehensibility of God belongs not at the margins or the end of the road in theology but at its very heart, insofar as God's inexhaustibility is the very condition for the possibility of the human spirit's self-transcendence in knowledge and love. Without the incomprehensible God as horizon and ultimate fulfillment, the human project itself would meet an impenetrable limit such that the human spirit would shut down, having no further depths to plumb.[19] Revelation does not signify an "enlightenment," writes Walter Kasper, such as would enable human beings to penetrate divine mystery. Rather, it is the revelation precisely of mystery even with regard to the Trinity:

The trinitarian profession of faith is therefore not only the summation of the revelation of the mystery of God; it is also the concrete exposition of the hiddenness of God, which is the origin, goal and essential content of all revelation.[20]

And in response to the question of whether in the act of revelation God ceases to be wholly other and so incomprehensible, von Balthasar is eloquent in defense of the "powerful incomprehensibility of the biblical God" whose love raises divine mystery far beyond any philosophical notion of incomprehensibility. God has not eliminated divine hiddenness even in self-revealing:

The statement therefore that God is "triune," all this is and remains discourse about incomprehensible mystery. It is only analogously (where the similarity is overruled by a greater dissimilarity!) that we can speak of persons in God; only analogously (where the similarity is overruled by a greater dissimilarity!) that we can speak of "begetting" and either "spiration" or "breathing forth"; only analogously (where the similarity is overruled by a greater dissimilarity!) that we can speak of "three," for what "three" means in relation to the absolute is in any case something quite other than the inner-worldly "three" of a sequence of numbers.[21]

Suffering adds a sharper edge to this doctrine of divine hiddenness. Jewish reflection on the European holocaust and liberation theology's search for God in situations of extreme poverty and violence point to the incomprehensibility of God not as a philosophical doctrine but as a datum of faith shaped by the anguish of history. Only lament and the courage of hope against hope enable the community to continue walking by divine light, inextricably darkened by the power of evil.[22]

It is abundantly clear in classical theology and its contemporary retrievals that human words, images, and concepts with their inevitable relationship to the finite are not capable of comprehending God, who by very nature is illimitable and unobjectifiable. Absolutizing any particular expression as if it were adequate to divine reality is tantamount to a diminishment of truth about God. The First Vatican Council, so clear about the intelligibility of divine truths in order to counteract fideism, was just as clear, against rationalism, about their perduring depths: "Divine mysteries of their very nature so excel the created intellect that even when they have been given in revelation and accepted in faith, that very faith still keeps them veiled in a sort of obscurity, as long as 'we are exiled from the Lord' in this mortal life, 'for we walk by faith and not by sight' (2 Cor 5:6–7)."[23] Anyone who would claim a knowledge of God greater than this on the grounds of "revelation" is ignoring the situation of being created and forgetting this deep wisdom of the tradition. We are dealing here with mystery that goes beyond all thematizing.

The experience of women today provides a powerful catalyst for reclaiming this classic wisdom as an ally in emancipating speech about God. Feminist critique of patriarchal discourse is surfacing the false assumptions that underlie insistence on exclusively male symbols and thereby propelling new discovery of holy mystery which we call God. Made in the image and likeness of God, women participate in the fire of divine being and signify the excellence of the Creator in a creaturely way. Correlatively, God can be pointed to in symbols shaped by women's reality as well as in imagery taken from the world of nature and of men. Not doing so has allowed one set of images to become a block to remembrance of the incomprehensible mystery of God. Doing so, on the other hand, has the immediate effect of bringing to light the true nature of language about divine mystery in male terms, namely, that it is as legitimate and inadequate as female and cosmic terms to express what is ultimately inexpressible. In the scope of the height and depth, the length and breadth of the incomprehensible God, language can be set free.

Analogy

If God is essentially incomprehensible, above all names and thought, beyond every ideal and value, a living God! — how is it possible to say anything at all about the divine? When we do dare to speak, what is the import of the names, images, stories, and concepts that are used? Obviously the only building blocks near to hand are creaturely experiences, relationships, qualities, names, and functions. From among these, in response to experiences of absolute mystery present and active in the world and its history, or in contrast to experiences of suffering and evil, the most esteemed of our relationships and qualities are articulated as words pointing to God.

In order to prevent affirmations about God from being interpreted as direct transcripts of reality, early Christian theology articulated the idea that speaking about God involves a threefold motion of affirmation, negation, and eminence. In this process the play of the mind is supple. A word whose meaning is known and prized from human experience is first affirmed of God. The same word is then critically negated to remove any association with creaturely modes of being. Finally, the word is predicated of God in a supereminent way that transcends all cognitive capabilities. For example, when we say that God is good, the movement of meaning carried in the reference to God also indicates that God is not good the way creatures are good, but God is good in an excellent way as source of all that is good. At this point we can no longer conceive the meaning of the word good, although it continues to point in the direction of holy mystery. Every concept and symbol must go through this purifying double negation, negating the positive and then negating the negation, to assure its own legitimacy. In the process an unspeakably rich and vivifying reality is intuited while God remains incomprehensible.

According to Aquinas, whose various uses of analogy have kept generations of commentators busy, this threefold movement of analogy is clarified by contrast with two other possibilities. On the one hand, words about God are not univocal, having the same meaning as when they are said of creatures, for that would ignore the difference between God and creatures. On the other hand, neither are they equivocal, having no association to their creaturely meanings, for that would yield only meaninglessness. Instead they are analogical, opening through affirmation, negation, and excellence a perspective onto God, directing the mind to God while not literally representing divine mystery.

Analogical predication rests on an interpretation of the doctrine of creation that sees all things brought into being and sustained by God who is cause of the world, causality itself being an analogical notion. Similar to the way fire which is hot by nature makes wood hot by setting it on fire, the whole world exists by being lit with the fire of being itself, which people call God. Every creature that exists does so through participation in that fire, the mystery of divine being. The free overflowing of the fire of being who shares this gift with creatures, without necessity or pressure, sets up a relationship of participation. All creatures participate to some degree in "being," the very dynamism of existing which God in essence is. Thanks to this ontology of participation, every creature in some way shares in divine perfection, although in no way does God resemble creatures. Looking at creatures we can glean clues about the characteristics of that primordial fire which is their origin and sustenance. Hence it is possible to speak positively of God, creator of all, through terms drawn from our knowledge of creaturely qualities, but always with the proviso that the reality of which we speak cannot be contained in this language, the burning wood not being fire itself. Thanks to the relationship of creation, words are but pointers to the origin and source of all.

The "knowing" of God accomplished in the analogical process is a dynamic of relational knowing. It is accomplished not in a concept but in a judgment of the human spirit that affirms God to be inconceivable while at the same time intuiting that the perspective opened up by the intelligible contents of a concept gives a view of God that is trustworthy. The creaturely roots of speech about divine reality give assurance that words have a certain measure of meaningfulness, that we are not launching into a black hole, so to speak, at the same time as their meaning escapes us. God is darkly surmised while remaining in essence conceptually inapprehensible.

Analogy shapes every category of words used to speak about God. Metaphoric terms involve some form of concrete bodiliness as part of what they mean: God is a rock, a lion, a consuming fire. Relational terms name God on the basis of divine relationship to the world: God is creator, redeemer, gift. Negative terms state that God lacks a given imperfection: God is infinite, immutable, impassible, perfections thought necessary according to the presuppositions of Greek philosophy. In these cases religious language which is metaphorical, relative, or negative does not intend to name directly and positively what God is *in se*, and to this extent the play of analogy is easily shown. The same is true of more formal substantive terms, words that can stretch to unmeasured lengths and so are used to point to excellences characteristic of God's very being in itself: God is good, living, wise; God is personal; God exists. Even these substantive terms never include a *ratio* that directly represents divine reality. In every case the same simultaneous movement of affirmation, negation, and letting-go in a transcending affirmation is required in order for the words to be true. The speech must intend yes and no and yes again if language is to avoid the danger of ascribing existence, reality, or personality to God in the same sense in which they are ascribed to creatures. There is always more in the concept than the concept itself can bear. Analogy breaks this open in an affirming movement of the human spirit that passes from light into darkness and thence into brighter darkness. "All affirmations we can make about God," Aquinas points out, "are not such that our minds may rest in them, nor of such sort that we may suppose God does not transcend them."[24]

The way in which negation may evoke a sense of the unknown God is marvelously illustrated by Aquinas's contemporary, the Jewish philosopher Moses Maimonides. According to his hypothetical case:

A person may know for certain that a "ship" is in existence, but may not know to what object the name is applied, whether to a substance or to an accident; a second person then learns that the ship is not an accident; a third, that it is not a mineral; a fourth, that it is not a plant growing in the earth; a fifth, that it is not a body whose parts are joined together by nature; a sixth, that it is not a flat object like boards or doors; a seventh, that it is not a sphere; an eighth, that it is not pointed; a ninth, that it is not round-shaped nor equilateral; a tenth, that it is not solid. It is clear that this tenth person has almost arrived at the correct notion of a "ship" by the foregoing negative attributes, as if he had exactly the same notion as those who imagine it to be a wooden substance which is hollow, long, and composed of many pieces of wood, that is to say, who know it by positive attributes. . . . In the same manner you will come nearer to the knowledge and comprehension of God by the negative attributes. . . . Each time you ascertain by proof that a certain thing, believed to exist in the Creator, must be negatived, you have undoubtedly come one step nearer to the knowledge of God.[25]

For the medievals, the moment of negation in analogy does not shut down thought but corrects the inadequacy of the positive affirmation, compels it to transcend itself, pushes it to its term: God who is always ever greater. The negation does not deny or revoke the affirmation, leading to an agnostic void, but powerfully invalidates its limits, in the end giving off some light. In this sense analogical language is more akin to the reverential abstinence from the use of God's name that characterized later Judaism, than to any exaggeration of divine aloofness from the world. At the end of the process the mystery of the living God is evoked while the human thinker ends up, intellectually and existentially, in religious awe and adoration.

The history of theology shows that soon after the medieval synthesis was achieved, the negating power of analogy was forgotten in face of the onset of nominalism and of ecclesiastical desire to make simple positive and authoritative statements about the divine.[26] Consequently, there have been good grounds for the Reformation tradition's suspicion of analogy. Martin Luther criticizes it for alliance with a theology of glory that forgets the cross. Karl Barth sees it as the Antichrist, an epitome of the arrogance of human reason that claims to know God on its own through natural theology. Wolfhart Pannenberg insists that logically a univocal core of similarity is present in every analogical statement so that, all disclaimers to the contrary, we end up presiding over the reality of God in our concepts.[27]

Twentieth-century Catholic return to the historical sources, on the other hand, accomplished in light of the exigencies of a contemporary mentality at once more skeptical and more searching, has resulted in a strong recovery of the complexity of analogy including its negating moment. Karl Rahner refuses to understand analogy as a hybrid between univocity and equivocity; rather, he insists on the original nature of the analogical relationship that grounds subsequent speech. We *exist* analogously, in and through being grounded in holy mystery which always surpasses us. Holy mystery "always constitutes us by surpassing us and by pointing us toward the concrete, categorical realities which confront us within the realm of our experience. Conversely, then, these realities are the mediation of and the point of departure for our knowledge of God."[28] Erich Przywara's contemporary theory of analogical speech leads even in revelation to the God who is "always ever greater."[29] David Tracy's skillful comparison of the analogical with the dialectical imagination connects analogy with a community's deepest religious experience of the manifestation of grace in the world, all the while describing it with a strong shot of the negative.[30] The net result of these various recent studies is an understanding of analogy in the Catholic mind today that once again stresses its movement through negation toward mystery, and consequently the nonliteral although still meaningful character of its speech about God.

This is not to say that differences between the basic mentalities of the Reformation and Catholic traditions are thereby overcome. The Protestant critical principle, which is quick to object when any creature usurps the prerogatives of God, and the Catholic critical principle, which insists that the presence of the divine be recognized even when its mediating agencies are broken by sin, color the world differently in a religious sense.[31] But it is to note heightened Catholic consciousness of the obliqueness of speech about God through the idea of analogy, which converges with classical Protestant and contemporary academic concerns. Whether expressed by metaphorical, symbolic, or analogical theology, there is basic agreement that the mystery of God is fundamentally unlike anything else we know of, and so is beyond the grasp of all our naming.[32]

The understanding that all speech about God is analogical assumes a strongly critical function when the androcentric character of traditional speech is faced with the question of naming toward God arising from women's experience today. Introducing female symbols makes it acutely clear that analogy still has a job to do in purifying God-talk of its direct even if unintentional masculine literalism. Now it becomes clear that we have not yet sufficiently articulated that the critical negation of analogy must be stringently applied to male images and conceptualizations of God no less than to other aspects of divine predication. The designation "he" is subject to all the limitations found in any other positive naming of God, and in the end does not really tell us anything about the divine. Even in the case of the symbol of God the Father, "as if" must be understood in every instance. "Negations, revolts, oppositions, all the mind's refusals, insofar as they are well founded," de Lubac observes, "are explained by the demands of affirmation and adherence."[33] Women's refusal of the exclusive claim of the white male symbol of the divine arises from the well-founded demand to adhere to the holy mystery of God, source of the blessing of their own existence, and to affirm their own intrinsic worth. Analogy functions as a wheel on which they can spin out emancipatory language in fidelity to the mystery of God and their own good mystery which participates in that fire.

Many Names

We have seen that God dwells in unapproachable light so that no name or image or concept that human beings use to speak of the divine mystery ever arrives at its goal: God is essentially incomprehensible. We have also described how all words about the divine begin from the experience of the world, and then are negated insofar as they carry reference to the creaturely mode in which the spare, original, strange perfections of the world exist, ultimately being reaffirmed in a transcending movement of the human spirit toward God as eminent source of all: language about God is analogical. "From this," Aquinas concludes, "we see the necessity of giving to God many names."[34] The first expression of the unknowability of God is the proliferation of names, images and concepts, each of which provides a different perspective onto divine excellence. For if we were able to see into the very essence of God and wrap our minds around this, we would be able to express the divine by only one, straight-as-an-arrow name. As created beings, however, we can never do this. Instead, the diversity of the world offers fragments of beauty, goodness, and truth, both social and cosmic, facets of reality that point us in different ways to the one ineffable source and goal of all. None alone or even all taken together can exhaust the reality of divine mystery. Each symbol has a unique intelligibility that adds its own significance to the small store of collected human wisdom about the divine. In addition, as a concrete term balances an abstract one, and so forth, each operates as a corrective to any other that would pretend to completeness. The tradition of the many names of God results from the genuine experience of divine mystery, and acts as a safeguard for it.

The Bible and the Christian tradition as well as the world's religions give evidence of a revelry of symbols for the divine that nourish the mind and expand the spirit. In the Bible, as Paul Ricoeur has lucidly shown, there is a polyphony of forms of discourse, all of them radically nonmetaphysical, by means of which the community interprets its religious experience. Each of these forms of discourse — narrative, prophecy, command, wisdom writings, and hymns of celebration and lament — reflect different aspects of relationship to holy mystery. "The referent 'God' is thus intended by the convergence of all these partial discourses"; yet God is still a reality which eludes them all.[35] In the matrix of these discourses a plethora of images comes into play. In addition to terms taken from personal relationships such as mother, father, husband, female beloved, companion, and friend, and images taken from political life such as advocate, liberator, king, warrior, and judge, the Bible pictures God on the model of a wide array of human crafts and professions. God in action with the world is pictured as a dairymaid, shepherd, farmer, laundress, construction worker, potter, fisherman, midwife, merchant, physician, bakerwoman, teacher, writer, artist, nurse, metal worker, homemaker. Despite the predominance of imagery taken from the experience of men, feminist exegesis, as we have seen, brings to light the evocative vision of God as a woman giving birth, nursing her young, and dedicated to child care for the little ones. Pointers to the divine are drawn from the animal kingdom, with God as roaring lion, hovering mother bird, angry mother bear, and protective mother hen, and from cosmic reality such as light, cloud, rock, fire, refreshing water, and life itself.

Out of these concrete names, relationships, and images, more ineffable terms have been fashioned in the course of tradition: God as source and goal of all, the ground of our being, the depth of reality, the beyond in our midst, the absolute future, ultimate mystery, being itself.

Postbiblical Jewish usage is fertile ground for the many names of

God, as is shown in a study by A Marmorstein who has counted over ninety names used in the Mishnah and other influential sources developed in the first to fourth centuries.[36] Among them, in addition to the most popular terms Creator and Father (of mercy, of the whole world, in heaven), are: the Living God, Friend of the World, Mighty One, Searcher of Hearts, the One who knows the thoughts of all, Lord of Consolations, Height of the World, Eye of the World, Life of the World, Beloved, the One who dwells in hidden places, the Heart of Israel, the One who understands, the One who spoke and the world was, Justice of the World, Home of the World, Rock of the World, the Holy One, Holy Spirit, the One who hears, Peace of the World, Strong One, Merciful One.

In a more organized dramatic illustration of belief in divine incomprehensibility, Islamic tradition employs a litany of the ninety-nine names of Allah. The hundredth name, believed to be the true one which expresses the essence of divinity, is honored in silence. It is not pronounced because such a name does not exist: God is ineffable. Human silence after fruitful, imaginative naming pays the best tribute to divine mystery.[37]

Casting the net ever wider over all of the religious expressions of humankind gathers in an abundance of symbols almost too numerous to count. While these names of God originate outside the tradition that honors one God, they are instructive in the sense of the mystery and relatedness that they invoke. John Mbiti, for example, has compiled a list of the names for God used by distinct peoples throughout Africa where religious sensibility was originally shaped by strong communal experience and closeness to nature.[38] Outside the generic use of the term God with either a male or female referent, the most frequently used term for the divine is Creator. Even a partial sampling reveals how diverse are the ways in which that theme is played out: God is called the Great Mother, Supreme One, Fashioner, Designer, Father, Distributor, Carver, Molder, Hewer, Excavator, Architect of the world. The theme of creation involves both birth and death, as seen in the prayer over the dying said by the southern Nuba: "Our God who has brought us into this world, may she take you back." In addition, the ultimate mystery is Alone the Great One, the Powerful One, Wise One, Shining One, the One who sees all, the One who is everywhere. He or she is Friend, the Greatest of Friends, the One you confide your troubles to, the One who can turn everything upside down, the One there from ancient times, the One who began the forest, the One who gives to all, the Rain-giver. While called Highest of the Highest and the Unknown, the divine is also named Queen of Heaven whose glory shines in mist and rainbow; the Great Spider, Great Spirit, Great One of the Sky, Protector of the

Poor, Guardian of Orphans, the Chief, the Fire, the Almighty, Watcher of everything, Owner of everything, Savior of all. Many African terms for God translate as "the One who": the One who loves, who gives birth to the people, who rules, who makes children, who embraces all; the One who does not die, who has not let us down yet, who bears the world, who has seen many moons, who thunders from far-off times, who carries everyone on her back, who is heard in all the world; the One who blesses.

Indeed, Western language of recent centuries appears thin and paltry when brought into contact with this polyphony resulting from the human search for appropriate names for God. Western language has focused on male symbols to the virtual exclusion of female and cosmic ones, and has further restricted even male naming to the work of ruling men and the patriarchal relation of father. Remembering the Christian and indeed the world tradition of the many names for God opens up space for the renewal of God-language, showing that such pluriform speech is not only legitimate but religiously necessary for a proper discourse about the mystery of God.

Even in the face of all this richness, however, what Aquinas calls the "poverty of our vocabulary" perdures.[39] Taking all the names together will not deliver definitive understanding of God. To borrow a metaphor from Henri de Lubac, persons who seek to know God by compiling the names of God do not resemble misers amassing a heap of gold, a summa of truths, which can go on increasing until a rare purchase can be made. Rather, such persons are better compared to swimmers who can only keep afloat by moving, by cleaving a new wave at each stroke. They are forever brushing aside the representations that are continually reforming, knowing full well that these support them, but that if they were to rest for a single moment they would sink.[40] If you have understood, then what you have understood is not God.

In sum, the classical themes of the incomprehensibility of God, the analogical nature of religious language, and the necessity of many names for God are a heritage most useful to women's desire to emancipate speech about God. They shift the debate from the narrow focus on one or two patriarchal symbols to a field at once more ancient and more living. Along with biblical usage this classical legacy sketches out a place to stand in order to move speech about God into directions more sensitive to women's interpreted experience and ultimately more liberating for all creatures, human beings, and the earth.

PART III

SPEAKING ABOUT GOD
FROM THE WORLD'S HISTORY

For centuries, ever since Aquinas's *Summa* ousted Lombard's *Sentences* as the preferred university textbook in theology, it has been customary to organize material on God into two distinct and ordered treatises. The first tract treats of the one God and divine existence, concentrating on divine nature and its metaphysical properties (*De Deo Uno*); the second tract focuses on the inner life of the triune God, treating the three divine persons and their appropriated activities in a sequence from first to third, from Father to Son to Holy Spirit (*De Deo Trino*). As with any systematization this approach has its strengths as well as its weaknesses. On the positive side its largely deductive arrangement yields a high clarity in the logical order and a neat organization of material. On the debit side not the least of its weaknesses lies in its poor integration of the two treatises, with the one nature of God and the divine triunity seeming to dwell in two different regions of the mind. In addition an abstractness colors this entire systematic ordering "from above," rendering it remote from the historical experience of the triune God in the economy of salvation and therefore from the actual life of believing persons.[1]

I began this study having in mind the traditional order. After many tense hours, feminist consciousness subverted it in an irresistible way. Hewing closely to women's experience made it extremely difficult to begin anywhere other than the juncture where the dialectic of God's presence and absence shapes life in all its struggle. Consequently, the

121

present exploration starts not with the unity of divine nature nor even with the "first person" of the Trinity, but with the Spirit, God's livingness subtly and powerfully abroad in the world. What results is a theology of the triune God that sets out from the experience of Spirit.

Careful attentiveness to women's experience in the church brings to light how, excluded by patriarchy from official responsibility for the channels of grace, that is, word and sacrament, they have traditionally expressed their religious seeking and finding in myriad forms of spirituality associated, more often than not, with care for those whom they love, with the earth, with creative personal prayer and poetry, with the labor, beauty, and conflicts of everyday life. Women know the power and the pain of bearing and birthing new life, and caring for it even to the point of exhaustion or death. The renewal of the fabric of life, the replenishment of physical and spiritual sustenance, has traditionally fallen to them. Women of spirit have also consistently found ways to resist the official constriction of their lives, at times mounting public challenge in the spirit of prophecy. All of this is traditionally the field of the Spirit.[2]

Women's critique of the patriarchal God and the hierarchical arrangement of the world that "he" authorizes brings this whole arena of women's religious experience, daily and peak, to the fore. In itself the thirst for less officially structured, more creative engagement with the mystery of God along with search for freer articulation is interpreted as a call of the liberating Spirit of God who, like the wind, blows where she wills and cannot be chained down in official precepts. Beginning with interpreted experience of the Spirit and thinking through to the living triune God is one way of speaking in the light of insights generated by the pattern of women's religious experience in the structural margins, a way that as a bonus brings to light much that has been largely ignored in the deductive approach.

In addition to coherence with women's experience, other reasons also commend this approach. It allows a starting point more closely allied to the human experience of salvation, without which there would be no speech about the triune God at all. Reflection on experience in its ordinariness and as it reaches its heights, depths, and limits links theology first of all to the doctrine of the Spirit, identified as God present and active in the world, as God who actually arrives and is effective wherever fragments of freedom and healing gain a foothold in the struggling world. The dialectic of the Spirit's presence and absence is known in effects — new life and energy, peace and justice, resistance and liberation, hope against hope, wisdom, courage, and all that goes with love. There is a sense in which we have to be touched first by a love that is not hostile (the "third" person), before we are moved to inquire after a definitive historical manifestation of this love (the "second" person), or point from there toward the mystery of the primordial source of all (the "first" person).

Furthermore, according to the Christian narrative it is the case that even before there is an incarnation of God in Christ and even today where belief in such an incarnation does not exist there is a universal presence of the Spirit of God freely pervading the world, quickening creation, and working toward the renewal of all creatures, both human beings and the earth. Indeed, without the power of the Spirit Jesus' own life and mission within the tradition of Judaism is unthinkable, to say nothing of his life's destiny in risen glory and the church. Starting with the Spirit thus coheres not only with the existential but also with the historical pattern by which faith in the triune God arises.

An inductive approach to speaking about the triune God, moreover, has the power of making this doctrine more intrinsically intelligible to many contemporary minds. A theology of the triune God "from below" will not seek to prove the existence of such a God by reasoning but, more closely allied with experience, will engage in the hermeneutical task of interpreting the meaning of this doctrine that far transcends any esoteric puzzles of one or three in a literal mathematical sense. In this sense the logic of an inductive approach is more apt to nourish religious sensibility. Most of these reasons have been noted before by theologians who have affirmed and even encouraged a starting point in the realm of experience for speaking about the triune God.[3] In sum, to begin speaking of the living God from the experience of Spirit corresponds with certain broad streams of existential, historical, religious, logical, theological, and feminist wisdom. Equipped with insight from women's experience, Scripture, and Christian tradition, this study now embarks on such discourse, seeking a way to speak about the mystery of God from a feminist theological perspective.

Chapter 7

SPIRIT-SOPHIA

I, the highest and fiery power, have kindled every living spark and I have breathed out nothing that can die. . . . I flame above the beauty of the fields; I shine in the waters; in the sun, the moon and the stars, I burn. And by means of the airy wind, I stir everything into quickness with a certain invisible life which sustains all. . . . I, the fiery power, lie hidden in these things and they blaze from me.

—Hildegaard of Bingen[1]

Divinity Drawing Near and Passing By

At the root of all religious imagery and its doctrinal elaboration lies an experience of the mystery of God. Since what people call God is not one being among other beings, not even a discrete Supreme Being, but mystery which transcends and enfolds all that is, like the horizon and yet circling all horizons, this human encounter with the presence and absence of the living God occurs through the mediation of history itself in its whole vast range of happenings. To this movement of the living God that can be traced in and through experience of the world, Christian speech traditionally gives the name Spirit.

If we ask more precisely which moments or events mediate God's Spirit, the answer can only be potentially *all* experience, the whole world. There is no exclusive zone, no special realm, which alone may be called religious. Rather, since Spirit is the creator and giver of life, life itself with all its complexities, abundance, threat, misery, and joy becomes a primary mediation of the dialectic of presence and absence of divine mystery. The historical world becomes a sacrament of divine presence and activity, even if only as a fragile possibility. The complexities of the experience of Spirit therefore, are cogiven in and through the world's history: negative, positive, and ambiguous; orderly and chaotic; solitary and communal; successful and disastrous; personal and political; dark and luminous; ordinary and extraordinary; cosmic, social, and individual. Wherever we encounter the world and ourselves as held by, open to, gifted by, mourning the absence of, or yearning for something ineffably more than immediately appears, whether that "more" be mediated by beauty and joy or in contrast to powers that crush, there the experience of the Spirit transpires. Within this wide horizon of historical experience language about the Spirit of God finds its origin and home.[2]

The breadth and depth of experience that may mediate holy mystery is genuinely inclusive. It embraces not only, and in many instances not even primarily, events associated with explicitly religious meaning such as church, word, sacraments, and prayer, although these are obviously intended as mediations of the divine. But since the mystery of God undergirds the whole world, the wide range of what is considered secular or just plain ordinary human life can be grist for the mill of experience of Spirit-Sophia, drawing near and passing by. Consider at least three historical mediations:

1. The natural world mediates the presence and absence of Spirit. However valuable it may be as an epistemological orientation, the Kantian turn to the subject resulted in an unfortunate constriction of theological interest to human phenomena alone. Until recently there has been little sustained reflection on what J. B. Metz has informally called "the Alps experience," a moment of wonder when we are overtaken by the grandeur of the natural world as it exists beyond us and without us, simply there in its own givenness and beauty, fragility and threatened state. The mediating power of what I would call "the Chernobyl experience," a moment of self-transcending protest when we are appalled at the ruination of nature and its life-giving qualities, has likewise been ignored by theology although that is slowly changing under pressure of the present ecological crisis of the earth. Nevertheless, while neglected in theory it has remained the case even in these anthropocentric centuries that the world will tell of the glory of God. Anyone who has ever resisted or mourned the destruction of the earth or the demise of one of its living species, or has wondered at the beauty of a sunrise, the awesome power of a storm, the vastness of prairie or mountain or ocean, the greening of the earth after periods of dryness or cold, the fruitfulness of a harvest, the unique ways of wild or domesticated animals, or any of the other myriad phenomena of this planet and its skies has potentially brushed up against an experience of the creative power of the mystery of God, Creator Spirit.

2. Personal and interpersonal experience likewise mediates the presence and absence of Spirit to human life. As the Bible's love songs show, the love of God for the world is revealed through the depths of love human beings can feel for one another. We seek and are found by Spirit in the person-creating give and take of loving relationships, in each fresh, particular discovery of the other's beauty, in the strength

of ongoing fidelity. The anguish of broken relationships, by contrast, mediates traces of divine absence and, perhaps, divine compassion. Moreover, the dynamism of questioning, of arriving at insight in clarity or darkness, of imagining new possibilities, of artistic and scientific creation conveys the fire of the intelligent Spirit, source of all creativity. Finding one's own voice, however haltingly, imparts the power of Spirit crying out. The boldness to hear the claim of conscience and follow its deep impulses even in the face of loss; the courage to taste righteous anger and allow it to motivate critical resistance to evil; the willingness to utter the prophetic word — these occurrences inscribe the movement of the Spirit's compassion into the ambiguity of the world. In the sheer joy and pain of bearing, birthing, and rearing; in everyday, commonplace work; in living out freedom with its considered choices; in taking responsibility for our own life and its impact on others; in the depths of sin, despair, and emptiness; in accepting forgiveness and bestowing it; in the outbreak of joy and celebration; in befriending the stranger and caring for the truly helpless; in meeting limits and making peace with our finitude; in hoping against hope in the face of overwhelming oppression, suffering, or death or, in the absence of felt hope, in the sheer grit still to go on — the mystery of God's Spirit, present and absent, is cogiven in every instance.

3. On the level of the macro systems that structure human beings as groups, profoundly affecting consciousness and patterns of relationship, experience of the Spirit is also mediated. Whenever a human community resists its own destruction or works for its own renewal; when structural changes serve the liberation of oppressed peoples; when law subverts sexism, racism, poverty, and militarism; when swords are beaten into ploughshares or bombs into food for the starving; when the sores of old injustices are healed; when enemies are reconciled once violence and domination have ceased; whenever the lies and the raping and the killing stop; wherever diversity is sustained in *koinōnia;* wherever justice and peace and freedom gain a transformative foothold — there the living presence of powerful, blessing mystery amid the brokenness of the world is mediated. And it is known not in the open, so to speak, but as the ground of the praxis of freedom that survives and sometimes even prevails against massive violence; as the ground, in Peter Hodgson's telling words, of those partial, fragmentary, disconnected, transient, tiny, yet transforming rebirths that enable history to go on at all in the midst of vast discontinuities and meaninglessness.[3]

So universal in scope is the compassionate, liberating power of Spirit, so broad the outreach of what Scripture calls the finger of God and early Christian theologians call the hand of God, that there is virtually no nook or cranny of reality potentially untouched. The Spirit's presence through the praxis of freedom is mediated amid profound ambiguity, often apprehended more in darkness than in light. It is thwarted and violated by human antagonism and systems of collective evil. Still, "Everywhere that life breaks forth and comes into being, everywhere that new life as it were seethes and bubbles, and even, in the form of hope, everywhere that life is violently devastated, throttled, gagged and slain — wherever true life exists, there the Spirit of God is at work."[4] This is not to say that every person who reflects on the world would arrive at this same conclusion. But within the tradition of Jewish and Christian faith, the Spirit's saving presence in the conflictual world is recognized to be everywhere, somehow, always drawing near and passing by, shaping fresh starts of vitality and freedom.

Some early Christian images illustrate the theological meaning of speech about the Spirit by locating it within a trinitarian framework. If God as primordial origin is pictured as the sun, and God incarnate as a beam of that same light streaming to the earth (Christ the sunbeam), then Spirit is the point of light that actually arrives and affects the earth with warmth and energy. And it is all the one shining light. Again, triune holy mystery may be pictured as an upwelling spring of water, the river that flows outward from this source, and the irrigation channel where the water meets and moistens the earth — again, Spirit. And it is all the one flowing water. Yet again, the triune God can be compared to a flowering plant with its deep, invisible root, its green stem reaching into the world from that root, and its flower (Spirit) which opens to spread beauty and fragrance and to fructify the earth with fruit and seed. And it is all the one living plant.[5] The point for our pondering is that calling the mystery of God Spirit signifies the active presence of God in this ambiguous world. Whether the Spirit be pictured as the warmth and light given by the sun, the life-giving water from the spring, or the flower filled with seeds from the root, what we are actually signifying is God drawing near and passing by in vivifying, sustaining, renewing, and liberating power in the midst of historical struggle. So profoundly is this true that whenever people speak in a generic way of God, of their experience of God or of God's doing something in the world, more often than not they are referring to the Spirit, if a triune prism be introduced.

Given the diverse experiences that mediate the mystery of the ever-coming God, language about the Spirit consistently breaks the boundaries of neat codification or one single metaphor. In the course of her visionary work on Christian doctrine the medieval theologian Hildegaard of Bingen spun out a plethora of images that brings this home in a vivid way. The Spirit, she writes, is the life of the life of all creatures;

the way in which everything is penetrated with connectedness and relatedness; a burning fire who sparks, ignites, inflames, kindles hearts; a guide in the fog; a balm for wounds; a shining serenity; an overflowing fountain that spreads to all sides. She is life, movement, color, radiance, restorative stillness in the din. Her power makes all withered sticks and souls green again with the juice of life. She purifies, absolves, strengthens, heals, gathers the perplexed, seeks the lost. She pours the juice of contrition into hardened hearts. She plays music in the soul, being herself the melody of praise and joy. She awakens mighty hope, blowing everywhere the winds of renewal in creation.[6] And this is the mystery of God, in whom we live and move and have our being.

Forgetting the Spirit

What then has gone wrong? For despite the pervasiveness of the dialectic experience of Spirit, theological articulation about the Spirit has traditionally lagged considerably behind reflection on God unoriginate source of all and God incarnate, classically named Father and Son respectively. The history of doctrine shows that the Spirit, while the first and most intimate way God is experienced, was yet the last to be named explicitly divine.[7] Even after this was done in fourth-century theology and officially expressed in the expanded Nicene creed's confession that the Spirit is Lord and life-giver, to be worshiped and glorified together with the Father and the Son — even then the Spirit did not receive attention commensurate with this confession. In most patristic texts and in Western medieval treatises after the split with the East, the Spirit is dealt with "in third place" after questions of divine creation and redemption and the intricate relationship of the Father and Son have been explored in detail. Perhaps the understanding of Spirit receives such short shrift due to this placement itself, coming at the end when a great deal about divinity and God's ways with the world has already been explicitly discussed. Perhaps, especially in the West, the neglect is due to the nature of the thought systems that emphasize divine transcendence in a less than relational way. Perhaps toward the end of their long constructive treatises theologians simply got tired. For whatever reasons, theology of the Spirit remained in an embryonic state. The situation is well symbolized by Aquinas's poignant difficulty in even finding an appropriate proper name for the Spirit:

While there are two processions in the God, one of these, the procession of love, has no proper name of its own. . . . Hence the relations also which follow from this procession are without a name: for which reason the person proceeding in that manner has not a proper name.[8]

The legacy of the already overlooked reality of Spirit underwent a further constriction after the sixteenth-century ecclesiastical split in the West. Protestant theology and piety traditionally privatized the range of the Spirit's activity, focusing on the justifying and sanctifying work of the Spirit in the life of the individual believer and emphasizing the Spirit's gift of personal certitude. Working in this tradition, for example, Karl Barth, while crediting the Spirit with the gathering, upbuilding, and sending of the Christian community, portrays the Spirit in his main metaphor chiefly as the subjective side of the event of revelation. The Spirit is God's own revealedness who makes revelation effective by enabling human beings to respond to Christ in faith.[9] The extreme of the Protestant tendency can be seen in the emphasis of some pentecostal groups on the emotional effects of life in the Spirit with undirected enthusiasm.

Post-Tridentine Catholic theology, on the other hand, traditionally tended in the opposite direction toward institutionalizing the Spirit, tying the Spirit's activity very tightly to ecclesiastical office and ordained ministry. The widely used neo-scholastic manuals of this period arranged their material in sequential blocks progressing from God to Christ to Church, thus ensuring that the radical freedom of the Spirit is controlled by subordination to ecclesiastical order and discipline. This mindset is crystallized in the words of even the enlightened thinker Karl Adam: "The structure of Catholic faith may be summarized in a single sentence: I come to a living faith in the triune God through Christ in His Church. I experience the action of the living God through Christ realizing himself in His Church. So we see that the certitude of the Catholic faith rests on the sacred triad: God, Christ, Church."[10]

Catholic piety of this period, as Yves Congar has analyzed, tended to displace many functions of divine Spirit onto the pope, the cult of the Blessed Sacrament, or the Virgin Mary.[11] Regarding Mary, for example, it is said that she is spiritually present to guide and inspire; that she forms Christ in believers and is the link between themselves and Christ; and that one goes to Jesus through her. In the Scriptures these are the actions of the Spirit. Furthermore, Mary is called intercessor, mediatrix, helper, advocate, defender, consoler, and counselor, functions that biblically belong to the Paraclete (Jn 14:16 and 26; 15:26; 16:7). A great deal of preaching and piety followed the focus delineated by Pope Leo XIII who wrote, "Every grace granted to human beings has three degrees in order; for by God it is communicated to Christ, from Christ it passes to the Virgin, and from the Virgin it descends to us,"[12] a precise substitution of Mary for the Spirit in the trinitarian gift of grace to the world. As one Protestant student bemusedly observed, "When I began the study of Catholic theology, every place I expected to find an exposition of the doctrine of the Holy Spirit, I found Mary. What Protestants universally attribute to the action of the Holy Spirit was attributed to Mary."[13] This critical observation has been basically substantiated by a number of contemporary Catholic theologians who attribute it to the undeveloped state of pneumatology in medieval Latin theology and the post-Tridentine world of thought.[14]

The cumulative effect of this rather meager Western pneumatological tradition has been that the full range of the reality and activity of God the Spirit has been virtually lost from much of Christian theological consciousness. As Heribert Mühlen observes, when most of us say God, the Holy Spirit never comes immediately to mind; rather, the Spirit seems like an edifying appendage to the doctrine of God.[15] Without a proper name, the Spirit is widely acknowledged by theologians today, usually in colorful language, to be the forgotten God. The Spirit is "faceless," as Walter Kasper phrases it; something "shadowy," in John Macquarrie's words; even "ghostly," a vague something or other according to Georgia Harkness. Of the three divine persons the Spirit is the most "anonymous," in Norman Pittenger's view, indeed the "poor relation" in the Trinity. Many have written of Spirit as the "unknown" or at least the "half-known" God, as Yves Congar has pointed out. In Joseph Ratzinger's analysis doctrine about the Holy Spirit has gone "homeless" in the West; when it does appear, Wolfhart Pannenberg notes, it seems curiously "watered down" from its biblical fullness. G. J. Sirks even calls the doctrine of the Spirit the "Cinderella" of theology.[16]

More recently yet another reason has been proposed for neglect of the Spirit. While Scripture considers the Spirit more of an impersonal than a personal power, the resonances of some ancient language and symbols indicate that it is appropriate to speak of Spirit in metaphors of female resonance. Such is the case, as we saw in chapter 5, with at least three terms: spirit, indwelling, and wisdom, or *ruah*, *shekinah*, and *hokmah/sophia*. So powerful is the association of Spirit with the meaning evoked by these female images that in recent years the theory has grown that one of the key if unarticulated reasons for the tradition's forgetfulness of the Spirit lies precisely here, in the alliance between the idea of Spirit and the roles and persons of actual women marginalized in church and society. There is a point to this, I think, when we realize that in the Bible the Spirit's work includes bringing forth and nurturing life, holding all things together, and constantly renewing what the ravages of time and sin break down. This is surely analogous to traditional "women's work," which goes on continuously in home, church, and countless social groupings, holding all things together, cleaning what has been messed up, while seldom if ever noticed and hence anonymous. Neglect of the Spirit and the marginalizing of women have a symbolic affinity and may well go hand in hand.

Faceless, shadowy, anonymous, half-known, homeless, watered down, the poor relation, Cinderella, marginalized by being modeled on women — such is our heritage of language about the Spirit. Kilian McDonnell's wry observation bears out, that "Anyone writing on pneumatology [theology of the *pneuma*, the Greek word for spirit] is hardly burdened by the past."[17] What is most baffling about forgetfulness of the Spirit is that what is being neglected is nothing less than the mystery of God's personal engagement with the world in its history of love and disaster; nothing less than God's empowering presence dialectically active within the world in the beginning, throughout history and to the end, calling forth the praxis of life and freedom. Forgetting the Spirit is not ignoring a faceless, shadowy third hypostasis but the mystery of God closer to us than we are to ourselves, drawing near and passing by in quickening, liberating compassion.

The Human Analogue

To refer to God's ongoing transcending engagement with the world, theology, following one option among the several used in Scripture, traditionally uses the word Spirit: the Spirit, Holy Spirit, Spirit of God and, much less frequently, Spirit of Christ.[18] The term signifies a power that does not arise from human initiative but undergirds and surrounds it in a relation that makes all else possible: the Creator Spirit at the very heart of the world. This nomenclature seems particularly effective in signifying divine elusiveness and the fact that no human concept can ever circumscribe it, for the Spirit as such escapes concrete depiction. This is signaled in the cosmic images that Scripture associates with Spirit: blowing wind, flowing water, burning fire, light. None of these elements has a stable definite shape, nor can they be grasped; yet each has a clear impact on the world it touches. The human world also provides a point of intelligible comparison. Scripture uses the same Hebrew word, *ruah*, for both divine Spirit and human spirit, the latter evoking the breath which a living person draws in and expels, as well as that utterly personal life force unique to each person that anchors identity at the same time that it gives aliveness and energy. Like all words used of God, the term Spirit is an analogy, God being more unlike than like anything we know in the world as spirit. But the term's elusive and dynamic qualities enable it to express human experience of God who transcends all things while yet remaining in communion with all of reality in a dialectic of presence and absence that knows no bounds.

In recent decades the use of this term Spirit for God has been called into question for a number of compelling reasons. To follow Sallie McFague's statement of the argument, the model of God as Spirit is rather personally amorphous, being ethereal and vacant in what it evokes, thus lacking interest and force. Furthermore, its effective history reveals that it has been used to concentrate on divine immanence among human beings to the practical neglect of God's presence in the cosmic world, and within that human world to focus on the relation of the individual to God to the neglect of human community and its often debilitating structures. Finally, the very notion of spirit tends to play into the intractable dualism of Western thought, which dichotomizes body and spirit, matter and spirit, flesh and spirit; hence it does not lead into a theology characterized by wholeness. In her own wonderful thought experiment McFague proposes instead that the relation with God traditionally spoken of in spirit language be reimagined in the model of God as friend. Such a model overcomes each of the above objections, concretely imaging holy mystery in beneficent relation to the whole cosmos and giving rise to an ethic of human companionship toward all creatures as we enter into friendly relation with the friend of the world.[19]

In light of the Western theological tradition the difficulties raised by this critique are obviously real ones. McFague's creative work on God as friend provides a superb model to which we shall return later in this chapter. Given the project afoot here to bring classical theology and feminist theology into dialogue, however, I propose to keep the traditional language of Spirit and test whether it is capable of a feminist retrieval, not to the exclusion of the model of God as friend but toward the expansion of language. It may be that the amorphous character of the Spirit allows a particular openness to being appropriated in female images; that the Spirit's traditional concentration on the human race and its individuals hides an alternative stream of cosmic and community activity waiting to be rediscovered; and that feminist envisioning of reality in patterns of wholeness that undercut dualism has advanced far enough that the idea of the Spirit in creation may serve an integrative rather than a divisive function.

One clue to the kind of language we seek is found in Native American ways of speaking. Paula Gunn Allen, a Laguna Pueblo/Sioux and scholar writes:

There is a spirit that pervades everything, that is capable of powerful song and radiant movement, and that moves in and out of the mind. The colors of this spirit are multitudinous, a glowing, pulsing rainbow. Old Spider Woman is one name for this quintessential spirit, and Serpent Woman is another . . . and what they together have made is called Creation, Earth, creatures, plants and light.[20]

This spirit, this power of intelligence, is also called Mother of us all, Thought Woman, Corn Woman, Earth Woman, Hard Beings Woman, Sky Woman, Spirit Creatrix. What is evoked by this language is transcendent power pervading the earth and all peoples to bless and challenge. Does the Christian tradition of the Holy Spirit bear any possibilities for similar speech about God?

As already pointed out in chapter 3, simply identifying the Spirit with the stereotypical "feminine" leaves the total symbol of God fundamentally unreformed and boxes actual women into a restrictive ideal. But if with critical feminist consciousness we speak in terms of Spirit using metaphors coined from women as *imago Dei*, this could be a gain to language. Such speech is not a creation of rigid, logical rules, but of disciplined theological imagination. Drawing on the biblical imagery of spirit/*shekinah*, wisdom, and mother, which has already set language about Spirit in a certain direction, this chapter canvasses the classical heritage for understandings of the Spirit of God that cohere with women's experience of the holy and press toward renewed speech about the mystery of God.

Spirit-Sophia in Action

Since language about the Spirit arises through historical experience of the world, it takes shape according to the great diversity of moments from birth to death that orient interpretation. People say here, in this instance, or there, in that, God is acting in ways analogous to what is being experienced. There is no neat way to catalogue the verbs that come into language by way of analogy with human deeds. What cannot be lost from view is that in speaking of Spirit-Sophia's deeds we are pointing to the gracious, furious mystery of God engaged in a dialectic of presence and absence throughout the world, creating, indwelling, sustaining, resisting, recreating, challenging, guiding, liberating, completing. While separated out for the sake of logical discussion, these discrete activities are in reality but aspects of the one engagement, the one economy of God with the world. Let us speak of the Spirit's actions, drawing attention to the affinity of such language with feminist values, highlighting as it does freely moving, life-giving, nonviolent power that connects, renews, and blesses.

Vivifying

The whole universe comes into being and remains in being through divine creative power, *Creator Spiritus*. This creative function relates the Spirit to the cosmos as well as to the human world, to communities as well as individuals, to new productions of the mind and spirit as well as to new biological life. All creatures receive existence as her gift, she who is named in the Nicene-Constantinopolitan creed giver of life, the vivifier.

While not a frequently repeated theme in Scripture, this activity is commonly presupposed in the biblical association of divine Spirit with life and with the breath of life. In the beginning she hovers like a great mother bird over her egg, to hatch the living order of the world out of primordial chaos (Gn 1:2). The unfathomable mystery of this original beginning is matched by the continuous beginning of new life which her creative presence energizes. This is as true for the intricate pattern of the world as a whole: "Let all your creatures serve you, for you spoke and they were made. You sent forth your Spirit and she formed them" (Jdt 16:14), as it is for the life of every individual: "The Spirit of God has made me, and the breath of the Almighty gives me life" (Jb 33:4).

Creation is not a one-time event, an act that produces the world and then departs. In this sense the Creator Spirit is as far as possible from the distant, detached God envisioned by Enlightenment deism. Rather, her creative activity involves a continuous energizing, an ongoing sustaining of the world throughout the broad sweep of history. She is the giver of life and lover of life, pervading the cosmos and all of its interrelated creatures with life. If she were to withdraw her divine presence everything would go back to nothing.

God's energizing presence can be spoken of in spatial metaphors that point in their contrasting ways to her life-giving, beneficent power: the Spirit dwells within all things (Wis 12:1); she encompasses the struggling world as a great matrix (Acts 17:28); she pervades the universe as one who holds all things together (Wis 1:7). These metaphors point to a powerful connectedness as the hallmark of her touch. All creatures from the personal self to the nonsentient cosmos are mutually related and exist in an interplay of communion thanks to her presence. At the same time each individual is gifted with its own integrity, the Spirit being at once the source of individuation and community, of autonomy and relation. Patterns of enduring, delighting, suffering, sympathizing, participating, playing, and glorifying characterize the community of life between the Spirit of God and the world.[21]

A ninth-century hymn still sung at significant moments in church life gives expressive voice to this sense of relationality. *Veni Creator Spiritus*, the people sing, Come Creator Spirit. This prayer acknowledges the "not yet" of the Spirit's presence with its cry "Come": creation is still underway. At the same time it acknowledges that the energizing power of

God is in a most profound way already here. She vivifies, knits together, and upholds the world in pervading and unquenchable love.

Renewing and Empowering

Brokenness and sin are everywhere, a situation that makes the full life and harmony of creation exist more as future hope than as past or present fact. In this intractable circumstance the vivifying power of divine Spirit comes to expression most intensely in fragmentary moments of renewing, healing, and freeing when human imbecility and destructive ill will are held at bay or overcome and a fresh start becomes possible. This is eloquently spoken in the creation-oriented psalm that describes an amazing variety of creatures and then acknowledges: "When you send forth your Spirit, they are created; you keep on renewing the face of the earth" (Ps 104:30). Renewal is an ever-present need.

Spirit-Sophia is the source of transforming energy among all creatures. She initiates novelty, instigates change, transforms what is dead into new stretches of life. Fertility is intimately related to her recreative power, as is the attractiveness of sex. It is she who is ultimately playful, fascinating, pure and wise, luring human beings into the depths of love. As mover and encourager of what tends toward stasis, Spirit-Sophia inspires human creativity and joy in the struggle. Wherever the gift of healing and liberation in however partial a manner reaches the winterized or damaged earth, or peoples crushed by war and injustice, or individual persons weary, harmed, sick, or lost on life's journey, there the new creation in the Spirit is happening.

It is happening when the earth is renewed. Striking symbols of the greening power of the Spirit occur visibly in spring with the blossoming of the earth, and in autumn with the fruitfulness of earth being harvested. Even more crucially her renewing power is made manifest in the overcoming of rapacious human habits that extinguish other living species, devise instruments of universal death, and foul the human habitat of fresh air, soil, and water itself. The resilience of earth's systems, within finite limits, is one sign of the Spirit's efficacy. Yet those limits are indeed finite. The ecological crisis of our day makes all too concrete the Pauline insight that in the Spirit all creation is groaning, waiting for its redemption that is tied to human freedom, itself not yet whole (Rom 8:22). Responsible care for the network of earth's life and its systems aligns human beings in cooperative accord with the renewing dynamism of God's Spirit, an alignment essential for the very future of the earth, and is in truth a major critical gestalt in which the renewing power of the Spirit becomes historically present for the earth.[22]

It is happening when social and political structures are renewed. In the biblical prophetic tradition the Spirit's presence is consistently linked with the power to denounce social wrongdoing, announce comfort for those who are suffering, and bring about justice for the poor. "The Spirit of the Lord God is upon me," the scroll of Isaiah announces. And what is the result? Action on behalf of justice and peace: bringing good tidings to the afflicted, binding up the brokenhearted, proclaiming liberty to captives, releasing those who are bound, comforting all who mourn (Is 61:1–2). In the absence of the Spirit devastation plagues the world. But when "the Spirit is poured upon us from on high," then:

> the wilderness becomes a fruitful field,
> and the fruitful field is deemed a forest.
> Then justice will dwell in the wilderness,
> and righteousness abide in the fruitful field.
> And the effect of righteousness will be peace,
> and the result of righteousness quiet and peace forever.
> My people will abide in a peaceful habitation,
> in secure dwellings and in quiet resting places. (Is 32:15–17)

Given the despoiling and polluting of the earth by greedy or fearful human beings, and given the plight of so many millions of people plagued by war, by domestic violence, by fear of the knock on the door at night, and by circumstances that send them fleeing as vulnerable refugees, Isaiah's choice of the Spirit's blessings — fruitful fields and a peaceful home — has an eerie contemporary relevance. Justice and peace throughout the world of nature and the human world are the effects of the Spirit's renewing power, coming to fruition whenever human beings find community in mutual relations of sympathy and love.

In history, however, these moments are few. Violence and injustice in the form of massive poverty, sexism, racism, and war destroy the lives of millions of human beings who die before their time. The radical transformation of crushing structures and murderous situations does not happen automatically but only through human effort that through active nonviolent resistance struggles for justice and against suffering. In the midst of this agony, Spirit-Sophia who loves people teaches the ways of justice and courage (Wis 8:7). Like a midwife she works deftly with those in pain and struggle to bring about the new creation (Ps 22:9–10). Through the mediation of human praxis she comes to wash what is unclean; pour water upon what is arid; heal what is hurt; make flexible what is rigid; warm what is freezing; straighten out what is crooked and bent.[23] Wherever she moves, there awakens modest and even bold engagement against the principalities and powers that crush and oppress. Wherever she succeeds, structures are transformed and liberation and community gain a foothold. The Spirit's renewing power thus manifests itself historically in shaping the praxis of freedom, those myriad forms of peoples' struggle toward more peaceful and equitable circumstances, a stunning example being women's struggle against sexism.

For some this means the call to utter the dangerous, critical word of prophecy. In a unique metaphor John's Gospel speaks about the Spirit as paraclete, meaning literally advocate or helper. In a courtroom drama of shifting scenes she acts first as a defense attorney bearing witness to Jesus Christ (15:26–27); then her role shifts to that of a prosecuting attorney having her day in court against the powers of this world; finally she is imaged as a judge handing down the verdict that convicts the world of sin because it does not believe, which in the Johannine context is proved by not loving one's neighbor in need (16:7–11; 1 Jn 4). The power of the Spirit-Paraclete to convict and sentence is conveyed in the human act of judging the powers and principalities of this world and turning to deeds of compassion.

For others it means announcing and actually bringing into being new events of freedom. For still others it means summoning the awesome courage to keep on with the struggle even in the absence of visible success. In the midst of downtrodden people, Leonardo Boff has eloquently written,

the Spirit appears as resistance, rising above all hatred, hoping against all hope. The Spirit is that little flicker of fire burning at the bottom of the woodpile. More rubbish is piled on, rain puts out the flame, wind blows the smoke away. But underneath everything a brand still burns on, unquenchable.... The Spirit sustains the feeble breath of life in the empire of death.[24]

Inspiring the denunciation of evil, the announcement of the good news of freedom, and courageous efforts of resistance and imagination to bring it about, the Spirit's renewing presence is always and everywhere partial to her beloved creatures suffering from socially constructed harm, working to liberate oppressed and oppressors from the distorted systems that destroy the humanity of them both. Like a baker-woman she keeps on kneading the leaven of kindness and truth, justice and peace into the thick dough of the world until the whole loaf rises (Mt 13:33).

In addition to cosmic and social renewal, Spirit-Sophia's deeds take place when the life of every person is renewed. Jaded, discouraged, hurt, exhausted, worried, people have human need for comfort, healing, and new enthusiasm for life that arises every day. Nonviolently but persistently the Spirit who dwells at the center of personal existence creates a clean heart, a new spirit, a heart of flesh and compassion instead of a stony heart (Ez 36:26). Like a washerwoman scrubbing away at bloody stains till the garment be like new, she works forgiveness and reconciliation in tortured hearts (Is 4:4; Ps 51:7). Hers is the power of person making among those diminished by pain who do not know their own dignity; hers the grace of conversion to turn from dead-end ways to walk the path of newness of life; hers the light of conscience; hers the power to shake up assured certainties and introduce the grace of a new question; hers the strength to foment discomfort among the unduly comfortable; hers the oil of comfort (*cum + fortis*, "making strong") known in experiences that heal, refresh, and invigorate; hers the vigor that energizes the fire of active, outgoing love. The creative power that knits us into life continuously mends the torn fabric of our lives, forming in the process fine new and possibly surprising patterns.

While history goes on the suffering continues, the red thread of suffering that unites all life. Yet, incorrigibly, hope keeps rising that, in the words of the mystics, all will be well. The direction of this hope, this hope against hope, points to Spirit-Sophia's shaping the world toward an ultimate end: the liberation of the world in God. There is an eschatological orientation to the Spirit's recreative work, and metaphors abound to articulate it. "On that day" the Spirit will be poured out like refreshing rain to end the time of drought (Is 44:3). Thanks to her power the dry bones of a whole people will reconnect, be enfleshed, and live (Ez 37:14). Justice will be radiant; there will be plenty to eat; even maidservants will prophesy and dream (Jl 2:26–29).

When creation is seen together with its future of liberation in God, any residual dualism or overspiritualizing regarding the scope of the Spirit's agency is put to rest. Her recreating includes the integrity of nature, the liberation of peoples, the flourishing of every person, and the shalom of the whole world in rescue from the powers of evil, which foster sin and destruction. The present arrangement of the Bible urges this insight if we view its opening and closing scenes together. The first thing God does in the Book of Genesis is create; the Spirit broods over the formless void of the earth and the dark deep of the waters to bring forth a world. At the end of the Book of Revelation this same world, now riddled with suffering and death, is recreated: "See, I am making all things new" (Rv 21:5). The Spirit is the agent of this renewal, coming to dwell among the people. In an incredibly tender gesture most often observed in the interaction of a mother with her child or lovers with each other, she will wipe away every tear from their eyes; there will be no more death or mourning or crying or pain, for the former things have passed away (Rv 21:3–4). This vision indicates that meanwhile, in the conflict of history still underway, every shred of renewal that transpires through the praxis of freedom is a fragmentary anticipation of the Spirit's victory in shaping creation into the new creation.

Gracing

Up to this point the Spirit's vivifying and recreative functions have been contextualized within the widest possible world of everything that exists. Nothing explicitly religious has been singled out as the field of her play, although the flourishing of the earth, of social structures, and of every person's life is of immeasurable religious significance. The world of the specifically religious, however, is also an arena for Spirit-Sophia's presence, and in an explicit way the vivifying, renewing Spirit dwelling within the whole world is associated with the life and development of religious traditions. While the offer of grace is universal, it is the religions which thematize this offer in narrative and ritual, thereby clearly focusing on the Spirit's deeds of drawing all creation toward the holiness of God.

As Irenaeus saw, "There is but one and the same God who, from the beginning to the end by various dispensations, comes to the rescue of humankind."[25] As the experience of finding wholeness and meaning comes to expression in diverse cultures and ages, the panoply of the world's religious traditions takes shape. No people are devoid of the inspiration of the Spirit. In ways known only to herself, she orients human beings toward ultimate mystery and the fullness of coming blessing through movements of their conscience and the rays of goodness and truth found in their diverse religious communities.

The Jewish tradition explicitly acknowledges the Spirit as the prime shaper of the community. The Hebrew Scriptures credit all of the gifts that build the life of the community to her inspiring, resting upon, or moving within different persons. The courage and wisdom of national leaders, the strength of defenders, the energy of seers, the wisdom of teachers, the creativity of musicians, poets, dancers, and artists are all gifts of the Spirit. Above all, prophecy with its strong ethical dimension is a sign of special endowment by her power. Abiding with the people and accompanying them through the vicissitudes of history, even absenting herself in what are experienced as times of dryness and exile, the Spirit creates the covenantal bonds that make Israel the people of God.

The Christian community originates in the tradition of the covenant people and inherits the latter's understanding of the Spirit. Accordingly, virtually every New Testament author identifies the history and destiny of Jesus the Jew, become the Christ, as a Spirit phenomenon.[26] The infancy narratives of Matthew and Luke see the Spirit as the creative power responsible for Jesus' very coming into the world. In this new beginning Spirit-Sophia overshadows Mary just as she hovered over the beginning of the world so that, in the words of the Nicene creed, the Messiah is "conceived of the Holy Spirit." All four Gospels begin the narrative of Jesus' ministry with his encounter with the baptizing John. On this occasion as described in the synoptic Gospels the Spirit, whose outpouring will seal the end-time, descends upon Jesus, expressing the theological point that the eschatological time of salvation has begun. Jesus is the Christ, the messianic bearer of the Spirit of God, the servant of God who will not break the bruised reed but enacts compassion and justice for the weak.

After being "led by the Spirit" through fasting, prayer, and temptation in the desert, Jesus' opening words in his hometown synagogue echo Isaiah in pointing to empowerment by the Spirit: the Spirit anoints him to preach good news to the poor, to proclaim release to captives and recovering of sight to the blind, to set at liberty those who are oppressed. Spirit-Sophia creates Jesus' solidarity with the poor so that in his ministry this prophecy is coming to fruition. The preaching and healing characteristic of his days are done in the power of the Spirit. He remains faithful in the Spirit throughout the suffering of a terrible death on the cross. Through the vivifying power of the Spirit this crucified victim of state terror is raised from the dead into glory, an act of new creation that defines the very essence of the God in whom Christians believe: a God "who gives life to the dead and calls into existence the things that do not exist" (Rom 4:17). Through the same Spirit Jesus the Christ becomes in turn a life-giving spirit for others. The various strands of Christian biblical tradition do not harmonize in their particulars but all do make clear that in the entire life, death, and resurrection of Jesus Christ the Spirit is present and active in a singular way to initiate the eschatological time of blessing.

"You shall receive power when the Holy Spirit has come upon you," the risen Christ promises the community of disciples, a power to witness to the ends of the earth (Acts 1:8). Starting from the foundational event when the Spirit descends upon the gathering of women and men in fire and wind, inspiring boldness and facility in preaching the gospel, those who believe in Jesus Christ interpret their community to be the creation of the Spirit.[27] Most essentially it is in and through Spirit-Sophia that Jesus Christ risen is now continuously present to believers. She illuminates and inspires their narrative memory, teaching them all things and bringing to mind all that Jesus had said. Spirit of Truth, she guides them into all truth as history moves on. She empowers Christian mission, inspiring disciples' enthusiasm for sharing the good news, their imagination and creativity in presenting it within different cultural situations, and their courage and strength under persecution. She is especially manifest when the *koinōnia* of believers is built up in joy and justice. Though they are many and diverse in gender, race, and class, they are conscious of themselves as one people since all drink of the one Spirit in the waters of baptism. The variety of personal charisms that go to build up their one body are the gifts of the Spirit given freely, without regard to social rank or gender. Every member of the community is justified, redeemed from sin and set right with God by her grace. In her power they know themselves to be set free from the ultimate control of sin and death and "born of the Spirit" (Jn 3:8). No longer strangers, they are now friends of God. Thanks to her movement in their prayer they are free to address God in an intimate way as Abba. Important decisions about life in Christ in the face of new situations are made with her help: "It has seemed good to the Holy Spirit and to us" (Acts 15:28). While plagued by human foibles and sinfulness, this community tries to manifest her fruits of love, joy, peace, patience, kindness, goodness, faithfulness, gentleness, and self-control. In short, biblical narratives of origin show that Christian life is unthinkable apart from the presence and activity of the Spirit who animates and makes holy the church.

Speaking about Spirit

Classical Metaphors

The deeds of Spirit-Sophia encompass the breadth, depth, and historical length of the whole world. In the course of history Western theology has attempted to synthesize these manifold activities by means of terms that would crystallize the meaning of the Spirit of God within a trinitarian framework and give ontological grounding to her influence. The most influential attempt has been that of Augustine who on the basis of the *imago Dei* doctrine used analogies from human self-consciousness to point to the triune God. In the so-called psychological analogy based on a person's remembering, knowing, and loving oneself, the Spirit is usually characterized as love, that is, a certain unutterable mutual communion, and as gift, which stands in reciprocal reference to the giver.[28] One of the difficulties with associating the Spirit exclusively with love, as von Balthasar has wryly noted, is that in the Johannine tradition it is the Father and Son who do the loving, while the Spirit is the Spirit of Truth who has the function of reminding, teaching, and guiding the disciples into all truth.[29] Here the Spirit is a spirit of intelligence, a thinking spirit. Nevertheless, the words love and gift became common currency in theology and were brought to a peak of systematization by Aquinas. We examine this theological discourse with the understanding that it offers limited but real clues for feminist speech about the Spirit of God.

We can only name God from creatures, argues Aquinas in his empirical fashion, and the human experience of love is so profoundly life-giving that it provides a key analogy for divine mystery.[30] God is Love, and so penetratingly is this the case that love can be spoken of as the very essence of God. Divine love is similar to human love in the sense that it is a binding, unitive force, always tending toward the ones loved and willing the good for them. Unlike human love, however, which is a response to goodness already there, God's love creates goodness, making the creature lovable.

Now, while love characterizes God as a whole, it is an especially apt term for that distinct manner of divine subsistence which is actually present and active in the world and which people call Spirit. We have already seen the difficulty Aquinas had in finding a proper name for the Spirit. In spite of "the poverty of our vocabulary"[31] he settled on love as an appropriate word, thanks not only to the psychological model of the Trinity that required a procession by way of the will along with that of the intellect (Word or Logos), but also because of the affinity between spirit and love in terms of what they mutually signify:

For the name spirit in corporeal things seems to signify impulse and motion; for we call the breath and the wind by the term spirit. Now it is the property of love to move and impel the will of the lover towards the object loved.... Therefore because a divine person proceeds by way of the love whereby God is loved, that person is rightly called Holy Spirit.[32]

Having established that the Spirit is fittingly called love, Aquinas notes that this love has two key characteristics. In a trinitarian perspective the Spirit stands in distinct relation to the other two divine persons by virtue of being breathed forth or spirated. Her standing forth in this way marks her as "love proceeding," *amor procedens*, an evocative phrase that emphasizes the mobile, outgoing, living essence of love, the very antithesis of stasis. Furthermore, love proceeding is precisely the love of the other two divine persons who are equal, though not the same, in every way. Hence the Spirit is "mutual love," *mutuus amor*, the love of reciprocal relation rather than the love of one superior or inferior to another.[33]

From the name of Spirit as love, proceeding and mutual, Aquinas sees that the Spirit may also rightly be called gift. Arguing, as in the case of love, from the meaning of the term among human beings he figures:

A gift is literally a giving that can have no return, i.e., it is not given with the intention that one be repaid and it thus connotes a gratuitous donation. Now, the basis for such free giving is love; the reason we give something to others freely is that we will good to them. Therefore what we give first to others is the love itself with which we love them. And so it is manifest that love has the quality of a first gift, through which all other free gifts are given.[34]

Humanly speaking a genuine gift is given freely, out of love and not out of necessity; its reception is occasion for gratitude and joy. In the divine freedom to be present to all creatures, empowering them to birth and rebirth in the midst of the antagonistic structures of reality, the Spirit is intelligible as the first gift, freely given and giving. Her loving in the world is gracious and inviting, never forcing or using violence but respectfully calling to human freedom, as is befitting a gift.

Each of these names for the Spirit, love and gift, is intended to point to both the inmost nature of divine mystery and the outermost reach of God's power freely streaming around creation to quicken and renew. In the richly condensed words of Paul, "The *love* of God is poured forth in our hearts by the *Holy Spirit* who is *given* to us" (Rom 5:5). Each has potential to contribute to feminist discourse about God but must be appropriated critically for truly liberating language to emerge.

Speaking of the Spirit as the power of mutual love proceeding has strong affinities with the model of relationship most prized by feminist thought. Love is the moving power of life, that which drives everything that is toward everything else that is. When love is mutual it signifies a respect, a prizing, and a bondedness that subvert the potential for domination inherent in peoples' concrete differences. Spoken of in terms of mutual love proceeding, God who is Spirit cannot be used to legitimize patriarchal structures but signals a migration toward reciprocity in community as the highest good. As the creative dynamic of mutual love, the Spirit vitally moves, attracts, impels, connects, and sets up a solidarity of reciprocal, freeing relation throughout the whole world as well as between herself and creation.

An innate difficulty with the notion of proceeding, however, lies in the secondary status sometimes ascribed to one thing that issues from another.[35] If the Spirit proceeds from the Father as the East confesses, or from the Father and the Son as is believed in the West, either way the metaphor of proceeding in its human usage implies a priority of the origin of the procession, since what proceeds inevitably "comes after," either chronologically or ontologically. Whenever the mind succumbs to its perennial temptation to literalize, this language implicitly leads to the subordination of Spirit to the first and/or second person. If the Spirit is then envisioned in female metaphors and associated with women, the subordination of women is powerfully reinforced.

In contrast to this, the classical doctrine of the Trinity has always insisted that all three persons are coeternal and equally divine, as fire cannot burn without its brightness and warmth. This interesting tension between trinitarian doctrine of coequal persons and the analogy used to interpret it, specifically, the tension between the confession that the Spirit is to be equally worshiped and glorified and the metaphor of proceeding with its connotation of possible subordination, heightens awareness that the model of love proceeding is only a partial one. But insofar as it bespeaks the living God who is neither isolated, nor static, nor driven, but who from profound mutual relatedness freely goes forth to quicken and renew, then it is a way of talking that blesses mutuality and outgoing compassionate love among human beings, women as well as men. Mutual love and love proceeding, the Spirit is the pure unbounded love that turns the hearts of human beings toward compassionate care as well as moves the sun and the other stars.[36]

A critical retrieval is also needed to ensure that speaking about the Spirit as gift will be liberating. As we saw in chapter 4, feminist theological anthropology has critically analyzed women's propensity, due to cultural nurture if not nature, to give themselves without stint to others. Commendable when it is the chosen action of a mature personality, this orientation has as its potential dark side the possibility that women may never develop a personal, subjective center from which to give. Concern for the genuine personhood of women as human subjects necessitates that the metaphor of gift be contextualized within the broad horizon of freedom. This is in fact what classical theology does, connecting the Spirit's giving and the gratuity of the gift in an intrinsic way: it is the very nature of a gift not to be owed. To acknowledge the dynamic freedom of the Spirit in all her operations and simultaneously to name the Spirit gift are to speak about God as a mystery of self-giving who liberally graces all creation, not from any constraint or determination of nature but freely, in accord with her own design. Like the wind she blows where she wills (Jn 3:8), a particularly apt biblical image for the freedom of the giver who is herself the gift, one capable of signifying the value of mature self-giving in freedom for women and men alike.

Feminist Metaphors

Given the experience that "in every generation she passes into holy souls and makes them friends of God, and prophets" (Wis 7:27), Spirit-Sophia herself may also be named friend, a particularly captivating variant of the more abstract love and gift. This metaphor for God was not much favored by classical theology. Augustine's search for the right word for the Spirit led him to conclude, "If the term 'friendship' is suitable, then let us use it, but it would be more exact to speak of love."[37] Aquinas develops the analogy of human friendship with a bit more detail. "Since by the Holy Spirit we are established as friends of God," then as we do with human friends we can share secrets, goods, and conversation with God; find delight, joy, and security in the divine presence; seek comfort in sorrow, and freely seek to please God. The difficulty with Aquinas's discussion, however, is that while he is eloquent about how the Spirit "constitutes us as God's friends," and about charity as "a kind of friendship" between a human person and God,[38] God is never named a friend in return, and thus the mutuality inherent in the idea of friendship is not brought fully to expression.

Images of God's power and action as Spirit, however, convey a way of relating that is mutual, reciprocal, full of friendship from God's side, so to speak, as well as the human side. In her own thought experiment on this subject Sallie McFague's analysis of the model of God as friend beautifully demonstrates that friendship (*philia*) is the most free relation known to adult human beings.[39] Presuming a genuine side-by-sidedness in its participants, it is characterized by mutual trust and responsibility, absorption in common interests, and inclusivity toward others, which may extend even to the stranger and alien. What is relevant in speaking about Spirit in this model is that friendship entails a reciprocity of relationship that exists independently of one's place in the social order, making it possible to cross boundaries of race, sex, class, and even natures. Since the Spirit not only makes human beings friends of God but herself befriends the world, she can rightly be named friend par excellence. In her friendship human beings can know themselves to be never alone with their personal and globe-encircling anxieties but supported and energized by gracious compassion and powerful sympathy, similarly directed.

Women's experience of being a sister, both in the family and in the circle of friends, so emphasized in feminist prizing of women's relations with each other, has the potential to specify further the model of friend. At its best the relationship of sister is one of solidarity on a peer level, one based on having much in common both in terms of heritage and goals. With those who are one's sisters the relation can be comfortable and challenging by turn, but always mutual and profoundly supportive. In this sense Spirit-Sophia, love, gift, and friend of the world, can be spoken about in sisterly metaphor. As Brian Wren, the hymn-maker, would have us sing,

> Dear Sister God,
> you held me at my birth.
> You sang my name, were glad to see my face.
> You are my sky, my shining sun,
> and in your love there's always room
> to be, and grow, yet find a home,
> a settled place.[40]

The ancient tradition of the maternity of the Spirit brings yet another nuance to the connectedness carried in the metaphor of friend, coloring her vivifying, renewing, and gracing activity with the strength and love of a mother. Relationship with the mothers of our mothers likewise offers strong metaphor for speech about the Spirit. A Puerto Rican woman named Inez expresses this beautifully when, after noting that God is to her above all a dark mystery, she observes:

But if they would ask me to draw God, I would draw my grandmother smiling. Because she is the only person that I believe has filled me or filled me so much that I can compare her with God. I would draw a picture of my grandmother with her hands open, smiling, as if to say, "Come with me because I am waiting for you." God is strength for the *lucha* [struggle], strength to keep going, to encourage.[41]

Spirit-Sophia, friend, sister, mother, and grandmother of the world builds relationships of solidarity, not antithesis, between God and human beings and among human beings with each other and the earth. Held in her affection, human beings are called to be genuine companions of all creatures, advocating justice and partnering life, while not being diminished or overpowered by a dominating will. As with love and with gift these summary metaphors point to the Spirit of God dialectically present and active in the world, galvanizing human praxis in alliance with her purpose of flourishing for all. Speaking about the Spirit in names of love proceeding, mutual love, gift freely given, and in images of friend, sister, mother and grandmother indicates an agenda for human life: we are loved in order to love; gifted in order to gift; and befriended in order to turn to the world as sisters and brothers in redeeming, liberating friendship.

Speaking about God

Where have we come in tracing the question of the right way to speak about God? The Spirit is the living God present throughout the world and in the struggle of human history. That being so, whatever is said about the Spirit is in fact language about the mystery of. God. The activities of vivifying, renewing, empowering, and gracing with their consequent names and images bring us in an initial way to three key insights important for feminist theology of God, namely, the transcendent God's immanence, divine passion for liberation, and the constitutive nature of relation.

1. God's indwelling nearness, spoken of as immanence in philosophical terms, is greatly neglected by classical theism. Far from being simply distant, above and beyond the world, however, Spirit-Sophia is the living God at her closest to the world, pervading the whole and each creature to awaken life and mutual kinship. Not existence over and against but with and for, not domination but mutual love emerge as the highest value as the Spirit of God dwells within and around the world with all its fragility, chaos, tragedy, fertility, and beauty.

It is not the case, however, that the Spirit is to be identified with immanence alone. At the same time that the Spirit animates, pervades, and quickens the world, differentiating and uniting simultaneously, she is also marked by the same transcendence that characterizes the whole biblical and theological conception of God, who is distinct from the world with a difference that is as essential to our humanity as to divine mystery. She is in the world but not bound by it; present and active, mutually engaged, but freely so, not amenable to human manipulation or exploitation. The experience of Spirit-Sophia directs language to do justice to divine immanence and transcendence simultaneously, showing that these two are not opposite poles but correlative concepts.

2. The ways of the Spirit likewise show that classical theism's presupposition about God's neutrality in situations of conflict is mistaken. The Spirit is the Spirit of freedom, partial to freeing captives rather than keeping them bound, biased in favor of life's flourishing rather than its strangulation. Divine freedom is not sheer indeterminacy, as Peter Hodgson so well writes, but is bound to compassion for the world: "just as love signifies the immanence of God in the world, so freedom signifies the immanence of the world in God."[42] There in God, encompassed by the Spirit, which is a metaphorical way of speaking but a real situation for faith, the world finds God's intent and power for its healing and liberation from the disfiguring history of evil. Divine power to keep on shaping "fragmentary shapes of freedom," which survive and sometimes even prevail, points to the Spirit's liveliness dedicated to liberation.

3. Can the Spirit dwell within creation, on fire for its flourishing, without being related to it in a real way? For classical theism the answer to this question is yes. The monarchical God exists simply beyond the world as "being itself" marked by no real relation to the world. But this

traditional assertion and its intent, which can be interpreted as a noble one insofar as it sought to protect divine freedom, must be set in tension with the activity of the Spirit.[43] What is immediately striking is that there is no possible aspect of the Spirit of God, either *ad intra* or *ad extra*, that can be spoken about without factoring in the idea of relation in an essential way. Can there be an unrelated Spirit, existing in splendid isolation? The history of theology shows that the notion has been and is unthinkable. Relationality is intrinsic to her very being as love, gift, and friend both to the world and within the holy mystery of God. At the same time that she is intrinsically related, the Spirit is essentially free, blowing like the wind where she wills, not, as feared, cramped, or diminished by relation but being distinctively Spirit precisely in and through relation. In contrast to the idea of God that equates relation with necessity or dependence and thus opposes relation and freedom, the ways of the Spirit show divine being to be characterized by a dynamic relational autonomy that overcomes such dichotomies. In fact, her ways of operating signal that far from being contradictory these two elements, freedom and relation, are essential to one another and enhance one another in a correlative way: "While remaining in herself, she renews all things" (Wis 7:27).

Setting biblical and classical teaching on the Spirit in dialogue with insights of feminist theology leads to interesting theological results. The Spirit's deeds, when pictured as the work of a female acting subject, enable speech about God in ways previously closed to imagination. Simultaneously such language adds density to feminist speech about God, directing attention to the vast scope of divine activity. This kind of speech strengthens the understanding that women's reality is *capax Dei*, capable not only of receiving and bearing the divine, but of symbolizing absolute mystery as well.

In the light of the full range of the Spirit's activities the insufficiency of those theological efforts that associate women with the Spirit simply through so-called feminine traits becomes clearer. The Spirit is much more than the stereotypical, patriarchal feminine; she is, in the words of one early Christian theologian, "intelligent, boundless in power, of unlimited greatness, generous in goodness, whom time cannot measure."[44] When women are considered *imago Dei* with Spirit-Sophia in view, a possibility of female integrity beyond dichotomizing comes into view. Not only creative but also recreative presence, not only nurturing but justice-making activity, not only sustaining but liberating power, not only love but truth, not only relationality but freedom are the capacity of human women in her image. What the Spirit delivers is a symbol of wholeness rather than the diminishment of only the first of each pair, valuable in itself but all too often held out as a partial ideal of women's existence.

The Spirit's pattern of wholeness is beneficial for all human beings, women as well as men, and for language about the holy mystery of God. In fact, the longest-reaching effect of considering the Spirit first and from a feminist perspective may well lie precisely here, in subverting at the outset the dominance of the patriarchal image of God so detrimental to the mystery of God and the well-being of human community. Language about the compassionate, liberating Spirit shapes into an unbroken whole dichotomies that have plagued both the classical idea of God, rendering divine being distant, patriarchal, and unrelated on the one hand, and the interpretation of the nature of women, rendering women half human on the other.

In the end, of course, these theological motifs about the Spirit play off one another to hint at the reality of the mystery of God to whom the universe owes its very breath but whom we never comprehend. What is intellectual darkness, however, emits existential light, once it is understood that the world is held in existence by her compassionate power while human beings are challenged to be allies of her liberating grace.

•

So comprehensive are the operations of the Spirit and so vast the corresponding human experiences by which the Spirit's presence is known that one might think that speaking about God had exhausted its material once the Spirit had been considered. But in the Christian dispensation this is not the case. God is God another way, not only vivifying, renewing, liberating, and gracing all creation but becoming one with its very flesh.

Chapter 8

JESUS-SOPHIA

But you too, good Jesus, are you not also a mother?
Are you not a mother who like a hen gathers her chicks beneath her
wings?...
And you, my soul, dead in yourself,
run under the wings of Jesus your mother
and lament your griefs under his feathers.
Ask that your wounds may be healed
and that, comforted, you may live again.
Christ, my mother, you gather your chickens under your wings;
This dead chicken of yours puts himself under those wings. . . .
Warm your chicken, give life to your dead one, justify your sinner.

—Anselm of Canterbury[1]

Wisdom Made Flesh

Christian faith is grounded on the experience that God who is Spirit, at work in the tragic and beautiful world to vivify and renew all creatures through the gracious power of her indwelling, liberating love, is present yet again through the very particular history of one human being, Jesus of Nazareth. The one who is divine love, gift, and friend becomes manifest in time in a concrete gestalt, the loving, gifting, and befriending first-century Jewish carpenter turned prophet. According to the witness of Scripture, Jesus is a genuine Spirit-phenomenon, conceived, inspired, sent, hovered over, guided, and risen from the dead by her power. In its etymological and historical context, the early Christian confession that Jesus is the Christ means precisely this, that he is the Messiah, the anointed one, the one anointed by the Spirit.[2] Through his human history the Spirit who pervades the universe becomes concretely present in a small bit of it; Sophia pitches her tent in the midst of the world; the Shekinah dwells among the suffering people in a new way. In a word, Jesus is Emmanuel, God with us.[3] Given the specific direction of his life, this is profoundly good news for persons who are poor, denigrated, oppressed, struggling, victimized, and questing for life and the fullness of life, the majority of whom are women with their dependent children. The community of disciples formed in the power of his Spirit keeps alive the dangerous memory of his life, death, and resurrection as promise of a future for all the defeated and the dead. In the circle of life where Christ's way is followed, a new possibility of shalom, of redemptive wholeness, is made experientially available and can be tasted in anticipation, even now, as the struggle of history goes on.

Distorting the Christ

What then has gone wrong? For despite the potential benefit devolving from the history of Jesus the Christ feminist theology raises a most stringent critique, pointing out that of all the doctrines of the church Christology is the one most used to suppress and exclude women.[4] At root the difficulty lies in the fact that Christology in its story, symbol, and doctrine has been assimilated to the patriarchal world view, with the result that its liberating dynamic has been twisted into justification for domination. Historically, as the early church became inculturated in the Greco-Roman world, it gradually shaped itself according to the model of the patriarchal household and then to the model of the empire. The image of Christ consequently assumed contours of the male head of household or the imperial ruler, a move correlated with similar development in the idea of church office. Christ was then viewed as the principle of headship and cosmic order, the ruling king of glory, the Pantocrator par excellence, whose heavenly reign sets up and sustains the earthly rule of the head of the family, empire, and church.[5] Obedience to these authorities was obedience to Christ; disobedience to them called into question one's allegiance to Christ himself. Thus co-opted, the powerful symbol of the liberating Christ lost its subversive, redemptive significance.

The foregoing analysis of the "imperial Christ" is stringently carried out by Latin American liberation theologians and others concerned about releasing the power of the gospel for oppressed peoples.[6] What feminist theological analysis makes clear is that the imperial tradition that assimilated Christology is precisely patriarchal in character, resulting in a view of Jesus the Christ that functions as a sacred justification for male dominance and female subordination. In particular, when Jesus' maleness, which belongs to his historical identity, is interpreted to be essential to his redeeming christic function and identity, then the Christ serves as a religious tool for marginalizing and excluding women.

Let me be very clear about what is at issue here. The fact that Jesus of Nazareth was a male human being is not in question, nor, in a more just church, would it even be an issue. Jesus' maleness is a constitutive element of his identity, part of the perfection and limitation of his historical contingency, and as such is to be respected. It is as intrinsic to his historical person as his familial, ethnic, religious, linguistic, and cultural particularity, his Galilean village roots, and so forth. The difficulty arises, rather, from the way Jesus' maleness is construed in official androcentric theology and ecclesial praxis, a way that results in a christological view that effectively diminishes women. Feminist theological analysis lays bare at least two ways in which such distorted interpretation occurs, and one logical anomaly that results.

First, at a level that is more often implicit than explicit, the maleness of Jesus is used to reinforce a patriarchal image of God. If Jesus is a man, so uncritical reasoning goes, and as such the revelation of God, then this must point to maleness as an essential characteristic of divine being itself. It indicates, if not an identification, then at the very least more of an affinity between maleness and divinity than is the case with femaleness. This interpretation is exacerbated by exclusive use of father and son metaphors to interpret Jesus' relationship to God. "Who has seen me has seen the Father" (Jn 14:9) — such language is thought to be not "mere metaphor" but is taken literally to mean that the man Jesus is the revealer of a male Father-God, despite the evidence in Scripture and tradition that the mystery of God transcends all naming and also creates female reality in the divine image and likeness. The knot is tied tighter by use of the concept of *logos*, long connected in Greek philosophy with the male principle, to articulate Christ's personal identity as God's self-expression in the world. Once the Logos is identified with the man Jesus precisely as male, then, as Rosemary Ruether has pointed out, "the unwarranted idea develops that there is a necessary ontological connection between the maleness of Jesus' historical person and the maleness of Logos as male offspring and disclosure of a male God."[7] So strong is this connection in the literal imagination that even the authoritative doctrine of Chalcedon is overruled. While there it is confessed that between the human nature and divine nature of Jesus Christ there is no mixing, no confusion, so that each nature keeps its own properties, still the androcentric imagination occasions a certain leakage of Jesus' human maleness into the divine nature, so that maleness appears to be of the essence of the God made known in Christ.

Second, the fact that Jesus was a man is construed to strengthen not only a patriarchal notion of God but also an androcentric anthropology, in the belief that a particular honor, dignity, and normativity accrues to the male sex because it was chosen by the Son of God himself for the enfleshment of incarnation. What androcentric anthropology already holds as a basic assumption, Christology confirms: men are not only more truly theomorphic but, in virtue of their sex, also christomorphic in a way that goes beyond what is possible for women. As stated in an official argument against women's ordination, for example, men, thanks to their "natural resemblance" enjoy a capacity for closer identification with Christ than do women.[8] While women may be recipients of divine grace, they are unsuited to carry out christic and especially eucharistic actions publicly due to their sexual difference from his maleness. Thus men alone among human beings are able to represent Christ fully. Women's physical embodiment becomes a prison that shuts them off from God, except as mediated through the christic male. For this mentality, the idea that the Word might have become female flesh is not even seriously imaginable, so thoroughly has androcentric Christology done its work of erasing the full dignity of women as christomorphic in the community of disciples.

As a logical outcome of this exacerbated stress on Jesus' maleness in the context of dualistic anthropology that essentially divorces male from female humanity, women's salvation is implicitly put in jeopardy, at least theoretically. The Christian story of salvation involves not only God's compassionate will to save but also the method by which this will becomes effective, namely, by God's plunging into sinful human history and transforming it from within. The early Christian aphorism "What is not assumed is not redeemed, but what is assumed is saved by union with God" sums up the insight that God's saving solidarity with all of humanity is what is crucial for the birth of the new creation. *Et homo factus est:* thus does the Nicene creed confess the universal relevance of the incarnation by the use of the inclusive *homo*. But if in fact what is meant is *et vir factus est*, with stress on sexual manhood, if maleness is essential for the christic role, then women are cut out of the loop of salvation, for female sexuality is not taken on by the Word made flesh. If maleness is constitutive for the incarnation and redemption, female humanity is not assumed and therefore not saved.

Dualistic anthropology solves this problem by understanding man as the head of woman. In his role as microcosm his eminence includes her reality along with all other creatures on the lower rungs of the ladder of being. Thus, in assuming male humanity, the savior in fact includes the female, and women are thereby saved. However, when this androcentric Christology meets an egalitarian anthropology that holds that women and men are equally created in the image of God, and are equally one in Christ through the waters of baptism, such a solution is ruled out. If women are not a lower order of creature subsumed in male humanity but co-partners in essential humanity along with men, then they are not connected to what is most vital for salvation, according to the logic of a male-centered Christology. If Christology now remains androcentric, the logical answer to the searching question "Can a male savior save women?" can only be *no*.[9] The negative response will perdure until the inner structure of Christology and its effective history are transformed to cohere with the liberating impulse of the gospel, valuing women as full participants in the mystery of redemption with capacity by nature and grace to represent Jesus the Christ.

The way forward to a genuinely liberating Christology is made up of several interrelated steps. At a foundational level anthropology must be envisioned anew to overcome the gender dualism that haunts traditional interpretation of Christ. That done, this chapter respeaks Christology by telling the gospel story of Jesus as the story of Wisdom's child, Sophia incarnate; by interpreting the symbol of the Christ to allow its ancient inclusivity to shine through; by explicating christological doctrine to unlock what is of benefit. In the end we return to the above distortions to see how they may have been transformed by a feminist reading of the christological tradition.

The Human Analogue

The social location of the distorted interpretation of Jesus' maleness in the Christian tradition is an ecclesial community where official voice, vote, and visibility belong by law only to men. Rising into intellectual expressions that support the status quo, this patriarchy is bedrock for the androcentric construction of gender differences shaping the misuse of maleness in Christology. Envisioning a different kind of community laced by relationships of mutuality and reciprocity allows feminist thought to rethink anthropology in an egalitarian gestalt, to practical and critical effect. Then Jesus' maleness is open to interpretation at once less theologically important and more liberating.

In the beginning of this intellectual effort it was clear what model of anthropology feminist thought did not want, namely, the prevailing dualistic model that casts women and men as polar opposites, each bearing unique characteristics from which the other sex is excluded. In this view male and female are related by the notion of complementarity, which rigidly predetermines the qualities each should cultivate and the roles each can play. Apart from naiveté about its own social conditioning, its reliance on stereotypes, and the denial of the wholeness of human experience that it mandates, this position functions as a smokescreen for the subordination of women since by its definition women are always relegated to the private, passive realm.[10]

In contrast to this dualistic anthropology feminist thinkers at first developed a single-nature anthropology, which views sexual difference as biologically important for reproduction but not determinative of persons as such. Since the meaning of male and female is still historically emerging, each is free to develop the best of traditional masculine or feminine characteristics in the search for wholeness, and may assume public and private roles according to their giftedness. In this view the stress is on basic similarity rather than difference, to the point where differences become relatively inconsequential. Apart from its neglect of the importance of sexual embodiment, which affects far more than reproduction in the life of every person, this view also comes under criticism for tending to hold out a single human ideal, possibly androgynous, which can be destructive of genuine human variety.

On the one hand, feminist thought resists an unrelieved binary way of thinking, a notion of human nature polarized on the basis of sex, which inevitably leads to a dominant/subordinate pattern. On the other hand, reduction to an equality of sameness by ignoring sexual difference is also unacceptable. Two separate types of human nature, or unisex?

A way beyond the impasse of these options is emerging: one human nature celebrated in an interdependence of multiple differences.[11] Not a binary view of two forever predetermined male and female natures, nor abbreviation to a single ideal, but a diversity of ways of being human: a multipolar set of combinations of essential human elements, of which sexuality is but one. Human existence has a multidimensional character. If maleness and femaleness can be envisioned in a more wholistic context, their relationship to each other can be more rightly conceived.

All persons are constituted by a number of anthropological constants, essential elements that are intrinsic to their identity. These include bodiliness and hence sex and race; relation to the earth, other persons and social groupings; economic, political, and cultural location, and the like.[12] These constants mutually condition one another, and in their endless combinations are constitutive of the humanity of every person. Significantly change any one of them, and a different person results.

It is shortsighted to single out sexuality as always and everywhere more fundamental to concrete historical existence than any of the other constants. Age, race, period in history, bodily handicap, social location, and other essential aspects of concrete historical existence are at least as important in determining one's identity as sex. Focusing on sexuality to the exclusion of other equally constitutive elements is the equivalent of using a microscope on this one key factor of human life when what is needed is a telescope to take in the galaxies of rich human difference. In a multipolar model, sexuality is integrated into a holistic vision of human persons instead of being made the touchstone of personal identity and thus distorted.

The anthropological model of one human nature instantiated in a multiplicity of differences moves beyond the contrasting models of sex dualism versus the sameness of abstract individuals toward the celebration of diversity as entirely normal. The goal is to reorder the two-term and one-term systems into a multiple-term schema, one which allows connection in difference rather than constantly guaranteeing identity through opposition or uniformity. Respect can thus be extended to all persons in their endless combinations of anthropological constants, boundlessly concrete. And difference itself, rather than a regrettable obstacle to community, can function as a creative community-shaping force. As poet Audre Lorde appreciates, diversity is a boundless resource:

Difference must be not merely tolerated, but seen as a fund of necessary polarities between which our creativity can spark like a dialectic. Only then does the necessity for interdependency become unthreatening. Only within that interdependency of different strengths, acknowledged and equal, can the power to seek new ways of being in the world generate.... Difference is that raw and powerful connection from which our personal power is forged.[13]

A multipolar anthropology allows Christology to integrate Jesus' maleness using interdependence of difference as a primary category, rather than emphasizing sexuality in an ideological, distorted way. Amid a multiplicity of differences Jesus' maleness is appreciated as intrinsically important for his own personal historical identity and the historical challenge of his ministry, but not theologically determinative of his identity as the Christ nor normative for the identity of the Christian community. Story, symbol, and doctrine then assume an emancipatory gestalt.

Jesus-Sophia in Action

The community of disciples is charged with keeping alive throughout the ages the good news let loose in the struggling world through the history and destiny of Jesus of Nazareth. An excellent way of doing so is provided by the wisdom tradition, which since the first century has allowed all the power of the figure of Sophia to focus and filter the significance and identity of the Messiah. Jesus is Sophia incarnate, the Wisdom of God: "but she was sent in one way that she might be with human beings; and she has been sent in another way that she herself might be a human being."[14] Not only does the gender symbolism cast Jesus into an inclusive framework with regard to his relationships with human beings and with God, removing the male emphasis that so quickly turns to androcentrism. But, the symbol giving rise to thought, it also evokes Sophia's characteristic gracious goodness, life-giving creativity, and passion for justice as key hermeneutical elements in speaking about the mission of Jesus.

Preaching, Ingathering, Confronting

In his brief ministry Jesus appears as the prophet and child of Sophia sent to announce that God is the God of all-inclusive love who wills the wholeness and humanity of everyone, especially the poor and heavy-burdened.[15] He is sent to gather all the outcast under the wings of their gracious Sophia-God and bring them to shalom. This envoy of Sophia walks her paths of justice and peace and invites others to do likewise. Like her he delights in being with people; joy, insight, and a sure way to God are found in his company. Again and again in imaginative parables, compassionate healings, startling exorcisms, and festive meals he spells out the reality of the gracious goodness and renewing power of Sophia-God drawing near. He addresses her, in all trust, as Abba; he also likens her to a shepherd searching for a lost sheep, a woman looking for her lost coin, a father forgiving his wayward child, a bakerwoman kneading yeast into dough, a mother giving birth. Scandalous though it may appear, his inclusive table community widens the circle of the friends of God to include the most disvalued people, even tax collectors, sinners, prostitutes. In all, his compassionate, liberating words and deeds are the works of Sophia reestablishing the right order of creation: "Wisdom is justified by her deeds" (Mt 11:19).

Through his ministry Jesus unleashes a hope, a vision, and a present experience of liberating relationships that women, the lowest of the low in any class, as well as men, savor as the antithesis of patriarchy. Women interact with Jesus in mutual respect, support, comfort, and challenge, themselves being empowered to acts of compassion, thanksgiving, and boldness by Spirit-Sophia who draws near in him. Although long neglected by the later tradition, these women emerge in feminist interpretation in significant ways. They befriend, economically support, advise, and challenge Jesus, break bread with him and evangelize in his name. Others receive the gift of his healing, being empowered to stand up straight beyond physical or mental suffering, spiritual alienation, or social ostracism. One woman whose name has been forgotten by patriarchal tradition prophetically anoints his head in an act that commissions him toward his death. New possibilities of relationships patterned according to the mutual services of friendship rather than domination-subordination flower among the women and men who respond and join his circle. They form a community of the discipleship of equals.[16]

All of this is too much for those heavily invested in the political and religious status quo. Mortally threatened, they conspire to be rid of him. In the end Jesus' death is a consequence of the hostile response of religious and civil rulers to the style and content of his ministry, to which he was radically faithful with a freedom that would not quit. The friendship and inclusive care of Sophia are rejected as Jesus is violently executed, preeminent in the long line of Sophia's murdered prophets.

Dying and Rising

Jesus' death included all that makes death terrifying: state torture, physical anguish, brutal injustice, hatred by enemies, the mockery of their victorious voices, collapse of his life's work in ruins, betrayal by some close friends, the experience of abandonment by God, and of powerlessness in which one ceases to be heroic. Indeed, he descended into hell, being "shattered," a term used elsewhere in the Gospels only of women.[17] *Ecce homo:* Christ crucified, the Wisdom of God.

For the Christian community the story does not end there. Faith in the resurrection witnesses that Sophia's characteristic gift of life is given in a new, unimaginable way, so that the crucified victim of state injustice is not abandoned forever. Her pure, beneficent, people-loving Spirit seals him in new, unimaginable life as pledge of a future for all the violated and the dead. This same Spirit is poured out on the circle of disciples drawn by the attractiveness of Jesus and his gracious God, and they are missioned to make the inclusive goodness and saving power of Sophia-God experientially available to the ends of the earth.

Along with other forms of political and liberation theology, feminist theology repudiates an interpretation of the death of Jesus as required by God in repayment for sin.[18] Such a view today is virtually inseparable from an underlying image of God as an angry, bloodthirsty, violent and sadistic father, reflecting the very worst kind of male behavior. Rather, Jesus' death was an act of violence brought about by threatened human men, as sin, and therefore against the will of a gracious God. It occurred historically in consequence of Jesus' fidelity to the deepest truth he knew, expressed in his message and behavior, which showed all twisted relationships to be incompatible with Sophia-God's shalom. Challenging the validity of powerful relations normed by dominance and submission, his liberating life bore the signature of his death; in that sense, suffering was most probable. What comes clear in the event, however, is not Jesus' necessary passive victimization divinely decreed as a penalty for sin, but rather a dialectic of disaster and powerful human love through which the gracious God of Jesus enters into solidarity with all those who suffer and are lost. The cross in all its dimensions, violence, suffering, love, is the parable that enacts Sophia-God's participation in the suffering of the world.

The victory of love, both human and divine, that spins new life out of this disaster is expressed in belief in the risen Christ. There is nothing imaginable here — can the caterpillar picture what it is like to be a butterfly? What is affirmed as faith, for evidence continues to contradict this, is that overwhelming evil does not have the last word. The crucified one is not, in the end, abandoned. Sophia-God gathers her child and prophet into new transformed life, promise of a future for all the dead and the whole cosmos itself. The feminist vision of wholeness, of the value of the bodily integrity of each, even the most violated, and the interconnectedness of the whole, is here inscribed at the very center of the Christian vision.

Christ crucified and risen, the Wisdom of God, manifests the truth that divine justice and renewing power leavens the world in a way different from the techniques of dominating violence. The victory of shalom is won not by the sword of the warrior god but by the awesome power of compassionate love, in and through solidarity with those who suffer. The unfathomable depths of evil and suffering are entered into in friendship with Sophia-God, in trust that this is the path to life. Guided by wisdom categories, the story of the cross, rejected as passive, penal victimization, is reappropriated as heartbreaking empowerment. The suffering accompanying such a life as Jesus led is neither passive, useless, nor divinely ordained, but is linked to the ways of Sophia forging justice and peace in an antagonistic world. As such, the cross is part of the larger mystery of pain-to-life, of that struggle for the new creation evocative of the rhythm of pregnancy, delivery, and birth so familiar to women of all times.[19]

Let it be noted that at the moment of final crisis Mary Magdalene, Mary the mother of James and Joseph, Salome, and "many other women" disciples (Mk 15:41) appear strongly in the story, and in fact are the moving point of continuity between the ministry, death, burial, and resurrection of Jesus. Near or afar they keep vigil at the cross, standing in a solidarity with this vilified victim that gives powerful witness to women's courage of relation throughout the ages. Their presence is a sacrament of God's own fidelity to the dying Jesus, their faithful friendship a witness to the hope that he is not totally abandoned. Not in hiding like others of their circle, they know the path to the tomb.

Grieving, but on the way to do what needs to be done, they are the first to encounter the risen Christ, to recognize him, to be charged with the mission to tell the good news to those in hiding. This they do: "Now it was Mary Magdalene, Joanna, Mary the mother of James, and the women with them who told this to the apostles" (Lk 24:10), persisting despite ridicule and unbelief.

It is fascinating to see how the church today asks to hear the words that the men disciples originally disparaged. The Sequence for the Mass of Easter Sunday, sung just before the great Alleluia and reading of the Gospel, urges, "Tell us, Mary, what you saw on the way?" To which she replies with ringing witness:

> I saw the tomb of the living Christ
> and the glory of his rising;
> angelic witnesses, the towel and the linen cloths.
> Christ my hope is risen;
> he goes before his own into Galilee.

Mary Magdalene now speaks throughout the whole world wherever Easter is celebrated in the Catholic liturgy.

Women form an intrinsic part of the circle in the upper room when the Spirit energizes the community in wind and fire at Pentecost. They move out as committed and creative coworkers for the gospel throughout the empire — apostles, prophets, preachers, missionaries, healers, leaders of house churches, carrying on through history the healing, liberating mission of Jesus-Sophia in the power of the Spirit. The story of Jesus-Sophia cannot be rightly told without at the same time weaving in the stories of the circle of "his own," women as well as men.

Feminist hermeneutics has blazed a trail showing how the gospel story of Jesus resists being used to justify patriarchal dominance in any form. His preaching about the reign of God and his inclusive life-style lived and breathed the opposite, creating a challenge that brought down on his head the wrath of religious and civil authority. They crucified him, but Sophia-God receives that death and transforms it to life. When the story of Jesus is told in this way, a certain appropriateness accrues to the historical fact that he was a male human being. If in a patriarchal culture a woman had preached compassionate love and enacted a style of authority that serves, she would most certainly have been greeted with a colossal shrug. Is this not what women are supposed to do by nature? But from a social position of male privilege Jesus preached and acted this way, and herein lies the summons.

Above all, the cross is raised as a challenge to the natural rightness of male dominating rule. The crucified Jesus embodies the exact opposite of the patriarchal ideal of the powerful man, and shows the steep price to be paid in the struggle for liberation. The cross thus stands as a poignant symbol of the "kenosis of patriarchy," the self-emptying of male dominating power in favor of the new humanity of compassionate service and mutual empowerment.[20] On this reading Jesus' maleness is prophecy announcing the end of patriarchy, at least as divinely ordained. Bernard Häring realizes this when he writes:

If someone would argue that humankind could be saved only by the incarnation of the Word in maleness, although I could not accept the argument, I would still find some meaning in it, since throughout history men have far outstripped women in domineering attitudes. Hence, it might be appropriate, according to our own limited human thinking, that Christ became a man to break the fetters of sexism by his absolute humility and liberty for others. Surely, anyone who wants to overemphasize Christ's maleness in order to establish prerogatives of males ("priests") over females has not understood Jesus as the liberator of all people, men and women, and has not understood the way he liberated us.[21]

In the light of the original gospel story of Sophia's envoy and prophet it becomes clear that the heart of the problem is not that Jesus was a man but that more men are not like Jesus, insofar as patriarchy defines their self-identity and relationships. Reading Scripture through feminist hermeneutics makes it possible to affirm that despite subsequent distortion something more than the subordination of women is possible, for Jesus-Sophia's story of ministry, suffering, final victory, and new community signify love, grace, and shalom for everyone equally, and for the outcast, including women most of all.

Speaking about Christ

The Whole Christ

After his death and resurrection, the focus of the ongoing story of Jesus-Sophia shifts from his concrete historical life with its contexts and relationships to the community of sisters and brothers imbued with the Spirit. From the beginning this community is marked by the confession that Jesus-Sophia is the Christ, the anointed, the blessed one. Intrinsic to this confession is the insight that the beloved community shares in this Christhood, participates in the living and dying and rising of Christ to such an extent that it too has a christomorphic character. Challenging a naive physicalism that would collapse the totality of the Christ into the human man Jesus, biblical metaphors such as the Pauline body of Christ (1 Cor 12:12–27) and the Johannine branches abiding in the vine (Jn 15:1–11) expand the reality of Christ to include potentially all of redeemed humanity, sisters and brothers, still on the way. Amid the suffering and conflicts of history, members of the community of disciples are *en christō* and their own lives assume a christic pattern. Biblical cosmic Christology expands the notion of Christ still further (Col 1:15–20), seeing that the universe itself is destined to be christomorphic in a reconciled new heaven and new earth.[22]

The fundamental nature of Christian identity as life in Christ makes clear that the biblical symbol Christ, the one anointed in the Spirit, cannot be restricted to the historical person Jesus nor to certain select members of the community but signifies all those who by drinking of the Spirit participate in the community of disciples. Christ is a pneumatological reality, a creation of the Spirit who is not limited by whether one is Jew or Greek, slave or free, male or female. To use the Pauline phrases, the body of the risen Christ becomes the body of the community; all are one in Christ Jesus (1 Cor 12; Gal 3:28). Sandra Schneiders explains it well:

the Christ is not exclusively the glorified Jesus, but the glorified Jesus animating his body which is the Church. Christ said to Paul "Why do you persecute *me*?" (Acts 9:4) because the literal fact is that the Christ is composed of all the baptized. This means that Christ, in contrast to Jesus, is not male, or more exactly not exclusively male. Christ is quite accurately portrayed as black, old, Gentile, female, Asian or Polish. Christ is inclusively all the baptized.[23]

This understanding of the inclusive meaning of Christ already undergirds a number of significant aspects of traditional ecclesial life. The church's mission is pervaded by the sense that in the neighbor or stranger whom we greet with a cup of cold water or stand with in resistance to oppressive power, solidarity with Christ is being forged. The focus is not on Jesus alone in a sort of Jesus-ology, but on looking with him in the same direction toward the inclusive well-being of the body of Christ, that is, all suffering and questing people: "just as you did it to one of the least of these who are members of my family, you did it to me" (Mt 25:40). Moreover, the liturgical place of encounter with Christ is not only word and sacrament taken in isolation but the assembled community itself, including the ministers and all women and men who pray and sing; for "Where two or three are gathered together for my sake, there am I in the midst of them" (Mt 18:20, a Gospel saying evocative of the Shekinah).[24] Again, while Jesus is named the Christ in a paradigmatic way, multiple redemptive role models are available within the community and may inspire and guide by their example, however strong, however fragile. The heritage of the saints, including Mary of Nazareth, embodies this insight in an ongoing way. In a word, the story of the prophet and friend of Sophia, anointed as the Christ, goes on in history as the story of the whole Christ, *christa* and *christus* alike, the wisdom community.

To speak rightly of Christ, feminist theology, in addition to honoring the inclusive intent of the Christ-symbol, genuinely respects the eschatological character of the risen Christ Jesus. The resurrection is an unimaginable event enveloped in the mystery of God. This negates a simple literalism that imagines Jesus still existing as in the days of his earthly life, only now invisible to our eyes. The truth is rather that Jesus has truly died, with all that this implies of change: he is gone from the midst of history according to the flesh. Faith in the resurrection affirms that God has the last word for this executed victim of state injustice and that word, blessedly, is life. Jesus in all his physical and spiritual historicity is raised into glory by the power of the Spirit. What this ringing affirmation precisely means is inconceivable. His life is now hidden in the glory of God, while his presence is known only through the Spirit wherever two or three gather, bread is broken, the hungry fed. But this indicates a transformation of his humanity so profound that it escapes our imagination. As the first Christian writer on this subject exclaimed,

But someone will ask, "How are the dead raised? With what kind of body do they come? You foolish one! What you sow does not come to life unless it dies. And what you sow is not the body which is to be, but a bare kernel. . . . So it is with the resurrection of the dead. What is sown is perishable, what is raised is imperishable. . . . It is sown a physical body, it is raised a spiritual body." (1 Cor 15:35–45)

The humility of the apophatic approach acknowledges that language about the humanity, and more precisely the maleness, of Jesus the Christ at this point proceeds under the negating sign of analogy, more dissimilar than similar to any maleness known in history.

With the inclusive and eschatological character of the Christ kept firmly in view, the maleness of Jesus can be reprised in the whole Christ and interpreted without distortion. Jesus' sex is simply an intrinsic part of his own identity as a finite human being in time and space, essential to his personal experience of the world along with other anthropological constants that made up his historical identity. In view of all the non-negotiable concreteness of his person, it is clear that Jesus' own historical humanity is not inclusive at all but a very particular crystallization of our common humanity, which can be actualized in a dizzying multiplicity of ways. Von Balthasar captures this limitation in a revealing observation about the condition of Jesus' humanity when he began his ministry at the age of thirty:

In this human fullness the essence of childhood and youth has not been lost; yet it is a fullness that still needs completion, because it is the fullness of a man and not a woman. It is a fullness also that pours itself out in the kenosis of the Son of God, overshadowed by approaching death for — as if it were incapable of further early growth — it is snatched away at the moment of highest potency. There is no experience of the process of growing old.[25]

Feminist theological language about Christ bears the insight that the inevitable limitations of Jesus' humanity *are* completed in the wholeness of the human race anointed with the Spirit, women and the elderly included. Maleness is not constitutive of the essence of Christ but, in the Spirit, redeemed and redeeming humanity is.

Vere Deus, Vere Homo

Just as biblical speech about Christ has elements that can subvert the androcentric construction of Christology, so too does the classical language of doctrine. Hammered out through centuries of controversy, this language affirms that in Jesus Christ human nature and divine nature concur in one hypostasis: Jesus Christ is *vere Deus, vere homo* in *una persona*. Do these words intend an essential connection between maleness and the mystery of God made flesh? The history of the struggle that generated these phrases shows that such is not the case.

Apart from the major Arian position that sought to protect the transcendence of God by relegating the Logos to the status of a superior creature, thereby denying genuine divinity to Logos/Sophia incarnate, most of the other conflicts circle around the authentic character of Jesus' humanity. From Arianism itself, to Docetism with its denial of real human flesh, to the Apollinarian solution of excising a rational soul, to the monophysite tendency to blur the distinction of natures, to the monothylite surgery on the human will, virtually every disputed position sought to shortchange the genuine quality of Jesus' humanity.[26] What was at issue was not his sex, race, class, nor any other concrete particularity but the completeness of his humanity precisely as human. And the stakes were very high, for what is not assumed is not redeemed.

Ultimately, Christian faith opted to affirm the genuine and complete humanity of Sophia incarnate, and to do so in the strongest possible language. The earlier Nicene confession that "God from God" became a human being (*et homo factus est*) was further specified by the Council of Chalcedon to mean a genuine human being (*vere homo*). This latter council also pressed into service the controversial word *homoousios*, "one in being," previously used in the Nicene creed to forge Jesus' identity of nature with God, to forge another identification, namely, Jesus is also "one in being with us as to his humanity." Given the anthropology then current, this signified a body of real flesh that could feel passions, suffer and die, and a soul with its own spiritual and psychological powers. According to this doctrinal language, whatever else it may mean, incarnation does not involve the mystery of God in merely dressing up like a human being and living a pretended life, a physical and psychological charade. Rather, one in being with us as to his humanity, Jesus is born to a life of creaturely finitude marked by the pleasures and pains of the body, nescience and growth in wisdom, and freedom with the need to risk.[27] These texts in their historical context make clear that it is not Jesus' maleness that is doctrinally important but his humanity in solidarity with the whole suffering human race. The intent of the christological doctrine was and continues to be inclusive.

Christ the Wisdom of God (1 Cor 1:24).

Using the female figure of personified Wisdom so influential in biblical Christology to speak about Jesus the Christ offers an augmented field of metaphors with which to interpret his saving significance and rootedness in God in ways that relieve the monopoly of male images of Logos and Son. In wisdom categories we can say that Sophia's intimate solidarity with the unoriginate God and her equally compassionate, life-giving solidarity with human beings whom she makes into friends of God are embodied in Jesus-Sophia, whose person is constituted by these two fundamental relations. Such a way of speaking breaks through the assumption that there is a "necessary ontological connection" between the male human being Jesus and a male God. This leads to the realization that as Sophia incarnate Jesus, even in his human maleness, can be thought to be revelatory of the graciousness of God imaged as female. Likewise, divine Sophia incarnate in Jesus addresses all persons in her call to be friends of God, and can be truly represented by any human being called in her Spirit, women as well as men. Not incidentally, the typical stereotypes of masculine and feminine are subverted as female Sophia represents creative transcendence, primordial passion for justice, and knowledge of the truth while Jesus incarnates these divine characteristics in an immanent way relative to bodiliness and the earth. The creative, redeeming paradox of Jesus-Sophia points the way to a reconciliation of opposites and their transformation from enemies into a liberating, unified diversity. In the end gender is not constitutive of the Christian doctrine of incarnation.

In addition to helping untie the knot of sexist Christology, wisdom categories bring other benefits to the fore:

1. A relation to the whole cosmos is already built into the biblical wisdom tradition, and this orients Christology beyond the human

world to the ecology of the earth, and indeed, to the universe, a vital move in this era of planetary crisis. As the embodiment of Sophia who is fashioner of all that exists, Jesus the Christ's redeeming care intends the flourishing of all creatures and the whole earth itself. The power of Christ's Spirit is seen wherever human beings share in this love for the earth, tending its fruitfulness, attending to its limits, and guarding it from destruction.

2. Wisdom discourse likewise directs belief toward a global, ecumenical perspective respectful of other religious paths. The imagery of wisdom operates today much the way the *logos* metaphor functioned in the early Christian centuries to signify the play of God's goodness and just order throughout the world, a function now somewhat curtailed for the *logos* due to its long association with androcentric theology and imperialistic ecclesial history. Sophia, however, is people loving; her light shines everywhere, and those whom she makes to be friends of God and prophets are found throughout the wide world. Jesus-Sophia personally incarnates her gracious care in one particular history, for the benefit of all, while she lays down a multiplicity of paths in diverse cultures by which all people may seek, and seeking find her.

3. By becoming one with humanity in incarnation and suffering, Sophia, whose paths are justice and peace, shows that the passion of God is clearly directed toward the lifting of oppression and the establishing of right relations. The table is set for those who will come, the bread and wine ready to nourish the struggle. What is needed is to listen to the loud cries of Jesus-Sophia resounding in the cries of the poor, violated, and desperate, and to ally our lives as the wisdom community to the divine creative, redeeming work in the world.

In sum, the doctrine of the incarnation confesses that in Jesus the Christ God has truly entered human history, for the sake of our salvation. Neither the divinity nor the humanity referred to in that confession requires maleness as an exclusive, constitutive condition. On the one hand God is not male. The metaphors of Word and Son most often used to articulate the relation between Jesus the Christ and God's absolute mystery signify not maleness in God but a certain divine relationality that can be superbly reprised in the symbol of Sophia. On the other hand, human history signifies the whole human race in a solidarity of sin and suffering, as the classical doctrine has always affirmed. The historical particularities of Jesus' person, including his sex, racial characteristics, linguistic heritage, social class, and so on do not signify that God is more appropriately incarnate into these realities than into others. As Rosemary Radford Ruether has tellingly observed, this point has always been clear with regard to Jesus' ethnic and social identity, but has been obscured with regard to sexual identity, leading to the prevalent view that the male represents Christ better than the female. But:

> It is impossible, theologically, to vindicate this view without rejecting the universality of the incarnation and making it an exclusive doctrine that redeems only those like Jesus in these particularities, rather than those unlike him. The historical particularities of Jesus' person only make clear that all persons exist in historical particularities. But the significance of the incarnation lies in the ability of this person to stand for us all, to be paradigmatic of human nature and the human condition generically.[28]

Given the affirmation that the incarnation is inclusive of the humanity of all human beings of all races and historical conditions and both genders, it becomes clear that Jesus the Christ's ability to be savior does not reside in his maleness but in his loving, liberating history in the midst of the powers of evil and oppression. In face of this, the trivialization introduced into the doctrine of the incarnation by androcentric stress on the maleness of Jesus's humanity fully warrants the charge of heresy and even blasphemy currently being leveled against it.[29]

Theology will have come of age when the particularity that is highlighted is not Jesus' historical sex but the scandal of his option for the poor and marginalized in the Spirit of his compassionate, liberating Sophia-God. That is the scandal of particularity that really matters, aimed as it is toward the creation of a new order of wholeness in justice. Toward that end, feminist theological speech about Jesus the Wisdom of God shifts the focus of reflection off maleness and onto the whole theological significance of what transpires in the Christ event. Jesus in his human, historical specificity is confessed as Sophia incarnate, revelatory of the liberating graciousness of God imaged as female; women, as friends of Jesus-Sophia, share equally with men in his saving mission throughout time and can fully represent Christ, being themselves, in the Spirit, other Christs. These are steps on the way to a community of equals interrelated in genuine mutuality, in theory as well as practice.

Speaking about God

Where have we come in tracing the question of the right way to speak about God through the thorny thicket of Christology? Jesus the Christ is the Wisdom of God in a concrete, historical gestalt. That being the case, language about the mystery of God receives a new precision when it is focused and filtered through Jesus-Sophia's history and destiny. The story of the liberating mission of this prophet and child of Sophia, the

narrative of his own desperate outcastness unto death ultimately involving the victory of life, and the consequent doctrine of his profound
relatedness to all human beings and to God's own being, which we
speak about as incarnation, limn with startling clarity insights important
for a theology of God: the transcendent God's capacity for embodiment,
divine passion for liberation, and the constitutive nature of relation.

The inner dynamic of the doctrine of incarnation sounds a ringing
affirmation of the cherished feminist value of bodiliness, even for God.
In the light of Jesus-Sophia we can see that the living God is *capax
hominis*, capable of personal union with what is not God, the flesh
and spirit of humanity. Here divine immanence or universal presence
through the indwelling Spirit takes on an intensely clear gestalt in divine embodiment, enabling God to dwell in a small segment of historical
time. Bodiliness opens up the mystery of God to the conditions of history, including suffering and delight. She becomes flesh, choosing the
very stuff of the cosmos as her own personal reality forever. She thereby
becomes irrevocably, physically connected to the human adventure, for
better or worse. Far from functioning as the index of creaturely separation from the divine, human bodiliness is manifest as irreplaceable
sacrament of mutual communion between heaven and earth, not only
in Jesus' case but ontologically for all.

In light of Jesus-Sophia we can say something more. Divine mystery proceeds not only universally in love but particularly in love.
God's friendship, everywhere present in the vivifying, renewing, gracing power of the Spirit in conflict with the powers of destruction, is
capable of a particular gestalt as the partisan friendship of Jesus-Sophia
for the poor and marginalized, including women, a friendship aimed at
empowering their growth in dignity as well as the conversion of those in
dominating positions. His solidarity with suffering people in the name
of God even to death diagrams the heart of Sophia-God, the essence
of her way with the world. As enfleshed image of divine goodness, his
history and destiny of suffering to life give divine compassion a precise
historical expression that can never be erased. Henceforth it is impossible, or if not impossible at least incorrect and even blasphemous, to
speak about God's stance as other than a passion for human and cosmic
flourishing.

Sophia herself, while radically distinct from the world, "remaining
in herself" (Wis 7:26), is always profoundly related to the world — "she
renews all things" (7:26). Her essence, in fact, might well be called connectedness, for in play with the world she is a breath, an emanation, a
radiance of unquenchable light (Wis 7:27). The power of relation built
into wisdom metaphors comes to unique fruition in the doctrine of

Jesus-Sophia, Sophia incarnate. Sophia is present in and with her envoy Jesus, pervading and embracing, containing and sustaining, indeed personally grounding him. His own relationality with others aimed at building up a community of shalom embodies her inclusive outreach in historical time where wholeness of relationship is shattered. Herein is glimpsed the nature of divine relatedness to the world as a whole: not a distant, dominating transcendence but otherness that freely draws near, bringing new life, sustaining all loves.

Anamnesis of Jesus, the Wisdom of God, connects God once for all to concrete embodiment, to the world, to suffering and delight, to compassion and liberation, in a way that can never be broken. Longstanding dichotomies are herein brought into mutual coinherence: creator and creature, transcendence and immanence, spirit and body, all splits which have fed into patriarchal obsession with power-over.

•

We have explored two ways in which historical experience leads to distinct speech about God. The hidden God is known in myriad ways as the power of life, truth, and hope against hope: Spirit-Sophia who pervades the world to vivify and renew. The incomprehensible God is also known in the encounter with Jesus the Christ, carried on through narrative remembrance and continued unleashing of the power of the Spirit within his circle of disciples: Sophia-God who joins the world in the flesh to heal, redeem, and liberate. There is still more to say. For in tracing human openness to the world and beyond the world we are pointed toward a relationship of origin and a hope for future homecoming that goes beyond anything we can concretely grasp. God is God yet another way, as absolute mystery, unoriginate origin and goal of the whole universe.

Chapter 9

MOTHER-SOPHIA

I saw that night, for the first time, a Mother in the Deity. This indeed was a new scene, a new doctrine to me. But I knowed when I got it, and I was obedient to the heavenly vision. . . . And was I not glad when I found that I had a Mother! And that night She gave me a tongue to tell it! The spirit of weeping was upon me, and it fell on all the assembly. And though they never heard it before, I was made able by Her Holy Spirit of Wisdom to make it so plain that a child could understand it.

— Rebecca Jackson[1]

Unoriginate Origin

The mystery of Sophia-God, moving as Spirit in the dialectical praxis of freedom and walking through time in the history and destiny of Jesus the Christ, is, even in being manifest, always and forever absolute mystery. This is not a provisional circumstance, able to be cleared up at some future moment such as at our personal death or the end of the world. Rather, it belongs to the very essence of God as God so to *be* that human minds can never exhaust that livingness: if you have understood, then what you have understood is not God.[2] The story of Jesus reprised in history through the power of the Spirit manifests the character of God's absolute mystery as one of graciousness and compassion, bent especially upon the hurt, captive, and lost. This but intensifies the mystery, turning it into the absolute mystery of love. Without origin, without source, without beginning, what people call God generates everything and seeks its flourishing. From this unoriginate radiance stream forth all the little lights and the power to resist the night.

Virtually every religious tradition ancient and modern acknowledges this situation in some way, that is, gives voice to the realization that human beings and their world are related to a divine origin. This relation is expressed in different narratives of the beginning wherein male or female deities, or both together, hatch, spin, speak, murder, artistically shape, give birth, or otherwise act to bring the world into being. Variously conceptualized as emanation, creation out of previously exist-

170

ing matter, or creation out of nothing, divine action "in the beginning" bespeaks human persons' experience that ultimately we cannot credit our existence or the being there of this world to our own devices. Just to be is a gift.

How are we to speak about God in face of the contingency and gift-character of existence? The most fundamental human relationship ready to hand as an analogue is that of parent and child. All human beings owe their existence to a woman and man who existed before them and whose cells united to conceive them. Given the generative power of human sexuality to produce new persons in the concrete, and the resulting life-long relationships between all persons and their parents, known or unknown, speaking about God who is origin of all on the analogue of mother and father, either or both, is genuinely appropriate, although such language can never be taken literally.

Since it is women whose bodies bear, nourish, and deliver new persons into life and, as society is traditionally structured, are most often charged with the responsibility to nurture and raise them into maturity, language about God as mother carries a unique power to express human relationship to the mystery who generates and cares for everything. As Adrienne Rich's groundbreaking study of motherhood points out:

All human life on the planet is born of woman. The one unifying, incontrovertible experience shared by all women and men is that months-long period we spent unfolding inside a woman's body. Because young humans remain dependent upon nurture for a much longer period than other mammals, and because of the division of labor long established in human groups, where women not only bear and suckle but are assigned almost total responsibility for children, most of us first know both love and disappointment, power and tenderness, in the person of a woman.[3]

The Jewish and Christian Scriptures recognize the importance of the mother-child relationship when they use the metaphors of pregnancy and birth, suckling and feeding, carrying and training, the anger of the mother bear and the protective wing of the mother hen to refer to God's creative relationship with the world.

So too did John Paul I when he startled the church with his singular reference to divine maternity. The setting was his Sunday address delivered to people gathered in St. Peter's Square at the historic moment in 1978 when the Camp David meeting between the leaders of Egypt, Israel, and the United States was underway. Hope for peace in a tortured region was in the air and, as each of these leaders had strong religious beliefs, they had made public references to God's care as a motive for negotiation. The pope took note of this and quoted them. President Sadat had referred to the Islamic saying "There is pitch darkness, a black stone, and on the stone a little ant; but God sees it and does not forget it." As a Christian President Carter had read, "even the hairs of your head are all numbered." Premier Begin had recalled the Jewish biblical text that even if a mother should forget her own child, God will never forget the covenant people. Inspired by these references to inclusive divine care, John Paul I went on:

Also we who are here have the same sentiments; we are the objects of undying love on the part of God. We know he always has his eyes open on us, even when it seems to be dark. God is our father; even more God is our mother. God does not want to hurt us, but only to do good for us, all of us. If children are ill, they have additional claim to be loved by their mother. And we too, if by chance we are sick with badness and are on the wrong track, have yet another claim to be loved by the Lord.[4]

While at that point in time the pope's use of both genders may have been unusual, this is a legitimate way to speak. God whose mystery cannot be expressed by any name nevertheless creates both male and female in the divine image, and can be spoken about in metaphors derived from either. Each brings its own sense of God. Here the intensifier "even more" connects speech about God with a typical experience of a woman with her sick child to signify a certain kind of divine concern for the well-being of sinners and those who are lost, in which group John Paul I includes the war-sick world. With a mother's love God keeps vigil through the long night of our sickness and tries everything to break the fever, in both personal and political realms. Altogether an excellent address.

Eclipsing the Mother

What then has gone wrong? For despite the value of maternal metaphors in human language and the legitimacy of their occasional appearance in biblical texts and theological tradition, it is highly characteristic of Christian speech that the origin and care-giver of all things is named almost exclusively in terms of the paternal relationship. The ancient words in Moses' mouth are still borne out in Christian discourse: "You forgot the God who gave you birth" (Dt 32:18). Omitting maternal imagery in official and unofficial speech about God is a hallmark of our heritage. "We believe in one God, the Father, the Almighty, maker of heaven and earth, of all that is seen and unseen": the opening words of the Nicene Creed repeated week after week, century after century bear witness to the grip that the image of the one, all powerful father who makes the world has on the Christian imagination.

Even when used almost exclusively, the paternal symbol never signifies theologically that God is a father in a literal or ontological sense, as if fatherhood constituted the divine essence. This name, like all human names for divine mystery, proceeds by way of analogy, which means that while it starts from the relationship of paternity experienced at its best in this world, its inner dynamism negates the creaturely mode to assert that God is more unlike than like even the best of human fathers, transcending fatherhood in a way that escapes our grasp. In a positive sense the name father derives from a certain kind of relationality that we experience vis-à-vis God, and connotes a divine way of acting. As Catherine LaCugna explains, "to say that God's behavior toward us can be characterized as fatherly (or motherly) is a statement about how God exercises divinity *with us*. It is a functional assertion, not an ontological claim."[5] Men's experience of originating another person into being, the human experience of having our life as a bequest from a man, and the basic relationship thereby set up between father and offspring point to an analogous relationship with the divine origin of all creatures. "For the name Father signifies relation," as Aquinas observes, the relation of generativity on the one hand and of being brought into being on the other.[6] To call God Father is to say that coming from no one prior, God relates to the world *as* a good father in human society relates to his offspring. But there is no point for point correspondence between human paternity and God the Father in either the immanent or economic trinity. All this, however, has not been remembered. God the Father has become an overliteralized metaphor, so monopolizing Christian speech about God that the equally legitimate and in some ways even more appropriate symbol of God as mother is eclipsed.

It is not simply the case that the predominance of the paternal metaphor happened somehow unself-consciously, as if by default. The maternal relationship as a pointer to the divine has been actively derogated and consciously erased from the repertoire of suitable images. This erasure accompanied the emergence of patriarchy as the dominant ideology within the Christian community. Religious imagery and social practice mutually influence each other, and the move to an all-male hierarchical priesthood necessitated exclusively male, ruling images for God. Elaine Pagels's careful work with the gnostic gospels shows how maternal imagery did not go down without a struggle, but nevertheless lost out as a corollary of the suppression of ministry by women in the second century.[7]

After a thousand years of the virtual nonexperience of women in public ecclesial roles, the inadequacy of maternal images for God was sealed for the official language of future generations by Aquinas's systematic incorporation of ancient Greek biology into his theological anthropology. According to Aristotle, in the act of conceiving life the male is the active partner who provides the vital form and originating movement, while the female is the passive partner providing the inert matter that receives the form. The resulting child is a creation of male energy working on inactive female matter. The two are radical opposites, the man being a vigorous actor and the woman comparable to a lifeless object:

Regarding the male as active and causing movement, and the female as passive and being set in movement, we see that the thing which is formed can be said to be formed "from them both" only in the sense in which a bed is formed from the carpenter and the wood.[8]

Taking this analysis at face value, Aquinas's anthropology characterizes female nature as the inert wood, passive in the quintessential women's act of pregnancy and birthing. From this passivity he draws several conclusions. Because it has no part in the active principle, which is superior to mere potency, female nature is fundamentally inferior to male nature and the maternal principle is inferior to the paternal one. In this assessment a mother, embodying an inferior and passive principle, obviously cannot provide suitable metaphor for the mystery of God who is the active source of all creation. In fact, to use such imagery would be to demean the dignity of God, who is pure act untainted by the shadow of passivity or unrealized potency.

It is obvious today that Aquinas's definitive exclusion of the maternal in speech about God is based on faulty biology raised to a metaphysical level. It is a biology that is nowhere any longer credible. But though the physical underpinnings have long since disappeared, the resulting philosophical evaluation of women especially in their maternal function has not similarly evaporated. It is the implicit premise undergirding virtually all statements of men theologians and the official magisterium that assign women certain preordained "roles" according to the order of nature. Even when women's receptivity is benevolently characterized as "active," the idea that women in their own right may take initiative and be the acting person who galvanizes the response of others escapes the comprehension of such thinkers trapped in a dualistic anthropology. When this long-standing, now officially disavowed but nevertheless still influential anthropology of women's passivity joins forces with Jung's psychological assessment of the feminine anima, which is void, waiting, and darkness, the results can be deadly. Bringing this subterranean characterization of mothering into the light enables us at least to make a clear-eyed judgment about its inadequacy, and to begin to remove one more tenacious obstacle blocking speech about God in the likeness of women.

In the contemporary world the human analogue for the dominant father symbol is threatened insofar as the rule of privileged fathers in civil and religious society is widely challenged. Feminist theology in particular, as we saw in chapter 2, delivers a sharp analysis of how the paternal metaphor has coupled with the values of dominance and authoritative rule in a patriarchal setting to yield speech about God that subordinates women and blocks their access to divine mystery both sociologically and psychologically. But in addition to women resisting male domination, all other forms of master-servant relations are also being rejected today as seen in youth against authoritarian fathers, nations against dictatorial rulers, colonialized nations against imperialists, and laity against representatives of ecclesiastical paternalism. This widespread phenomenon is bringing the Almighty Father God into difficulty on many fronts.[9]

Even if this were not the case, it would obviously be advantageous to reclaim the power and vulnerability of mothering as metaphor for God. The experience of originating others and of nurturing them into maturity is not solely a male one but is intensely female on a fundamental biological and psychological level. Women conceive, bear in their own bodies, and give birth to new persons; human beings receive life and nurture from their mothers in a diversity of ways; and the consequent complex relationship is profoundly formative of persons and society. Human relationship to the creative origin of the world traditionally expressed in relation to God as father is thus excellently carried in the symbol of God as mother. Speaking about God critically in these terms yields an understanding of divine reality shaped by the wonder, greatness, and hard work of a particular female experience, suggesting that where good mothering is found there we have hints to divine relationality with the world. In the patriarchal social context the maternal metaphor brings to bear a different vision. Language traced on this female pattern intimates that birth-giving, nurturance, play and delight in the other, unmerited love, fierce protectiveness, compassion, forgiveness, courage, service, and care for the weak and vulnerable characterize what surrounds us as absolute mystery. Women's living and life-giving experience as mothers is fitting metaphor for speech about the gracious Sophia-God of Jesus and her world-renewing Spirit.

The Human Analogue

Even if the monopoly of the almighty father image is dislodged, and even if female nature along with maternal experience receives a new positive valuation, another difficulty besets the use of mother as analogy for God. This is the social construction of motherhood in institutions shaped by patriarchy. Feminist analysis has brilliantly laid bare how male theorists have equated reproductive and child-rearing activities with the very essence of women's nature, asserting that women find their true fulfillment only in that role, and casting its meaning in terms that enhance the work of men. Adrienne Rich, for example, has developed the remarkably helpful distinction between women's experience of motherhood, that is, "the potential relation of any woman to her powers of reproduction and to children," and the institution of motherhood, "which aims at ensuring that potential — and all women — shall remain under male control," through cultural, ideological, political, economic, social, medical, and religious structures.[10] The effect of the institution of motherhood and its equation that woman equals mother, exclusively and without remainder, is sociological and political. It allows women no say in the exercise of their reproductive capacities if they are to live up to traditional society's expectations, and then, when they do have children, relegates women out of the public domain into the private realm of domesticity where they sacrifice themselves to serve the next generation and, not incidentally if a husband is in the picture, attend to men's needs as well.

Benevolent paternalism in the church and society waxes eloquent about the values of this ideal of motherhood. But such romanticizing, while defining the role positively, actually limits and effectively subordinates women. Idealizing mothers functions as the reverse side of exploitation, being an attempt to give back to women as mothers what has been taken from them as human subjects: dignity, autonomy, choice of their own path in life, and the chance to participate in the public upbuilding of society. One Latin American woman astutely sums up the dynamic: "Praising mothers can serve as the best disguise for a male ideology."[11] Such praise is also illogical, as Adrienne Rich points out: "there has been a basic contradiction throughout patriarchy between the laws and sanctions designed to keep women essentially powerless, and the attribution to mothers of almost superhuman power (of control, of influence, of life-support)."[12]

The romantic idealization of motherhood has lost its power to convince, given women's articulated experience of their own human dignity. There is more to being a woman than being a mother, even for women who are rearing children, even while that experience is crucially and irreplaceably important. Even on a practical level, equating women's nature with motherhood is not accurate. Given today's extended life-span, a statistical First World woman can expect to live more than half her adult life after her childbearing and nurturing years are over. Language must attend to the critical difference between the concrete experience of women as mothers and the way this is codified in patriarchal institutions if speech about God as mother is to reclaim mothering as a liberating power, rather than sail off into romantic ideology.

There is yet more to the situation. Physicality is constitutive of human persons. As spirit-in-the-world, women are embodied differently from men; the physical difference is not extrinsic to self-identity or relationship with others. The range of experiences associated with a personal embodiment capable of physically bearing, delivering, and nourishing new life shapes women's subjectivity in unique ways. Moreover, actually giving life and rearing children are formative experiences which affect not only individual women but the whole fabric of society. This is a realm belonging to more than half the human race that has seldom been articulated by those whose experience it actually is, until now. Feminist theory is thus working two sides of the barricade at once. It critiques patriarchal ideology that idealizes motherhood as a universal norm but that simultaneously relegates the role of mother to the private order. At the same time it seeks to honor the distinctiveness of women's embodiment and creativity, including the powerful experience of being mothers. It seeks to see with new eyes the worth of what has been trivialized and devalued in patriarchal judgment on female experience, and to avoid the trap of holding male experience to be the norm.

Several factors qualify linguistic use of the mother symbol for God. Given the patriarchal construction of motherhood, there is a danger that the mother image in speech about God, especially if it is the only female symbol used, may subtly undermine women's search for identity in their own whole person apart from the relationship and role of mothering. In real life the human analogue includes the experience of women who bear children against their will, and who are unable to provide basic necessities or to protect their children from danger and abuse. As with father or any other metaphor drawn from human relationship, ambiguity also exists insofar as the inherent goodness of the maternal relationship can be distorted. Mothers are not always unalloyedly good; there are inadequate and abusive mothers as well as strong and loving ones, making discernment essential from beginning to end. Moreover, children grow up and need to seek their independence from parents in order to be capable of adult relationships in their own right. Speaking about God as mother, as is obvious from the tradition of God as father, could be used to perpetuate psychological immaturity, maintaining childish dependence on a comforting authority figure rather than encouraging adult responsibility for the world.

All of this complexity informs the symbol of God as mother. The intricacy of the bond between mother and child and its social construction makes it crucial to remember that speech about God proceeds by way of analogy, God being more unlike than like what we know in the best of mothers. This being the case, there is nevertheless powerful and largely untapped truth available in the range of women's experience of having and being mothers that can reshape speech about the mystery of God.

As a resonant metaphor the human analogue of mother connotes at least the following elements. To this point in time every human being on this earth is of woman born, spending months in the womb of a woman before taking a first breath and uttering a first cry: there is a creative source of our life who precedes and generates us. In addition to being knitted into life within a woman, human beings are born not fully developed but need to be nurtured and socialized into the human community for many years by a mother or others who assume this mothering role, including with more frequency today, fathers, day care givers, and members of the extended family: there is an ongoing power that cares for our life. Taking the best of this experience from the child's perspective, mothering is associated with primordial experiences of comfort, play, discovery, nurture, love and compassion, security in being held and sheltered, and basic trust in being taught, disciplined, and led forth. From the woman's perspective, mothering involves the creative activity of beginning life, giving birth, and providing for the child's growth, food first of all and then emotional and intellectual nourishment. This is an active experience of involvement in the flourishing of another, potentially "one of the most ecstatic and humanly rewarding experiences there is."[13] There is power in the delivery of new life, warmth and strength in freely given love that bears responsibility to rear what one has created, and vulnerability in the ways a woman can be hurt by what damages her child. For both mother and child in different ways the relationship connotes interdependence and mutuality of life at the deepest level, a quality of intimacy and familiarity that is genuinely person creating. For neither does it exhaust the possibilities of their capacity for relationship. It is with these associations in mind that the relationship of mothering, when critically relieved of restrictive anthropological and sociological strictures, offers an excellent metaphor for language about God the Creator of heaven and earth, of all that is seen and unseen.

Mother-Sophia in Action

Mothering the Universe

When, energized by the Spirit and focused by the story of Jesus-Sophia, human speech tries to articulate the absolute point of origin that is no point, the primordial, free, hidden depths of absolute divine mystery, it speaks always about an unoriginate source of all there is. Naming toward this absolute mystery with the analogue of mother dares to celebrate in a female gestalt divine being, that is primordial upwelling of the power of being and divine acts of giving life, sustaining it, and encouraging it to grow. Wiser than Solomon, those who speak this way do not have to admit with regret in the face of the marvels of creation, "but I did not know that she was their mother" (Wis 7:12).

Holy Wisdom is the mother of the universe, the unoriginate, living source of all that exists. This unimaginable livingness generates the life of all creatures, being herself, in the beginning and continuously, the power of being within all being. "From whose womb did the ice come forth, and who has given birth to the hoarfrost of heaven?" (Jb 38:29). The answer is God the Mother. She freely gives life to all creatures without calculating a return, loving them inclusively, joyfully saying the basic words of affirmation, "It is good that you exist."[14] Her creative, maternal love is the generating matrix of the universe, matter, spirit, and embodied spirit alike. This is true not only in the case of human persons but of all living and inanimate creatures and the complex interrelationships between them that constitute "the world." All creatures are kin to one another and therefore, where spirit has reached the breakthrough of human intelligence, creatively responsible for one another. All creatures are siblings from the same womb, the brood of the one Mother of the universe who dwells in bright darkness. In her, as once literally in our own mother, we live and move and have our being, being indeed her offspring (Acts 17:28).

Delivering every creature into the integrity of its own existence, Mother-Sophia ceaselessly cares for the well-being of the world that exists only as a result of her free initiative. This too can be spoken about fittingly in maternal metaphors. God the Mother rejoices in the world's flourishing, has compassion on its weakness, and pours forth her powerful love to resist what damages or destroys.

Reprising biblical metaphors gives concreteness to this broad sweep of God's maternal, compassionate power. She cries out in terrible labor to deliver the new creation of justice (Is 42:14). She suckles the newly born, teaches toddlers to walk, bends down to feed them, and carries them about, bearing them from birth even to old age with its gray hairs (Is 46:3–4). As a mother comforts her child, so too she comforts those who lament (Is 66:13). But unlike some human mothers, God the Mother will never forget the children of her womb (Hos 11:3–4; Is 49:15).

At the same time that she carries and comforts, the Mother-Creator seeks to overcome whatever destroys beloved creation. The prophetic image of God as furious as a mother bear deprived of her cubs is one scriptural witness to this phenomenon: "I will fall upon them like a bear robbed of her cubs; I will tear open their breast" (Hos 13:8). This is no sweet mother, but one moved to awful deeds to protect what is hers. She pledges to attack the destroyers and tear their hearts out.

The religious experience of divine mercy is made luminous in maternal metaphors. By the power of her mighty Spirit she gives birth anew to those who receive her word, and these are in an unfathomable way her children, born not of blood nor of the will of the flesh nor of human will, but born of God (Jn 1:13). Her great compassion or womb-love wipes out offenses, restoring a clean heart to those who seek forgiveness. The result of her ministrations is a new spirit in the one who turns to her, issuing in "the joy of salvation," restoration of the well-being that comes with right relation to the one who gave you birth (Ps 51).

The compassion of God the Mother insures that she loves the weak and dispossessed as well as the strong and beautiful. We do not have to be wonderful according to external norms to elicit her love, for this is freely given by virtue of the maternal relationship itself. God looks upon all with a mother's love that makes the beloved beautiful. Human persons cannot earn or merit this love, but it is freely and abundantly given. In this regard, it appears that in the midst of a juridical experience of salvation controlled by a patriarchal church, Martin Luther was on to a rediscovery of the maternal love of God, although he did not realize it or speak about it this way.[15] Thanks to Christ we are justified by the grace of God freely given: this has nothing to do with deservingness and everything to do with divine love meeting human need, for which a mother's love is an excellent paradigm. The absolute mystery of the unoriginate origin of the universe has the character of a mother's compassion.

These shifting metaphors depict divine acts of creation and compassion as women's work, both biologically and in roles traditionally assigned in society. The inner dynamic of this maternal symbol steers clear of the idea associated with classical theism that God creates the world while remaining unrelated to it. Freely and abundantly giving life, she continues to be intensely involved with creation, caring, fostering, training.

The maternal source and compassionate matrix of the universe is also its goal, the point of homecoming at the end of the journey. Christian eschatological hope can be expressed in images of birth and new life redolent of the experience of mothering. When human energy collapses, Mother-Sophia has the last word as she had the first, and it is the word of life. With the same maternal creativity and largess by which in the beginning she brings into being the things that do not exist, she gives life to the dead with an outpouring of power that radically empowers (Rom 4:17). The beloved offspring return whence they come, mothered into life.

Establishing the Mercy of Justice

In speaking about God as mother-creator Sallie McFague makes a particularly interesting connection between motherly care and justice, bringing to light the toughness inherent in the maternal experience. At first glance the juxtaposition of maternal care and the judgment of justice may seem jarring, especially in the face of a romanticized view of mothering. But mothers have a stake in the well-being of their children and do stand in judgment on whatever hurts them. As this theologian explains:

The metaphor of God as mother which we have been considering is built not upon stereotypes of maternal tenderness, softness, pity, and sentimentality, but upon the female experience of gestation, birth and lactation. This experience in most animals, including human beings, engenders not attributes of weakness and passivity but qualities contributing to the active defense of the young so that they may not only exist but be nourished and grow. Whatever thwarts such fulfillment is fought, often fiercely, as mother bears and tigers amply illustrate. ... Those who produce life have a stake in it and will judge, often with anger, what prevents its fulfillment.[16]

Creating and sustaining the universe, God as mother is concerned not only with the good of privileged individuals but with the well-being of the entire household of the world. Aquinas glimpsed this when he set up the analogy: as human justice is to the community or the household, so the justice of God is to the whole universe.[17] Because God desires the growth and fulfillment of the whole interconnected world, the *oikoumenē*, her attention is turned in a special way toward the ones most in need. Their deprivation and suffering is not only their personal concern — and indeed it is that — but shows that something is wrong with the way things are ordered in the larger world. God's maternal will for the good of the whole world motivates a preferential option for the last, lowest and least, espied in human acts that attempt to redress imbalance and bring about right order. God as mother is therefore allied with concern for justice and calls forth an ethic of care for justice in those who are "born of God."

The actions of contemporary mothers in situations of oppression bear eloquent witness to this powerful aspect of the maternal relationship. One Central American woman writes of her Christian base community's growth in consciousness under a violent dictatorship:

I recall that it was women who most insisted on discovering God as a God of Life.... Being bearers and sustainers of life women found new meaning in God as God of life, and themselves became stronger as defenders and bearers of life, not only in the biological sense but in all its dimensions.... In this journey women discover feminine elements in God: care and concern for children, even those who are not their own, defense of life, love, affection, and empathy for suffering. Such characteristics — more feminine, if you will — of a God found to be close to us and more tender-hearted, led to a rediscovery of God as mother, not just as father, not just as protector, but as one who is immensely concerned for the poor and for the least, for those who have been left unattended.... [Hence] women walk beside their people in creating new life, in giving a meaning to life, taking part in and actively defending a project in history, one that is liberating and is generating new rights to justice. [18]

This is an extraordinary report of the intertwining of maternal self-consciousness, compassion for the weak, concern for justice, and speech about God as mother spun out of growth in responsibility amid daily occurrences of violent death. The power of mothering in situations of danger and need points language toward God's passion for justice precisely as she is Mother-Creator of all.

The dynamic of maternal love is visible in the mothers and grandmothers of Argentina's Plaza de Mayo who courageously demonstrated in public against a repressive government on behalf of their disappeared children.[19] It appears in alliances of South African mothers who love their children and therefore speak out at great personal risk to abolish apartheid:

Let's say: we are the mothers. We are mothers — see what is taking place in this country. A mother will hold the knife on the sharp end. Today we see our people being sent to jail every day — there's detentions, the courts are crowded everyday, people in exile, people rotting in jails. Now we, as mothers, what must we say? We say to you — we are sick and tired of what is happening. We see our children being sent to jail for nothing.... We have got people who are rotting in the jails — we say we want those people to come home![20]

Mother love motivates women who treasure their children and therefore march to stop the fratricide in Northern Ireland; who cherish their children and therefore advocate dismantling nuclear arsenals; who value their children and therefore organize to get drunk drivers who kill off the road; who are desperately grieved over their dead children and so organize a mothers' front against the death squads in Sri Lanka. The record of mothers' resistance is long and painful. It also includes "mothers in slavery who fought for the survival and freedom of their children; mothers in ghettos and camps who shielded their children or comforted them when protection was no longer possible; ... welfare mothers in the United States fighting for minimal health and security."[21] The phenomenon is visible in those with a mother's sensibility wherever poverty and tyranny endanger children and others for whom they care. Their fundamental stance is shaped by the question, "Did I conceive to throw away?"[22] Concern for justice in the concrete marks these terrible mothers, the fiercely loving ones whose desires model God the Mother's own will that everyone live and have enough bread. The experience of these women generates insight into the kind of love poured out by God as mother, standing for justice with a passion born of compassion for all her children.

It is becoming unmistakably clear that the scope of inclusive justice must broaden to catch all creatures of this planet, present and as yet unborn, in the net of concern. Most liberation theologies have yet to join the justice issue with ecological and nuclear exigencies. Without care for the world that provides the goods that we would distribute justly, however, and without harnessing the destructive power of nuclear weapons that can kill even birth itself, there will be no future for liberated people to inhabit. Human beings must become guardians of the world, as good parents of a large household that includes vulnerable but necessary nonhuman creatures with their own beauty, value, and integrity. This essential quality of wholistic concern for universal justice is implied in the image of God the Mother, creator of heaven and earth and of all that is seen and unseen. The Colombian Indians express this in a religious song filled with a sensibility badly needed in rapacious society:

> She is the mother of all races, the mother of all tribes.
> She is the mother of the thunder, mother of the rain and rivers,
> the mother of trees and all living things.
> She is the mother of the animals, the only one,
> and the mother of the Milky Way.
> And the mother has left in us a memory ...
> She left songs and dances as a reminder.[23]

As creative, life-giving mother of all that is, God has at heart the well-being of the whole world, its life-systems and all its inhabitants. Preserving resources and endangered species, rightly reordering economic relationships, equitably redistributing goods, and banning whatever damages and defiles creation are human activities that make present Wisdom's maternally interested love.

It is helpful to clarify the terminology being used here, for different areas of scholarship use the term *justice* in different ways. In moral philosophy, an ethic of justice or rights commonly refers to a position that considers a mature moral agent to be one who respects the rights of others while pursuing his or her own good according to the individual's own inalienable rights. According to this view, moral maturity is reached when a person is able to engage in self-motivated acts on the basis of the application of principle, avoiding harm to others except in extreme circumstances when principles permit exceptions. This is called an ethic of justice or an ethic of rights, with focus on the individual moral agent and the just exercise of individual rights.

As is well-known today, the research of Carol Gilligan and others who attend to female experience in their data is bringing to light the fact that a significant number of girls and adult women, while knowing moral principles as well as boys and men do, resolve moral dilemmas by a method that is more flexible with regard to principle because they are seeking to preserve relationships. Their reasoning resounds "in a different voice."[24] Gilligan has accordingly proposed the existence of an alternative system that she names an ethic of care, in which moral maturity is evidenced by the moral agent's response to the needs of others while seeking to maintain the network of relationships in which all dwell. In this pattern of the moral life, the emphasis is on personal responsibility within the context of relationship rather than on individual rights against the background of the rights of others. In recent work Gilligan has theorized that it is not the case that these two ethics are polar opposites or mirror images of one another, one having what the other lacks. Neither can they be reconciled in a complementary way. Rather, like the famous line drawing of gestalt psychology, which can be perceived as either a duck or a rabbit, they are two distinct ways of arranging the same material, expressive of a different understanding of self in society and of a different interpretation of the moral good.[25]

On balance, the concern for justice promoted by the spirituality of the justice and peace movements, the Catholic social justice tradition, and feminist liberation theology is more closely aligned with an ethic of care than with an ethic of justice or rights, despite the ambiguity of vocabulary. Stress on the interrelatedness of all creatures with each other provides the context for responsible attention to the needs of others inclusively, especially therefore those who are most deprived.[26]

Within a traditional dualistic framework compassion and justice are cast as polar opposites. The first has to do with the heart showing mercy, the other with the intellect meting out what is due. In the transformative gestalt of a feminist paradigm, the justice orientation of God as creative mother does not stand in contrast to her compassion but is rather an indispensable expression of it. God Mother-Creator "knows" the suffering of beloved creatures but desires that they should flourish. The journey of the metaphor from the wombs of women to the compassion of God extends even further, from the compassion of God to her passion for justice for the whole world. God as mother is dangerous language. It summons those "born of God" to maternal thinking as a moral project.

Speaking about God

In the end Holy Wisdom is mystery beyond all telling. Speaking about God as mother points to the depth of that absolute mystery, expressing God as unoriginate origin, primordial being, hidden source of all that is, creator without beginning yet ever young and fresh, absolutely free, fount of outpouring, root of life. And even these words proceed by way of analogy. When the intelligibility of the symbol of God as mother informs speech about divine mystery, then again, as in the case of Spirit and Jesus-Sophia, theology of God transforms some of the deficiencies of classical theism. Maternity with its creativity, nurturing, and warmth, its unbounded compassion and concern for justice, its sovereign power that protects, heals, and liberates, its all-embracing immanence, and its recreative energy shapes a new understanding of divine relationality, mystery, and liberating intent.

The mother image points to an intrinsic relatedness between God and the world, a loving relationality that belongs to the very essence of being a mother and never ends. In and through the experience of birthing and rearing an orientation emerges that fights against alienation, that resists seeing things and people as separate but instead fosters a vision of connection with them and oneself. The vision validates itself because as a mother one *is* connected with another in a way that is constitutive of the self.[27] Speaking about God as mother fixes as bedrock the idea that relationship is a constitutive way in which divine freedom enacts itself.

This symbol gives to divine immanence and transcendence a distinctive cast. Because of the human experience that undergirds it, mothering leads quickly toward the idea of immanence, a mother being intimately involved in the life of her infant or small child. But in addition to this idea of God in our midst, closer to us than we are to ourselves, the mother image makes immanence mutual. The implicit memory of dwelling in a mother's womb gives rise to the thought that in God too we live and move and have our being, a mutual indwelling that issues in autonomy. Furthermore, in a feminist framework, the immanence of God as mother does not supplement or complement an overly transcendent father God, bringing closer to the world a God who otherwise would dwell in splendid isolation free of any real relation to the other. This is the inevitable result if a dualistic framework is maintained and male and female principles are stereotyped. But the mother-creator image itself is capable of evoking divine transcendence in a new gestalt. Her transcendence consists precisely in her free existence in lasting relation springing from a depth so profound as to escape finite concepts. In human experience a mother is intensely mysterious to her young child. Her daily abilities and skills upon which a child depends for survival are great and powerful. In addition much of her life is unknown, either having been lived before the child came on the scene, or taking place in the company of others, husband, friends, colleagues at work, or other adults with whom she is in relation. This is simple human experience pointing to the infinite depths of God the Mother's hiddenness, her vast freedom forever incomprehensible to our minds. Speech about God as mother refuses to polarize divine immanence and transcendence but, guided by the symbol, thinks these to be code words signifying human experience of God's nearness in mystery, and pointing to divine being as freely relational.

It is human experience that we do not remain small children, but grow up into adults. Relationship with one's own mother or the mothering persons in one's life reaches maturity when in addition to rooting us in our origins it incorporates elements of mutual friendship and help. Speaking about God as mother does not bind us into prestructured patterns arising from the relationship of childhood but brings about a mature realization of mutuality with God, shown in human responsibility to cooperate with God's transforming design for the world's salvation. All creatures, human beings and the earth, exist in relations of mutual kinship with each other and with God their mother, creator of heaven and earth, who delights in creation and whose passion it is to bring the whole world to the fullness of life in justice, peace, and universal harmony.

•

In human language we have charted something of the dialectical movement of Spirit-Sophia present and absent in the world, remembered the conflictual, liberating story of Jesus-Sophia ongoing as the Christ, and modeled the absolute mystery of unoriginate origin in the gestalt of Mother-Sophia. A trinitarian pattern of experience has emerged, as was intended. What is the right way to speak about the one God in the face of this multidimensional encounter?

PART IV

DENSE SYMBOLS AND THEIR DARK LIGHT

Chapter 10

TRIUNE GOD:
MYSTERY OF RELATION

Who is She, neither male nor female, maker of all things,
only glimpsed or hinted, source of life and gender?
She is God,
mother, sister, lover: in her love we wake, move, grow,
are daunted, triumph and surrender.

Who is She, mothering her people, teaching them to walk,
lifting weary toddlers, bending down to feed them?
She is Love,
crying in a stable, teaching from a boat,
friendly with the lepers, bound for crucifixion.

Who is She, sparkle in the rapids, coolness of the well,
living power of Jesus flowing from the Scriptures?
She is Life,
water, wind and laughter, calm, yet never still,
swiftly moving Spirit, singing in the changes.

—Brian Wren[1]

Tradition and Its Discontents

As we trace the vivifying ways of the Spirit, the compassionate, liberating story of Jesus Sophia, and the generative mystery of the Creator
Mother, it becomes clear that the Christian experience of the one God
is multifaceted. The God of inexhaustible mystery who is inexpressibly
other is also with the world in the flesh of history, and is furthermore
closer to us than we are to ourselves. Sophia-God is beyond, with, and
within the world; behind, with, and ahead of us; above, alongside, and
around us. The religious experience of being met in this diversity of saving ways functioned historically and continues to be the starting point
for seeking the intelligibility of speech about God in the Christian tradition. Shaped by this encounter, thought discerns a distinct kind of
monotheism: the one God enjoys a trinitarian existence.[2]

191

At its most basic the symbol of the Trinity evokes a livingness in God, a dynamic coming and going with the world that points to an inner divine circling around in unimaginable relation. God's relatedness to the world in creating, redeeming, and renewing activity suggests to the Christian mind that God's own being is somehow similarly differentiated. Not an isolated, static, ruling monarch but a relational, dynamic, tripersonal mystery of love — who would not opt for the latter?

The fact is, however, that the doctrine of the Trinity in recent centuries has run into a thicket of problems, which were verbalized in the nineteenth and twentieth centuries, although building long before that. These difficulties have considerably lessened appreciation of trinitarian speech about God. One fundamental obstacle arises from the fact that over time the triune symbol has been divorced from the original multifaceted, life-giving experiences that gave it birth in human understanding. This separation has been aided and abetted by extraordinary forgetfulness of the nature of theological language and of the indirect way it points to holy mystery. Clear and distinct trinitarian terms give the impression that theology has God sighted through a high-powered telescope, with descriptions of the interactions between three persons intended to be taken in some literal sense. Increasing philosophic refinements within refinements present the triune symbol not as a revered expression of the historical experience of salvation, that is, not as an asymptotic interpretation of the gracious God encountered through Jesus in the Spirit, but as a mind-bending mathematical puzzle, a mystery in the sense of a problem that can be solved or at least clarified with enough intellectual keenness and hubris.

Consequently, the triune symbol and the thought to which it gives rise have become unintelligible and religiously irrelevant on a vast scale, appearing as esoteric doctrine that one could well do without. This attitude is superbly represented in the way Friedrich Schleiermacher relegates the Trinity to the closing pages of his magisterial *The Christian Faith*. His controlling motive is the conviction that the doctrine, derived as it is from several more basic elements and being of little practical value, had little to do with the essence of this faith.[3] The Trinity continues to be found in the appendix of the personal catechism of many minds and hearts, as compared with its place in official church teaching and prayer and in ecumenical statements. To paraphrase an observation by Karl Rahner, if people were to read in their morning newspaper that a fourth person of the Trinity had been discovered it would cause little stir, or at least less than is occasioned by a Vatican pronouncement on a matter of sexual ethics — so detached has the triune symbol become from the actual religious life of many people.[4]

A paradox ensues. On the one hand, people think of God in a monolithic monopersonal way because trinitarian doctrine is simply too separated from experience and too complicated to understand. On the other hand, if the triune God is thought about at all it is with a strong tendency toward tritheism, as if God were three people, three persons in the modern psychological sense of the term. Either way, the liberating point of the symbol is lost.

In addition to critical concern about the Trinity's loss of connection with religious experience and its overliteralization in Christian imagination, feminist theology raises another critique, that this symbol is used to sustain the patriarchal subordination of women. It does this through both its male imagery and the hierarchical pattern of divine relationships inherent in the structure of reigning models of the symbol itself.

Imagery

The exclusive use of male imagery is the first difficulty to surface when the Trinity is addressed from a feminist perspective. At least two male figures, a father who generates a son, breathe forth a third more amorphous figure who is nevertheless referred to as "he." Trinitarian theology focuses on the pattern of relationship between these male-envisioned "persons," as does liturgy and catechesis. The evocative power of the deeply masculinized symbol of the Trinity points implicitly to an essential divine maleness, inimical to women's being *imago Dei* precisely as female. Giving rise to the uncritically held assumption that maleness is of the essence of the triune God, it has the sociological effect of casting men into the role of God while women stand as dependent and sinful humanity. In the West it has not been imagined any other way. In his argument for the shape of the trinitarian God as the one who loves in freedom, Peter Hodgson captures the theological frustration arising from the intransigence of this imagery with the observation, "It is so obviously misleading to think of God as a fraternity of male beings who are begetting, spirating, and proceeding from one another that it is best to drop this language entirely."[5] Searching for new ways of expressing ancient truth that is still compelling, women propose a variety of options: using both male and female imagery, using personal imagery without gender (friend, redeemer), using nonpersonal terms, using biblical names such as Abba, Servant, Paraclete, or retrieving the nonpatriarchal meaning of the Father of Jesus Christ.[6]

Structure

Beyond the male imagery, however, a further problem keeps surfacing from the relational pattern within the Trinity itself as usually presented in classical theology. At first, under pervasive, Neoplatonic influence, early formulations assumed that the one high God could act on the world only through intermediaries. The trinitarian schema thus started with a notion of the first "person" of the Trinity as *fons divinitatis*, or principle and originating source of divinity itself. The Word and Spirit were then understood philosophically as emanations from the Father, or more picturesquely as the one God's two hands held out to the world. Such a model carries an implicit subordinationism, for the second and third persons are in some sense aspects of the first and can never be genuinely and equally persons as is the first. Insofar as they devolve from the first person who realizes divinity most fully, they have a diminished divinity. The being of God, whose unity is preserved by reductively referring the second and third persons to the unoriginate source, is thus structured in a hierarchical pattern rather than according to the equality of mutual relations.

The alternative vision of three equal persons struggled to come to light in the Nicene debate and its aftermath, successfully breaking through in the *homoousios* of the Nicene confession and the expansion of the article on the Spirit in the Nicene-Constantinopolitan creed. In theology three *hypostases* were posited as equally related, one to another, while remaining distinct.[7] This explicit faith affirmation did not resolve the theoretical problem, however, as later theological development and use of trinitarian doctrine show. In classic form the doctrine of the Trinity presents the unoriginate Father as the principle and source of the whole of deity. He generates a Son, word, or image who proceeds from his substance in the procession known as generation. Between them is set up the relations of paternity and filiation, with emphasis on the way the Father gives everything to the Son and the Son receives everything totally from the Father. In turn, both Father and Son in the Western tradition, as compared to the Father alone in the Eastern, breathe forth the divine Spirit in the procession for which it is difficult to find a name, but may be called spiration, or simply procession itself. This sets up a relation of active spiration on the one hand, and passive spiration on the part of the Spirit who receives all from the one or the two who breathe "him" forth.

Classical theology insists with great rigor on this pattern of proceeding, which is indeed reflective of certain biblical narratives in which the Father sends the Son and, together with the Son or alone, also sends

the Spirit (see Jn 20:21; 14:26). It is argued that in this order and its resulting relations lies the identity of the three persons. What keeps them
distinct is the way they do or do not proceed from one another. That
is why friendship does not provide a particularly apt model for, as Augustine argues, "a friend is so called relatively to his friend, and if they
love each other equally then the same friendship is in both."[8] But this
would be to blur the differences between them, which would endanger
their uniqueness. Only trinitarian names that imply a relation of origin
preserve the distinction of persons in God. By Aquinas's time these relations of ordered origin are referred to in the paradoxical language of
opposition; they are relations of opposition. Interpreted according to
the minds of the authors, this language intends to safeguard personal
distinctiveness. So long as these relations are in place the persons are
not interchangeable: a father can never be his own son. Distinction of
persons is maintained at the same time that the unity of the one God is
preserved through a system of processions in a certain strict order.

When the totality of biblical witness is taken into account, it becomes apparent that theology has been highly selective in its focus on
the Father-Son-Spirit pattern, for other options are also realizable. In
a key Lukan passage, for example, it is not the Father but the Spirit
who sends Jesus to bring good news to the poor and proclaim liberty
to the oppressed (Lk 4:16-20). Jürgen Moltmann has organized the rich
scriptural data in a helpful way to show its witness to several orders of
proceeding. Before the resurrection the sequence reads Father-Spirit-
Son, for the Spirit is so powerfully active in the birth, baptism, and
passing over of Jesus' life in death and resurrection that Jesus can be
said to live from the works of the creative Spirit. After the resurrection
the order becomes Father-Son-Spirit, for Jesus is now made a life-giving
spirit and himself joins in the sending of the Spirit to the community of
disciples. Finally, when we consider the eschatological transformation
of creation the sequence becomes Spirit-Son-Father, for the Spirit is the
power of the new creation and brings all to rebirth. In this last sequence
the Spirit is not the energy proceeding from the Father or the Son, but
the glorifying God from whom Father and Son receive their glory; the
unifying God who gives them their union; the active subject from whom
Father and Son receive the world as their home.[9] These various scriptural options make it possible to conceive of the trinitarian persons in
different patterns of relation from a set series of sequential processions.
Instead, the three interweave each other in various patterns of saving
activity and can be spoken about in concepts such as giving over and
receiving back, being obedient and being glorified, witnessing, filling,
and actively glorifying.

In addition to limiting attention to only one of several trinitarian languages, the structure of the processional model carries an inherent difficulty. While affirming and promoting the equality of divine persons and their mutual interrelation, it nevertheless subverts this by its rigid hierarchical ordering. The Father gives everything and receives back nothing that could be considered ontologically essential. The Spirit on the other hand receives everything and gives nothing essential in return. Even where the entire process is characterized as the movement of love, as for example in Walter Kasper's retrieval of the trinitarian tradition through the love categories of Richard of St. Victor, the relations are asymmetrical:

In the Father, love exists as pure source that pours itself out; in the Son it exists as a pure passing-on, as pure mediation; in the Spirit it exists as the joy of pure receiving. These three modes in which the one being of God, the one love, subsists, are in some sense necessary because love cannot be otherwise conceived.[10]

But the experience of mutual love so prized in feminist reflection shows that love can in fact be conceived another way, namely, in a relational pattern of mutual giving and receiving according to each one's capacity and style. When the model used, however, focuses on the procession of first to second to third, a subtle hierarchy is set up and, like a drowned continent, bends all currents of trinitarian thought to the shape of the model used. Through insistence on the right order of certain processions, ontological priority inevitably ends up with the Father while at the other end of the processions the Spirit barely trails along, as we have seen.

The irony is that the classical tradition also carries within itself a corrective to this implicit trinitarian hierarchy dogging both Eastern and Western conceptions. This corrective lies in the insistence that each of the three persons of the Trinity is radically equal to each of the others, their difference lying only in their ways of being related to each other. As Augustine figures, it is true that when we say the words Father, Son and Spirit, each syllable is separated from the other in a sequence of time; but these intervals belong to the nature of words as bodily sounds and not to God's Trinity. In God there is no sooner or later, no before or after, no intervals of time or place. Jointly, inseparably, mutually the three persons dwell within each other and exercise powerful activity.[11] Sequence, then, does not necessitate subordination. When trinitarian language is thus pondered as a whole, it is clear that the fundamental attempt of the doctrine is to secure an understanding of God as a profound relational communion.

Yet the basic metaphors being used necessarily signify an order of precedence in their human gestalt. Processions, whether academic, liturgical, funeral, and so on, imply rank. Parents exist before their children, and are responsible for their existence. A gift implies a giver who is already there. While trinitarian equality is affirmed, the images falter and are simply not capable of bearing the burden of the mutuality to be expressed. The Father generates the Son and from one or both proceeds the Spirit, a pattern that presses headlong toward a first followed by a second and a third, in fact if not in intent. The impression is consistently given of an inherent inconsistency in classical trinitarian theology itself, which struggles to insist on equality of persons at the same time that it uses constructs that by their very design undermine equality and mutuality and introduce subordination in a subtle way. Different metaphor systems are needed to show the equality, mutuality, and reciprocal dynamism of trinitarian relations.

From the asymmetry of trinitarian relations in the classical model a practical inequality follows, with neither Son nor Spirit attaining the authority of the Father. All originates from the first person, the apex of the divine pyramid. Such a model is clearly coherent with the existence of patriarchal structures in church and society, and is in functional rapport with them. It both reproduces and supports such structures. Argumentation in its favor betrays a mindset which assumes that if a certain order of precedence is not kept, with a single ruler at the top and all proceeding from there, then chaos will break out, personal identity become indistinct, and harmony be destroyed. A different order of unity based on mutual personal relations and shared responsibility is not envisioned. The caution sounded by feminist thinkers from Virginia Woolf to Mary Daly is as relevant to the hierarchical model of trinitarian theology as it is to human cavalcades: beware the processions of the sons of educated men.[12]

Freeing the Symbol from Literalness

First steps toward a feminist theological interpretation of trinitarian language are taken when it is remembered that this symbol of holy mystery arises from the historical experience of salvation, and that it speaks about divine reality not literally but by way of analogy.

Rooted in Experience

An encounter with holy mystery lies at the root of all religious doctrine. So too with the Trinity. It is a symbol that develops historically out of the religious experience of the gracious God who encountered

Jews and then Gentiles through Jesus of Nazareth in the power of the Spirit.[13] Christian experience of faith, therefore, is the generating matrix for language about God as triune. Conversely, the Trinity is a legitimate but secondary concept that synthesizes the concrete experience of salvation in a "short formula." It is a theological construct that codifies the liberating God encountered in history. Without attentiveness to this rootedness in experience, speculation on the Trinity can degenerate into wild and empty conceptual acrobatics.[14]

The first Christian believers symbolized God in accord with their Jewish monotheistic tradition as YHWH, the God of Israel. Without abandoning this tradition they increasingly focused on how this same God mysteriously encountered them in the person and mission of Jesus the Christ. Again, they experienced this same God's continuing presence and activity through the power of the Spirit in their midst after Jesus' death had removed him from ordinary human interchange. In each of these ways they were engaged in a religious experience of divine mystery acting in a very particular gracious way within their history. The biblical writing created by these first-century communities does not contain any developed trinitarian doctrine. What it has instead are stories and words of praise, narratives and doxologies cast in threefold symbols of God that arose spontaneously out of Christian experience of holy mystery in its character of being transcendently mysterious, historically mediated, and liberatingly immanent. The primary concern of these narrations and doxologies is soteriological: to announce and celebrate the good news of human liberation and cosmic reconciliation coming from God through Jesus the Christ in the Spirit.

This experience and its literary precipitate form the matrix for the development of later centuries when the Trinity in the form of doctrine gradually came to speech. The intellectual trigger for its growth was reflection about Jesus' relationship with God, thinking that was carried out within the Hellenistic framework of thought. There was need for the Christian symbol of God to become more complex to embrace the christological mystery. Far from being a simple intellectual search, however, the basic motivation was religious, empowered by the question of how the one and only God could be so envisioned that each of the ways in which the community encountered divine mystery could be affirmed as genuinely an experience of God. As Norman Pittenger has so well put it, this was not a case of an experiential tritheism seeking a monotheistic expression, but a monotheistic belief seeking a way for triadic experience to be preserved.[15]

A certain logic ordered the progression of thought. Three experiences come to human beings from one God. Therefore three sorts of relationship are possible with one God. Therefore three corresponding distinctions may be said to exist within one God. Why the latter insight? It is based on the conviction that God is utterly faithful, and does not self-reveal in any guise other than the one which actually coheres with the essence of divine being. The symbol of the Trinity thus intends to safeguard the reality of liberating experience both as given by God, and as giving the one true God. The whole ensuing apparatus of theological terminology about the Trinity, its language of one *ousia* in three *hypostases*, or of one divine nature and three divine persons, is the result of this attempt to interpret the experience of God at the very center of Christian faith. Far from being literally descriptive, the trinitarian symbol desires to express and protect the fundamental Christian experience of shalom drawing near. It is shorthand for the dynamic, inexpressible Sophia-God of compassionate, liberating love who is involved in history in multifaceted ways.

If this is true of the origin and historical development of the doctrine, it is no less so regarding its present intelligibility. For it is the case that the Trinity has lost its mooring in experience. One way to enable the Trinity to make sense is to explore its originating history in religious experience: to seek to link later conceptual clarifications with that experience as its own interpretation in a particular cultural milieu, and then to lift up the threefold experience of the mystery of God even today as point of departure for understanding. For believers today no less than in the first century it remains the case that "All our thinking moves from the world to God, and can never move in the opposite direction."[16]

Perhaps no contemporary axiom has been more influential in showing this linkage between Christian experience of God and the mystery of God's own being than the epistemological axiom that "the economic Trinity is the immanent Trinity, and vice-versa," formulated in this fashion by Karl Rahner.[17] *Economic* signifies an arrangement, a plan, or the administration of such social groupings as a household. In this trinitarian adage it refers to the economy (Greek, *oikonomia*) of salvation, God's plan to redeem the whole sinful world by lavishing on it the riches of grace (Eph 1:10). The economic Trinity signifies God's redeeming relatedness to the world in liberating love, God *pro nobis*. On the other hand, the *immanent* of the axiom refers to God's own being considered in itself, God *in se*.[18] The axiom expresses the epistemological truth that it is given to us to point to the latter only through the former.

The point of affirming that the economic Trinity is the immanent Trinity is that there are not two Gods, one who encounters us in the world and another different one who is totally other than what we experience. In Jesus Christ God does not wear a mask; the power of the Spirit does not hide a deity who is fundamentally cruel and enslaving rather than compassionate and liberating; neither of these encounters is with a false God; nor are they extrinsic to God's own being. Basic trust in the experience of God's threefold relatedness to us suggests that a certain corresponding threefoldness characterizes God's own true being. As Rahner has argued, God is not so little involved in relationship with us that the distinctions we experience in divine encounter are only on our creaturely side; instead, the triadic character of our religious experience indicates a threefold character even of God's own way of being God. The concrete ways that God is given to us in history point to three interrelated ways of existing within God's own being. God really corresponds to the way we have encountered the divine mystery in time.

At this point a strong objection is offered by some contemporary theologians who hold that it simply is not given to human beings to talk about the inner life of God. Such language is a bold overreach of human capabilities which must inevitably fail. The most we can do is suspect some kind of self-differentiation in God, possibly even glimpse it; but we must respect it as a mystery, in silence. There should be no speculation about the inner being of God. We may speak of the economic but not of the immanent Trinity, so-called. James Mackey even calls this axiom that so enables speech about God's immanent being "one of the greatest red herrings ever drawn on the confused history of the trinitarian doctrine."[19] These cautions are intensely reflective of contemporary sensibility in a postmodern world, and function as a valuable critique of the overrationalized condition of much trinitarian theology. It is indeed too often forgotten that we see only through a glass, darkly, and have no knowledge of God in the order of empirical facts.

Given the triune symbol's rootedness in salvific experience and its intent to point via analogy to the holy mystery so experienced, however, we would lose a great deal if we ceased speaking altogether of the immanent triune God. For this language is not a literal description of the inner being of God who is in any event beyond human understanding. It is a pointer to holy mystery in trust that God really is the compassionate, liberating God encountered through Jesus in the Spirit. It is language which affirms that what is experienced in Christian faith really is of God; that what we are involved with is nothing other than saving divine mystery. At rock bottom it is the language of hope. No one has ever seen God, but thanks to the experience unleashed through Jesus in the Spirit we hope, walking by faith not by sight, that the livingness of God is with us and for us as renewing, liberating love. We hope that it is the livingness of *God* who is with us in the suffering of history, and so we affirm that God's relation to the world is grounded in God's own being capable of such relation. To hold that the economic Trinity is the immanent Trinity and vice-versa is to dare to say that divine mystery is the power of love for us springing from God's being love from all eternity. In other words, "In knowing the God who is our origin, ground and goal, we do not know a shadow image of God but the real living God of Jesus Christ in their Spirit. The God who saves — this *is* God."[20] Such understanding betrays the presence of deep hope, the very essence of the risk of faith.

Probing the significance of trinitarian language as an interpretation of religious experience provides a point of entry for feminist theological reflection. The threefold, interwoven aspects of encounter with the one holy mystery point to Sophia-God who is not a monolithic block but a living mystery of relation, to us and to herself.

Spoken Allusively

What is true of theological language about God in general remains the case when speech turns to the triune mystery. Since "we cannot know what God is, but only what God is not,"[21] such speech is always indirect, having a metaphorical, analogical, or symbolic character. Even when taken from the language of Scripture, no similarity can be predicated between God and creatures without the dissimilarity being always ever greater. No concept is adequate, no model mirrors directly. This is more obviously true of picturesque terms taken from the human world such as father and son, the acts of generation, of breathing, of being related, of mutually loving. But even highly abstract philosophical terms such as nature, person, and being are at root analogical when used to refer to God. While they have no particular concrete referent or picture content, the concepts they signify are bound by human finitude and do not reach their intended goal without first being negated with respect to their creaturely content. In the colorful language of Gregory of Nazianzus,

What, then, is procession? Do tell me what is meant by the unbegottenness of the Father, and I will explain to you the physiology of the generation of the Son and the procession of the Spirit, and we shall both of us be frenzy-stricken for prying into the mystery of God. And who are we to do these things, we who cannot even see what lies at our feet, or number the sands of the sea, or the drops of rain, or the days of eternity, much less enter into the depths of God, and supply an account of that nature which is so unspeakable and transcending all words?[22]

All our speech is earthbound or spacebound, so to speak. There is the greatest possible unlikeness between all analogies used and the holy mystery of the triune God who is their intended referent.

This has not always been remembered in the course of theology's history. Trinitarian discussion in particular has given the impression of being highly specialized, esoteric knowledge about God intended in a literal sense, rather than allusive language about a religious symbol. It is interesting to note in this regard that the most influential book on the Trinity in the West, Augustine's *De Trinitate*, is simply peppered with comments about the inadequacy of his reflections, so blessed and incomprehensible is the triune mystery of God. This thinker, who could be so wrong about some crucial things such as the nature of women, got it precisely right when he observed at the end of his fifteen books of strenuous effort to illumine the triune God by multiple human analogies:

Here by experience itself it has appeared to me so difficult. . . . As often as I have desired to illustrate it by the creaturely image of it which we ourselves are, so often, let my meaning be of what sort it might, did adequate utterance utterly fail me; nay, even in my very meaning I felt that I had attained to endeavor rather than accomplishment.[23]

Two examples of terms used in speaking about God's Trinity, namely, "person" and the numbers "one" and "three," may serve to illustrate the allusive character of language about the triune God. First, the one God subsists in three divine persons, according to the formulation of the classical doctrine. Laboring to understand what this means, Augustine explores why the word person is used to speak about God's threefoldness. There is a need to find some word to say about Father, Son and Spirit in common, although no word is adequate:

When it is, therefore, asked what the three are or who the three are, we seek to find a generic or a specific name which may include the three together. But we come across none, because the supereminent excellence of the divinity transcends all the limits of our customary manner of speaking. For God is thought more truly than can be uttered, and exists more truly than can be thought.[24]

Theology seeks a general word for the three, however. It cannot be Father or Son or Spirit, for these words name what is distinctive; there is only one of each. It would not be right to say that they are three essences or three somewhats, for that would deliver to us more than one God. In the end it is legitimate to say that they are three persons, provided that this be understood as mystery and not in any usual or known sense:

When it is asked three what, then the great poverty from which our language suffers becomes apparent. But the formula three persons was coined not in order to give a complete explanation by means of it, but in order that we might not be obliged to remain silent.[25]

Person recommends itself because it is the term used by theological tradition, because Scripture does not contradict it, but most of all because it is necessary to say *something* when the question arises about what the three are. In explaining Augustine's point, Edmund Hill suggests that we try referring to the persons as three *x*'s in God, or as A,B,C, so unknown is the threesomeness to which the term refers.[26] Centuries later Anselm of Canterbury will even speak of "three something-or-other," "three I know not what" (*tres nescio quid*).[27] In speaking of the triune mystery, person is perhaps the least inconvenient of labels, but it is highly inadequate, in fact, improper.

For contemporary theology the intrinsic difficulty of the meaning of person is further compounded by the semantic drift of this term in the course of the centuries. The word first came into trinitarian language as the Greek *hypostasis*, a philosophical term that is virtually untranslatable into modern English. Its approximate meaning connotes a firm base from which an existing thing stands forth and develops; or a full-stop to a nature; or the fundamental subsistence of a thing. The Latins meanwhile used *persona*, a term with a certain human personal density but also intended in a philosophical sense. Since the Enlightenment, however, the arcane philosophical meaning of person has receded in favor of an understanding of person as an individual center of consciousness and freedom; personalist and postmodern philosophy insists on the qualification that the autonomous person is relational through and through. Now to say that God is three "persons" inevitably gives rise to a picture of God as three distinct people with separated consciousnesses who are personally interrelated and somehow one. Tritheism becomes endemic. With the analogical nature of theological language firmly in view, it must be said that God is not a person in the modern sense; neither is God three such persons. God transcends what we understand to be person as source of all that is personal, and thus is not less than personal. God is interpersonal and transpersonal in an unimaginably rich way. In any event, the point that guides this discussion is that we do not have hold of a clear and distinct idea when speaking about God as a Trinity of persons. Whether understood in the classic philosophical way or the modern personalist way, person refers to God only indirectly, metaphorically. The understanding of person in the trinitarian symbol escapes our grasp.

This is the case not only for the term person but also for the numbers one and three. These terms are not intended to denote anything positive in God, but to remove something. This is difficult to remember, however, for we inevitably think in quantitative terms when such numbers are mentioned, so that two or three together add up to more than one. But in God, none of the three persons together are "more" God than one person taken singly. It is not similar to the case of human beings, where one alone is less than three together. Nor, to use Augustine's example of gold statues:

And in equal statues, three together amount to more of gold than each singly, and one amounts to less of gold than two. But in God it is not so; for the Father, the Son, and the Holy Spirit together is not a greater essence than the Father alone or the Son alone; but these three substances or persons, if such they must be called, together are equal to each singly; which the natural human being does not understand. For we cannot think except under conditions of bulk and space, either small or great, since phantasms or as it were images of bodies flit about in our mind.[28]

In thinking about the one God in three persons, this theologian urges, let whatever occurs to us that is substantially greater in three than in one alone, or less in one than in two, be rejected without any doubt.[29] This is not a caution that has been widely heeded. Forgetting the analogical nature of number, theology and preaching have too often spoken of three persons in one God in such a way as to give rise inevitably to the idea that God, like Gaul, is divided into three parts.[30] The intent of the numbers in talk of the Trinity, however, is much more subtle. To say that God is one is intended to negate division, thus affirming the unity of divine being. To say that the persons are three is intended to negate singleness, thus affirming a communion in God.[31] Number, when said of God, cannot be taken in a quantitative sense. Rather, as Augustine writes,

in that highest trinity one is as much as the three together, nor are two anything more than one. And they are infinite in themselves. So both each are in each, and all in each, and each in all, and all in all, and all are one.[32]

Where does this brief excursus through classical sources bring us? We emerge with the strong realization that the symbol of the Trinity is not a blueprint of the inner workings of the godhead, not an offering of esoteric information about God. In no sense is it a literal description of God's being *in se*. As the outcome of theological reflection on the Christian experience of relationship to God, it is a symbol that indirectly points to God's relationality, at first with reference to the world and then with reference to God's own mystery. The Trinity is itself an analogy referring to divine livingness. Our speech about God as three and persons is a human construction that means to say that God is *like* a Trinity, *like* a threefoldness of relation. Negating the literalness of this symbol enriches understanding, loosening the hold of particular philosophical interpretations and setting our minds in the direction of holy mystery. As Augustine concludes, "For things incomprehensible must be so investigated that no one may think they have found nothing, when they have been able to find how incomprehensible that which they were seeking really is."[33] The triune God is not simply unknown, but positively known to be unknown and unknowable — which is a dear and profound kind of knowledge.

Directing the Symbol toward Meaning

A second step toward feminist theological speech about God's triune livingness is dialogue with other theological efforts to resituate this symbol in postclassical categories. Twentieth-century theology's attempts to reknit the triune symbol back to its foundational experiences of salvation and to release the religious power of its allusive language result in new ways of conceptualizing God as triune.[34] While the classical form of the doctrine grounded the unity of the three divine persons in the unoriginate first person (the Eastern model) or in the one divine nature or essence (the Western option), other options now emerge. In one instance, talk of three persons is replaced by the language of modality or manners of subsistence while divine unity is conceptualized in analogy with a single acting subject. In another instance, three persons precisely in the modern sense are envisioned while divine unity is modeled on social communion. Each of these gestalts of trinitarian doctrine contributes in its own way to feminist speech about God.

The most influential designers of the single subject pattern are without question Karl Barth and Karl Rahner. In their efforts to recapture the plausibility and religious power of the triune symbol, each has returned to the experience of God in history, alternately interpreted as divine self-revelation or self-communication in accord with each one's religious tradition's emphasis on word or sacrament. Fundamentally, each works with the basic model of absolute mystery who exists in three self-differentiated ways.

Karl Barth's neo-orthodox reconstruction construes divine self-relatedness as the power of God's own being to become the God of another. In revelation God reveals God's ownself, not some other thing: God reveals, through himself, himself (*sic*). Since we have to do with

God in a threefold way in the revelatory event, the divine being is known to be structured in a threefold relationship. For God corresponds to himself, that is, God really is as he has shown himself to be in revelation. The moments of self-revelation are not foreign to the being of God; rather, the one who meets us as Father, Son, and Spirit is already the God who meets himself and has community in this way. The three aspects of the event of revelation, which lead us to speak about God as the Revealer, the Revelation, and the Revealedness, do not point to plurality of parts in God but are actually a threefold repetition of the whole divine being:

The name of Father, Son and Spirit means that God is the one God in threefold repetition; and this in such a way that the repetition itself is grounded in His Godhead, so that it implies no alteration in His Godhead; and yet in such a way also that He is the one God only in this repetition.[35]

Hence we can say that the one God is God in the threefold mode of his own self-relatedness. This, of course, is the language of faith that perceives an analogy between God's being for us and God's being for himself in the event of revelation.

Rahner's fundamental insight, worked out in categories of transcendental theology, springs from Christian experience of Jesus in the Spirit interpreted as the very self-communication of God. In incarnation and grace God imparts the divine being to created nature: to Jesus in the incarnation and to the rest of humanity in the gift of grace, in radical proximity. God communicates himself (*sic*) in his own person to the creature so absolutely that no third thing comes between God and the creature. Rather, the Giver himself is the gift. So radical is this triune self-giving in incarnation and grace that, unless we are duped, God's relationship to us known in these ways is the reality of God as he is in himself. Divine self-communication does not coincide with God in lifeless identity but evokes the ways that from all eternity God has of being himself. Hence we can say that "the one God subsists in three distinct manners of subsisting."[36] When speaking of the unoriginate source of all, tradition calls God Father; as self-expressing and spoken out into history, God is called Word or Son; as uniting in love given and received by us, God is Spirit. This all refers to only one God, the holy mystery whose own dynamic self-distinctions ground his saving relation to the world. As Rahner observes, lifeless self-identity is not the most perfect way of being absolute.

Both of these interpretations are contemporary repristinations of the ancient Greek design of Trinity where a single divine origin has two distinct but essentially interrelated issues. The Father is the principle of the godhead, and goes forth through the Word in the Spirit. Theologians who prefer a more distinct *communio* model of Trinity note an inherent difficulty within this model, namely, that a subtle subordinationism asserts itself when the first person is made the originating source who issues in the second and third persons as modalities of his own being. The first person is endowed with a covert priority to which the second and third persons are referred. Whether Barth's and Rahner's interpretations totally escape the charge of such subordinationism is a matter of debate. The alternative approach found in Moltmann and Boff, which sees three persons in the modern sense forming an ultimate community, however, is also not without its difficulties.

Jürgen Moltmann's reconceptualization of the Trinity likewise starts from salvific experience. However, his narrative rendering of the relationships of Father, Son, and Spirit occasions critique of Barth's and Rahner's idea of the Trinity as an absolute subject existing in inner modality. The idea of one divine subject giving himself (*sic*) simply does not do justice to the biblical history of the Father who sends his Son, whose faithful suffering in union with the Father releases the Spirit of love even for the most godforsaken. Neither does it do justice to the fellowship among these three, nor to their open relationship to the world. Thus each of the three persons must be characterized by his own substantiality and intellectuality, and the unity of the divine Trinity must be seen to consist not in the identity of an absolute subject but in the living *koinōnia*, the community, among three distinct divine persons:

If we take Boethius' definition, the trinitarian Persons are not "modes of being"; they are individual, unique, non-interchangeable subjects of the one, common divine substance, with consciousness and will. Each of the Persons possesses the divine nature in a non-interchangeable way; each presents it in his own way.[37]

This social Trinity forms the grid against which the story of salvation can be told as God's history with the world, which also happens among the three divine persons. Unlike the Trinity as absolute subject, here the inner divine life is inclusive of the world with all its joy and pain. Redemption, for example, belongs to the history of God: the Father hands over his Son, who in obedience undergoes the cross; in the abandonment of the cross both suffer loss in different ways; their mutual love in grief releases the Spirit upon the godless world. The cross is a trinitarian event opening up a path for the suffering of the world to enter the very being of God, there to be redeemed finally in the eschatological victory of divine life. This approach through saving history is crystallized in the programmatic statement, "Any one who talks of the trinity talks of the cross of Jesus, and does not speculate in heavenly riddles."[38]

Moltmann's idea of the triunity of God as a fellowship of persons with a dynamic openness to the joy and pain of the world has burst with vigor upon the theological imagination. Strongest critique is directed toward that aspect of his thesis which claims that since the Father handed Jesus over to be crucified, it can rightly be said that Jesus died of his Father. This is to blame Jesus' Abba, critics argue, for what rightly should be laid at the doorstep of the history of human injustice. It leaves us with the repellent view of a sadistic God rather than a God who loves life and hates injustice. One can imagine a loving father or mother suffering the grief of the loss of a son due to an unjust death; how terribly often this happens in our world. But to think that the parent takes the initiative in arranging the sacrifice — here imagination reaches its limits and humanistic values rise up in protest. Nevertheless, Moltmann's central thesis about the triune God's involvement with the pain of the world continues to gain adherents, not least because of its pastoral and sociopolitical implications before the endless mystery of human suffering.

Latin American liberation theology has likewise found in the social Trinity a more adequate pattern for ultimate reality. In the beginning is not the single subject subsisting in distinct modes; rather, says Leonardo Boff, in the beginning is communion.[39] Divine unity is an integrating union of three unique persons, each unique while intrinsically related to the other two. The true God exists as a mystery of communion of Father, Son, and Spirit. The diversity of the persons does not break up divine unity but reveals its profound richness, which is greater thanks to the distinction of the persons than it would be with a single subject alone. Accordingly, the triune God whom we encounter in history as the origin, mediator, and driving force of liberation dwells as a community of love wherein there is total equality amid mutuality and respect for difference. The triune symbol thus understood is a model of the highest ideal for humanity. It lays the foundation for a liberated society of equal brothers and sisters, critiques patterns of unjust domination, and offers a source of inspiration for change.

In the background of these designs in political and liberation theologies that reformulate Trinity as a community of three distinct persons lies the common assumption of the political danger of nontrinitarian monotheism. One single God reigning in absolute power calls for one emperor or dictator similarly ruling. Imperial rule receives easy theological justification while human political dependency and attitudes of servitude are legitimated.[40] In this context, the trinitarian doctrine takes on a corrective and liberating role insofar as it replaces the concept of a divine monarch with the social character of the triune God. Such a *communio* model of ultimate reality carries a political program, putting an end, in Walter Kasper's words, "to a particular political theology that serves as an ideology to justify relations of domination in which an individual or a group tries to impose its ideas of unity and order and its interests to the exclusion of others."[41] The trinitarian view of God tends to support political theory that is oriented toward social interaction and participation rather than submission to the absolute ruler.

Moltmann develops this thesis with particular reference to patriarchy. The solitary, ruling male God envisioned as a single, absolute subject and named father can hardly help but have a dominating relationship to the world. This in turn justifies the social and political structures of patriarchy with the solitary human patriarch at the head of the pyramid of power. Conversely, the triune God who exists essentially in mutual inner relationships provides a different model for human interaction, pointing to a community without supremacy or subjection where differences flourish in the matrix of a relationship of equals. As monotheism was and is the religion of patriarchy, and as pantheism may be supposed to be the religion of the early matriarchy, the triune idea of God points to a community of brothers and sisters in which all are one in shared responsibility without subordination or privilege.[42]

It seems to me that such analysis is altogether too sanguine about the liberating character of the triune symbol, for history shows how easily patriarchy in church and society has coexisted with trinitarian belief. Even the *homoousios* of Nicea did not basically alter the patriarchal notion of God, shaped by images of empire. Nor do we yet have the human experience of an integral, harmonious society upon which this model is predicated. The nature of its unity escapes us experientially, if not in theory. Yet the liberating possibility of the social model of the Trinity points in the right direction. Rather than fight the semantic drift of the word person into its modern sea of individual consciousness, theologians of this mindset flow with the current, encouraging development of the ancient notions of *hypostasis/persona* in such a way as to undergird a human community of justice, peace, and love.

These two major patterns of interpreting the triune symbol, the modalistic limned by Barth and Rahner and the communitarian reprised by Moltmann and Boff, do not exhaust contemporary options although they provide particularly fruitful instances of retrieval of the Trinity and its plausibility coherent with feminist perspectives.[43] Many other renamings of the triune God combine aspects of each pattern, or strike out on yet new paths. The diversity is reflective of the genuine need to make sense of this central but somehow esoteric Christian symbol.

In existential-ontological terms John Macquarrie works out the notion of Being as the energy of letting-be and self-spending. God who is Being itself is constituted by three persons, which are movements within the mystery of Being: primordial Being, deep overflowing source of all; expressive Being, mediating the dynamism outward; unitive Being, closing the circle to accomplish a rich unity in love.[44] Constructing the concept of God, Gordon Kaufman imagines God's absoluteness, humaneness, and present presence as dimensions of the one living God, a concept which relativizes all idols and judges all human inhumaneness.[45] Modeling God for a nuclear, ecological age, Sallie McFague experiments with God as mother, lover, and friend of the world which is God's body.[46] Tracing the logic of love, Walter Kasper envisions a giver, a receiver and giver, and a receiver; or a source, a mediation, and a term as the three modes in which divine love subsists.[47] Heribert Mühlen uses communications theory to illuminate divine reality as the I, Thou, and We of love.[48] Correlating the blessing of God to the human dilemma, Paul Tillich posits God as creative power vis-à-vis our finitude, saving love addressing human estrangement, and ecstatic transformation in the face of the ambiguity of human existence; or more philosophically, the element of abyss, the element of form, and the unity of the two.[49] Dorothy Sayers likens the triune God to a book as thought, written, and read.[50] Positing time to be of the divine essence, Eberhard Jüngel conceptualizes the Trinity as the passion history of God: God comes from, to, and as God at the heart of the mystery of the suffering world.[51] In process categories, Norman Pittenger interprets God who is love as the creative source of all initial aims, the self-expressive act which lures by being the model of the goal, and the responsive movement motivating creature to respond.[52] In more functional terms Letty Russell conceives the Trinity as Creator, Liberator, and Advocate who calls human beings into partnership with divine care for the world.[53] Langdon Gilkey speaks of God as divine being, divine logos, divine love; or source, principle of possibility and order, and recreative, reuniting power.[54] Emphasizing that our images reveal God precisely as imageless, Nicholas Lash speaks of the Trinity as eclipse, word, and presence.[55] Peter Hodgson limns the triune figuration as the one (Father) who loves (Son) in freedom (Spirit).[56] Conscious of the threefold experience at the heart of Hindu as well as Christian faith, Raimundo Panikkar interprets holy mystery as source, being, and return to being, which is analogous to the biblical affirmation that God is above all, through all, and in all (Eph 4:6).[57]

The threes keep circling round. Whatever the categories used, there is reflected a livingness in God; a beyond, a with and a within to the world and its history; a sense of God as from whom, by whom, and in whom all things exist, thrive, struggle toward freedom, and are gathered in. To use one more model, this time from the eleventh-century theologian Hildegaard of Bingen, there is a brightness, a flashing forth, and a fire, and these three are one, connecting all creation together in compassion.[58] All these metaphors express the trinitarian structure of Christian belief in God.

Female Metaphors

The symbol of the triune God is the specific Christian shape of monotheism. As a symbol it points to the livingness of God come to speech through human experiences of being vivified, liberated, and created in the midst of the ambiguity of history. In and through such experiences the community comes to trust that holy mystery really is this way, whirling everywhere to renew and set free, enfleshed in historical joy and pain, deep wellspring of the universe. The trinitarian symbol radically affirms the hope that God really is in accord with what has been mediated through experience, in other words, that Sophia-God corresponds to herself in bedrock fidelity. The thought to which it gives rise evokes a sense of ultimate reality highly consonant with the feminist values of mutuality, relation, equality, and community in diversity.

Throughout this theological exploration I have been operating on the theological assumption that all three *hypostases* of the Trinity transcend categories of male and female. I have also been arguing the case arising from the equal human dignity of women that each *hypostasis* may be spoken of in female metaphors, and seeking to show how this may in fact occur. While this thesis has gone forward with the help of Scripture and tradition in the case of each "person" taken singly, the difficulty becomes more dense with divine Trinity as a whole. The overwhelming weight of usage has been on the side of the male imagery of father and son, with some few lesser images taken from the natural world (wellspring, river and irrigation channel, or fire, its brightness and warmth). With one or two exceptions, female imagery for the Trinity as a whole has been stunningly absent.

There is nothing essentially necessary about this state of language, however. Scattered throughout Scripture and tradition is an interesting fluidity of usage that gives the lie to the idea that certain trinitarian names must be rigidly attributed to one person rather than the others. Take, for example, the metaphors of spirit, wisdom, and mother. Each of these metaphors may be and in fact have been spoken variously about each of the trinitarian persons. The one high creator God is Spirit (Jn 4:24); so too is Christ the Lord (2 Cor 3:17–18). All three persons may be called Spirit, for all are holy and all are Spirit, as Augustine and many others have observed.[59] As for Wisdom/Sophia, her biblical figure reflects the roles of all three persons as she creates, liberates, and graces human beings in various strands of the wisdom tradition. Working with a less personified, more essentialist view of wisdom, Augustine at least implicitly recognizes this point: "And so the Father is wisdom, the Son is wisdom, and the Holy Spirit is wisdom, and together not three wisdoms but one wisdom."[60] While acknowledging that the Word of God is called Wisdom/*sapientia* in a special way in the Scriptures, he writes that the name is not inappropriately used of the whole triune mystery:

Therefore both the Father himself is wisdom, and the Son is called the wisdom of the Father in the same way as he is called the light of the Father; that is, in the same manner that the Son is light from light and yet both are one light, so we are to understand wisdom from wisdom, and yet both one wisdom; and therefore also one essence.[61]

Similarly, "the Holy Spirit also is wisdom proceeding from wisdom,"[62] so that in the end Augustine reflects: "I know not why Father and Son and Holy Spirit should not be called love, and all together one love, just as Father and Son and Holy Spirit are called wisdom, and all together not three but one wisdom."[63]

Even mother is not said exclusively of the first person. While Isaiah and other biblical writers use the metaphor to speak of the unoriginate God's strong and compassionate maternal care, the prayers of early Syriac Christianity refer to the Holy Spirit as mother, and the medieval mystical tradition finds it suitable even for Jesus and for the whole triune mystery of God. Julian of Norwich, for example, writes:

I understand three ways of contemplating motherhood in God. The first is the foundation of our nature's creation; the second is his taking of our nature, where the motherhood of grace begins; the third is the motherhood at work. And in that, by the same grace, everything is penetrated, in length and in breadth, in height and in depth without end; and it is all one love.[64]

It is not essential for the truth of God's triune mystery to speak always in the metaphors of father, son, and spirit, although virtually exclusive use of these names over the centuries in liturgy, catechesis, and theology has caused this to be forgotten. At this point in the living tradition I believe that we need a strong dose of explicitly female imagery to break the unconscious sway that male trinitarian imagery holds over the imaginations of even the most sophisticated thinkers. What is the right way to speak about the triune God? One right way is to speak about the Trinity as a symbol of the mystery of salvation, in the midst of the world's suffering, using female images.

Holy Wisdom Who Is with and for the World

All creation is groaning, pressing toward a peace and well-being that continually elude us with every new outbreak of political, personal, and natural disaster. In the Christian community women and men experience that they are inspired and galvanized by God's Spirit to be wise and bold of speech and courageous in action, engaging the many tasks involved in renewing, healing, and liberating the world from the grip of sin and suffering. Toward this end they find their path along the way of Jesus, empowered by the narrative memory of his ways, his imaginative stories of God, his drinking the cup of pain and death, and the ringing hope and life that flow from this to their own life praxis. In the solidarity of community they experience at the same time that their own lives and the whole earth are gifts, at once tenacious and fragile, freely given from an unspeakably rich source of life that they mirror in their own creative generativity. The threefold, interwoven aspects of encounter with the one holy mystery point to God who is not a monolithic, undifferentiated block but a living mystery of relation, bent on the world.

God is God as Spirit-Sophia, the mobile, pure, people-loving Spirit who pervades every wretched corner, wailing at the waste, releasing power that enables fresh starts. Her energy quickens the earth to life, her beauty shines in the stars, her strength breaks forth in every fragment of shalom and renewal that transpires in arenas of violence and meaninglessness. From generation to generation she enters into holy souls, and not so holy ones, to make them friends of God and prophets, thereby making human beings allies of God's redeeming purpose. What we can say is this: Sophia-God dwells in the world at its center and at its edges, an active vitality crying out in labor, birthing the new creation. Fire, wind, water, and the color purple are her signs.[65]

God is God again as Jesus Christ, Sophia's child and prophet, and yes, Sophia herself personally pitching her tent in the flesh of humanity to teach the paths of justice. The shape of the historical life of this crucified prophet, risen from the dead, reveals the shape of Holy Wisdom's love for the world. It is a love that enters in and takes part, that revels at the feasting of outcasts in inclusive table community, that suffers relegation to the margins of defeat by dominating power, that wins a new kind of advance in the great "nevertheless" of the resurrection. What we can say is this: Sophia-God is irreversibly connected with the joy and anguish of human history, in the flesh; in the power of Spirit-Sophia Jesus now takes on a new communal identity as the risen Christ, the body of all those women and men who share in the transformation of the world through compassionate, delighting, and suffering love. In solidarity with his memory and empowered by the same Spirit, the little flock is configured into a sacrament of the world's salvation, empowered to shape communities of freedom and solidarity.

God is God again as unimaginable abyss of livingness, Holy Wisdom unknown and unknowable. She is the matrix of all that exists, mother and fashioner of all things, who herself dwells in light inaccessible. Without this still-point of the turning world there would be no dance, and there is only the dance;[66] without this silence there would be no music or word, which is where she can be heard; without this eclipse the rays of her fiery spirit would consume the world. What we can say is this: Holy Wisdom is a hidden God, absolute holy mystery. And this is an absolutely holy mystery of love, bent on the world's healing and liberation through all of history's reversals and defeats.

Holy Wisdom in Herself

Theology typically moves from speaking about God with us to God *in se*; from the functional to the ontological spheres; from the economic to the immanent Trinity. Here language is stretched to the breaking point, for God's inner Trinity remains a mystery, strictly speaking, even including the meaning of the word *inner*. All kinds of analogies from the psychological, social, and natural world have been pressed into service. They point to the livingness of God as a mystery of dynamic communion, related not only to the world but internally alive in relation as well. The traditional trinitarian names of Father, Son, and Spirit are correctly construed when it is remembered that they are symbols or figures of divine relations. Speaking from a perspective that prizes the equal humanity of women as *imago Dei*, *imago Christi*, *imago Spiritus*, we can enlist female metaphors in the task of speaking the unspeakable.

Holy Wisdom does not exist in lifeless self-identity but corresponds to herself in a threefold repetition by virtue of which she can freely encompass the world. Unoriginate source, unknowable mother of all, she forever comes forth from hiddenness as her distinct self-expressing Word. The Word is Wisdom in the movement outward from light inaccessible: "I came forth from the mouth of the Most High," Sophia says (Sir 24:3), and this eternal divine movement of self-distinction, when posited externally, grounds creation, becomes personally concrete in incarnation, and takes shape in ongoing fragmentary anticipations of the world's salvation. Simultaneously, Holy Wisdom forever unfurls as distinct self-bestowing Spirit. The Spirit, holy, intelligent, free-moving, steadfast, is Holy Wisdom in the spiraling movement of liberating love freely and inclusively given. So genuine is the historical gift of herself in the streaming forth of her Spirit that in grace we are not dealing with some third thing; rather, the giver herself is the gift.

Through Holy Wisdom's approach in incarnation and grace, then, we are enabled to speak about the reality of her own inner relatedness in terms of the livingness of unoriginate Mother, her beloved Child, and the Spirit of their mutual love; or the vitality of Wisdom's abyss, her personal word and her energy; or Sophia's eternal communion in personal mystery, hidden, uttered, and bestowed; or the relations of Spirit, Wisdom, and Mother in encircling movement. Each are in each, and all in each, and each in all, and all in all, and all are one. Holy Wisdom's livingness in three distinct movements, shapes, manners of subsistence, *hypostases*, modes of being, persons, has as its correlative a benefit and blessing for all who are lost and forsaken. For through the solidarity created by Wisdom incarnate on the cross and the liberating praxis set loose by Wisdom's Spirit, those who suffer are connected with divine life, the ultimate ground of hope. The historical world is interwoven in its time with the eternal livingness of Holy Wisdom.

This language too is allusive and indirect. Spoken this way, the triune symbol depicts in female metaphor a threefold reality, hidden in the fullness of her power, eternally uttering the distinct word of herself, and pouring forth her personal love. And the threefold movement, in eternal and hypostatic distinction, is all the one mystery. What is modeled in this language is the exuberant dignity and life-giving power of women, for here divine mystery, darkly known through creation, salvation, and the ongoing dialectic of presence and absence, appears in female gestalt, and divine blessing comes as a female gift. Such a symbol of God signifies for women the call to grow into the abundance of their human powers, to be creative, self-expressive, and loving together in ways that address human brokenness, violence, and the destruction of the earth. It points to the mystery of triune Holy Wisdom as *imago feminae*.

The Symbol Gives Rise to Thought

When language about the triune God in female metaphor is spoken from an explicitly feminist theological stance, it becomes clear that central aspects of classical trinitarian doctrine are strongly compatible with insights prized by this perspective. As the sustaining ground and ultimate reference point for the human and natural world, the trinitarian symbol for God may function in at least three beneficial ways. The God who is thrice personal signifies that the very essence of God is to be in relation, and thus relatedness rather than the solitary ego is the heart of all reality. Furthermore, this symbol indicates that the particular kind of relatedness than which nothing greater can be conceived is not one of hierarchy involving domination/subordination, but rather one of genuine mutuality in which there is radical equality while distinctions are respected. The trinitarian God, moreover, cannot be spoken about without reference to divine outpouring of compassionate, liberating love in the historical world of beauty, sin, and suffering, thus leading us to envision a God who empowers human praxis in these same directions. With this idea of God we have come just about as far from the isolated patriarchal God of Enlightenment theism as is possible.

Mutual Relation

Trinitarian speech is most obviously about three persons in God, but the notion of trinitarian persons in both ancient and modern senses conveys, and in fact is equivalent with, the category of relation. From the Cappadocian theologians through Augustine on up to Aquinas and beyond, the affirmation is made that what constitutes the trinitarian persons is their relationality. Aquinas crystallizes this development with his definition of the persons as "subsistent relations."[67] This means that the persons are persons precisely *as* mutual relations and not as anything else apart from their mutual bonding. Relationality is the principle that at once constitutes each trinitarian person as unique and distinguishes one from another. It is only by their reciprocal and mutually exclusive relationships that the divine persons are really distinct from each other at all. Their uniqueness arises only from their *esse ad*, from their being toward the others in relation. Holy Wisdom *is* a mystery of real, mutual relations.

The ontological priority of relation in the idea of the triune God has a powerful affinity with women's ownership of relationality as a way of being in the world. It furthermore challenges classical theism's typical concentration on singleness in God that has been so consistently reprised in a patriarchal sense. Since the persons are constituted by their relationships to each other, each is unintelligible except as connected with the others. Relation is the very principle of their being. No statement about one is true if taken in isolation from the other relations that equally constitute God's holy being. What this indicates in simple terms is that there is no absolute divine person. There are only the relative three: "They are always one in relation to the other, and neither the one nor the other alone."[68] At the heart of holy mystery is not monarchy but community; not an absolute ruler, but a threefold *koinōnia*.

How to characterize this relatedness? The mutuality experienced in genuine friendship offers one fertile clue. Friendship is the most free, the least possessive, the most mutual of relationships, able to cross social barriers in genuine reciprocal regard. Like all good relations friendship is characterized by mutual trust in the reliability of the other(s), but what makes it unique is that friends are fundamentally side-by-side in common interests, common delights, shared responsibilities. Mature friendship is open to the inclusion of others in the circle, assuming an essential stance of hospitality. Even in the case of parent and child, the relationship reaches its most interpersonally successful stage when the two negotiate the changes of the years to become related as adult friends, mutually giving and receiving across the generational line.

Classical theology hesitates to use friendship to model the trinitarian relationships, thinking that such a characterization sets up so much mutuality that the persons become indistinct. But if in view of the christological mystery it becomes clear that friendship with God and genuine human autonomy grow in direct and not inverse proportion, how much more intensely is it not the case that Holy Wisdom's own inner befriending is constitutive of "personal" distinctiveness. In love unity and differentiation are correlates rather than opposites of each other. Far from blurring individual uniqueness, adult friendship enhances it. As with other forms of healthy love, the stronger the bond, the more creative of personhood the relationship is. It is the peculiar genius of the relation of friendship to be able to create powerful and beneficent bonds of mutuality among distinct human beings and between people and other realities without regard for origin. Nor are true friends interchangeable with one another.

Jewish and Christian faith traditions carry a fundamental sense of God's friendliness toward the world, and from here Holy Wisdom's triune mystery can be spoken about in the language of friendship. The empowering Spirit befriends us in situations beautiful and wretched alike, making generation after generation into friends of God and prophets. Jesus-Sophia is the incarnation of divine friendship, hosting meals of inclusive table community and being hospitable to people of all kinds, even responding to prodding to widen his circle of care, as in the case of the Canaanite woman whose daughter was ill (Mt 15:21-28). He calls the women and men of his circle not children, not servants, not even disciples, but friends (Jn 15:15); one can only surmise that they called him friend in return. The creative love of Mother Wisdom reaches throughout the universe and all of its embedded individual lives with a friendship brimming with desire for the well-being of the whole of her creation. Human beings experience that the vivifying, liberating, and creating power of the holy mystery of God engages us in partnership to renew the earth and establish justice in such a way as to turn us also in an attitude of profound friendship toward all others, even those most unlike ourselves.

From these saving and challenging religious experiences the metaphor of Sophia-God as a Trinity of friendship can be spun out. Holy Wisdom, the horizon encircling all horizons, is a profound mystery of relatedness, whose essential livingness consists in the mutuality of friendship. The love of friendship is the very essence of God. Hidden Abyss, Word, and Spirit mutually indwell in a companionable communion of unimaginable strength. In Simone Weil's evocative words, "Pure friendship is an image of the original and perfect friendship that belongs to the Trinity, and is the very essence of God."[69] In this living friendliness the hypostases are not determined by their point of origin or rank in the order of procession but exist in each other in genuine mutuality. The image of a woman being herself, expressing herself, and befriending herself in an inclusive movement that issues in care for the world forms one remote human analogue. So too does the image of three women friends circling around together in the bonds of unbreakable friendship. In threefold "personal" distinctiveness Holy Wisdom embraces the world with befriending power as unreachable Abyss, as self-expressive Word that joins history in the flesh, as overflowing Spirit that seeks out the darkest, deadest places to quicken them to new life. The eternal friendship that is the triune mystery of Sophia opens to encompass the whole broken world through awakening friends of God to the praxis of compassion and freedom. Modeling the triune symbol on relations of friendship and speaking it in wisdom metaphors offers one alternative to the exclusive male imagery of the classical model and the hierarchical pattern of relationship that frequently though subtly attends it.

Radical Equality

While theology from the perspective of women's experience identifies relation as central to reality, it has also flagged the crisis in self-identity occasioned by the tendency of women to be poorly related to others, that is, to be so concentrated on the needs of others or so dependent on their direction that one's own personal center is diffused. Not just any kind of relationality is to be advocated. Early on, Rosemary Radford Ruether described the search for new patterns of relation on which women, rejecting both sexist stereotypes and androgyny, are embarked: "Authentic relationship is not a relation between two half selves, but between whole persons, when suppression and projection cease to distort the encounter. We seek a new concept of relationship which is not competitive or hierarchical but mutually enhancing."[70] The nature of the divine relations is such that the persons do not lose their distinctiveness by being so related. On the contrary, the relations not only bond the persons but establish them in personal uniqueness. With the usual male imagery Augustine makes this point well: "Wherefore if the father also is not something in respect to himself, then there is no one at all that can be spoken of relatively to something else."[71] Trinitarian relations do not occasion a homogenized blur. While mutual in quality they are mutually exclusive in the identity they give each person. Thus they constitute each one as distinct from each other, so that they cannot be interchanged. The triune symbol safeguards the idea that the distinctiveness or self-transcending uniqueness of each person is essential, belonging to the very being of God.

At this point classical doctrine and feminist insight again vigorously coalesce (strange bedfellows!). The centuries-long controversy over subordinationism left the tradition with the explicit affirmation that the persons of the Trinity, the subsistent relations, are radically equal though distinctly different from each other. The three persons are coeternal, just as fire cannot burn without its attendant brightness and warmth. They are coequal in divinity, greatness, and love. To use Augustine with his own images again:

[there is] so great an equality in that trinity, that not only is the Father not greater than the Son as regards divinity, but neither are the Father and Son together greater than the Holy Spirit; nor is each individual person, whichever it be of the three, less than the trinity itself.[72]

There is no subordination, no before or after, no first, second, and third, no dominant and marginalized. There is only "a trinity of persons mutually interrelated in a unity of equal essence."[73] The trinitarian symbol intimates a community of equals, so core to the feminist vision of ultimate shalom. It points to patterns of differentiation that are non-hierarchical, and to forms of relating that do not involve dominance. It models the ideal, reflected in so many studies of women's ways of being in the world, of a relational bonding that enables the growth of persons as genuine subjects of history in and through the matrix of community, and the flourishing of community in and through the praxis of its members. In this vision personal uniqueness flourishes not at the expense of relationship but through the power of profound companionship that respects differences and values them equally: an aim mirrored in the symbol of the Trinity.

Community in Diversity

When Holy Wisdom is spoken about as a *koinōnia* of mutual, equal relations of friendship, then divine unity itself must be understood in interrelational fashion. While the solitary God of classical theism is associated with a bare, static, monolithic kind of unity, a unity of divine nature, the triune symbol calls for a differentiated unity of variety or manifoldness in which there is distinction, inner richness, and complexity. How to envision such a oneness?

Eastern theology points to it with the Greek term *perichōrēsis*, a word that signifies a cyclical movement, a revolving action such as the revolution of a wheel.[74] Secured in the theological lexicon by the usage of John Damascene, this term evokes a coinherence of the three divine persons, an encircling of each around the others. It may be interpreted in two ways. One, more static sense, means something simply dwelling or resting within another. This sense appears in the Latin translation of the term as *circuminsessio*, from the words for sitting and seat (*sedere*, *sessio*). The other sense indicates more dynamically an interweaving of things with each other, leading to its translation into Latin as *circumincessio* (from *incedere*, "to permeate" or "encompass"). The net effect of these metaphors gives strong support to the idea that each person encompasses the others, is coinherent with the others in a joyous movement of shared life. Divine life circulates without any anteriority or posteriority, without any superiority or inferiority of one to the other. Instead there is a clasping of hands, a pervading exchange of life, a genuine circling around together that constitutes the permanent, active, divine *koinōnia*.

In explaining the sense of *perichōrēsis* Edmund Hill muses that it conjures up the rather lovely picture of an eternal divine round dance, noting that "indeed a pun in this sense is possible in Greek, where the word for 'dance round' or 'dance in a ring' is *perichoreuō*, with a short o in the middle."[75] This is not to say that the etymology of the theological term *perichōrēsis* lies in the Greek word *perichoreuō* (to dance around), for it does not. Rather, it comes from *perichōreō* which signifies cyclical movement or recurrence.[76] In what they connote if not in etymology, however, the two words are closely related, and a divine round dance modeled on the rhythmic, predictable motions of a country folk dance are one way to portray the mutual indwelling and encircling of God's holy mystery. I would extend the metaphor further to include the art form created by modern choreographers in their drive to express the anguish and ecstasy of the contemporary spirit. Dancers whirl and intertwine in unusual patterns; the floor is circled in seemingly chaotic ways; rhythms are diverse; at times all hell breaks loose; resolution is achieved unexpectedly. Music, light and shadow, color, and wonderfully supple motion coalesce in dancing that is not smoothly predictable and repetitive, as is a round dance, and yet is just as highly disciplined. Its order is more complex.[77] Casting the metaphor in yet another direction, we can say that the eternal flow of life is stepped to the contagious rhythms of spicy salsas, merengues, calypsos, or reggaes where dancers in free motion are yet bonded in the music. Perichoretic movement summons up the idea of all three distinct persons existing in each other in an exuberant movement of equal relations: an excellent model for human interaction in freedom and other regards. Precisely as community in diversity Holy Wisdom has the capacity to be the ground of the turning world.

In the end it becomes clear that one way of speaking alone is never adequate. Psychological and social models, male and female images or both together, personal and impersonal references — every one contributes insight that the others do not, for God's livingness moves in a saving relationality that escapes our imagination. In this light even personalist language drives beyond itself to include cosmic shapes. From this realm another model suggests itself which is compatible with feminist perspectives. Using geometric figures, Walter Kasper suggests that classical trinitarian theology of the East can be illustrated by a straight line: divinity proceeds from Father through Son to Spirit, and thence on to the world. The Western view meanwhile, is better described by a triangle or circle, the Spirit closing the divine processions in reference back to the Father.[78] Being neither classical Greeks nor Latins, let us envision neither a straight line nor a self-enclosed circle but a triple helix. Biologically the double helix is the carrier of the genetic code of all human life. In this sense it is one of the most mysterious, powerful shapes in all creation. The strands of the helix do not originate from each other but are simply there together, not statically but moving in a dance of separation and recombination, which creates new persons. The image of a triple helix intensifies this life-giving movement. It connotes the unfathomable richness of holy triune mystery, inwardly related as a unity of equal movements, each of whom is distinct and all of whom together are one source of life, new just order, and quickening surprise in an infinite mix. Analogous to Wisdom's joyous movement of shared life, or perichoretic dance, the triple helix twirls around in a never-ending series of moves, which includes human partners and their decisions for good or ill, toward the fullness of shalom for all creatures, human beings and the earth, especially the most discarded. Such a model soon transcends itself toward personalist categories once again, as do brightness, the flashing, and the fire and all such images taken from the natural world. The point of all of these theological constructions is not to describe the inner being of God but to articulate the radical livingness of God's holy mystery encountered in multifaceted ways.

The mutual relation, radical equality, and communal unity in diversity inherent in the triune symbol preclude the patriarchal idea of God as a self-enclosed absolute. Instead, Sophia-God's holy mystery is spoken about as self-communicating mystery of relation, an unimaginable, open communion in herself that opens out freely to include even what is not herself. The circular dynamism within God spirals inward, outward, forward toward the coming of a world into existence, not out of necessity but out of the free exuberance of overflowing friendship. Spun off and included as a partner in the divine dance of life, the world for all its brokenness and evil is destined to reflect the triune reality, and already does embody it in those sacramental, anticipatory moments of friendship, healing, and justice breaking through.

Speaking about the Triune God

Speaking about the Trinity expresses belief in one God who is not a solitary God but a communion in love marked by overflowing life. In no way is it a picture model that signifies secret information about the inner life of God, but a genuine symbol arising from divine-human relation in this ambiguous world and pointing to dimensions of that relation that we trust are grounded in no less a reality than the very mystery of God. Its language is analogical at all times: Holy Wisdom is like a Trinity, like a threefoldness of personal relation. The relations may be modeled on human analogies taken from what is known about the interaction of male and female, parent and child, lover and beloved, friend and friend. Through the ages different interpretations have sought to release the symbol's religious power creating psychological or social analogies, using terms such as persons or modes of being, bringing to bear the models of a self-communicating or self-revealing power or of a loving community. The point of all of these theological constructions is to give voice to fragmentary saving experiences as experiences of *God*, in the living tradition of the Christian story.

In the end, the Trinity provides a symbolic picture of totally shared life at the heart of the universe. It subverts duality into multiplicity. Mutual relationship of different equals appears as the ultimate paradigm of personal and social life. The Trinity as pure relationality, moreover, epitomizes the connectedness of all that exists in the universe. Relation encompasses and constitutes the web of reality and, when rightly ordered, forms the matrix for the flourishing of all creatures, both human beings and the earth. As Anne Carr summarizes in lovely cadences:

The mystery of God as Trinity, as final and perfect sociality, embodies those qualities of mutuality, reciprocity, cooperation, unity, peace in genuine diversity that are feminist ideals and goals derived from the inclusivity of the gospel message. The final symbol of the God as Trinity thus provides women with an image and concept of God that entails qualities that make God truly worthy of imitation, worthy of the call to radical discipleship that is inherent in Jesus' message.[79]

If the image of God is the ultimate reference point for the values of a community, then the structure of the triune symbol stands as a profound critique, however little noticed, of patriarchal domination in church and society. The power of an interpersonal communion characterized by equality and mutuality, which it signifies, still flashes like a beacon through a dark night, rather than shining like a daytime sun. Human community in a relationship of equals has yet to be realized save in isolated and passing instances. Yet the central notion of divine Trinity, symbolizing not a monarch ruling from isolated splendor but the relational character of Holy Wisdom points inevitably in that direction, toward a community of equals related in mutuality. The mystery of Sophia-Trinity must be confessed as critical prophecy in the midst of patriarchal rule.

Chapter 11

ONE LIVING GOD: SHE WHO IS

Blessed is She who spoke and the world became. Blessed is She.
Blessed is She who in the beginning gave birth.
Blessed is She who says and performs.
Blessed is She who declares and fulfills.
Blessed is She whose womb covers the earth. . . .
Blessed is She who lives forever, and exists eternally.
Blessed is She who redeems and saves. Blessed is Her Name.

— Sabbath Prayer[1]

"No Real Relation" and Women's Sensibility

As already noted, the sequence characteristic of classical theism separates the question of the nature of divine being, codified in the treatise *De Deo Uno*, from the historical experience of the mystery of God come to expression in trinitarian language, and places it prior to the study of God's multifaceted relation to the world. Consequently, the one divine essence as a whole is spoken about in isolation from God's own intrinsic personal relationality, and metaphysical properties are assigned to that essence in abstraction from God's free, historic involvement with the struggle and life of the world. The result in many a Western imagination is the notion that there are really four elements to be looked at in the study of God, namely, one divine nature plus three divine persons.

Furthermore, classical thought classifies relation in the category of accident, thereby rendering it unsuitable for predication about divine nature in which nothing accidental inheres. Thus while the persons may be relational, relationship with the world is banned from God's essential nature. The relation between God and the world is said to be "real" on the world's side toward God but not "real" in a mutual way from God to the world. Aquinas, who exemplifies this view, uses the example of a column that can be spoken of relationally as being "on the right" only if it stands to the right side of an animal, in which case the relation is not really in the column but in the animal:

224

Since therefore God is outside the whole order of creation, and all creatures are ordered to Him, and not conversely, it is manifest that creatures are really related to God Himself; whereas in God there is no real relation to creatures, but we speak about God as related inasmuch as creatures are referred to Him.[2]

The effective history of theological speech about this nonrelational God, supported by rigorous philosophical argument in a patriarchal system, invites widespread repugnance today. Such language in its multifaceted use has bequeathed to modern persons the image of a God fundamentally uninvolved with the world, a God who is, in Walter Kasper's pointed phrase, a "solitary narcissistic being who suffers from his own completeness."[3] This God is an "indifferent metaphysical iceberg," as W. Norris Clarke would have it, a transcendent giver to be sure, but one whose being is unreceptive in turn to the life of the world.[4] Clarke who has wrestled long and honorably with this built-in problem of scholastic theology concludes: "The Thomistic metaphysical doctrine that there are no 'real relations' in God to the world should be dropped — not denied perhaps but quietly shelved as being no longer illuminating."[5]

From a feminist perspective the denial of divine relation to the world codified in the highly specialized scholastic language reflects the disparagement of reciprocal relation characteristic of patriarchy in its social and intellectual expressions. If the ideal is the potent, all-sufficient ego in charge of events and independent of the need for others, then to be connected in mutuality with others introduces "deficiency" in the form of interdependence, vulnerability, and risk. Genuine mutuality threatens any form of domination, including the paternalistic ordering of things. Thus it is not accidental that classical theism insists on a concept of God with no real relation to the world, even when this is interpreted as an affirmation of divine transcendence. Unrelated and unaffected by the world, such a theistic God limns the ultimate patriarchal ideal, the solitary, dominant male.

But there is another human experience that finds self-transcendence enacted precisely through affinity rather than quarantine; another interpretation of fullness of being that includes rather than excludes genuine, reciprocal relations with others who are different; another pattern of life that values compassionate connectedness over separation; another understanding of power that sees its optimum operation in collegial and empowering actions rather than through controlling commands from on high. Women typically witness to deep patterns of affiliation and mutuality as constitutive of their existence and indeed of the very grain of existence itself. From this perspective the image of an unrelated or only superficially related God is a distortion.

Before the God of no real relation disappears from view altogether, however, something is to be retrieved that is of benefit to feminist reflection. By laying bare the precise, eccentric meaning of the term "real relation" when used in this context, contemporary interpreters of Aquinas provide an intriguing clue to something valuable that must not be lost. The text itself discloses the meaning that is intended by the use of such a phrase. God, writes Aquinas, "does not produce the creature by necessity of His nature, but by His intellect and will, as is explained above. Therefore there is no real relation in God to the creature."[6] Seen against its complex philosophical background, "real" here has the narrow technical meaning of "belonging to nature," that is, of happening out of necessity or according to a natural process. Since, however, God creates creatures not necessarily but in an exuberance of divine freedom, then relationship to a world is not a must. Hence in this system to say that God's relation to the world is not "real" but rather in the order of personal intention (*relatio rationis*) is language that upholds divine freedom and the gift-character of creation. It is to assert that God relates to the world not because of a requirement that is mandated by nature but freely, out of love.[7]

It is the emphasis on freedom in personal relation that must not slip from view in the search for right speaking about God and the world. While emerging feminist ontology is articulating the insight that no reality can be construed apart from its constitutive network of relationships, feminist wisdom also emphasizes the importance for every woman of centering herself, affirming herself, and choosing her own life's directions. The strategic reasons for this are to cultivate women's underdeveloped sense of themselves as active subjects of history and to counteract culturally induced habits of drift and self-denigration. Emphasis on respecting difference, one's own and that of others, deepens this trajectory of autonomy, creating a condition that nourishes mature relationship in freedom. "Without the love of the other as other, made possible only when self is distinct from other," argues Catherine Keller, " 'love' turns out upon closer inspection to be a case of egoistic self-love, which attempts to encase the other within the self."[8] Women seek to articulate an extensively relational self grounded in a community of free reciprocity. What is slowly coming to light is a new construal of the notion of the person, neither a self-encapsulated ego nor a diffuse self denied, but selfhood on the model of relational autonomy. Discourse about God from a perspective of women's experience, therefore, names toward a relational God who loves in freedom. It prizes a genuine dialectic between God and the world that safeguards difference while preserving connection.

Useful though the precise retrieval of historical meaning in the "no real relation" idea may be, however, the original phrasing is too esoteric to contemporary ears to serve further speech. No amount of explanation suffices to overcome the instant and deep impact on the human spirit today of talk about God who has no real relation to the world. And in truth, Aquinas insists that having no real relation to the world rightly places God "outside" the whole order of creation, beyond mutuality in any sense. Medieval and early modern theology emphasized this sense of the phrasing much more than it did divine freedom from necessity. The notion has outlived whatever usefulness it might have had.

Divine Nature: A Communion

Keeping a finger on the pulse of the religious experiences whose interpretation gives rise to speech about the trinitarian, relational God in the first place, contemporary theology has become aware that, given the presupposition that there is only one God, God's being is by nature relational. As Augustine noticed, even essential things said of the three divine persons are spoken in a way that connotes relationalty. "But from this is educed a most unexpected sense: that essence itself is not essence, or at least that, when it is called essence, not essence but something relative is intimated."[9] Trinitarian communion itself is primordial, not something to be added after the one God is described, for there is no God who is not relational through and through.

The mutual coinherence, the dancing around together of Spirit, Wisdom and Mother; or of mutual Love, Love from Love, and unoriginate Love; or of the three divine persons — this defines who God is as God. There is no divine nature as a fourth thing that grounds divine unity in difference apart from relationality. Rather, being in communion constitutes God's very essence. Divine nature exists as an incomprehensible mystery of relation. *What* the divine nature is is constituted by *who* God is in triune relationality without remainder.

The axiom that the economic Trinity is the immanent Trinity and vice-versa, so productive for theological thought, can therefore be extended. If relation in God is not posited accidentally but is constitutive of divine nature, then the immanent Trinity is the nature of God and vice-versa. "There is not some fourth reality 'behind,' as it were, the Father, Word, and Pneuma," argues William Hill; "there is no divine nature subsistent in itself in addition to the three Persons."[10] For all that he divided the treatises on God one and three, Aquinas did see this clearly: "relation really existing in God is really the same as His essence, and only differs in its mode of intelligibility . . . in God relation and essence do not differ from each other, but are one and the same."[11] In Catherine LaCugna's succinct paraphrase, "To be God is to be to-be-relationally."[12] Nature and relation in God differ in our conceptuality because, historical and finite, we tend to consider things first under one aspect, then under another. But for God as God, divine nature is fundamentally relational.

Here is another arresting point of coherence between contemporary retrieval of Christian tradition and feminist theological interest. Being related is at the very heart of divine being. God's being is not an enclosed, egocentric self-regard but is identical with an act of free communion, always going forth and receiving in. At the deepest core of reality is a mystery of personal connectedness that constitutes the very livingness of God. The category of relation thus serves as a heuristic tool for bringing to light not just the mutuality of trinitarian persons but the very nature of the holy mystery of God herself. Divine unity exists as an intrinsic *koinōnia* of love, love freely blazing forth, love not just as a divine attitude, affect, or property but as God's very nature: "God is Love" (1 Jn 4:16).

Bespeaking God's Solidarity with the World

The nature of God as inherently *communio* makes it possible to speak of how the mystery of God is capable of relating to what is creaturely and laced with history. Incomprehensible depth of personal communion, Sophia-God is free to create the historical universe and relate to it not out of necessity but out of overflowing graciousness. In so doing, Holy Wisdom whose very being is relational dwells not in isolation from the world nor in ontological opposition to it but in reciprocal relation, sustaining its life, continuously resisting destructive powers of nonbeing, appearing in the myriad shapes of the historical praxis of freedom, approaching from the future to attract it toward shalom. Reflecting its Creator, the universe has relationship as its fundamental code. Hence Sophia-God and the historical world exist in mutual, if asymmetrical, relation. Insofar as each is directed toward the other with reciprocal interest and intimacy, the relation is mutual. Insofar as the world is dependent on God in a way that God is not on the world, the relation is not strictly symmetrical. God in the world and the world in God: this is one way to summarize these radically distinct yet mutually related realities.

God in the World

Most Christian language, biblical, liturgical, catechetical, theological, draws attention to divine presence and action in the world. In line with the author of Ephesians who affirms that there is one God "who is above all and through all and in all" (Eph 4:6), Christians attest to God's presence in the midst of beauty and the coming of justice, lean on the strength of this presence in the midst of struggle and suffering, mourn its absence and even rail against it when radical evil casts divine nearness into the dark.

The one relational God, precisely in being utterly transcendent, not limited by any finite category, is capable of the most radical immanence, being intimately related to everything that exists. And the effect of divine drawing near and passing by is always to empower creatures toward life and well-being in the teeth of the antagonistic structures of reality. Exemplifying the Catholic imagination at work, Aquinas works with a fine analogy to explain this. God's presence among creatures touches them with power the way fire ignites what it brushes. We know that fire is present wherever something catches on fire. Everything that exists does so by participation in the fire of divine being. Everything that acts is energized by divine act. Everything that brings something else into being does so by sharing in divine creative power. Since something is present wherever it operates, and since God operates in the existence and working of all things, we can avow that God is present in all things.[13]

The trinitarian template discloses this one God in the world in multifaceted ways. Spirit-Sophia who blows where she wills, pervading the world with vitalizing and liberating power, brings divine presence in the world to its widest universality. Jesus-Sophia, preaching the nearness of the reign of God, embodying in his own relationships with the poor and outcast the compassionate love of heaven for earth, being crucified for it, and raised to glory in the Spirit as pledge of the future for all, brings divine presence in the world to the point of its most precise particularity. Holy Wisdom, the unoriginate Mother of all things, upholding the world as the generating and continuously sustaining source of the being and potential for new being of all creatures, radicalizes divine presence in dark mystery.

For the analogical imagination, the fact that God's creative, liberating power can be effective in everything that exists does not diminish the autonomous power of the creature. On the contrary, such power increases in direct proportion to one's communion with the source of all power. Similarly, the glory of God is being manifest to the degree that creatures are most radically and fully themselves. Consequently, divine presence in the world should not be spoken about in terms of a suffocating, overwhelming shadow but rather as the ground of freedom itself. Similarly, referring to God in the world does not connote an occasional intrusion or intervention, God, as it were, "perforating an otherwise closed system from without," as Karl Rahner phrases it. Rather, religious discourse about divine presence should point to "the infinite incomprehensible mystery and absolute future, present intrinsically in the world all along as that which provides its ultimate consummation and so sustains its movement towards this from within."[14] God is in the world as ground, support, and goal of its historical, struggling existence.

The World in God

All Christian speech about God, including classical theism with its heavy stress on transcendence, affirms that God dwells intimately at the heart of the world. But it is quite otherwise with the question of whether the indwelling is reciprocal, that is, whether the world is likewise present in God. The spectrum of theological options includes at least two ways of saying no to that question and one way of coherently thinking through a yes.

For classical theism the world exists always and everywhere "outside" divine being. That the world might dwell within God is virtually an ontological impossibility, given the structure of theism's idea of God as Pure Act, intrinsically incapable of being affected by anything created. While Aquinas, for example, makes an occasional intriguing reference to the fact that people speak as if it were so, writing that "by a certain similitude to corporeal things, it is said that all things are in God, inasmuch as they are contained by Him,"[15] such a notion never functions significantly in his thought. Within the constraints of this system, if the world did make a difference to God, it would necessarily entail diminishment to divinity itself, for by definition divine being must transcend any outside influence. The divorce between God, cast in terms of a divine nature with no real relation to anything created, and the finite world quickly shifts into an unbridgeable dualism, as the history of classical theism demonstrates.

At the opposite end of the spectrum lies classical pantheism, the notion that God and the world are virtually identical, existing in so intertwined a way that divine being is the substance or essence of all things. Here the radical distinction between unoriginate mystery and creature is blurred. The infinite God merges with the finite being of things, thus ceasing to be their creative, transcending ground. Correspondingly, there is no substantial independence or freedom in anything finite, since the divine is the essence of all essences. While divine immanence is clearly maintained, this concentration on divine nearness results in such a lack of differentiation between God and the world that no true relation is actually possible.

A feminist perspective that prizes mutuality in relations quickly parts company with classical theism, critiquing its isolationist and dualist patterns. Reflection arising from women's experience also finds pantheism wanting. The culturally induced tendency for women to submerge themselves in the "all" of a man or family or institution to the detriment of their own genuine personhood is a perennial temptation, as is plasticity to the direction of dominant others rather than free self-actualization. In these circumstances, the pantheistic paradigm that holds God to be totally identified with the world is a suffocating deception. Insofar as some form of freedom-in-relation is a hallmark of the feminist ideal as well as of mature human personhood, a model that combines the core insights of both theism and pantheism is sought, one that safeguards the radical distinction between God and the world while also promoting their mutual, if asymmetrical, relationship.

A third position, variously known as dialectical theism, neoclassical theism, or, more typically, panentheism, offers another, more congenial model. As defined in *The Oxford Dictionary of the Christian Church*, panentheism is "The belief that the Being of God includes and penetrates the whole universe, so that every part of it exists in Him, but (as against pantheism) that this Being is more than, and is not exhausted by, the universe."[16] Here is a model of free, reciprocal relation: God in the world and the world in God while each remains radically distinct. The relation is mutual while differences remain and are respected. As with classical theism no proportion between finite creatures and divine mystery is set up; the disparity between them is absolute. But the absolute difference between Creator and creature is encircled by God who is all in all.

If theism weights the scales in the direction of divine transcendence and pantheism overmuch in the direction of immanence, panentheism attempts to hold onto both in full strength. Divine transcendence is a wholeness that includes all parts, embracing the world rather than excluding it, as the etymology of panentheism, "all-in-God," suggests, while divine immanence is given as the world's inmost dynamism and goal. Transcendence and immanence are correlative rather than opposed. At root this notion is guided by an incarnational and sacramental imagination that eschews any fundamental competition between God and the world in favor of the power of mutually enhancing relation. As a working paradigm panentheism would be false only if God is dissolved into the world or the world identified with God in some monistic fashion. Otherwise it is a view that operates with a certain "logic of the infinite," as Karl Rahner observes, whereby connectedness between creatures and their Creator does not diminish the difference between them but rather enhances it in direct proportion to the strength of their union.[17]

This fundamental vision of mutual coinherence in which Holy Wisdom is present throughout the universe while everything is embraced in her inclusive freedom and compassionate love is highly compatible with feminist values. The accent on divine relatedness to the world overcomes the isolation of the patriarchal God of classical theism. At the same time positing relation as the principle of self-distinction thwarts the tendency toward absorption that marks the stereotypical feminine of pantheism. When in the freedom of love Holy Wisdom chooses to share her life with others and so creates, and there is no "time" when this will of divine love is not the case, then the inner trinitarian relatedness of divine mystery circles outward in genuine, free, personal relation to the world. It is precisely this divine living embrace that frees the world into its own integrity and self-transcendence. What this model brings into view is a dialectic in which human beings are created *capax infiniti* and the mystery of God perdures as *capax finiti*, capable of mutual relation with what is not divine. The world then, although not necessary in a hypothetical sense, does make a difference to God. She would not be creator, vivifier, redeemer, liberator, companion, and future without it.

Further light is shed on panentheism's intelligibility by an imaginative exercise dear to philosophers. Imagine the infinite and the finite together, although, granted, the infinite is unimaginable. Where should one draw the line that divides them? To draw such a line would be to delimit what is infinite, and it would then not be infinite at all. To transpose this example into theology, where is the line that separates God and the world? The boundary between God and the finite world is only creation's boundary, not God's, if God is incomprehensible mystery beyond every category. To press this point in a koan reminiscent of Zen, "What is the boundary if only one country is bounded?"[18] We cannot draw a line and say, "Thus far shall you come, and no farther" (Jb 38:11), as the Creator originally said to the sea, if the One we are addressing is the sheer livingness of the mystery of God. She cannot be so constricted. Rather, she is like the boundless sea encompassing a tiny island. And so, continuing with spatial metaphors, God cannot be circumscribed over against the finite world, for this would be an unwarranted and indeed impossible restriction. Rather, the universe, both matter and spirit, is encompassed by the matrix of the living God in an encircling which generates uniqueness, futurity, and self-transcendence in the context of the interconnected whole. Holy Wisdom transcendingly embraces all of finite existence in an inclusive relation that sets it free and calls it to communal, personal, and cosmic shalom. Arriving at this well-being is thwarted by the evil of radical suffering and sin, both personal and social, that destroys the good of others and leaves relationships in tatters. Therefore the congruence of the parties in this relationship occurs at the point of praxis, God being present in history in the myriad shapes of freedom and love. But the very possibility of resistance, ongoing fidelity, and renewal exists because of the power of the relation between God and the world that is stronger than death.

Female Metaphors

In a unique way the paradigm of panentheism opens speech about God to a fruitful use of metaphors gleaned from women's existence, especially maternal and friendship imagery.

To begin with, consider the notion of the world's dwelling in God. One of the most intriguing ways of explaining how this can be so is found in the kabbalistic doctrine of the self-limitation of God, that spins out an elliptical narrative about God's special preparation for the creation of the world.[19] In the beginning a dilemma exists because, since the infinite God is the fullness of being, boundless, there is no room for anything finite to exist. For the world to be possible at all some space must be hollowed out for finite being to exist in its own integrity, without being swallowed up by God's overwhelming infinity. In the act of creating, therefore, divinity withdraws. God makes room for creation by constricting divine presence and power. There is a contraction or concentration or infolding of the divine being in order to clear a space for the world to dwell. Into the resulting void shaped by divine self-limitation the creative word is spoken and the world is brought forth. Thus creation "outside" of God nevertheless remains "in" God, in the primordial space made possible by the self-contraction of the infinite. God's generous self-emptying is the condition for the possibility of finite existence in its own autonomy, while the difference between Creator and creature is embraced by the One who is all in all.

Variously printed as *zimsum* or *tsimtsum*, the idea of God's self-limitation in creation has recently gained currency in Christian theology where it is linked with the divine *kenōsis* paradigmatically enacted in Christ Jesus,

> who, though he was in the form of God,
> did not regard equality with God as something to be clung to
> but emptied himself, taking the form of a slave,
> being born in human likeness.
> And being found in human form, he humbled himself

> and became obedient to the point of death —
> even death on a cross. (Phil 2:6–8)

Within the Christian story it is possible to see that divine self-emptying in the incarnation and passion of Christ is not an uncharacteristic divine action. Rather, this historical moment discloses the pattern of Sophia-God's love always and everywhere operative. Divine freely self-giving love did not begin with God's personal entering into human history but is so typical that it plays out at the dawn of creation itself. "Creation is an abdication," writes Simone Weil; "God has emptied himself. This means that both the Creation and Incarnation are included with the Passion."[20] From a Thomistic perspective William Hill concurs: "the deepest implication of St. Thomas's understanding of the reality of the finite order is that it exists only 'in' God; in the creative act God empties himself out kenotically, as it were, making room 'within' himself for the nondivine."[21] In his own narrative retelling of the trinitarian history of God with the world, Jürgen Moltmann makes the same point: "God 'withdraws himself from himself to himself' in order to make creation possible.... This self-restricting love is the beginning of that self-emptying of God which Philippians 2 sees as the divine mystery of the Messiah."[22] Such a theologoumenon, implying that *kenōsis* characterizes the very essence of God, points effectively to cosmic generosity rather than divine stinginess at the heart of the world.[23]

What is striking about these and virtually all discussions of the kenotic, self-limiting God is the continuous, almost exclusive use of male imagery and pronouns for God. Moltmann does note that unlike the story of God's creation by the word which is best expressed in masculine metaphors — itself a highly debatable position — this notion of creation by making room is better interpreted by motherly categories;[24] but his subsequent writing does not do so. Such exclusive use of male metaphors is a blatant anomaly because to be so structured that you have room inside yourself for another to dwell is quintessentially a female experience. To have another actually living and moving and having being in yourself is likewise the province of women. So too is the experience of contraction as a condition for bringing others to life in their own integrity.

Quite literally every human person yet born has lived and moved and had their being inside a woman, for the better part of the year it took for them to be knit together. This reality is the paradigm without equal for the panentheistic notion of the coinherence of God and the world. To see the world dwelling in God is to play variations on the theme of women's bodiliness and experience of pregnancy, labor and giving birth. Correlatively, this symbol lifts up precisely those aspects of women's reality so abhorred in classical Christian anthropology — the female body and its procreative functions — and affirms them as suitable metaphor for the divine. More than suitable in fact, for they wonderfully evoke the mystery of creative, generative love that encircles the struggling world, making possible its life and growth in the face of the power of nonbeing and evil. As some of our poets now say, "in her we live and move and have our being" (gloss on Acts 17:28).

Maternal metaphors, as is the case with all metaphors, eventually reach a point where they are not applicable. In the course of life we are born and grow up, relinquishing childlike dependence upon our mothers as a condition for mature personhood. Another metaphor system needs to come into play in order to evoke mutual indwelling in the fullness of personal autonomy.

The feminist retrieval of the power of friendship turns thinking in this direction. Genuine friends, whether of the same or different sex, age, race, or class, whether married to each other or not, whether family members, neighbors, professional colleagues, or any of the myriad combinations possible to human friendship, dwell within each other, in each other's hearts and minds and lives, with an affection that engenders broad scope for individuality to develop. The better the friendship the more potent its capacity to generate creativity and hope, as experiences of trust, care, delight, forgiveness, and passion for common interests and ideas flow back and forth. In addition to its person-creating power, the love of mature friendship has the potential to press beyond its own circle to offer blessing to others. Befriending the brokenhearted, the poor, or the damaged earth with its threatened creatures are but some of the ways the strength of this relation can overflow.

To see God and the world existing in a relationship of friendship, each indwelling the other, has deep affinity with women's experience. It also corresponds to several key biblical themes. Wisdom's path is one, for a characteristic activity of Sophia is friend making: "From generation to generation she passes into holy souls and makes them friends of God, and prophets" (Wis 7:27). Being friends and prophets are not antithetical conditions, for entering into friendship with God sets up a mutuality of interests that turns God's friends to enact her word of challenge and comfort in situations of suffering and distress. Friendship with God in Christ is another. At the climactic supper in John's Gospel, Jesus calls his disciples no longer servants but friends. Such they are not only to him but to God, sharing in the mutual knowledge and indwelling characteristic of Jesus' own relation with God (Jn 15:15; 17:21). What comes to light in these traditions, wisdom and Johannine, and in the

Jewish and Christian mystical traditions that reprise and develop them, is a powerful friendliness between Sophia-God and the world. Their mutual relation is structured not according to the model of domination-submission but of genuine partnership in the freedom of difference. God dwells within the world and the world dwells in her: when this relationship is endorsed by human beings, they become as friends who make passionate common cause for the well-being of the whole and each one.

Divine Being, Sheer Liveliness

If the relational God and the world coinhere in mutual if asymmetrical reciprocity, is it appropriate to speak about God in the singular and as such? Speaking about God without including the historical world in every sentence does not mean that the relation no longer exists nor that it is not vitally important in shaping discourse about God. But there is theological legitimacy to focusing solely on God, who is never not related to the world, and asking about the singularity and character of divine mystery beyond all telling.

Pondering the nature of God from the vantage point of earth and its variety of creatures, classical theology, as exemplified in Aquinas, uses the term "being" to define what best specifies that mystery, namely, incomprehensible liveliness. In God essence and existence are one and the same so that God's very nature is *esse*, to be. Everything that exists does so through participation in divine being, given to each thing as its own discrete finite act of existence. God is self-subsisting being, being itself, *ipsum esse subsistens*.[25]

The difficulties with this notion of being today are legion. We in the West inherit the legacy of nominalism that collapsed being into a genus and so rendered it incapable of disclosing the living mystery of God. Even Thomistic neo-scholastic metaphysics spoke of being in substantialist terms, giving rise to the impression that it signifies some kind of objective essence. The notion of being, moreover, when traditionally attributed to God, does not immediately call to mind anything relational, further compromising its effectiveness. To most Western minds today the language of being connotes something static, limited, abstract and impersonal, and thus unfit to signal the dynamic and inherently relational nature of incomprehensible mystery. At first glance it certainly seems of limited usefulness in bringing forth speech about God coherent with feminist reflection.

Yet a long philosophical and theological tradition from Philo to the early Mary Daly has found that an intuition of being arising from the actual existence of things and from their struggle toward existence against the forces of evil and nonbeing provides a choice analogue for speaking about God. I suggest that the ontological language of being has the advantage of providing an all-inclusive category for reality at large, leaving nothing out, and thereby entailing that the cosmos does not slip from view by too heavy a concentration on the human dilemma. Connected with the idea of God, language about being indicates that all things that exist are related to God as the source of their existence, and hence to each other. It is thus a code word for the universe's status as creation. Predicated of God, being symbolizes sheer livingness, which is also a going forth, an unimaginable act of communion that issues in everything. It is thus a code word for God as source of the whole universe, past, present, and yet to come, and as power that continuously resists evil. In this light the notion of being has a contribution to make to feminist discourse about God.

Philosophical Dimension

Our intuition of being arises from both negative and positive experiences. Though classical discussion deals almost exclusively with the latter, the idea of being is born in the dialectic of the negative contrast experience as much as, if not more than, in the analogical movement of mind from the wonder of things. Powerful negative experiences of the destruction of life and goodness call forth protest from deep within the human spirit, a crying out in anguish against the evil that devastates. In acts that can never be underestimated, people resist and strive for an increase of life and freedom. These moments of a definitive *no* to the denigration of creation offer a glimpse of being as though in a mirror. Being is darkly surmised in contrast to the suffering, as what should be there but is lacking. It is affirmed in contrast to the power of nonbeing which is having its day. As the struggle against wretchedness continues, being is espied as a horizon of promise. Because there is something more, despair is encompassed. From these experiences being can be articulated as a *puissance*, a force that empowers resistance to evil and radical suffering.

In a happier sense the notion of being arises from amazement at the world, from wonder that anything exists at all. This wonder assumes the character of a "metaphysical shock" when the possibility that there might have been nothing at all, including the one who is doing the wondering, dawns.[26] Thought seeks out what it is that energizes all things to exist and arrives at the idea of being, a notion like no other.

One way to catch its meaning is to enumerate everything that is found in the world such as stars, animals, persons, mountains, and so on. Clearly one would not add being to this list for it is not a particular thing in its own right and does not belong in the same category as the things listed. "Yet in some way," John Macquarrie points out, "being is common to all the beings."[27] It is the very actuality of things, their act of being there at all.

Again, one can imagine something white, round, and hard, able to fit into the palm of a hand. The difference between the ball thus sum-moned up in imagination and a ball that someone is actually holding is named in the term being. It is something that cannot be classified along with whiteness, roundness, and hardness, possibly the same in both cases, but is seen in the fact that the ball in your hand really exists. Being, then, is not a property such as color, shape, weight or size, or even all of them taken together, which determines the particular indi-viduality of the ball. Rather it is the ball's sheer actuality, its existence in its own right, the act which gives all of its properties existence in reality.

Being evokes a most dynamic and living although elusive reality, the act of being-there of things. When spoken with regard to the world and all its creatures, it signifies neither a particular being nor the sum of beings, neither a property of things nor a whole class of things, neither a substance nor an accidental quantity or quality inhering in a substance. Not belonging to any usual category of thought, it is an idea that is sui generis. It points to the reality that undergirds all else, in virtue of which everything exists.

Theological Dimension

When this philosophical notion is reprised in theological speech to re-fer to God, it signifies that the mystery encompassing the world is more being-ful than all finite creatures combined; in fact, that God is the fire of sheer aliveness whose act of being overflows, bringing the universe into existence and empowering it to be. This language carries the compan-ion recognition that all things are on fire with existence by participation in God's holy being which is unquenchable.

Two explicit stipulations are particularly apt at this point, given the blind alleys down which being has wandered in the history of theology. The first is that in its pristine theological sense, being is not a concept to which the category of relation is external. The being of God that we are speaking of is essentially love. God's being is identical with an act of communion, not with monolithic substance, and so is inherently relational.

The second qualification to be remembered is that being, when predicated of God, does not refer to a specific property or attribute of any kind, nor does it indicate some sort of superior genus of which

God is the primary member. To affirm that God is "being itself" is precisely to deny that God is a particular being located on an ontological continuum that also includes the world. Every time this is overlooked the misunderstanding transpires whereby God is reduced to an element within a larger whole, made part of the totality of reality. Divinity is captured in the category of being, just one bigger and better instance of being itself. When this happens, Eriugena's insistence that God is "the One who is more than being" rings true.[28] So too does Abraham Heschel's insight that "The statement 'God is' is an understatement."[29] God who is pure being transcends any genus, any concept, even being itself if that be considered an overarching category. The horizon itself cannot be present within the horizon; the limit by which everything is defined cannot itself be defined by a still more ultimate limit: "God is not in any genus."[30]

This brings us to our conceptual limits. Divine aliveness cannot be thematically grasped in a concept but only pointed to in an affirmation of judgment. Religious thinkers who realize this suggest that being be uttered as something other than a noun in order to realize its transcending dynamism. In Mary Daly's early feminist vision, for example, there is a deep connection between women's becoming and the intuition of being. This word "Be-ing," referring to what some would call God, should be perceived not as a noun but as a verb, that part of speech which connotes dynamic action. Be-ing is the "Verb" in which all beings participate, live and move and have their being. It is an intransitive Verb, that is, not limited by any object but soaring everywhere. The universal presence of this Verb Be-ing is manifest throughout the world, grounding creative hope in resistance to the ravages of nonbeing. In the power of this active, unlimited Verb of Verbs women experience the courage *to be* over against patriarchal definition of their niggardly worth, and struggle toward a future of genuine personhood.[31]

In her structural study of the questions on God in Aquinas's *Summa* Catherine LaCugna adopts a similar expedient, translating the pivotal term *esse* not as a noun but as the predicate nominative "to-be."[32] William Hill interprets being not as a noun but as a participle, a form of speech that connotes not mere givenness but an act, the exercise of "to be."[33] This same stress on the dynamism of being is found in John Macquarrie's lovely rephrasing of God's being as the dynamic act of "letting-be." God as Being not only is, but more quintessentially lets be, not in the sense of ignoring creatures or of leaving them alone but by saying "Let there be," that is, by empowering, enabling, bringing them into being.[34] Since a noun presupposes that we comprehend what we are referring to, cautions Abraham Heschel, we should avoid nouns in speaking of the nature of God. Rather, since awareness of God dawns only in encounter, our words should bespeak a relationship that results from being sought, pursued, called upon. We therefore have no nouns by which to describe the divine essence; we have only adverbs by which to indicate the ways in which God approaches us.[35]

Verb, predicate nominative, participle, adverb, being that lets be — such language strains and breaks its bounds attempting to express the inexpressible fullness of Holy Wisdom's nature, pointing to eternal mystery so profound and absolute that some mystics can even name being eternal Nothingness. Being itself does not define divine being, which is always and everywhere beyond definition. Insofar as this consistent negation invalidates nothing except the limits of the affirmations we make about being, it actually can give off a little light. For the not-knowing that comes at the end of thought pursued to its limits is actually a deeply religious form of knowing.

What the language of being points to is the world's relation to God as the living God. To start from wonder at the being of created things, to stretch this idea toward infinite mystery until it escapes intelligibility, and then to say that the very essence of holy mystery is "to be" is to credit God with pure liveliness, with a superabundance of actuality that transcends imagination. It is to affirm of God in a surpassing and originating sense all the vitality, radical energy, originality, spontaneity, and charm encountered in the very being-there of created existence. To start from the passion for lost being in the struggle against suffering and evil, and to cry to God as the power of resistance, healing, and liberation is likewise to name God in terms of being. It is to affirm that in a surpassing and originating sense God is not undialectically the ground of everything that is but is the ground of what should be and we hope will be, the power of being over against the ravages of nonbeing. The intuition of divine being born in suffering points to eschatological shalom that challenges the present, in utter faithfulness.

Far from a dead-weight abstraction, the notion of God as being signifies ultimate reality as pure aliveness in relation, the unoriginate welling up of fullness of life in which the whole universe participates. It refers us to the creative ground of all that is and the recreative ground of the energy to resist nonbeing toward the good that may yet be, the future promised but unknown. This symbol of divine being can strengthen and embellish discourse about the mystery of God. It can also be expressed in female metaphor with the appellation SHE WHO IS.

Speaking about the Living God: SHE WHO IS

Near the start of the biblical story of deliverance and covenant stands an enigmatic encounter. A bush is burning in the wilderness without being consumed. In respect for the presence of the holy, Moses removes his shoes. From the bush he hears words of divine compassion for people who are enslaved, and feels challenged to partner this God of the Hebrews in winning their release. In this context the exiled shepherd asks the ancestral God for a self-identifying name. It is graciously given: "I AM WHO I AM" (Ex 3:14), *'ehyeh 'asher 'ehyeh*, safeguarded in the sacred tetragrammaton YHWH.

The exegetical difficulties of this passage are numerous, and have given rise to a variety of interpretations of the personal name of the liberating God.[36]

Given the virtually untranslatable nature of the name, some scholars see here an affirmation of the mystery of God. YHWH is a limit expression, not a defining name but an unnameable one. There is no name that we can comprehend that would satisfactorily designate the Holy One. We are left in salutary darkness.

Others argue that the name should be interpreted in a causative sense to signify that God brings about whatever exists and whatever occurs in history. Thus the name YHWH means "I bring to pass" or "I cause to be" or "I make to be whatever comes to be." This explanation builds on an affinity between the letters of the name and a Hebrew verb denoting *to be* to evoke the idea that God is the Creator of all things who lets creatures *be* in life-giving fashion.

Still another position holds that the name carries the promise of divine accompaniment to people struggling under bitter oppression. In uttering the divine name God is saying, "I shall be there, as who I am, shall I be there with you." In this reading the transcendent mystery of God ("as who I am") is made known in and through the promise to bring about deliverance from bondage and to initiate the covenant relationship. Here the sense of the verb *to be* is interpreted relationally and historically. To be means to be with and for others, actively and concretely engaged on their behalf.[37]

Of all the interpretations of the name given at the burning bush, however, the one with the strongest impact on subsequent theological tradition links the name with the metaphysical notion of being. YHWH means "I am who I am" or simply "I am" in a sense that identifies divine mystery with being itself. Biblical exegetes are unanimous in criticizing the anachronistic tendency to read this philosophical meaning back into the original text, let alone to the events that gave rise to it, for the

Hebrew mind did not resonate with such metaphysical nuances until it came into contact with Hellenistic culture. Nevertheless, from the Septuagint translation onward the idea that the name YHWH discloses the ontological nature of God gained precedence in Jewish circles and was widely used in early Christian theology.[38]

It is thus to a long and venerable tradition that Aquinas appeals when he calls on the metaphysical interpretation to support his demonstration that the divine essence is identical with divine existence, or that God's very nature is to be. He finds the term "being" particularly apt because it refers to no partial aspect of God but rather to the whole in an indeterminate way, as to an infinite ocean. Its excellence is further seen in that it highlights the uniqueness of God, for of no one else can it be said that their essence is to exist. At the climax of this argument he proposes that being can serve even to name God in a particularly apt way. He asks, "Is HE WHO IS the most appropriate name for God?" Referring to the burning bush scene interpreted metaphysically, he answers in the affirmative: "Therefore this name HE WHO IS is the most appropriate name for God."[39] Aquinas fills this name with all the transcendent significance that accrues to pure, absolute being in his system. God whose proper name is HE WHO IS is sheer, unimaginable livingness in whose being the whole created universe participates.

The androcentric character of the standard English translation of God's name as HE WHO IS is piercingly evident. That character is not accidental but coheres with the androcentric nature of Aquinas's thought as a whole, expressed most infamously in his assessment of women as deficient males. The original Latin, however, could be rendered differently. It reads, *Ergo hoc nomen, "qui est," est maxime proprium nomen Dei.*[40] *Qui est* is a construction composed of a singular pronoun and singular verb. The grammatical gender of the pronoun *qui* is masculine to agree with its intended referent *Deus*, the word for God which is also of grammatically masculine gender. The name could be translated quite literally "who is" or "the one who is," with the understanding that the antecedent is grammatically masculine.

Naming toward God from the perspective of women's dignity, I suggest a feminist gloss on this highly influential text. In English the "who" of *qui est* is open to inclusive interpretation, and this indicates a way to proceed. If God is not intrinsically male, if women are truly created in the image of God, if being female is an excellence, if what makes women exist as women in all difference is participation in divine being, then there is cogent reason to name toward Sophia-God, "the one who is," with implicit reference to an antecedent of the grammatically and symbolically feminine gender. SHE WHO IS can be spoken as a robust, appropriate name for God. With this name we bring to bear in a female metaphor all the power carried in the ontological symbol of absolute, relational liveliness that energizes the world.

But not only that. The light of the biblical burning bush narrative adds a further precision. The one who speaks there is mystery in a personal key, pouring out compassion, promising deliverance, galvanizing a human sense of mission toward that end. Symbolized by fire that does not destroy, this one will be known by the words and deeds of liberation and covenant that follow. SHE WHO IS, the one whose very nature is sheer aliveness, is the profoundly relational source of the being of the whole universe, still under historical threat. She is the freely overflowing wellspring of the energy of all creatures who flourish, and of the energy of all those who resist the absence of flourishing, both made possible by participating in her dynamic act. In the power of her being she causes to be. In the strength of her love she gives her name as the faithful promise always to be there amidst oppression to resist and bring forth.

SHE WHO IS: linguistically this is possible; theologically it is legitimate; existentially and religiously it is necessary if speech about God is to shake off the shackles of idolatry and be a blessing for women. In the present sexist situation where structures and language, praxis and personal attitudes convey an ontology of inferiority to women, naming toward God in this way is a gleam of light on the road to genuine community.

Spiritually, SHE WHO IS, spoken as the symbol of ultimate reality, of the highest beauty and truth and goodness, of the mystery of life in the midst of death, affirms women in their struggle toward dignity, power, and value. It discloses women's human nature as *imago Dei*, and reveals divine nature to be the relational mystery of life who desires the liberated human existence of all women made in her image. In promoting the flourishing of women SHE WHO IS attends to an essential element for the well-being of all creation, human beings and the earth inclusively.

Politically, this symbol challenges every structure and attitude that assigns superiority to ruling men on the basis of their supposed greater godlikeness. If the mystery of God is no longer spoken about exclusively or even primarily in terms of the dominating male, a forceful linchpin holding up structures of patriarchal rule is removed.

In a word, SHE WHO IS discloses in an elusive female metaphor the mystery of Sophia-God as sheer, exuberant, relational aliveness in the midst of the history of suffering, inexhaustible source of new being in situations of death and destruction, ground of hope for the whole created universe, to practical and critical effect.

To Practical and Critical Effect

When done with eyes open to the magnitude of evil plaguing the world, speaking about God in the language of being moves from the ontological to the historical in short order. This is due to the belief that God's passion is for the world, which is under duress. Any words that are true must take this care into account. J. B. Metz sums this up in an illuminating way:

The idea of God to which Christian orthodoxy binds us is itself a practical idea. The stories of exodus, of conversion, of resistance and suffering belong to its doctrinal expression. The pure idea of God is, in reality, an abbreviation, a shorthand for stories without which there is no Christian truth in this idea of God.[41]

Speaking rightly about God from a feminist perspective means weaving the stories of women and women's ways of being into the stories of God that the Jewish and Christian traditions habitually tell. This in turn bubbles up to color even the "pure idea of God," in the direction of the praxis of freedom. And so we say:

The mystery of God, Holy Wisdom, SHE WHO IS, is the dark radiance of love in solidarity with the struggle of denigrated persons, including long generations of women, to shuck off their mean estate and lay hold of their genuine human dignity and value. Wherever the human project comes crashing down through systemic oppression, through the sin of others that delights in hurting or remaining indifferent, through personal folly and wrongdoing, through any contingent combination of factors, or wherever the earth and its life-systems are being damaged or destroyed, there the pain and suffering and degradation do not necessarily have the last word. They are bounded by the livingness of Sophia-God who gives life to the dead and calls into being the things that do not exist (Rom 4:17). She accompanies the lost and defeated, even violated women, on the journey to new, unimaginable life.

Conversely, mutuality in relation with God calls forth human responsibility for the good of the world. Alive in the *koinōnia* of SHE WHO IS, women and men are called to be friends of God and prophets, that is, appreciators of her wonders, sympathizers with her resistance to whatever degrades beloved creation, companions to her passion for the world's flourishing, starting with the nearest neighbor in need and extending to the farthest flung system by which we order, or disorder, our common life. The nearest woman in need with her dependent children and systemic sexism are prime candidates for transforming attention.

This way of speaking crafts a partnership amid the ambiguity of history: SHE WHO IS, Holy Wisdom herself, lives as the transcendent matrix who underlies and supports all existence and potential for new being, all resistance to oppression and the powers that destroy, while women and men, through all the ambivalence of their own fidelity, share in her power of love to create, struggle, and hope on behalf of the new creation in the face of suffering and evil.

Chapter 12

SUFFERING GOD: COMPASSION POURED OUT

Where love is a scream of anguish....

— Maya Angelou[1]

Speaking about SHE WHO IS in the dynamic terms of mutual and equal trinitarian relations and the essence of liveliness opens the door anew to ancient language about divine *pathos* or involvement in the suffering of the world. In the midst of distress religious experience at times senses the presence of Sophia-God drawing near and accompanying people down the dark road of pain; at other times the intuition of faith finds that God has already passed by and is terrifyingly absent. What is the right way to speak about God in the constant happening of woe? Are human beings the only ones who weep and groan, or can this also be predicated of the holy mystery of God who cherishes the beloved world? In the quest for language about God coherent with women's experience, although divine mystery is always greater than any human thought, the classical attribute of impassibility becomes a test case for reinterpretation. Joining a critical conversation that has been in process for some time, feminist theology has its own reconstructive contribution to make.

The Apathic, Omnipotent God and "His" Critics

Classical theism has long thought that, along with female experience, the experience of suffering is an inappropriate field from which to glean words for divine mystery. In its own frame of reference, some of the reasons for barring suffering from language about God can be admired for their noble intent. Classical theism understands that at times suffering may be a punishment for sin; obviously, the all-holy one can never be stricken with this. Suffering is also a sign of creaturely finitude, belonging to transitory moments of time; the eternal Creator cannot be marked by it. Pain, moreover, is an imperfection arising from a deficiency in

246

one's being; hence it is incompatible with the greatness of God who is the source of all perfection.

In the metaphysical discourse characteristic of scholasticism these theological insights are expressed in the notion of God who is being itself, *actus purus*, whose very nature is to be, to be totally in act while unmoved by any other. To say that God cannot suffer or be affected by the suffering of creatures is a philosophical deduction from this view of divine nature. Since suffering is a passive state requiring that one be acted upon by an outside force, there is no possibility of this occurring in divine being which is pure act. Furthermore, since God is always totally in act, the divine being is altogether unchangeable, that is, never passing from act to potency or vice-versa. As pure act or the fullness of being, God has no potentiality for either gaining or losing. Therefore change is impossible (the attribute of immutability). Consequently, since suffering implies movement from one state to another in response to what happens, it too is impossible for God. From every angle suffering is a vulnerable state incompatible with divine nature as being itself.[2]

Both theologically and philosophically, language about the apathic God, from the Greek *a-patheia* meaning no pathos or suffering, seeks to preserve divine freedom from a dependency on creatures that would in fact render God finite. Incapable of being affected by outside influences, the classical apathic God acts not out of need or compulsion but from serene self-sufficiency. Negating passion and vulnerability as divine qualities enables God's universal goodness to operate without fear or favor. As Moltmann benevolently interprets the usage of Judaism and early Christianity, "The apathic God could therefore be understood as the free God who freed others for himself."[3] Independent of the world, God can act to save with sheer gratuitous love.

The symbol of the impassible God is made more complex when it is combined with the classical attribute of omnipotence. Modeled on the all-determining power of a patriarchal ruler, divine power is traditionally interpreted to mean that God is ultimately in control of whatever happens so that nothing occurs apart from the divine will. This ruler may well be benevolent but "his" exercise of power is unilateral and brooks no opposition except what "he" allows. The classical form of the theodicy problem is predicated on this unexamined assumption, namely, that divine omnipotence means God can do directly whatever "he" wants. The fact that destructive events are not prevented indicates not that God actually wills them, for God wills only the good, but that the divine will permits them to happen for some purpose. To punish wrongdoing, to test character, to educate or form personality, or to bring forth a greater good — these are the religious reasons traditionally given to the anguished question, why? In this perspective famine and other disasters can be called "acts of God," a linguistic usage which has entered into official legal employ and continues to warp even the secular imagination. No matter the extent of the personal or global devastation, classical theodicy knows that God's glory is being served. As one manual of theology attested, "In the final end, moral evil will serve the supreme aim of the world, the glorification of God, inasmuch as it reveals His mercy in forgiving and His justice in punishing."[4]

Thanks to the powerful logic of Greek philosophy, classical theism succeeds in keeping even affirmations about God's involvement in the cross of Jesus from transforming the basic idea of God. In a unique way Christians confess that in Jesus who was wrongly tortured to a god-forsaken death, God has identified with the depths of human woe in order to save. Even here, however, classical thought protects the apathic God by maintaining that Jesus' anguish affects only his finite human nature. Because there is already a definition in place that affirms God as impassible, the suffering of Jesus belongs to God insofar as the Logos has assumed a human nature; but it cannot be predicated of God as such.

This can lead to very poignant theological probing, as seen in the dilemma posed by Anselm of Canterbury. Experiencing the effects of divine mercy and yet under the sway of the notion of the impassible God, he queries with inexorable logic: "But how art thou compassionate, and at the same time passionless? For if thou art passionless, thou dost not feel sympathy; and if thou dost not feel sympathy, thy heart is not wretched from sympathy with the wretched; but this it is to be compassionate. But if thou art not compassionate, whence cometh so great consolation to the wretched?" To do justice to all the points of his dilemma, Anselm's solution is to figure that "thou art compassionate in terms of our experience, and not compassionate in terms of thy being,"[5] a peculiarly unsatisfactory answer, which nevertheless in its dualism has held sway for most of a millennium.

It is true that Jewish and Christian belief has always affirmed God's living care in the midst of human woe and pain.[6] But in the last analysis, classical theism's view is that suffering lies exclusively on the human side of things and is not allowed to influence God's own happiness, a notion that reaches far into popular and theological imagination. It is consequently not exactly a caricature that Camus bitterly depicts when he says that God is like an eternal bystander with his back turned to the woe of the world.

And yet. . . . There is in our history a barbarous excess of suffering, a violence and destructiveness so intense in quality and extensive in scope that it can only be named genuine evil. These centuries have witnessed millions of people gassed, burned, tortured, bombed and shot out of existence. Millions more continue to have the life ground out of them by the misery of poverty. Within patriarchal systems women in large numbers are the recipients of male aggression expressed in sexual assault, wife battering, and murder as well as in the institutionalized violence of sexism. Within racist societies people of color or different ethnic origin are violated in ways that kill the body and demean the spirit. Everywhere is the suffering of illness, aging, and death. Social conflict, interpersonal pain, personal loneliness and meaninglessness are endemic. Both in the natural world and among human beings a history of suffering weaves in and out of every moment so profoundly that suffering can be called the "red thread" that connects all living things in history. There is suffering, in other words, that does not simply punish or test or educate or work a greater good. Instead, it destroys. In Wendy Farley's careful description this is called radical suffering:

Radical suffering is present when the negativity of a situation is experienced as an assault on one's personhood *as such*. . . . This assault reduces the capacity of the sufferer to exercise freedom, to feel affection, to hope, to love God. . . . In radical suffering the soul itself has been so crippled that it can no longer defy evil. The destruction of the human being is so complete that even the shred of dignity that might demand vindication is extinguished.[7]

Radical suffering afflicts millions of people the world over in intense and oppressive ways.

In face of the suffering of one innocent child, described so graphically by Dostoevsky; in face of the unfathomable degradation of the Jewish holocaust narrated so searingly by Elie Wiesel; in face of the boundless affliction of a freed slave woman explored so hauntingly by Toni Morrison;[8] in face of these and all the singular and communal ills which plague living creatures in history, the idea of the impassible, omnipotent God appears riddled with inadequacies. The idea of God simply cannot remain unaffected by the basic datum of so much suffering and death. Nor can it tolerate the kind of divine complicity in evil that happens when divine power is conceived as the force that could stop all of this but simply chooses not to, for whatever reason. A God who is not in some way affected by such pain is not really worthy of human love and praise. A God who is simply a spectator at all of this suffering, who even "permits" it, falls short of the modicum of decency expected even at the human level. Such a God is morally intolerable. Thus, spurred on primarily by growing consciousness of the massive suffering of the world, but also by developments in biblical studies and philosophy, large numbers of thoughtful people in the nineteenth and twentieth centuries have rejected the classic idea of the impassible, omnipotent God, finding it both intellectually inadequate and religiously repugnant.[9]

The whole modern movement of protest atheism springs from this reaction. So too does some of the most creative theological thinking of the twentieth century.

Abraham Heschel mines the Jewish Scriptures and brings to new light the prophetic understanding of the biblical God of pathos, the suffering God. Freely, and with care for justice, God enters into a relationship of passionate participation with the world and responds in grief, gladness, anger, and challenge to events in history. Divine power here shows itself as compassion in the call to human deeds of righteousness.[10] Postholocaust Jewish thinkers, wrestling with the terror of the experienced absence of the God of the covenant while history was interrupted by such destructive evil, carve out new notions of divine agency. To believe at all some retrieve the notion of divine self-limitation and consequent suffering, at times expressed in the symbol of the weeping Shekinah: God was silent not because he chose to be, argues Hans Jonas, but because he could not intervene due to self-divestiture of power (*zimsum*).[11] Others insist that the effectiveness of divine power is intrinsically linked to active human responsibility: God was silent because human beings would not listen and act upon the commandments of love and justice.[12]

Protestant theology typically finds its clue in the cross, from which it speaks about the genuine involvement of the trinitarian God in history's agonies. The cross reveals that God is found precisely in the midst of such pain, and shares it in a way that leads to salvation. In Moltmann's formulation, "Only if all disaster, forsakenness by God, absolute death, the infinite curse of damnation and sinking into nothingness is in God himself, is community with this God eternal salvation,"[13] because in God all of this tragedy is transmuted into life, on the model of the death and resurrection of Jesus Christ. Here God's power is often spoken about under the rubric of radical *kenōsis* and therefore as weakness, in the manner of the dialectical imagination.

Process theology's concepts of the reciprocal relation between God and the world, and the consequent nature of God, which receives back all that has passed into the world, give theoretical structure to the brief Galilean vision of God who is neither an eternal, aseptic being, a dominating ruler, or a stern moralist. In Whitehead's now famous words,

What is done in the world is transformed into a reality in heaven, and the reality in heaven passes back into the world. By reason of this reciprocal relation, the love in the world passes into the love in heaven, and floods back again into the world. In this sense, God is the great companion — the fellow-sufferer who understands.[14]

This pattern of thought has developed the appealing notion that divine power operates through persuasion rather than coercion, luring rather than giving orders.

Pursuing the great via media, John Macquarrie argues for a God who is both passible and impassible, a dialectical theism that attempts to do justice to both sides of the dilemma.[15]

European Catholic thinkers tend to take their cue from the incarnation, breaking with impassibility due to the kenotic aspect of the Word become flesh. They operate with the sensibility expressed by the Second Council of Constantinople in 553: "Our Lord Jesus Christ, crucified in his flesh, was true God, Lord of Glory, and one of the Trinity."[16] The personal union of divine and human natures in Christ is so profound that the cross belongs not to the human being Jesus alone but also to the person of the divine Logos. Hans Küng makes use of a uniquely Catholic analogy in this regard: just as through the *communicatio idiomatum* Mary can be called Mother of God, and this signifies not only a semantic but also an ontological reality, so too in view of the incarnation to say that God suffers intends something ontological about God.[17]

Prodded by the misery of millions of persons oppressed by poverty and violence, Latin American liberation theologians argue for the solidarity of God not only with the cross of Jesus but with all those who are suffering. From this vantage point Jon Sobrino proposes suffering as a mode of being for God, arguing that this is simply a concrete interpretation of the biblical intuition that God is Love.[18]

For all of these thinkers, divine capacity for suffering is a most characteristic expression of divine freedom active in the power of love. In an astute observation on the current theological scene, Ronald Goetz has commented that the move to integrate suffering into the idea of God is happening on so many points along the spectrum that it is tantamount to the rise of a new orthodoxy.[19] This is happening, furthermore, with very little theological dispute or accusations of heresy. If ever there were a *kairos*, a critical moment, for the religious symbol of the suffering God, that moment would seem to be now.

The classical attribute of impassibility, as the term itself suggests, is a negative concept. It removes from God the kind of suffering that implies finitude and creatureliness. In effect it affirms that God does not suffer the way creatures do. But in itself it does not block the idea that God may yet suffer in a way appropriate to divine being. The attribute as classically stated does not have a positive content, but points to the dark mystery of God. The way is open for creative respeaking in light of today's religious sensibilities. What then of theology from a perspective of women's experience? To the biblical, theoretical, and existential critiques of the classical idea of the impassible God, language arising from a feminist perspective adds a further precision.

Prizing connectedness, feminist analysis perceives how deeply the idea of the apathic God is shaped by the patriarchal ideal. For men in a dominant position, freedom has come to mean being in control, existing self-contained and self-directed, apart from entanglements with others. Thought from this stance has not shown itself theoretically capable of integrating freedom with genuine mutual relationship to others, posing them instead as incompatible states of being. Thus God is either free or genuinely related to and affected by the world and its suffering, a dualistic position that presents thought with an unhappy choice. Apart from a very sophisticated hermeneutic, the affirmation of divine freedom produces language about God as the quintessential macho man, unmoved and unfeeling in the face of human suffering.

Critics of the symbol of the suffering God, now often suggested as more adequate than the apathic God, charge that the former is simply an anthropomorphic construction, not as worthy of attention as the more purely metaphysical idea of impassibility. But from a feminist perspective it is clear that the attribute of impassibility as traditionally interpreted is equally anthropomorphic. In the patriarchal system the nonrelational human male exercising unilateral power sits at the pinnacle of perfection. Relationality and the inevitable vulnerability that accompanies it are correspondingly devalued as imperfections. Being free from others and being incapable of suffering in one's own person because of them become the goal. This patriarchal model has given the concept of impassibility its orientation and content in the human mind. To say, then, that speech about the suffering God is anthropomorphic does not count as a telling criticism. Rather, such language is simply drawing on a different set of human experiences from that which undergirds the classical ideal.

Feminist theology judges that the attribute of impassibility, even when posed as the ethical ideal of freedom, is found wanting when compared with the truth discerned in the lived experience characteristic of women. Self-containment and the absence of relationship are not necessarily the highest perfections but signify lack. Furthermore, the attribute of omnipotence, modeled on the power of an absolute monarch, reflects patriarchal preference for domination and control. Dorothee Soelle sums up this view of many feminist theologians in her choice words:

> But as a woman I have to ask why it is that human beings honor a God whose most important attribute is power, whose prime need is to subjugate, whose greatest fear is equality.... Why should we honor and love a being that does not transcend but only reaffirms the moral level of our male-dominated culture? Why should we honor and love this being, and what moral right do we have to do so if this being is in fact no more than an outsized man whose main ideal is to be independent and to have power?[20]

What is even worse than the dominating model of God's power in itself is its effect when introduced into the question of suffering, thereby linking destructive, radical suffering and evil to the permissive will of God. From a feminist perspective, the idea that God might permit great suffering while at the same time remaining unaffected by the distress of beloved creatures is not seriously imaginable. The connected self typical of women's way of being in the world demands a different concept of God in the midst of suffering.

But here a new caveat presents itself. Predicating suffering of God in such a way that suffering becomes a value in itself, or that God becomes essentially weak or powerless, and then holding up this model for emulation is a trap that ensnares women's struggle for equality and full humanity. Statements about "God's power that is weakness," claims about the Father's love shown in Jesus' abandonment on the cross, assertions that God was never so great as in humiliation, never so glorious as in self-surrender, and never so powerful as when impotent — such themes abound in current reformulations of impassibility and omnipotence.[21] Perhaps the vigor with which divine powerlessness in the midst of suffering is propounded is intended by some men theologians to challenge the abuse of power within patriarchy so marked by the domination of those in charge. Even so, when spoken to women, stress on the powerless suffering of God is particularly dangerous.

One of the key ingredients in the maintenance of systems of oppression is inculcating a feeling of helplessness in those oppressed. Without knowledge of their own power, those being victimized have no energy to resist. One of the first steps toward freedom occurs when, usually through the dynamics of a questioning, supportive community, oppressed people awaken to their own dignity and worth and begin to exercise their own power. Structurally subordinated within patriarchy, women are maintained in this position, not liberated, by the image of a God who suffers in utter powerlessness because of love. The ideal of the helpless divine victim serves only to strengthen women's dependency and potential for victimization, and to subvert initiatives for freedom, when what is needed is growth in relational autonomy and self-affirmation. The image of a powerless, suffering God is dangerous to women's genuine humanity, and must be resisted.

In face of this danger, might it not be better for feminist theology to forego any speaking about God's suffering? Perhaps. But there is another factor to consider, namely, the pathological tendency in the present culture of First World countries to deny suffering and death in human experience, which leads to banality in thought and superficiality in values.[22] In this context speech about redemptive suffering and the power of the suffering God is genuinely countercultural, and of benefit to women who know in their own experience a full cup of anguish.[23] In the long run the antidote to an impassible, omnipotent God is neither the reverse image of a victimized, helpless one nor silence on the whole subject. What is needed is to step decisively out of the androcentric system of power-over versus victimization and think in other categories about power, pain, and their deep interweaving in human experience. In what follows we touch once again the bedrock of women's interpreted experience, seeking to discover what the content of women's lives may contribute to a new realization of the power of the suffering God, and how speech about such a God may in turn promote the full and equal humanity of women.

Female Metaphors

Travail is a not inconsequential part of female life. Women's experiences of suffering the world over include the pain attending labor and childbirth, the penalty incurred for freely chosen actions for justice, the sorrow of grief over harm that comes to others, and the destruction known in personal degradation. Are women truly *imago Dei* even here, drinking the cup of sorrow? We are probing the capacity of symbols generated by experience of pain to evoke the mystery of God. Four such examples are adduced here, although the way God can be spoken about is not the same in all cases. In the first two instances women's suffering is the coin of creative advance. The pain of childbirth in a wanted, successful pregnancy is accompanied by a powerful sense of creativity and issues in the joy that a new child, one's own, is born. Likewise, in the midst of oppression women have consistently acted courageously and subversively for the betterment of their people. These acts, often unrecorded by official history and for which they have paid dearly, may issue in new fragments of justice and peace. But in the latter two situations we face the pit of darkness where there is no intelligibility at all. A loved one is disappeared; one's own self is violated. Even here women's courage to mourn and resist may lead to healing and new life, however scarred. Where it cannot, we are left with silence, narrative remembrance, and witness.

Birth

Thanks to the shape and creative potential of their own bodies, women know the pain of bringing new life into the world. Mercy Oduyoye observes, "At the age of sixteen I watched an eighteen year old woman having her first baby. From that time I understood why an Akan woman was said to have returned safely from the battle-front when she had successfully pulled through that whole experience and returned with herself and her baby."[24] In a way unique to half the human race, women labor in bearing and birthing each new generation, a suffering which can be woven round with a strong sense of creative power and joy: "The labor pains vanish; the chaos and darkness, the screams, sweat, swearing and the piercing cries are given a new quality. . . . A living being in the image of God has emerged."[25]

Feminist thinkers have criticized the practice of modern North American obstetrics for removing control of her body from a laboring woman and inducing passivity and dependence on medical authorities.[26] When actively engaged and experienced, however, this experience of labor and delivery offers a superb metaphor for Sophia-God's struggle to birth a new people, even a new heaven and a new earth. One biblical text makes this explicit as God says:

> For a long time I have held my peace,
> I have kept still and restrained myself
> now I will cry out like a woman in labor
> I will gasp and pant. (Is 42:14)

The loud birthing cries evoke a God who is in hard labor, sweating, pushing with all her might to bring forth justice, the fruit of her love. Intense suffering as an ingredient in intense creative power marks the depth of divine involvement in the process. And it is not over yet; only eschatologically will the delivery take place. In the course of history human beings are partners with Holy Wisdom in the birthing process, sharing in the labor of liberating life for a new future. Those who are suffering cry out in pain; but "the cry comes first from God, who is the champion and companion of the oppressed, who promises a new order in which the first shall be last and the last shall be first. The cry goes out to the people of God, compelling them to follow, to work together toward the new age."[27]

Justice and Anger

Women suffer when they choose to act in situations great or small to bring about the betterment of human life through the pursuit of human rights, healing, justice, and peace. This experience too betrays an admixture of creative power and pain, for the action being taken faces off with the antagonistic structures of sin, which are not deconstructed without fierce struggle. There are Lilian Ngoyi, Rahima Moosa, Sophie Williams, and Helen Joseph who at risk of being banned or worse, losing their very lives, led twenty thousand South African women, nonentities under apartheid, in a defiant peaceful march on the government buildings in 1956 to protest the hated pass laws. At the heart of a violent institution they stood in silent protest with right arms raised, and departed singing, "You have struck a rock; you have tampered with the women; you shall be destroyed." The price they paid went on for years, but the flame of freedom was kept alive.[28] There is Maria, one of the national organizers of rural, indigenous Guatemalan widows, traditionally the most marginalized group in that country's society. Fierce resistance from men led to threats from the civil patrols whose leaders mocked: "These women don't have husbands. That is why they go all over the place. What we are going to do is gather them all together and, if we don't kill them right away, divide them up. Each man will get seven widows."[29] There is Rosa Parks who for her people deliberately sat down on the bus knowing imprisonment would follow; her act provided the spark that lit the civil rights movement.[30] In every case these and other such women signal the presence of many others in the same context who commit countless acts of courage to resist injustice and bring about change, and who suffer the consequences.

This splendid and striking women's witness offers yet more imagery for speaking about Sophia-God who hears the cry of the poor, being "moved to pity by their groanings because of those who afflicted and oppressed them" (Jgs 2:18). As the voice in the flaming bush acknowledges, she knows experientially what the people are suffering and creates a solidarity with and among them that ultimately brings about change (Ex 3:7–8, reprised in Wis 10:15–19). In this Exodus story Wisdom's intent was already moving forward through the collaboration of women of different classes, races, and ages: through the crafty, defiant actions of the Hebrew midwives Shiphrah and Puah who refused to murder new life, through Moses' mother and sister Miriam who creatively hid and fed this little baby, and through Pharaoh's daughter who sheltered him (Ex 1, 2). She now shapes Moses' sense of prophetic mission and stokes up his courage. In every generation women who work and suffer for justice's sake, withstanding the indifference or the rage of the powerful, are coworkers with the burning flame of Wisdom, sacraments of her liberating intent. Their lives are metaphor for the suffering engagement of the God who loves justice.

A passion that often accompanies action on behalf of justice is righteous wrath. The violation of human beings is an outrage. When consciences and hearts awaken to this, then energy for resistance is born. Consciously appropriated, anger releases power for constructive work against injustice. Like oppressed groups everywhere but in a way specific to their gender, women are taught to suppress anger and to evaluate it consistently as something to be avoided, not nice, even sinful. To be sure, some forms of anger are destructive, escalating hostility that quickly leads to hate and violence. This is not the anger that we are speaking about here. But there is also righteous anger which waxes hot because something good is being violated. This is a genuine form of living care. It gives birth to courage and humor and unleashes energy for change.

When women awaken to the ravages wreaked upon them and those they love by unjust patriarchal systems, they typically get angry. This is a justifiable, forceful reaction to being deceived and diminished. In her pivotal essay "The Power of Anger in the Work of Love," Beverly Harrison argues that anger signals something amiss in relationship:

Anger is not the opposite of love. It is better understood as a feeling-signal that *all is not well* in our relation to other persons or groups or to the world around us. Anger is a *mode of connectedness* to others and it is always a *vivid form of caring*. To put the point another way: anger is — and it *always* is — a sign of some resistance in ourselves to the moral quality of the social relations in which we are immersed. Extreme and intense anger signals a deep reaction to the action upon us or toward others to whom we are related.[31]

Such anger is itself a mode of suffering. If integrated in the matrix of a befriending community, it gives birth to self-love in those who are abused and becomes a sharp fresh power, a cleansing and renewing energy that opens new channels of commitment. Where anger arises, there the energy to act and to resist is present. Nor is the power generated by moral outrage necessarily a temporary phenomenon. Mary Daly has rightly observed, "Rage is not a stage. It is not something to be gotten over. It is a transformative, focusing force."[32] Editing a wonderful book of photographs of African American women, Barbara Summers underscores how struck she was by the creative power in the anger of even the most accomplished of these women: "A truly beautifying discovery for me was to find so much love in anger. It was a fist-up, death-defying love that challenged the unfair conditions of life and muscled in on injustice as it nursed both sides of a nation."[33] This is not anger with the spirit of murder in it, but fury that is creative of life.

Women ablaze with righteous anger offer an excellent image of God's indignant power of wrath kindled by injustice. Apart from fundamentalist preaching, the wrath of God is not a subject frequently heard in our day. This is no doubt in reaction to the traditional stress on divine anger within a patriarchal framework that laid heavy, continuous guilt on consciences and obscured the saving message of divine mercy. But in a feminist framework the wrath of God is a symbol of holy mystery that we can ill afford to lose. For the wrath of God in the sense of righteous anger against injustice is not an opposite of mercy but its correlative. It is a mode of caring response in the face of evil, aroused by what is mean or shameful or injurious to beloved human beings and the created world itself. Precisely because Holy Wisdom cares with a love that goes beyond our imagining, the depths of divine anger are likewise immeasurable: "The exploitation of the poor is to us a misdemeanor; to God it is a disaster."[34] The religious symbol of divine wrath discloses God's outrage at the harm done to those she loves: this should not be. True, God's anger lasts but a moment; true, it is always instrumental, aimed at change and conversion. But it stands as an antidote to sentimentality in our view of God's holy mystery as love, and as a legitimation of women's anger at the injustice of their own diminishment and the violation of those they love.

The wisdom writings of Scripture carry just such an image of divine wrath in the female figure of Sophia. At her first appearance in Proverbs she is shouting in the streets, in the markets, on the top of the walls, at the entrance of the city gates — it seems no one can escape her voice:

> How long, O simple ones, will you love being simple?
> How long will scoffers delight in their scoffing ... ?
> Give heed to my reproof. ...
> Because I have called you and you refused to listen,
> have stretched out my hand and no one has heeded,
> and you have ignored all my counsel,
> and would have none of my reproof,
> I also will laugh at your calamity;
> I will mock when panic strikes you ...
> when distress and anguish come upon you. (Prv 1:23–27)

These are angry words, and for a purpose. Sophia here is one symbol of God as a furious woman who goes public with her anger in the mode of the prophets, to bring about conversion.

The prophet Hosea, as we have seen, portrays God, angered at injustice, like an angry mother bear who will go to any length to get back her cubs, even to tearing apart the predators (Hos 13:7–8). In these and other images reflective of women's experience of anger over injustice, the female symbol of the suffering God who cares for the oppressed is strengthened by a feminist retrieval of the wrath of God.

God as a woman in the labor of childbirth; God as a woman courageously engaged on behalf of justice; God as a woman angry against what harms and destroys — these images at their best are based on freely chosen acts that have the possibility of a fruitful outcome. But there is also suffering that is not a concomitant of creative power; it comes against our will like a thief in the night and works to destroy. Created by systemic injustice, historical chaos, and new initiatives of personal wrongdoing, this kind of suffering affects women through harm done to those whom they love and through abuse to their own humanity.

Grief

Women's relational way of being in the world typically creates in them a deep vulnerability to being rendered desolate when suffering visits those whom they love and care about. This experience is so powerful that feminist theorists are using it to rewrite the definition of evil. Whereas in the history of Western thought a preponderance of definitions of evil has concentrated on human disobedience to divine law and thus on "sin," some feminist ethical analysis now argues that women's experience identifies the most fundamental evil to be the phenomenological conditions of pain, separation, and helplessness.[35] When these conditions affect people within the circle of women's affection, boundless anguish ensues. From Rachel weeping for her children to the mothers and grandmothers of the Argentinian Plaza de Mayo, we could not measure the pain of women occasioned by harm done to those they love. "My heart cries out within me," writes South African poet Helen Kotze, "But my eyes are dry. And hollow is my hope."[36] With dry eyes or wet, women do more than a fair share of the crying in the world.

Women who experience this kind of desolation provide another reference point for speaking about God who grieves over the harm done to her beloved creation, a way, moreover, consonant with biblical tradition. In the Bible divine sorrow and lament appear in varied guises. At times God wails a funerary lament in the traditional undulating rhythms of mourning women; again, God takes up the cry of Rachel weeping for her children (Jer 31:15–20); at other times there are just heavy words of lamentation and woe. At the outbreak of war God grieves, "Therefore I weep with the weeping of Jazer for the vine of Sibmah; I drench you with my tears, O Heshbon and Elealeh; for upon your fruit and your harvest the battle shout has fallen" (Is 16:9). In such contexts of war and civil disaster the whole populace is weeping and mourning, so the text evokes the idea that God's lamentation is as broad and as deep as that of the people themselves.[37] Divine mourning also goes forth beyond Israel to include the whole suffering world, even those who appear to be enemies. Noting the devastation of a neighboring people God cries out, "Therefore I wail for Moab; I cry out for all Moab," and "my heart moans for Moab like a flute" (Jer 48:31, 36). In compassion and vulnerable love divine mystery takes up the cry of lament for beloved people who are broken and land that is devastated.

Jewish rabbinic and kabbalistic traditions are not embarrassed by this idea of divine sorrow. In one memorable gloss on the Exodus narrative, a rabbinic commentator notes that on the night when Israel escaped bondage by crossing the sea, they sang and danced on the far shore when their Egyptian pursuers were engulfed by the waves. In heaven the angels also wanted to celebrate. But God prevented this saying, "The works of my hands are drowning in the sea, and you want to sing songs!"[38] Grief for the destruction even of the enemy — so wide is the divine net that catches the pain of the world.

This same theme shifts explicitly into female imagery in the Jewish tradition of the Shekinah. Midrash depicts her going with the people into exile, their sorrowing companion in tragedy. What does the Shekinah say when a man is being hanged? "My head is heavy, my arm is heavy." Plumbing the depths of this symbol at a time of utter disaster, one twentieth-century rabbi in the Warsaw ghetto turned, like the prophets, to the image of divine weeping. The Holy One who seems to be absent has withdrawn into an inner chamber to mourn and weep over the distress and destruction of the people. In a unique twist on classical theism, this religious thinker surmises that precisely because God is infinite, divine suffering is infinite beyond human comprehension. Therefore not only the people but God too needs comfort, and human beings are called to assuage divine grief.[39]

Weeping women, women whose hearts moan like a flute because those they love have come to harm, are everywhere in the world. As *imago Dei* they point to the mystery of divine sorrow, of an unimaginable compassionate God who suffers with beloved creation. Holy Wisdom keeps vigil through endless hours of pain while her grief awakens protest. The power of this divine symbol works not just to console those who are suffering, but to strengthen those bowed by sorrow to hope and resist. If God grieves with them in the middle of disaster, then there may yet be a way forward.

Degradation

There is yet more, and it is terrible to speak of. In their own person women experience suffering that yields no discernible good but rather violates and destroys human dignity and even life itself. In Simone Weil's description such a situation is named affliction (French: *malheur*), a more or less attenuated equivalent of death, which takes possession of the soul and marks it with the brand of slavery. The occasions that bring on affliction may be physical, psychological, or social. But the effect is to squeeze out life, dry out power, introduce unwarranted guilt and self-hatred, plunge the sufferer into darkness.[40] Women experience affliction in myriad ways as they drink the cup of personal humiliation, fear, violation, and degradation. Very precisely, sexual embodiment as a female of the race within patriarchal society sets every woman in danger from rape, beatings, and other forms of male abuse. Too much of this suffering bears the mark of affliction. There is nothing redemptive about it.

In her *Texts of Terror* Phyllis Trible brings to light largely unnoticed biblical narratives of women who suffer appalling tragedy with no one to comfort or help them: the exiled slave woman Hagar, the raped princess Tamar, the young sacrificed daughter of Jephthah, the gang-raped and murdered nameless concubine from Bethlehem.[41] In three out of these four stories there is no biblical criticism of the perpetrators. And yet the sufferings they inflict on women are enormous. The Bethlehem woman, for example, was handed over to the rapists by her master who was seeking to protect himself while on a journey; after they "tortured her all night until the morning" (Jgs 19:25), she was taken home, dead or alive we know not, and her body hacked into twelve pieces. Trible's literary-feminist reading captures the torment here:

Of all the characters in scripture, she is the least. Appearing at the beginning and end of a story that rapes her, she is alone in a world of men. Neither the other characters nor the narrator recognize her humanity.... Without name, speech or power, she has no friends to aid her in life or mourn her in death. Passing her back and forth among themselves, the men of Israel have obliterated her totally. Captured, betrayed, raped, tortured, murdered, dismembered, and scattered — this woman is the most sinned against.... Her body has been broken and given to many. Lesser power has no woman than this, that her life is laid down by a man.[42]

This is suffering that does not come about because a woman has chosen to birth new life, or stand up for justice, or love someone. It is forced upon her by men, against her will, robbing her of everything, even life itself. What makes this text so intensely appalling is the fact that its torments continue to befall actual women to this very day.

A very public though by now suppressed chapter in the history of women's affliction is the trial and execution of women accused of being witches by the Inquisition. For reasons that had much to do with the threatened patriarchal dominance of spiritual and healing power, hundreds of thousands, perhaps more than a million women were annihilated in the name of God.[43] In the tradition of sorrowing witness, one poet has created a litany of remembrance of the holocaust of women:

- Margaret Jones, midwife, hanged 1648.

- Joan Peterson, veterinarian, hanged 1652.

- Isobel Insch Taylor, herbalist, burned 1618.

- Mother Lakeland, healer, burned 1645 . . .

- Barbara Gobel, described by her jailors as "the fairest maid in Wurzburg," burned 1645.

- Frau Peller, raped by Inquisition torturers because her sister refused the witch judge Franz Buirman, 1631 . . .

- Sister Maria Renata Sanger, subprioress of the Premonstratensian Convent of Unter-Zell, accused of being a lesbian; the document certifying her torture is inscribed with the seal of the Jesuits and the words, "AD MAJOREM DEI GLORIAM" . . .

- Anna Rausch, burned 1628, 12 years old.

- Sybille Lutz, burned 1628, 11 years old.

- Emerzianne Pichler, tortured and burned together with her two children, 1679.

- Agnes Wobster, drowned while her young son was forced to watch her trial by water, 1567 . . .

- Veronica Zerritsch, compelled to dance in the warm ashes of her executed mother, then burned alive herself, 1754, 13 years old.

- Frau Dumler, boiled to death in hot oil while pregnant, 1630.[44]

What makes these Inquisition murders particularly obnoxious is that they were performed with the official approbation of a powerful religious institution by male leaders who were sure that they were carrying out the will of God. But on the stage of world history this particular litany is practically endless and could be extended to include all the women throughout the generations who have been beaten, raped, killed, and ruined by male misogyny obsessed with its own righteousness and rule.

In our own day new brands of women's suffering come to expression in a poem by Michele Najlis, a Nicaraguan detained along with many others by the government:

> They pursued us in the night.
> They surrounded us,
> and left us no defense but our hands
> linked to millions of hands linked together.
> They made us spit up blood,
> they scourged us;
> they filled our bodies with electric shocks
> and they filled our mouths with lime;
> they put us in with beasts all night long,
> they threw us in timeless dungeons,
> they ripped out our nails;
> with our blood they covered even their rooftops,
> even their own faces,
> but our hands
> are still linked to millions of hands linked
> together.[45]

Is the raped and murdered concubine from Bethlehem *imago Dei?* Are the young and old women killed as so-called witches images of God? Are the victims of state torture in the likeness of God? Do these and all the violated women of the world offer yet another symbol of the suffering God? I think that they do. *Ecce homo:* in an unspeakable way they are images of the crucified.

In the Christian world view the paradigmatic locus of divine involvement in the pain of the world is the cross. In the human integrity of a broken human being, who prized truth and fidelity above his own safety and loved his friends in an ever-widening circle until the godforsaken end, something of the mystery of God is darkly manifest: Christ crucified, the wisdom and power of God. Here if anywhere it can be glimpsed that Wisdom participates in the suffering of the world and overcomes, inconceivably, from within through the power of love.

This vivid moment does not begin or end God's identification with the suffering world. In a memorable metaphor developed by Gerald Vann, the cross is like a dark ring around a tree that comes to light when the tree is cut; we see the ring only where it is cut across, but the dark ring goes on and on, up and down the whole tree.[46] Crosses of all kinds keep on being set up in history. The christological symbol of God's active suffering in Christ becomes a historically inclusive one, encompassing the suffering lives of women and men of all ages. The suffering body of Christ includes the raped and denigrated bodies of women. As Asian theologian Virginia Fabella writes, all over the world desperately poor women "are today the Christ disfigured in his passion."[47] It is a suffering that should not be.

This theological insight comes to concrete expression in the figure of the *Christa*, Christ as a crucified woman, first sculpted by Edwina Sandys and displayed in 1984 at the Cathedral of St. John the Divine in New York City. The figure does not intend to deny the male Jesus of history but to evoke the all-encompassing scope of God's identification with crucified people, including and in particular abused women. Touching off a storm of controversy as it did, this sculpture directs a question mark "at a male culture in which the tortured female body is regarded as pornographic, rather than the expression of the sufferings of God."[48] More theologically astute than the horrified reaction against *Christa* is the intuition voiced by Archbishop Oscar Romero in a homily on the feast of Corpus Christi: "It is most opportune to pay homage to the body and blood of Christ while there are so many outrages to his body and blood among us. I should like to join this homage of our faith to the presence of the body and blood of Christ, which we have shed, with all the blood shed, and the corpses piled up, here in our own land and throughout the world."[49]

Holy Wisdom does not abhor the reality of women but identifies with the pain and violence that women experience on the cross, of whatever sort. So we may ask again Elie Wiesel's terrifying question.[50] When a woman is raped and murdered, what does the Shekinah say? She says, my body is heavy with violation. Through the long night when the Bethlehem concubine is gang-raped and tortured, where is God? She is there, being abused and defiled. There too being burned to death by the Inquisition. There too being tortured by the male enforcers of unjust rule. Along with all abused women these women are *imago Dei*, *imago Christi*, daughters of Wisdom. Sophia-God enters into the pain of women whose humanity is profaned and keeps vigil with the godforsaken for whom there is no rescue. In turn, their devastation points to the depths of the suffering God. There is no solution here, no attempt at theoretical reconciliation of atrocity with divine will. Only a terrible sense of the mystery of evil and the absence of God, which nevertheless may betray divine presence, desecrated.

Divine Suffering

Attending to women's experience of suffering and response to suffering can shape language about God that makes divine mystery more religiously accessible in the midst of disaster. What theological concepts support this kind of speech? To what understanding of God does the symbol of the suffering God give rise?

God's Being as Love

Classical theism models its notion of divine being on the root metaphor of motion adapted primarily from the nonpersonal, physical world. If one uses that model it is clearly the case that something already purely in act cannot pass from potency into act, nor can something completely in motion be in any way passive or receptive. Hence, God cannot suffer. But this root metaphor of motion is hardly adequate to God's holy mystery, which is utterly personal, transpersonal, source of all that is personal. A different interpretation becomes possible when the root metaphor is taken from personal reality that is constitutively relational. Then the essence of God can be seen to consist in the motion of personal relations and the act that is love. With this in view it is possible to conceive of suffering as not necessarily a passive state nor a movement from potentiality to act. Rather, suffering can be conceived of ontologically as an expression of divine being insofar as it is an *act* freely engaged as a consequence of care for others. The personal analogy makes it possible to interpret divine suffering as Sophia-God's act of love freely overflowing in compassion.

Feminist theology is rightly wary of overstressing the value of love because of the attention traditionally devoted to agapaic or self-giving love which, without equal regard for self-affirmation and the excellence of mutuality, has operated in the sociological sphere to maintain women's subordination. Set within an inclusive context and continuously regulated by the value of relational autonomy, however, love may yet serve as a crystallization of the relational essence of God's being. We can say that the inconceivable power that gives life to the world, sustains it everywhere and always, joins its crucified history, empowers every event of healing and liberation, and is the deepest mystery toward which the world moves is essentially relational: Holy Wisdom as pure, unbounded love, utterly set against evil, totally on the side of the good.

Love Entails Suffering

Does love entail suffering in God? In the classical tradition with its apathic ideal, the answer is obviously no. Love is purely a matter of the will;

to love is to will the good of the one loved.[51] Defending this tradition William Hill reasonably argues that if someone I love is suffering it does them no good if I suffer too; what matters is that I *do* something to relieve the misery.[52] The difficulty with this argument, however, is that the notion of love as simply willing the good of others prescinds from the reciprocity entailed in mature relations. Of course love includes willing the good of the beloved, and the classical idea is right as far as it goes. But as actually lived, and paradigmatically so in the light of women's experience, love includes an openness to the ones loved, a vulnerability to their experience, a solidarity with their well-being, so that one rejoices with their joys and grieves with their sorrows. This is not a dispensable aspect of love but belongs to love's very essence. In fact, a chief source of the energy that generates "willing the good" and relieving misery lies precisely in this experience of compassionate solidarity with the suffering of those we love. In the light of the feminist prizing of mutuality as a moral excellence, love does entail suffering in God.

An Excellence

Speech about the suffering God who loves in solidarity with the conflictual world does not intend to say that God suffers because of some intrinsic deficiency; nor unwillingly through being overtaken by outside forces; nor necessarily under the constraint of nature; nor passively under the dictates of a stronger power. On the contrary, speech about Holy Wisdom's suffering with and for the world points to an act of freedom, the freedom of love deliberately and generously shared in accord with her own integrity. "This is the manner of God's suffering: to suffer as the fruit of love and of the infinite capacity of love for solidarity."[53] As a summation of compassionate love, the symbol of divine suffering appears not as an imperfection but as the highest excellence.

Language about the suffering God has a particular affinity with the experience of Spirit, named mutual love, love proceeding, freely given gift and friend of the world. In Scripture and rabbinic writing she is forever speaking, crying, admonishing, sorrowing, weeping, rejoicing, groaning, comforting.[54] But the meaning of this speaking ultimately includes the triune God in relation to the world. Interpreting the metaphysical notion of pure act through the relational lens of trinitarian life delivers a notion of Holy Wisdom *capax passionis*, capable of suffering, while as God she does not perish and can bring forth new life.

Only a Suffering God Can Help

Bonhoeffer's insight continues to inspire religious reflection: "God allows himself to be edged out of the world and on to the cross . . . and that is the way, the only way, in which he can be with us and help us. . . . Only a suffering God can help."[55] But how can a suffering God be of any help? There is an element of truth to one woman's appalled objection to this kind of language with which many would sympathize. If I were at the bottom of a deep pit, aching, cold, and nursing a broken arm, she writes, "what I want and urgently need is a Rescuer with a very bright light and a long ladder, full of strength, joy and assurance who can get me out of the pit, not a god who sits in the darkness suffering with me."[56] What she rightly rejects is the notion of a suffering God who is powerless, the antithesis of the omnipotent God. However, the human situation of agony and death is more internal to ourselves and more socially complex than this example would allow. Closer to the point is the reflection of another woman who spent endless days and nights on a hospital ward with her tiny, sick daughter, helping the nurses with the other babies when she could. It was a dreadful exposure to the meaningless suffering of the innocent. "On those terrible children's wards," she writes, "I could neither have worshipped nor respected any God who had not himself cried out, 'My God, My God, why hast thou forsaken me?' Because it was so, because the creator loved his creation enough to become helpless with it and suffer in it, totally overwhelmed by the pain of it, I found there was still hope."[57]

This is one way the symbol of a suffering God can help: by signaling that the mystery of God is here in solidarity with those who suffer. In the midst of the isolation of suffering the presence of divine compassion as companion to the pain transforms suffering, not mitigating its evil but bringing an inexplicable consolation and comfort. In her phenomenology of compassion Wendy Farley notes how compassion with its sympathetic knowledge:

does not stand outside the suffering in handwringing sympathy. It does not peer down on the victim and demand a stoicism that denies the pain. It begins where the sufferer is, in the grief, the shame, the hopelessness. It sees the despair as the most real thing. Compassion is with the sufferer, turned toward or submerged in her experience, seeing it with her eyes. This communion with the sufferer in her pain, *as she experiences it*, is the presence of love that is a balm to the wounded spirit. This relationship of shared, sympathetic suffering mediates consolation and respect that can empower the sufferer to bear the pain, to resist the humiliation, to overcome the guilt.[58]

Communion becomes a profound source of energy for the healing of suffering. Knowing that we are not abandoned makes all the difference.

Speaking about God's suffering can also help by strengthening human responsibility in the face of suffering. The impassible God models a dispassionate, apathic attitude that influences community ideals. Conversely, the suffering God reorders the human ideal toward compassionate solidarity. The logic of the symbol discloses that if God's compassionate love struggles against destructive forces, then being in alliance with God calls for a similar praxis. Living out this stance of "seeing the world feelingly"[59] empowers action on behalf of those who are suffering. Especially in situations of massive suffering due to injustice, such a symbol makes clear that God is to be found on the side of those who are oppressed, as a challenge to oppressors be they individuals or structures.[60] The close correlation between divine pathos and prophetic act in the Bible indicates that responsible action for resistance, correction, and healing are among the truest expressions of living faith.

Comfort and the challenge to responsible praxis do not of themselves resolve everything, especially death which in the end engulfs everyone. Human beings may be consoled, and pour out every effort to heal and liberate, but suffering continues in history. At the very limit of limit situations, the symbol of the suffering God can help by awakening hope that historical failure is not the last evidence of what the future holds. This is a deep mystery, how in the depths of suffering, hope against hope is born. "When all the immanent possibilities for continuation or renewal are exhausted," Peter Hodgson observes, "when persons and peoples are driven to the depths of defeat and despair, they can and do experience the 'miraculous' ability to start over, to build afresh, to maintain a struggle and a vision."[61] Grounding this energy is a sense of reality that can be interpreted as ultimately religious and spoken about in religious terms. If Holy Wisdom is in compassionate solidarity with suffering people in history, a future is thereby opened up through even the most negative experience. This is because we are speaking about *God*, than whose power of love nothing greater can be conceived. If there be God, then there are parameters to evil, and a terminus. The human struggle can go forward in hard-won hope against hope that the compassion of God will overcome chaos and death and set limits even to the unfathomable mystery of evil. Speech about the suffering God points forward: in the end all will be well, and so energy to resist despair arises.

As the foundation of this hope, Christian faith speaks about the paschal mystery, about Jesus Christ's death and resurrection as the first fruit of an inclusive harvest, about new unimaginable life breaking out through death itself and as a corrective to death. Although for a time there was no glimmer of hope, God was near at hand, nevertheless, and Jesus was not ultimately abandoned. The victory arrives through the living communion of love, overcoming evil from within. To say this is not to rationalize suffering or to find a solution to the problem of evil or to offer cheap consolation. The cross and resurrection scandalize and cannot be reconciled theoretically. Rather, this event deepens the mystery of how God's solidarity with the suffering world brings about a future even for the most godforsaken. It points to the real mystery of the trinitarian God as an ally against suffering and moves the community to the practice of love that corresponds to this mystery. The presence of the living God, even when darkly intuited in the mode of absence, offers new possibilities to the situation from within.

Only a suffering God can help. The compassionate God, spoken about in analogy with women's experience of relationality and care, can help by awakening consolation, responsible human action, and hope against hope in the world marked by radical suffering and evil.

Divine Power

Speaking of the suffering God from a feminist liberation perspective entails reshaping the notion of omnipotence. Both the classical model of power-over and the dialectical view of the absence of power in helpless suffering are riddled with inadequacies. We seek an understanding that does not divide power and compassionate love in a dualistic framework that identifies love with a resignation of power and the exercise of power with a denial of love. Rather, we seek to integrate these two, seeing love as the shape in which divine power appears.

One major resource for this language is the experience of women who know the breakthrough of their own strength, usually under duress: the nurturing power of a mother who enables her children to grow into their own personhood; the dynamic spirit of a preacher who galvanizes her community to take hold of their own dignity; the creative power of an artist who shapes a world with words or materials or movement; the justice-making vigor of women who know wrongs, both personal and structural, and stand as strong witnesses to resist and remake; the courage of sick, lonely, or violated women who reach out to establish connectedness, deriving energy that they critically turn toward the well-being of others. All of these and other like women fundamentally detest suffering and mobilize imaginatively and compassionately against it despite the price.

The kind of power they evidence is a vitality, an empowering vigor that reaches out and awakens freedom and strength in oneself and others. It is an energy that brings forth, stirs up, and fosters life, enabling autonomy and friendship. It is a movement of spirit that builds, mends, struggles with and against, celebrates and laments. It transforms people, and bonds them with one another and to the world. Such dynamism is not the antithesis of love but is the shape of love against the forces of nonbeing and death. And it operates in a relational manner.

Feminist theologians are grappling for language to give voice to this understanding of power arising from women's experience. Neither power-over nor powerlessness, it is akin to power-with.[62] Taking a clue from Audre Lorde, Rita Brock speaks eloquently of erotic power as the power of connectedness, which alone can heal the brokenheartedness that is patriarchy's legacy.[63] In proposing the models of God as mother, lover, and friend, Sallie McFague notes how they project a different view of power from the monarchical model: "It is not the power of control through either domination or benevolence but the power of response and responsibility — the power of love in its various forms (agape, eros, and philia) that operates by persuasion, care, attention, passion, and mutuality."[64] Sharon Welch probes the critical power of *jouissance* which subverts clear and distinct categories in favor of movement, fluidity, and the deep joy that comes from connectedness with others in life-pursuits.[65] Wendy Farley persuasively develops the notion of power in terms of compassionate love that resists tragic suffering. Compassion is an empowering power, an efficacy, a blazing fierceness, rather than an interior emotion, and it has an efficacy for transformation. Through its sympathetic knowledge of suffering it "contends for sufferers not like a white knight — steel on steel — but as a different *kind* of power."[66] In Anne Carr's summation, feminist theological probing of the experience of motherhood as a source for symbolizing God's ways opens rich ideas of power "as enablement of the autonomy of others, as gentle persuasion, as patient love and encouragement, themes consonant with the biblical descriptions of God."[67] Relational, persuasive, erotic, connected, loving, playful, empowering, resisting — such are some of the words we seek.

Thinking of Holy Wisdom's "almighty power" along these lines leads to a resymbolization of divine power not as dominative or controlling power, nor as dialectical power in weakness, nor simply as persuasive power, but as the liberating power of connectedness that is effective in compassionate love. We can say: Sophia-God is in solidarity with those who suffer as a mystery of empowerment. With moral indignation, concern for broken creation, and a sympathy calling for justice, the power of God's compassionate love enters the pain of the world to transform it from within. The victory is not on the model of conquering heroism but of active, nonviolent resistance as those who are afflicted are empowered to take up the cause of resistance, healing, and liberation for themselves and others.[68]

Speaking about the Suffering God

The depth of wrong in the history of the world goes beyond human comprehension. In the face of this *tremendum* we have been weighing the viability of language about the suffering God in feminist theology. Speaking of God this way is closely akin to what women articulate as multiple skeins of their experience, and has the capacity to unleash human compassion, responsibility, and hope. The dark side of such language is its potential to play into women's passive victimization by glorifying suffering. Only when set carefully and consistently within the context of a God who is utterly committed to the *humanum*, whose glory is the human being and, specifically, women, fully alive, does the symbol of the suffering God release its empowering power. Then it signifies the power of suffering love to resist and create anew.

In no way is this theological speech intended to yield a literal description of God. The rule of analogical language applies here in full strength. Even less does it attempt even remotely to reconcile the mystery of suffering and evil with the holy mystery of God. Such a conceptual solution is not possible. The most astute theodicies pale before the depth of torment in the history of the world. Evil is indeed the surd which shatters every rational system of thought. Anyone who works out a rational way to integrate evil and radical suffering in an ordered fashion into a total intellectual system of which God is a part thereby justifies it. Such efforts, in my judgment, are doomed to fail.

If evil and suffering cannot be explained away, given a positive interpretation, or made intelligible, what is the point of speaking of the suffering God, even in a feminist theology? Only this: that such discourse facilitates the praxis of hope. Against the background of the history of human injustice and suffering, the suffering God is a most productive and critical symbol for it cannot be uttered without human beings hearing the challenge to solidarity and hope. If the glory of God is the human being, woman, fully alive, then whatever destroys that aliveness is inimical to divine glory. And if God is in solidarity with violated women, the call to resist is born at the very core of faith. Speaking about the suffering God, consequently, is a companion to criticism of those conditions that dishonor women, and indeed all human beings and living creatures. Even then it is valid only if accompanied by the struggle to change the conditions in the direction of a new heaven and a new earth.

There is no theoretical solution to the mystery of suffering and evil, but there is the immense field of responsive action toward overcoming what kills women's human dignity. Here and there such action succeeds, granting fragmentary experiences of salvation, anticipations of the human condition where suffering and evil are overcome. Light dawns, courage is renewed, tears are wiped away, a new moment of life arises. Toward that end, speaking about suffering Sophia-God of powerful compassionate love serves as an ally of resistance and a wellspring of hope. But it does so under the rule of darkness and broken words.

EPILOGUE

What is the right way to speak about God in light of women's reality? Ideas of God are cultural creatures related to the time and place in which they are conceived. We have traced one pattern of Christian feminist language arising from diverse experiences: the Spirit's universal quickening and liberating presence, the living memory of Wisdom's particular path in the history of Jesus, and inconceivable Holy Wisdom herself who brings forth and orients the universe. We have explored the ways in which these discourses coalesce into the symbol of the Trinity, a living communion of mutual and equal personal relations. Divine capacity for relation has led to speaking about Sophia-God's participation in the suffering of the world that empowers the praxis of freedom, a discourse that takes place in the energizing matrix of the one God's sheer liveliness named with the symbol SHE WHO IS. All of the above chapters are clues, starting points, commencements. This generation needs to keep faith with this question, creating, testing, reflecting, discarding, keeping. No language about God will ever be fully adequate to the burning mystery which it signifies. But a more inclusive way of speaking can come about that bears the ancient wisdom with a new justice.

NOTES

Abbreviations

AH   Irenaeus of Lyons, *Adversus Haereses*. In *Ante-Nicene Fathers*. Vol. 1, edited by A. Cleveland Coxe. Edinburgh: T & T Clark, 1885. Reprint. Grand Rapids, Mich.: Eerdmans, 1989.

CTSAP   *Catholic Theological Society of America Proceedings*. Recent volumes are published by Mercer University Press, Macon, Ga. (vol. 46=1991).

De Trin   Augustine, *De Trinitate*. In *Nicene and Post-Nicene Fathers*. Vol. 3, edited by Philip Schaff. Grand Rapids, Mich.: Eerdmans, 1956.

DS   H. Denzinger and A. Schönmetzer, *Enchiridion Symbolorum. Definitionum et Declarationum de Rebus Fidei et Morum*. 36th ed. Freiburg im Breisgau: Herder, 1965.

DV   *Dei Verbum*, Dogmatic Constitution on Divine Revelation. In *The Documents of Vatican II*, edited by Walter A. Abbott. New York: America Press, 1966.

GS   *Gaudium et Spes*, Pastoral Constitution on the Church in the Modern World. In *The Documents of Vatican II*, edited by Walter A. Abbott. New York: America Press, 1966.

JAAR   *Journal of the American Academy of Religion*

JFSR   *Journal of Feminist Studies in Religion*

JR   *Journal of Religion*

LG   *Lumen Gentium*, Dogmatic Constitution on the Church. In *The Documents of Vatican II*, edited by Walter A. Abbott. New York: America Press, 1966.

NJBC   Raymond Brown, Joseph Fitzmyer, Roland Murphy, eds. *New Jerome Biblical Commentary*. Englewood Cliffs, N.J.: Prentice Hall, 1990.

PG   P. Migne, ed. *Patrologiae cursus completus. Series graeca*. 161 vols. Paris, 1857–1866.

PL   P. Migne, ed. *Patrologiae cursus completus. Series latina*. 221 vols. Paris, 1844–1864.

SCG   Thomas Aquinas, *Summa Contra Gentiles*. 4 vols. Garden City, N.Y.: Doubleday, 1957.

ST   Thomas Aquinas, *Summa Theologiae*. 60 vols. Blackfriars edition. New York: McGraw Hill, 1964.

TDNT   Gerhard Kittel and Gerhard Friedrich, eds., *Theological Dictionary of the New Testament*. 10 vols. Grand Rapids, Mich.: Eerdmans, 1964–1976.

TDOT   G. Johannes Botterweck and Helmer Ringgren, eds. *Theological Dictionary of the Old Testament*. 6 vols. Grand Rapids, Mich.: Eerdmans, 1974–1990.

TI   Karl Rahner, *Theological Investigations*. 23 vols. London: Darton, Longman & Todd, 1961–1992; New York: Crossroad, 1980–1992.

TS   *Theological Studies*

Chapter 1 / Introduction: To Speak Rightly of God

1. Adrienne Rich, from "Transcendental Etudes," in *The Fact of a Doorframe: Poems Selected and New 1950–1984* (New York: W. W. Norton, 1984) 268–69.

2. Gregory of Nyssa, "De deitate Filii et Spiritus sancti," *PG* 46.557. The importance of the role of the laity in this debate is demonstrated by John Henry Newman, *On Consulting the Faithful in Matters of Doctrine* (London: Collins, 1986).

3. These examples are adduced by Gordon Kaufman, *The Theological Imagination: Constructing the Concept of God* (Philadelphia: Westminster, 1981) 187–89. Kaufman argues here for the importance of the great symbol of Jesus Christ who, as the image of the invisible God, manifests a God who does not act in a violent way but rather creates a community of love and equality in a peaceable and free way.

4. Martin Luther, *Large Catechism*, in *The Book of Concord*, trans. Theodore Tappert (Philadelphia: Fortress, 1959) 365.

5. Elisabeth Schüssler Fiorenza and Mary Collins, eds., *Women: Invisible in Church and Theology* (*Concilium* 182) (Edinburgh: T & T Clark, 1985).

6. This experience has been perceptively analyzed by Constance Fitzgerald, "Impasse and Dark Night," in *Living with Apocalypse: Spiritual Resources for Social Compassion*, ed. Tilden Edwards (New York: Harper & Row, 1984) 95–116.

7. Rosemary Radford Ruether gives a theological and practical description of the gathering of women in *Women-Church: Theology and Practice of Feminist Liturgical Communities* (San Francisco: Harper & Row, 1985); critical and creative analysis is offered by Marjorie Proctor-Smith, *In Her Own Rite: Constructing Feminist Liturgical Tradition* (Nashville, Tenn.: Abingdon, 1990). Among a wealth of examples, see the prayer patterns limned by Arlene Swidler, *Sistercelebrations* (Philadelphia: Fortress, 1974); Miriam Therese Winter, *WomanPrayer/WomanSong: Resources for Ritual* (New York: Crossroad, 1987), and her *WomanWord: A Feminist Lectionary and Psalter* (New York: Crossroad, 1990).

8. Rebecca Chopp, *The Power to Speak: Feminism, Language, God* (New York: Crossroad, 1989) 7 and passim.

9. Mary Daly, *Beyond God the Father: Toward a Philosophy of Women's Liberation* (Boston: Beacon, 1973) 37 and passim.

10. Paul Ricoeur's lapidary axiom in *The Symbolism of Evil* (Boston: Beacon, 1967) 347–57, to which we shall return.

11. *ST* I, q. 29 a. 3.

12. Augustine, *Sermo* 52, c. 6, n. 16 (*PL* 38. 360). Anselm, *Proslogium* chaps. 2–3, in *Saint Anselm: Basic Writings*, trans. S. N. Deane (LaSalle, Ill.: Open Court, 1974). Hildegaard of Bingen, *Scivias*, trans. Mother Columba Hart and Jane Bishop (New York: Paulist, 1990), bk. 1, vision 1. *ST* I, q. 3, preface. Luther, theses 19 and 20, "The Heidelberg Disputation," in *Luther: Early Theological Works*, trans. and ed. James Atkinson (Philadelphia: Westminster, 1962) 290–91. Simone Weil, *Waiting for God*, trans. Emma Craufurd (New York: Harper & Row, 1973) 32. Sallie McFague, *Models of God: Theology for an Ecological, Nuclear Age* (Philadelphia: Fortress, 1987) 35 and passim.

13. Karl Rahner, "The Specific Character of the Christian Concept of God," *TI* 21:189.

14. *DV* 8.

15. Anne Carr, *Transforming Grace: Women's Experience and Christian Tradition* (San Francisco: Harper & Row, 1988). This is an excellent synthesis of the background and sweep of feminist theology, with extensive bibliography (pp. 245–66).

16. Despite its negative connotation in popular parlance, the word *feminist* is widely used in academic circles. Taken from the Latin *femina* (woman), it signifies a stance which advocates the flourishing of women as a precondition for genuine human community. In my view it is a perfectly suitable word, and I will use it in the sense described here. For background, see Anne Carr, "Is a Christian Feminist Theology Possible?" *TS* 43 (1982) 279–97, and Sandra Schneiders's eloquent lectures collected in *Beyond Patching: Faith and Feminism in the Catholic Church* (New York: Paulist, 1991).

17. In the words of Vatican II, "with respect to the fundamental rights of the person, every type of discrimination, whether social or cultural, whether based on sex, race, color,

social condition, language, or religion, is to be overcome and eradicated as contrary to God's intent" (*GS* 29).

18. Vatican II, *Nostra Aetate* ("Declaration on the Relationship of the Church to Non-Christian Religions") 2.

19. Two decades of pivotal North American feminist study are collected in Carol Christ and Judith Plaskow, eds., *Womanspirit Rising: A Feminist Reader in Religion* (San Francisco: Harper & Row, 1979), and idem, *Weaving the Visions: New Patterns in Feminist Spirituality* (San Francisco: Harper & Row, 1989).

Examples of feminist theology in Europe include Catharina Halkes, *Suchen, was verlorenging: Beiträge zur feministischen Theologie* (Gütersloh, 1985); Elisabeth Moltmann-Wendel, *A Land Flowing with Milk and Honey: Perspectives on Feminist Theology*, trans. John Bowden (New York: Crossroad, 1986); and Marie-Therese Wacker, ed., *Der Gott der Männer und die Frauen* (Düsseldorf: Patmos Verlag, 1987).

20. The following is but the tip of the iceberg. The global phenomenon of women's religious discourse is studied in Diana Eck and Devaki Jain, eds., *Speaking of Faith: Global Perspectives on Women, Religion, and Social Change* (Philadelphia: New Society, 1987); Barbel von Wartenberg-Potter, *We Will Not Hang Our Harps on the Willows: Global Sisterhood and God's Songs*, trans. Fred Kaan (Oak Park, Ill.: Meyer-Stone Books, 1987); and Melanie May, *Bonds of Unity: Women, Theology and the Worldwide Church* (Atlanta: Scholars Press, 1989).

Latin America: Elsa Tamez, ed., *Through Her Eyes: Women's Theology from Latin America* (Maryknoll, N.Y.: Orbis, 1989).

Asia: Virginia Fabella and Sun Ai Lee Park, eds., *We Dare to Dream: Doing Theology as Asian Women* (Maryknoll, N.Y.: Orbis, 1990); Chung Hyun Kyung, *Struggle to be the Sun Again: Introducing Asian Women's Theology* (Maryknoll, N.Y.: Orbis, 1990); and "Special Section: Asian Women Theologians Respond to American Feminism," *JFSR* 3 (1987) 103–34.

Africa: Mercy Amba Oduyoye, *Hearing and Knowing: Theological Reflections on Christianity in Africa* (Maryknoll, N.Y.: Orbis, 1986); Bénézet Bujo, "Feministische Theologie in Africa," *Stimmen der Zeit* 113 (1988) 529–38.

Intercontinental: John Pobee and Barbel von Wartenberg-Potter, *New Eyes for Reading: Biblical and Theological Reflections by Women from the Third World* (Oak Park, Ill.: Meyer-Stone Books, 1986); Virginia Fabella and Mercy Amba Oduyoye, eds., *With Passion and Compassion: Third World Women Doing Theology* (Maryknoll, N.Y.: Orbis, 1988); Letty Russell, Kwok Pui-lan, Ada Maria Isasi-Diaz, Katie Geneva Cannon, *Inheriting Our Mother's Gardens: Feminist Theology in Third World Perspective* (Louisville: Westminster, 1988), with extensive annotated bibliography.

21. Ada Maria Isasi-Diaz and Yolanda Tarango, *Hispanic Women: Prophetic Voice in the Church* (San Francisco: Harper & Row, 1988).

22. This is one of the most critical conversations now under way. Women's emancipation has different meanings for women of nondominant cultures and poor women due to the corrosive effects of racism and poverty, a reality that has not been carefully attended to by white, middle-class feminism. See Bell Hooks, *Ain't I a Woman? Black Women and Feminism* (Boston: South End Press, 1981); Cherríe Moraga and Gloria Anzaldúa, eds., *This Bridge Called My Back* (Watertown, Mass.: Persephone Press, 1981), with contributions from North American women of African, Asian/Pacific, Latin, and native descent; Bettina Aptheker, *Women's Legacy: Essays on Race, Sex and Class in American History* (Amherst: University of Massachusetts Press, 1982). The theological import of this criticism is explored by Pauli Murray, "Black Theology and Feminist Theology: A Comparative View," *Anglican Theological Review* 60 (1978) 3–24; Katie Geneva Cannon, "The Emergence of Black Feminist Consciousness," in *Feminist Interpretation of the Bible*, ed. Letty Russell (Philadelphia: Westminster, 1985) 30–40; and Delores Williams, "Black Women's Literature and the Task of Feminist Theology," in *Immaculate and Powerful: The Female in Sacred Image and Social Reality*, ed. Clarissa Atkinson, Constance Buchanan, and Margaret Miles (Boston: Beacon, 1985); idem, "Womanist Theology," in *Weaving the Visions*, 179–86. The dialogue continues in works by white women such as Susan Brooks Thistlethwaite, *Sex, Race, and God: Christian Feminism in Black and White* (New York:

Crossroad, 1989); and Sharon Welch, *A Feminist Ethic of Risk* (Minneapolis: Fortress, 1990).

23. Carr, *Transforming Grace*, 63–94, contextualizes this variety in society and the academy; Sallie McFague, *Metaphorical Theology: Models of God in Religious Language* (Philadelphia: Fortress, 1982) 152–77, gives a thorough description. Goddess feminism is explored by Carol Christ, "Symbols of Goddess and God," in *The Book of the Goddess, Past and Present*, ed. Carl Olson (New York: Crossroad, 1985) 231–51; Nelle Morton, "Goddess as Metaphoric Image," in her *The Journey Is Home* (Boston: Beacon, 1985) 147–75; and Maria Gimbutas, *The Language of the Goddess: Unearthing the Hidden Symbols of Western Civilization* (San Francisco: Harper & Row, 1989).

24. Susanna Heschel, ed., *On Being a Jewish Feminist* (New York: Schocken Books, 1983); Judith Plaskow, *Standing Again at Sinai: Judaism from a Feminist Perspective* (San Francisco: Harper & Row, 1990); Susan T. Foh, *Women and the Word of God: A Response to Biblical Feminism* (Grand Rapids, Mich: Baker, 1979) (an evangelical perspective); and Mary Jo Weaver, *New Catholic Women: A Contemporary Challenge to Traditional Religious Authority* (San Francisco: Harper & Row, 1985).

25. Carter Heyward et al., "Lesbianism and Feminist Theology," *JFSR* 2 (1986) 95–106; Mary Hunt, *Fierce Tenderness: A Feminist Theology of Friendship* (New York: Crossroad, 1990).

26. Josephine Donovan, *Feminist Theory: The Intellectual Traditions of American Feminism* (New York: F. Ungar, 1985), describes the Enlightenment liberal, cultural, Marxist, Freudian, existentialist, and radical options. Another typology is organized by Maria Riley, *Transforming Feminism* (Washington, D.C.: Center of Concern, 1989), in the categories of liberal, cultural, radical, and socialist feminism. Excellent background is given by Rosemary Radford Ruether and Rosemary Skinner Keller, eds., *Women and Religion in America: A Documentary History*, 3 vols. (San Francisco: Harper & Row, 1981, 1983, 1986).

27. Catherine Keller remarks that this new habit of identifying our social location is itself a kenotic practice, emptying our discourse of the false substance of inflated universals: "Scoop up the Water and the Moon Is in Your Hands: On Feminist Theology and Dynamic Self-Emptying," in *The Emptying God: A Buddhist-Jewish-Christian Conversation*, ed. John B. Cobb and Christopher Ives (Maryknoll, N.Y.: Orbis, 1990) 102–3.

28. Different presentations of this perspective are given by Letty Russell, *Human Liberation in a Feminist Perspective: A Theology* (Philadelphia: Westminster, 1974), and Elisabeth Schüssler Fiorenza, "Feminist Theology as a Critical Theology of Liberation," *TS* 36 (1975) 605–26.

29. See, for example, Adrienne Rich's use of the creative skills of the spider in her poem "Natural Resources," in *The Fact of a Doorframe*, 261; and Elisabeth Schüssler Fiorenza, "The Quilting of Women's History: Phoebe of Cenchreae," in *Embodied Love: Sensuality and Relationship as Feminist Values*, ed. Paula M. Cooey, Sharon A. Farmer, and Mary Ellen Ross (San Francisco: Harper & Row, 1987) 35–49.

30. Mary Collins, "Naming God in Public Prayer," *Worship* 59 (1985) 291–304.

31. Bernard Lonergan, *Insight: A Study of Human Understanding* (San Francisco: Harper & Row, 1978) 191–92, 222–25.

32. Paraphrase of *AH* 4.20.7; see also 3.20.2 and 5.3. Mary Ann Donovan, "Alive to the Glory of God: A Key Insight in St. Irenaeus," *TS* 49 (1988) 283–97, clarifies the context of this maxim in relation to the companion phrase with which it appears: *gloria enim Dei vivens homo, vita autem hominis visio Dei* (*AH* 4:20.7).

33. Juan Luis Segundo, *Our Idea of God*, trans. John Drury (Maryknoll, N.Y.: Orbis, 1974) 8.

34. Wolfhart Pannenberg, "Toward a Theology of the History of Religions," in *Basic Questions in Theology: Collected Essays*, 2 vols., trans. George Kehm (Louisville, Ky.: Westminster/John Knox, 1983) 2:65–118.

35. Gregory of Nyssa, "An Answer to Ablabius: That We Should Not Think of Saying That There Are Three Gods," in *Christology of the Later Fathers*, ed. Edward Hardy (Philadelphia: Westminster, 1954) 257.

Chapter 2 / Feminist Theology and
Critical Discourse about God

1. Sojourner Truth's address before an unruly New York audience in 1853 appears in *Feminism: The Essential Historical Writings*, ed. Miriam Schneir (New York: Random House, 1972) 96–97.

2. Roger Haight, *An Alternative Vision: An Interpretation of Liberation Theology* (New York: Paulist, 1985) 53.

3. H. P. Owen, *Concepts of Deity* (New York: Herder and Herder, 1971) 1.

4. McFague, *Models of God* (see chap. 1, n. 12) 63–69. This book is an outstanding example of constructive theology, to which I am indebted for inspiration and ideas.

5. Herbert Vorgrimler, "Recent Critiques of Theism," in *A Personal God?* (*Concilium* 103), ed. Edward Schillebeeckx and Bas van Iersel (New York: Seabury, 1977) 24. Credit for coining the word goes to the philosopher Ralph Cudworth in *The Intellectual System of the Universe* (London: printed for Richard Royston, 1678).

6. Michael Buckley, *At the Origins of Modern Atheism* (New Haven: Yale University Press, 1987); Marcel Neusch, *The Sources of Modern Atheism*, trans. Matthew O'Connell (New York: Paulist, 1982); Hans Küng, *Does God Exist? An Answer for Today*, trans. Edward Quinn (Garden City, N.Y.: Doubleday, 1980). One of the best popular statements of what is at stake in the atheistic debates remains John A. T. Robinson, "Can a Truly Contemporary Person Not Be an Atheist?" in *The New Christianity*, ed. William R. Miller (New York: Dell, 1967) 299–314.

7. Richard Rubenstein, *After Auschwitz: Radical Theology and Contemporary Judaism* (Indianapolis: Bobbs-Merrill, 1968); Arthur Cohen, *The Tremendum: A Theological Interpretation of the Holocaust* (New York: Crossroad, 1981). An incisive analysis of the difficulty is given by Paul Ricoeur, "Evil, A Challenge to Philosophy and Theology," *JAAR* 53 (1985) 635–48.

8. Victorio Araya, *God of the Poor: The Mystery of God in Latin America* (Maryknoll, N.Y.: Orbis, 1987); Jon Sobrino, "The Experience of God in the Church of the Poor," in *The True Church and the Poor*, trans. Matthew O'Connell (Maryknoll, N.Y.: Orbis, 1984) 125–59. For liberation theology from cultural contexts other than Latin America, see James Cone, *God of the Oppressed* (New York: Seabury, 1975); Vine Deloria, *God Is Red* (New York: Grosset & Dunlap, 1973); Albert Nolan, *God in South Africa* (Grand Rapids, Mich.: Eerdmans, 1988); and Aloysius Pieris, *An Asian Theology of Liberation* (Maryknoll, N.Y.: Orbis, 1988).

9. Cobb and Ives, eds., *The Emptying God* (see chap. 1, n. 27); Aloysius Pieris, *Love Meets Wisdom: A Christian Experience of Buddhism* (Maryknoll, N.Y.: Orbis, 1990); Raimundo Panikkar, *The Silence of God: The Answer of the Buddha* (Maryknoll, N.Y.: Orbis, 1990).

10. Martin Heidegger, *Identity and Difference*, trans. Joan Stambaugh (New York: Harper & Row, 1957) 72. Helpful analyses of the deficiencies of classical theism appear in Langdon Gilkey, "God," in *Christian Theology: An Introduction to Its Traditions and Tasks*, ed. Peter Hodgson and Robert King (Philadelphia: Fortress, 1985) 88–113; Schubert Ogden, "The Reality of God," in *The Reality of God* (New York: Harper & Row, 1963) 1–70; and Theodore Jennings, *Beyond Theism: A Grammar of God-Language* (New York: Oxford University Press, 1985) 13–28.

11. Walter Kasper, *The God of Jesus Christ*, trans. Matthew O'Connell (New York: Crossroad, 1984) 295.

12. Carr, *Transforming Grace* (see ch. 1, n. 15) 144–57.

13. For example, Jürgen Moltmann, *The Crucified God: The Cross of Christ as the Foundation and Criticism of Christian Theology*, trans. R. A. Wilson and John Bowden (New York: Harper & Row, 1973) 200–204; Walter Kasper, *Jesus the Christ*, trans. V. Green (New York: Paulist, 1976) 168; Jon Sobrino, *Christology at the Crossroads*, trans. John Drury (Maryknoll, N.Y.: Orbis, 1978) 218, 291; Leander Keck, *A Future for the Historical Jesus* (Philadelphia: Fortress, 1981) 210.

14. Yvone Gebara, "Option for the Poor as an Option for the Poor Woman," in *Women, Work and Poverty* (*Concilium* 194), ed. Elisabeth Schüssler Fiorenza and Anne Carr (Edinburgh: T & T Clark, 1987) 110–17.

15. Bell Hooks, *Feminist Theory: From Margin to Center* (Boston: South End Press, 1984) ix. Chopp, *The Power to Speak* (see chap. 1, n. 8) 15–18 and 115–24, offers a fine analysis of marginality.

16. Margaret Farley, "Sexism," *New Catholic Encyclopedia* (New York: McGraw Hill, 1978) 17:604.

17. Examples of patriarchy in the history of Western culture itself, in philosophy, law, medicine, political theory, education, marriage as well as religion are collated in Julia O'Faolain and Lauro Martines, eds., *Not in God's Image: Women in History from the Greeks to the Victorians* (New York: Harper & Row, 1973); and Marilyn French, *Beyond Power: On Women, Men and Morals* (New York: Ballantine Books, 1985). A sweeping review of the issues is found in Seyla Benhabib and Drucilla Cornell, eds., *Feminism as Critique: On the Politics of Gender* (Minneapolis: University of Minnesota Press, 1987).

18. *ST* I, q. 92, a. 1, ad. 1. See Maryanne Cline Horowitz, "Aristotle and Women," *Journal of the History of Biology* 9 (1976) 183–213. Excellent analysis of this thought pattern appears in Rosemary Radford Ruether, ed., *Religion and Sexism: Images of Woman in the Jewish and Christian Traditions* (New York: Simon and Schuster, 1974), especially Ruether's essay "Misogynism and Virginal Feminism in the Fathers of the Church," 150–83, and the textual study by Eleanor Commo McLaughlin, "Equality of Souls, Inequality of Sexes: Women in Medieval Theology," 213–66; see also Margaret Farley, "Sources of Sexual Inequality in the History of Christian Thought," *JR* 56 (1976) 162–76; and Kari Elisabeth Børresen, *Subordination and Equivalence: The Nature and Role of Woman in Augustine and Thomas Aquinas* (Lanham, Md.: University Press of America, 1981).

19. *ST* I, q. 92, a. 1, ad. 2.

20. *ST* I, q. 92, a. 4; q. 93, a. 4. Elizabeth Clark and Herbert Richardson call Aquinas "The Man Who Should Have Known Better," in *Women and Religion: A Feminist Sourcebook of Christian Thought* (San Francisco: Harper & Row, 1977) 78–101.

21. "World's Women Data Sheet" (Washington, D.C.: Population Reference Bureau in collaboration with UNICEF, 1985); *Report of the World Conference to Review and Appraise the Achievements of the United Nations Decade for Women: Equality, Development and Peace* (New York: United Nations, 1985).

22. Mary Daly's *Gyn/Ecology: The Metaethics of Radical Feminism* (Boston: Beacon, 1978) explores and powerfully indicts the physical degradation of women in diverse cultures. See also Mary D. Pellauer, "Moral Callousness and Moral Sensitivity: Violence against Women," in Barbara Hilkert Andolsen, Christine Gudorf, and Mary Pellauer, eds., *Women's Consciousness, Women's Conscience: A Reader in Feminist Ethics* (Minneapolis: Winston, 1985) 33–50; Susan Brooks Thistlethwaite, "Every Two Minutes: Battered Women and Feminist Interpretation," in *Weaving the Visions* (see chap. 1, n. 19) 302–13.

23. Ecclesiastical patriarchy's twin roots in Greek philosophy and Roman law are described by Mary Collins, "The Refusal of Women in Clerical Circles," in *Women in the Church*, ed. Madonna Kolbenschlag (Washington, D.C.: Pastoral Press, 1987) 1:51–63.

24. Paulo Freire, *Pedagogy of the Oppressed*, trans. Myra Bergman Ramos (New York: Seabury, 1970). The classic description of the result is given by Simone de Beauvoir, *The Second Sex* (New York: Alfred Knopf, 1953).

25. Nancy Miller and Kate Swift, *Words and Women: New Language in New Times* (Garden City, N.Y.: Doubleday, 1976) 34. In this regard Jürgen Habermas's analysis of the systematic distortion that institutional power imposes on communication to further its own self-interest has been found useful by many feminist theorists; see his *Toward A Rational Society: Student Protest, Science and Politics* (Boston: Beacon, 1971).

26. One of the earliest and most astute analyses of this interlocking of oppressions, including race, class, and the degradation of the earth, is Rosemary Radford Ruether's *New Woman, New Earth: Sexist Ideologies and Human Liberation* (New York: Seabury, 1975). See Beverly Lindsay, *Comparative Perspectives of Third World Women: The Impact of Race, Sex and Class* (New York: Praeger, 1980); M. Shawn Copeland, "The Interaction of Racism, Sexism and Classism in Women's Exploitation," in *Women, Work and Poverty*, 19–27; Betty Reardon, *Sexism and the War System* (New York: Teacher's College Press/Columbia University, 1985). The connection between suppression of women and rape of the earth is explored in Carolyn Merchant, *The Death of Nature: Women, Ecology*

and the Scientific Revolution (San Francisco: Harper & Row, 1980); conversely, reverence for the earth as a component of the emancipation of women is clarified by Irene Diamond and Gloria Feman Orenstein, eds., *Reweaving the World: The Emergence of Eco-Feminism* (San Francisco: Sierra Club Books, 1990); and Lois Daly, "Ecofeminism, Reverence for Life, and Feminist Theological Ethics," in *Liberating Life: Contemporary Approaches to Ecological Theology*, ed. Charles Birch, William Eakin, and Jay McDaniel (Maryknoll, N.Y.: Orbis, 1990) 88–108.

27. Gerda Lerner, *The Creation of Patriarchy* (New York: Oxford University Press, 1986). Also Peggy Reeves Sunday, *Female Power and Male Dominance: On the Origins of Sexual Inequality* (Cambridge, Eng.: Cambridge University Press, 1981).

28. Ruether, *New Woman, New Earth*, 4.

29. Elizabeth Fox-Genovese, *Within the Plantation Household: Black and White Women of the Old South* (Chapel Hill, N.C.: University of North Carolina Press, 1988).

30. Anselm, *Cur Deus Homo?* bk 1, chap. 21, in *Saint Anselm: Basic Writings* (see chap. 1, n. 12).

31. See chap. 4 below for development of this theme.

32. Elisabeth Schüssler Fiorenza, *In Memory of Her: A Feminist Theological Reconstruction of Christian Origins* (New York: Crossroad, 1983) is an outstanding example of this work of retrieval to which I am greatly indebted. Rosemary Radford Ruether and Eleanor Commo McLaughlin, eds., *Women of Spirit: Female Leadership in the Jewish and Christian Traditions* (New York: Simon and Schuster, 1979); Patricia Wilson-Kastner et al., eds., *A Lost Tradition: Women Writers of the Early Church* (Lanham, Md.: University Press of America, 1981).

33. The most comprehensive reconstructive effort in systematic theology to date is Rosemary Radford Ruether, *Sexism and God-Talk: Toward a Feminist Theology* (Boston: Beacon, 1983), which reformulates the traditional treatises from foundational theology to eschatology. I am much indebted to the ideas in this work.

34. Ground-breaking examples of the old "handmaid" receiving new life are Carol Gould, ed., *Beyond Domination: New Perspectives on Women and Philosophy* (Totowa, N.J.: Rowman & Allanheld, 1983); and Morwenna Griffiths and Margaret Whitford, eds., *Feminist Perspectives in Philosophy* (Bloomington: Indiana University Press, 1988).

35. Ruether, *Sexism and God-Talk*, 18–19.

36. Ibid., 19.

37. For development, see Edward Schillebeeckx, *Christ: The Experience of Jesus as Lord*, trans. John Bowden (New York: Seabury, 1980) 731–43.

38. Rebecca Chopp, "Feminism's Theological Pragmatics: A Social Naturalism of Women's Experience," *JR* 67 (1987) 255.

39. Rosemary Radford Ruether, "Feminist Theology and Spirituality," in *Christian Feminism: Visions of a New Humanity*, ed. Judith Weidman (San Francisco: Harper & Row, 1984) 25.

40. This is beautifully explained by Anne Carr, "Feminist Theology in a New Paradigm," in *Paradigm Change in Theology*, ed. Hans Küng and David Tracy (New York: Crossroad, 1989) 397–407; and Sallie McFague, "An Epilogue: The Christian Paradigm," in Gilkey, *Christian Theology*, 377–90.

For the impact of this paradigm shift on the academic study of religion, see Valerie Saiving, "Androcentrism in Religious Studies," *JR* 56 (1976) 177–97; Rosemary Radford Ruether, "The Feminist Critique in Religious Studies," *Soundings* 64 (1981) 388–402; idem, address on the occasion of the 75th anniversary of the American Academy of Religion, "The Future of Feminist Theology in the Academy," *JAAR* 53 (1985) 703–13; and Arlene Swidler and Walter Conn, eds., *Mainstreaming: Feminist Research for Teaching Religious Studies* (Lanham, Md.: University Press of America, 1985). A series of essays in *Horizons: Journal of the College Theology Society* consistently deals with the issue; e.g., Margaret Farley, "Feminist Ethics in the Christian Ethics Curriculum," 11 (1984) 361–72; Jane Kopas, "Teaching Christology in Light of Feminist Issues," 13 (1986) 332–43.

41. This analogy is effectively proposed by Jill Raitt in her presidential address to the American Academy of Religion, "Strictures and Structures: Relational Theology and A Woman's Contribution to Theological Conversation," *JAAR* 50 (1982) 3–17.

42. Gregory of Nazianzus, "The Third Theological Oration — on the Son," in *Christology of the Later Fathers* (see chap. 1, n. 35) 171.

43. The telling but common example offered by Ruether, *Sexism and God-Talk*, 67.

44. Julian of Norwich, *Showings*, trans. and intro. by Edmund Colledge and James Walsh (New York: Paulist, 1978) 298.

45. Marjorie Suchocki, "The Unmale God: Reconsidering the Trinity," *Quarterly Review* 3:1 (1983) 34.

46. *SCG* 4.11, 19.

47. Clifford Geertz, "Religion as a Cultural System," in *The Interpretation of Cultures* (New York: Basic Books, 1973) 90. A good analysis of the function of symbols in the thought of Geertz as well as other social anthropologists and philosophers is F. W. Dillistone, *The Power of Symbols in Religion and Culture* (New York: Crossroad, 1986).

48. Studies that helpfully analyze the dynamic relationship between God and social arrangements include Alain Durand, "Political Implications of the God Question," in *New Questions on God* (*Concilium* 76), ed. J. B. Metz (New York: Herder & Herder, 1972) 67–74; Charles Glock, "Images of God, Images of Man, and the Organization of Social Life," *Journal for the Scientific Study of Religion* 11 (1972) 1–15; David Nichols, "Images of God and the State: Political Analogy and Religious Discourse," *TS* 42 (1981) 195–215; and Segundo, *Our Idea of God* (see chap. 1, n. 33). None of these studies explicitly raises the question of women.

49. Paul Tillich, *Systematic Theology*, 3 vols. (Chicago: University of Chicago Press, 1951, 1957, 1963) 1:140–41.

50. Ibid.

51. Mary Daly, "Feminist Post-Christian Introduction," *The Church and the Second Sex* (New York: Harper & Row, 1975) 38, and her sustained analysis in *Beyond God the Father* (see chap. 1, n. 9).

52. Carol Christ, "Why Women Need the Goddess," in *Womanspirit Rising* (see chap. 1, n. 19) 275.

53. Kaufman, *The Theological Imagination* (see chap. 1, n.3) 32.

54. John Calvin, *Institutes of the Christian Religion*, ed. John McNeill (Philadelphia: Westminster, 1960) bk. 1, chap. 11, par. 8.

55. C. S. Lewis, *A Grief Observed* (London: Faber, 1966) 52.

56. Ruether, *Sexism and God-Talk*, 23. See Karen Bloomquist, "Let God Be God: The Theological Necessity of Depatriarchalizing God," in *Our Naming of God*, ed. Carl Braaten (Minneapolis: Fortress, 1989) 45–60; and the excellent discussion by McFague, "God the Father: Model or Idol?" in *Metaphorical Theology* (see chap. 1, n. 23) 145–92.

57. For literature on the critique of the model of God as father, see McFague, *Metaphorical Theology*, 215 n.1; Carr, *Transforming Grace*, 134–57; and Catharina Halkes, "Themes of Protest in Feminist Theology against God the Father," in *God as Father?* (*Concilium* 143), ed. J. B. Metz and Edward Schillebeeckx (New York: Seabury, 1981) 103–10. For retrievals see McFague, *Models of God*, 91–123 (the father symbol can continue to be fruitful if used in the context of the model of God as mother, for then it will signify a caring parent rather than a domineering patriarch); Sandra Schneiders, *Women and the Word: The Gender of God in the New Testament and the Spirituality of Women* (New York: Paulist, 1986) 11–15; Dorothee Soelle, *The Strength of the Weak: Toward a Christian Feminist Identity*, trans. Robert and Rita Kimbler (Philadelphia: Westminster, 1984) 114–17; Diane Tennis, *Is God the Only Reliable Father?* (Philadelphia: Westminster, 1985).

In my judgment the father-child relationship is too basic a datum of human experience and too important both for every human person as offspring and for men as generative persons to dispense with altogether and forever as metaphor for God. If it can be deconstructed as an idol and buttress of oppression and spoken in a community of the discipleship of equals, it may yet serve as an icon of divine creativity, protection, delight, and care.

Chapter 3 / Basic Linguistic Options:
God, Women, Equivalence

1. Meinrad Craighead, *The Mother's Songs: Images of God the Mother* (New York: Paulist, 1986) 15.

2. Ruether, *Sexism and God-Talk* (see chap. 2, n. 33) 46.

3. Chopp, *The Power to Speak* (see chap. 1, n. 8).

4. Martin Buber, *Eclipse of God: Studies in the Relation between Religion and Philosophy* (New York: Harper & Row, 1952) 7.

5. Ibid., 7–9.

6. Aquinas, here following Damascene: *ST* I, q. 13, a. 8.

7. This has been well noted by Rita Gross, "Female God Language in a Jewish Context," in *Womanspirit Rising* (see chap. 1, n. 19) 167–73.

8. Aquinas, *De Potentia* (Westminster, Md.: Newman Press, 1952) q. 7, a. 5.

9. Marcia Falk, "Notes on Composing New Blessings," in *Weaving the Visions* (see chap. 1, n.19) 132.

10. As Caroline Walker Bynum points out, "Gender-related symbols, in their full complexity, may refer to gender in ways that affirm or reverse it, support or question it; or they may, in their basic meaning, have little at all to do with male and female roles" ("Introduction: The Complexity of Symbols," *Gender and Religion: On the Complexity of Symbols*, ed. Caroline Walker Bynum, Stevan Harrell, and Paula Richman [Boston: Beacon, 1986] 2).

11. *ST* I, q. 12, a. 13.

12. The importance of image and the imagination has been an issue in religious studies for at least two decades, triggered into prominence by Ray Hart's insightful *Unfinished Man and the Imagination: Toward an Ontology and a Rhetoric of Revelation* (New York: Herder & Herder, 1968). The theme developed in the 1970s through studies such as Amos Wilder's, *Theopoetic and the Religious Imagination* (Philadelphia: Fortress, 1976), and John Bouker's, *The Religious Imagination and the Sense of God* (Oxford: Clarendon Press, 1978). David Tracy's analysis of ecumenical differences in imagination has become a classic in its own right: *The Analogical Imagination: Christian Theology and the Culture of Pluralism* (New York: Crossroad, 1981). I am indebted to the analysis of both Gordon Kaufman, *The Theological Imagination* (see chap. 1, n. 3), and Garrett Green, *Imagining God: Theology and the Religious Imagination* (San Francisco: Harper & Row, 1989), two very different approaches but both enlightening. Margaret Miles's excellent work *Image as Insight: Visual Understanding in Western Christianity and Secular Culture* (Boston: Beacon, 1985) exposes the power of the image to shape moral values; Nelle Morton shows a way forward in *The Journey Is Home* (see chap. 1, n. 23), especially "How Images Function," 31–39, "Beloved Image," 122–46, and "The Goddess as Metaphoric Image," 147–75.

13. Paul Tillich, *Dynamics of Faith* (New York: Harper & Row, 1957) 41–48. An enlightening treatise that further probes the symbolic mediation of religious knowledge is Avery Dulles, *Models of Revelation* (Garden City, N.Y.: Doubleday, 1983).

14. The reader is invited to dwell with the illustrations of God in this book as examples of the power of the image to move thought and praxis in specific directions. See Ricoeur, *Symbolism of Evil* (see chap. 1, n. 10) 347–57.

15. W. A. Visser't Hooft, *The Fatherhood of God in an Age of Emancipation* (Geneva: World Council of Churches, 1982) 133.

16. This list of feminine characteristics is taken from Daniel O'Hanlon, "The Future of Theism," *CTSAP* 38 (1983) 8.

17. Visser't Hooft, *Fatherhood of God*, 133; O'Hanlon, "Future of Theism," 7–8; Yves Congar, *I Believe in the Holy Spirit*, 3 vols., trans. David Smith (New York: Seabury, 1983) 3:155–64; Hans Küng, *Does God Exist?* (see chap. 2, n. 6) 673.

18. Küng, *Does God Exist?* 673.

19. Carr, *Transforming Grace* (see chap. 1, n. 15), chap. 4 surveys the academic study of gender.

20. Rosemary Radford Ruether, "The Female Nature of God: A Problem in Contemporary Religious Life," in *God as Father?* (see chap. 2, n. 57) 61–66. Much contemporary use of the concept of the feminine is related to the categories codified by Carl Jung; see Naomi Goldenberg, "A Feminist Critique of Jung," *Signs* (Winter 1976) 443–49, and "Important Directions for a Feminist Critique of Religion in the Works of Sigmund Freud and Carl Jung," Ph.D. diss., Yale University, 1976.

21. Robert Murray, "The Holy Spirit as Mother," in *Symbols of Church and Kingdom* (London: Cambridge University Press, 1975) 312–20; P. A. De Boer, *Fatherhood and Motherhood in Israelite and Judean Piety* (Leiden: Brill, 1974).

22. Kasper, *God of Jesus Christ* (see chap. 2, n. 11) 223.

23. Franz Mayr, "Trinitätstheologie und theologische Anthropologie," *Zeitschrift für Theologie und Kirche* 68 (1971) 474. This is reminiscent of Basil of Caesarea, who at one point held that the Holy Spirit was equal in nature but not in rank or dignity with the Father and the Son: *Contra Eunomium* 3.2 (*PG* 29.657c). While he later changed his position, the incident is illustrative of the tendency to subordinate the Holy Spirit.

24. Mario Bachiega, *Dio Padre o Dea Madre?* (Florence, 1976); H. H. Schrey, "Ist Gott ein Mann?" *Theologische Rundschau* 44 (1979) 233; Mayr, "Trinitätstheologie," 469.

25. John B. Cobb, "The Trinity and Sexist Language," in his *Christ in a Pluralistic Age* (Philadelphia: Westminster, 1975) 264. George Tavard sets up a similar polarity in *Women in Christian Tradition* (Notre Dame, Ind.: University of Notre Dame, 1973) 195–99, but then questions it on the basis of the difficulties it presents.

26. Congar, *I Believe in the Holy Spirit*, especially "The Motherhood in God and the Femininity of the Holy Spirit," 3: 155–64.

27. Leonardo Boff, *The Maternal Face of God: The Feminine and Its Religious Expressions*, trans. Robert Barr and John Diercksmeier (Maryknoll, N.Y.: Orbis, 1987) 101.

28. Ibid., 188–203 vs. 119 and passim.

29. Donald Gelpi, *The Divine Mother: A Trinitarian Theology of the Holy Spirit* (Lanham, Md.: University Press of America, 1984).

30. Phyllis Trible's expression, used throughout *God and the Rhetoric of Sexuality* (Philadelphia: Fortress, 1978).

31. Herbert Richardson recounts the following personal recollection. As a child he was taught to say a bedtime prayer "Father-Mother God, loving me, guard me while I sleep, guide my little feet up to thee." It was thereby borne in upon his young mind that if the divine is both Father and Mother, God is different from any one thing he experienced around him (*Women and Religion* [see chap. 2, n. 20] 164–65).

32. Ruether, *Sexism and God-Talk* (see chap. 2, n. 33) 52.

33. See the prayers in Frederick Grant, *Hellenistic Religions: The Age of Syncretism* (New York: Liberal Arts, 1953) 131–33; and historical studies by scholars such as Judith Ochshorn, *The Female Experience and the Nature of the Divine* (Bloomington: Indiana University Press, 1981). The use of equivalent imagery did not necessarily mean that these societies were egalitarian; the feminist liberation hermeneutic introduces something genuinely new in this regard.

34. Elizabeth A. Johnson, "The Incomprehensibility of God and the Image of God Male and Female," *TS* 45 (1984) 441–65. Dorothee Soelle puts the same idea more graphically: "We do not mean to substitute a dominant feminist exclusivity, but in a paternalistic culture language has to be turned on its head before anyone will begin to grasp what the problem is and to understand that human beings might chose another symbol to identify with" ("Mysticism — Liberation — Feminism," in *The Strength of the Weak* [see chap. 2, n. 57] 101).

Chapter 4 / Women's Interpreted Experience

1. The Latin text is printed in R. Laqueur, "Ephoros. Die Proömium," *Hermes* 46 (1911) 161–206, at 172; cited in James Crenshaw, "The Acquisition of Knowledge in Israelite Wisdom Literature," *Word and World* 7 (1987) 246. Lines 6 and 7 of the Latin text read:

> terra fortis est, at homo vincit eam.
> homo fortis est, at moeror vincit eum.

The Crenshaw translation renders *homo* in an inclusive sense, to read "humans." Thus "the earth is majestic, but humans master it." However, the punch line of the verse, *sed omnibus fortior est femina*, clearly intends to contrast men and women, not humans and women. The Crenshaw translation sets up an ironic situation where inclusivity effectively bars women from participation in what is named human. Thus I have rendered *homo* in the more limited sense.

2. See David Tracy, *Blessed Rage for Order* (New York: Seabury, 1975); Schillebeeckx, *Christ* (see chap. 2, n. 37) 27–79, interpreted by Mary Catherine Hilkert, "Discovery of the Living God: Revelation and Experience," in *The Praxis of Christian Experience: An Introduction to the Theology of Edward Schillebeeckx*, ed. Robert Schreiter and Mary Catherine Hilkert (San Francisco: Harper & Row, 1989) 35–51; Francis Schüssler Fiorenza, *Foundational Theology: Jesus and the Church* (New York: Crossroad, 1984) 296–301 especially; Jon Sobrino, "The Experience of God in the Church of the Poor" (see chap. 2, n. 8); and Nicholas Lash, *Easter in Ordinary: Reflections on Human Experience and the Knowledge of God* (Charlottesville: University Press of Virginia, 1988). Critique and warning are sounded by Owen Thomas, "Theology and Experience," *Harvard Theological Review* 78 (1985) 179–201.

3. The debate about women's experience is traced in Carr, *Transforming Grace* (see chap. 1, n. 15) 117–33. It continues in Sheila Greeve Devaney, "The Limits of the Appeal to Women's Experience," presentation to the Women and Religion Section of the American Academy of Religion, November 1986; Chopp, "Feminism's Theological Pragmatics" (see chap. 2, n. 38) 239–56; and Ann O'Hara Graff, "An Assessment of Women's Experience as a Starting Point for Theology," paper presented at the Catholic Theological Society of America, June 1991. See the analysis by Monika Hellwig, *Whose Experience Counts in Theological Reflection?* (Milwaukee, Wis.: Marquette University Press, 1982).

4. A key proponent of the category of contrast experience is Edward Schillebeeckx who first uses the notion in "The Magisterium and the World of Politics," in *Faith and the World of Politics* (*Concilium* 36), ed. J. B. Metz (New York: Paulist, 1968) 19–39.

5. Nelle Morton, *The Journey Is Home* (see chap. 1, n. 23), powerfully insists on the importance of women's hearing each other into speech; Sharon Welch, *Communities of Resistance and Solidarity: A Feminist Theology of Liberation* (Maryknoll, N.Y.: Orbis, 1985).

6. The pioneering essay on this subject is Valerie Saiving, "The Human Situation: A Feminine View," *JR* 40 (1960) 100–112, rep. in *Womanspirit Rising* (see chap. 1, n. 19) 25–42. Her thesis is probed and demonstrated by Judith Plaskow, *Sex, Sin and Grace: Women's Experience and the Theologies of Reinhold Niebuhr and Paul Tillich* (Washington, D.C.: University Press of America, 1980); see Ruether, "The Consciousness of Evil: The Journeys of Conversion," in *Sexism and God-Talk* (see chap. 2, n. 33) 159–92; Paula Cooey, "The Power of Transformation and the Transformation of Power," *JFSR* 1 (1985) 23–36. Foundational analysis of the conversion process is undertaken by Bernard Lonergan, *Method in Theology* (New York: Seabury, 1979) 235–66.

7. Madonna Kohlbenschlag, *Kiss Sleeping Beauty Good-Bye: Breaking the Spell of Feminine Myths and Models* (Garden City, N.Y.: Doubleday, 1979).

8. Karl Rahner, "Experience of Self and Experience of God," *TI* 13:125. For background, see his foundational work *Spirit in the World*, trans. William Dych (New York: Herder & Herder, 1968), and its development in *Foundations of Christian Faith*, trans. William Dych (New York: Seabury, 1978), chaps. 1–4. A lucid rephrasing of this position can be found in John Haught, *What Is God? How to Think about the Divine* (New York: Paulist, 1986).

9. Rahner, "Experience of Self," 129.

10. A highly instructive example of this critique is Francis Schüssler Fiorenza, *Foundational Theology: Jesus and the Church*.

11. Johann Baptist Metz, *Faith in History and Society: Toward a Practical Fundamental Theology*, trans. David Smith (New York: Seabury, 1980).

12. For these categories, see Paul Ricoeur, "Naming God," *Union Seminary Quarterly Review* 34 (1978–79) 215–27.

13. Daly, *Beyond God the Father* (see chap. 1, n. 9) 33.

14. Ntozake Shange, *for colored girls who have considered suicide / when the rainbow is enuf* (New York: Macmillan, 1976) 63. In this cry not only femaleness but blackness is endorsed as essential to this character's self-discovery: see analysis by Michelle Cliff, "I Found God in Myself and I Loved Her / I Loved Her Fiercely: More Thoughts on the Work of Black Women Artists," *JFSR* 2 (1986) 7–39; and Carol Christ, *Diving Deep and Surfacing: Women Writers on Spiritual Quest* (Boston: Beacon, 1980) 97–117.

15. For a recent overview of this field, see Lisa Cahill, "Feminist Ethics," *TS* 51 (1990) 49–64. Illuminating essays are collected in *Women's Consciousness* (see chap. 2, n. 22); Eva Feder Kittay and Diana Meyers, eds., *Women and Moral Theory* (Totowa, N.J.: Rowman and Littlefield, 1987); Beverly Wildung Harrison, *Making the Connections: Essays in Feminist Social Ethics*, ed. Carol Robb (Boston: Beacon, 1985).

16. Margaret Farley, "Feminist Ethics," *Westminster Dictionary of Christian Ethics*, ed. James Childress and John Macquarrie (Philadelphia: Westminster, 1986) 230.

17. Nancy Chodorow, *The Reproduction of Mothering* (Berkeley: University of California Press, 1978).

18. Catherine Keller, *From a Broken Web: Separation, Sexism and Self* (Boston: Beacon, 1986), gives an excellent analysis of the separate and connected self.

19. Carol Gilligan, *In a Different Voice: Psychological Theory and Women's Development* (Cambridge: Harvard University Press, 1982); Jean Baker Miller, *Toward a New Psychology of Women* (Boston: Beacon, 1976).

20. Mary Field Belenky, Blythe McVicker Clinchy, Nancy Rule Goldberger, Jill Mattuck Tarule, *Women's Ways of Knowing: The Development of Self, Voice, and Mind* (New York: Basic Books, 1986).

21. Barbara Hilkert Andolsen, "Agape in Feminist Ethics," *Journal of Religious Ethics* 9 (1981) 69–83; Christine Gudorf, "Parenting, Mutual Love, and Sacrifice," in *Women's Consciousness*, 175–91. A feminist critique of agapaic love arises not only because of its potential for idealizing the cultural ideal of women's already problematic loss of self, but because it subverts reciprocal regard. In women's understanding agape cannot be divorced from eros, and both move in the direction of mutuality.

22. *Embodied Love* (see chap. 1, n. 29); Susan Ross, " 'Then Honor God in Your Body' (1 Cor 6:20): Feminist and Sacramental Theology on the Body," *Horizons* 16 (1989) 7–27; Penelope Washbourn, "The Dynamics of Female Experience: Process Models and Human Values," in *Feminism and Process Thought*, ed. Sheila Greeve Davaney (New York: Edwin Mellen Press, 1981) 83–105.

23. Margaret Farley has inspired a generation of feminist theologians with this insight, which she closely relates to the development of ethical norms: "New Patterns of Relationship: Beginnings of a Moral Revolution," *TS* 36 (1975) 627–46. As an instance of how this consciousness works in practice, see her study of commitment, which is simply pervaded by the understanding of mutual relationship: *Personal Commitments: Beginning, Keeping, Changing* (San Francisco: Harper & Row, 1986).

24. Linell Cady, "Relational Love: A Feminist Christian Vision," in *Embodied Love*, 135–49; Carter Heyward, *The Redemption of God: A Theology of Mutual Relation* (Lanham, Md.: University Press of America, 1982).

25. Maryanne Cline Horowitz, "The Image of God in Man — Is Woman Included?" *Harvard Theological Review* 72 (1979) 175–206, presents the positive record in this regard. The dualistic anthropology typical of classical theology along with alternatives to it are analyzed by Carr, *Transforming Grace* (see chap. 1, n. 15) 117–33; Ruether, *Sexism and God-Talk*, 47–54, 93–115; Mary Aquin O'Neill, "Toward a Renewed Anthropology," *TS* 36 (1975) 725–36; Sara Butler, ed., *Research Report: Women in Church and Society* (Mahwah, N.J.: Catholic Theological Society of America, 1978); and Mary Buckley, "The Rising of the Woman Is the Rising of the Race," *CTSAP* 34 (1979) 48–63.

26. Trible, *God and the Rhetoric of Sexuality* (see chap. 3, n. 30) 1–30; and Phyllis Bird, "Male and Female, He Created Them: Gen 1:27b in the Context of the Priestly Account of Creation," *Harvard Theological Review* 74 (1981) 129–59.

27. Trible, *God and the Rhetoric of Sexuality*, 98; see 74–105.

28. See analysis of the *imago* by Green, *Imagining God* (see chap. 3, n. 12) 83–104; Wolfhart Pannenberg, *Anthropology in Theological Perspective*, trans. Matthew O'Connell

(Philadelphia: Westminster, 1985) 43–79; and Jürgen Moltmann, *God in Creation: A New Theology of Creation and the Spirit of God*, trans. Margaret Kohl (San Francisco: Harper & Row, 1985) 215–43.

29. Joseph Fitzmyer, "Pauline Theology," *NJBC* 82:112–27; and Pierre Benoit, Roland Murphy, Bastiaan van Iersel, eds., *The Presence of God (Concilium* 50) (New York: Paulist, 1969), especially Ulrich Luz, "New Testament Perspectives on the Image of God in Christ and Mankind," 80–92.

30. This issue is developed further in chap. 8 below. I am grateful to William Thompson of Duquesne University for the helpful distinction between the models of copying and participating that underlie debates over women as *imago Christi*. For the inclusive, pneumatological character of Christ, see John Zizioulas, *Being as Communion* (Crestwood, N.Y.: St. Vladimir's Seminary Press, 1985), especially 110–42. See also the thoughtful reflections by Monica Melanchton (India), "Christology and Women," in *We Dare to Dream* (see chap. 1, n. 20) 15–23.

31. This instance is brought to attention by Ruether, *Sexism and God-Talk*, 131. The account is found in Eusebius of Caesarea, *Hist. Eccl.* 5.1.1–63, at 41; in *Sources crétiennes* 41 (Paris: Editions du Cerf, 1955) 6–26, quote at 17.

32. Gustav Bardy, trans., *Sources crétiennes* 41, n. 47; see C. S. Song, *Jesus, The Crucified People* (New York: Crossroad, 1990).

33. *LG* 42.

34. Jon Sobrino, "The Martyrdom of Maura, Ita, Dorothy, and Jean," in his *Spirituality of Liberation* (Maryknoll, N.Y.: Orbis, 1988) 153–56.

35. *LG* 50.

36. Buber, *Eclipse of God* (see chap. 3, n. 4), 13–46.

Chapter 5 / Scripture and Its Trajectories

1. Dulles, *Models of Revelation* (see chap. 3, n. 13) 39.

2. Ibid., 209; see especially 131–54. The above models are developed at length in this work.

3. *DV* 11. This text's background and meaning are analyzed by Alois Grillmeier in *Commentary on the Documents of Vatican II*, ed. Herbert Vorgrimler (New York: Herder & Herder, 1969) 3:199–246.

4. See the application of this principle in the case made for pastoral interpretation of the Bible by Elisabeth Schüssler Fiorenza, " 'For the Sake of Our Salvation . . . ': Biblical Interpretation and the Community of Faith," in *Bread Not Stone: The Challenge of Feminist Biblical Interpretation* (Boston: Beacon, 1984) 23–42; and her presidential address to the Society of Biblical Literature, "The Ethics of Biblical Interpretation: Decentering Biblical Scholarship," *Journal of Biblical Literature* 107 (1988) 3–17. Questions of the authority of Scripture and methods of interpretation are further addressed in Adela Yarbro Collins, ed., *Feminist Perspectives on Biblical Scholarship* (Chico, Calif.: Scholars Press, 1985); Letty Russell, ed., *Feminist Interpretation of the Bible* (see chap. 1, n. 22); and Sandra Schneiders, "Does the Bible Have a Post-Modern Message?" in *Postmodern Theology: Christian Faith in a Pluralist World*, ed. Frederic Burnham (San Francisco: Harper & Row, 1989) 56–73. The whole issue of *Interpretation* 42/1 (1988) is dedicated to feminism and the Bible.

5. Joachim Jeremias, "Abba," in *The Central Message of the New Testament* (London: SCM Press, 1965) 9–30; and his *The Prayers of Jesus* (London: SCM Press, 1967) 11–65. This thesis is carefully explored and supported by Robert Hamerton-Kelly, *God the Father: Theology and Patriarchy in the Teaching of Jesus* (Philadelphia: Fortress, 1979). In Hamerton-Kelly's update "God the Father in the Bible and in the Experience of Jesus: The State of the Question," in *God as Father?* (see chap. 2, n. 57) 95–102, he notes that perhaps people today need a different symbol to express the same experience of liberating love expressed in Jesus' Abba. The philological and historical aspects of the problem are explored by Joseph Fitzmyer, "Abba and Jesus' Relation to God," in *À cause de l'évangile*, ed. R. Gantry (Paris: Editions du Cerf, 1985) 15–38.

6. *NJBC* 42:63. See Geza Vermes, *Jesus the Jew: A Historian's Reading of the Gospels* (Philadelphia: Fortress, 1973); E. P. Sanders, *Jesus and Judaism* (Philadelphia: Fortress, 1985); and the imaginative reconstruction of Jesus' prayer by Robert Aron, *The Jewish Jesus* (Maryknoll, N.Y.: Orbis, 1971).

7. Word count by Samuel Terrien, *Till the Heart Sings: A Biblical Theology of Manhood and Womanhood* (Philadelphia: Fortress, 1985) 139; slightly different count in Hamerton-Kelly, *God the Father*, 71–72.

8. James Dunn, *Christology in the Making* (Philadelphia: Westminster, 1980) 30.

9. E. Schüssler Fiorenza, *In Memory of Her* (see chap. 2, n. 32) 118–40; also Schneiders, *Women and the Word* (see chap. 2, n. 57) 37–49.

10. Raymond Brown, *The Gospel According to John I–XII* (Garden City, N.Y.: Doubleday, 1966) 533–38.

11. Edward Schillebeeckx has done more than anyone to highlight this meaning: *Jesus: An Experiment in Christology*, trans. Hubert Hoskins (New York: Seabury, 1979) 256–71.

12. Edward Schweizer, et al., *pneuma*, *TDNT* 6:332–451; George Montague, *The Holy Spirit: Growth of a Biblical Tradition* (New York: Paulist, 1976).

13. Jerome, *Comm. in Isaiam* 11 (*PL* 24.419b).

14. Ann Belford Ulanov, *The Feminine in Jungian Psychology and in Christian Theology* (Evanston, Ill.: Northwestern University Press, 1971) 325; see Leonard Swidler, *Biblical Affirmations of Women* (Philadelphia: Westminster, 1979) 58–60.

15. Schneiders, *Women and the Word*, 38.

16. Brown, "The Paraclete," in *The Gospel According to John XIII–XXI* (Garden City, N.Y.: Doubleday, 1970), appendix 5, 1135–44; Johannes Behm, "Paraclete," *TDNT* 5:800–14.

17. Jay G. Williams, "Yahweh, Women and the Trinity," *Theology Today* 32 (1975) 240.

18. Ludwig Blau, "Shekinah," *The Jewish Encyclopedia* (New York: Funk and Wagnalls, 1905) 11:258–60; Dale Moody, "Shekinah," *Interpreters Dictionary of the Bible* (Nashville, Tenn.: Abingdon, 1962) 4:317–19.

19. *Ab.* 3.2, in Moody, "Shekinah," 318.

20. Genesis *Rabbah* 86.6, Moody, in ibid.

21. *Bar. Meg.* 29a, ibid.

22. Quoted by Abraham Heschel, *God in Search of Man: A Philosophy of Judaism* (New York: Harper & Row, 1955) 21–22 and 80–87; see Gershom Scholem, *Major Trends in Jewish Mysticism*, 3rd rev. ed. (New York: Schocken Books, 1954): "no other element of kabbalism won such a degree of popular support" (229–33).

23. See the critical, creative use of the *shekinah* tradition by Rita Gross, "Female God Language in a Jewish Context," 167–73, and Naomi Janowitz and Maggie Wenig, "Sabbath Prayers for Women," 174–78, in *Womanspirit Rising* (see chap. 1, n. 19); Marcia Falk, "Notes on Composing New Blessings," 128–38, and Ellen Umansky, "Creating a Jewish Feminist Theology," 187–98, in *Weaving the Visions* (see chap. 1, n. 19).

24. In Murray, "Holy Spirit as Mother" (see chap. 3, n. 21) 315. For historical background and further examples, see P. J. Jacob, "The Motherhood of the Holy Spirit," *Journal of Dharma* 5 (1980) 160–74; Congar, *I Believe in the Holy Spirit* (see chap. 3, n. 17) 3:155–64; and Rosemary Radford Ruether, *Womanguides: Readings Toward a Feminist Theology* (Boston: Beacon, 1985) 24–31.

25. In E. Pataq-Siman, *L'Expérience de l'Esprit d'après la tradition syrienne d'Antioche*, Théologie historique 15 (Paris: Beauchesne, 1971) 155. See F. X. Durrwell, *Holy Spirit of God: An Essay in Biblical Theology*, trans. Sr. Benedict Davies (London: Geoffrey Chapman, 1986).

26. The scholarly literature is virtually unsurveyable. See Ulrich Wilckens, "Sophia," *TDNT* 7:465–528; R. B. Scott, "The Study of the Wisdom Literature," *Interpretation* 24 (1970) 20–45; Roland Murphy, "Hebrew Wisdom," *Journal of American Oriental Society* 101 (1981) 21–24. It should be noted that Sirach and the Book of Wisdom are considered part of the canon by the Roman Catholic and Orthodox traditions, but not by Protestant and Jewish traditions.

27. In the rabbinic tradition that follows, Torah assumes the character and roles of Sophia. Torah exists before the creation of the world; Torah is God's dear child; Torah gives life to the world — see Gerhard Kittel, "Logos," *TDNT* 4:132–36.

28. Respectively: Gerhard von Rad, *Wisdom in Israel* (Nashville, Tenn.: Abingdon, 1972); Bernhard Lang, *Frau Weisheit: Deutung einer biblischen Gestalt* (Düsseldorf: Patmos Verlag, 1975); R. N. Whybray, *Wisdom in Proverbs: The Concept of Wisdom in Proverbs 1-9* (Naperville, Ill.: A. R. Allenson, 1965); and Helmer Ringgren, *Word and Wisdom: Studies in the Hypostatization of Divine Qualities and Functions in the Ancient Near East* (Lund: H. Ohlssons, 1947).

29. James Dunn's argument, "Was Christianity a Monotheistic Faith from the Beginning?" *Scottish Journal of Theology* 35 (1982) 319–20.

30. C. Larcher, *Études sur le livre de la Sagesse* (Paris: J. Gabalda, 1969) 402–14. In Raymond Brown's judgment, while Hebrew thought would not say that Wisdom was God as John's Prologue says the Word was, nevertheless Wisdom is divine (*The Gospel According to John I–XII*, 522).

31. Canaanite and Semitic sources are supported by William Albright, "The Goddess of Life and Wisdom," *American Journal of Semitic Languages and Literature* 36 (1919/20) 258–94, and his *From the Stone Age to Christianity* (Garden City, N.Y.: Doubleday, 1957) 367–74. Maat is explored by Christa Kayatz, *Studien zu Proverbien 1–9* (Neukirchen-Vluyn: Neukirchener Verlag, 1966). Advocates of Isis include Wilfred Knox, "The Divine Wisdom," *Journal of Theological Studies* 38 (1937) 230–37; and Hans Conzelmann, "The Mother of Wisdom," in *The Future of Our Religious Past*, ed. James Robinson (New York: Harper & Row, 1971) 230–43.

32. So prays the deformed Lucius in Apuleius of Madauros, *Metamorphoses* 11.25, in J. Gwyn Griffiths, *The Isis Book* (Leiden: Brill, 1975). For *Kyria* as a title of Isis, see Martin Hengel, *The Son of God* (Philadelphia: Fortress, 1976) 77–78 n.135. For the cultural power of the Isis cult, see Françoise Dunand, *Le culte d'Isis dans le bassin oriental de la Méditerrané*, 3 vols. (Leiden: Brill, 1973); and Friedrich Solmsen, *Isis among the Greeks and Romans* (Cambridge: Harvard University Press, 1979).

33. Vera Vanderlip, *The Four Greek Hymns of Isidorus and the Cult of Isis* (Toronto: A. M. Hakkert, 1972) 18–19.

34. For discussion of particulars in the transference from Isis to Sophia, see Conzelmann, "The Mother of Wisdom," in *The Future of Our Religious Past* 230–43; and John Kloppenborg, "Isis and Sophia in the Book of Wisdom," *Harvard Theological Review* 75 (1982) 57–84, a study important for its methodological observations.

35. E. Schüssler Fiorenza, *In Memory of Her*, 133.

36. Martin Hengel, *Judaism and Hellenism* (London: SCM Press, 1973) 1:157–62.

37. E. Schüssler Fiorenza, *In Memory of Her*, 189.

38. Dunn, *Christology in the Making*, 195; M. Jack Suggs, *Christology and Law in Matthew's Gospel* (Cambridge: Harvard University Press, 1970) 58; Brown, *The Gospel According to John I–XII*, cxxv. For detailed background, see my study "Jesus, the Wisdom of God: A Biblical Basis for Non-Androcentric Christology," *Ephemerides Theologicae Lovanienses* 61 (1985) 261–94.

39. On the Mount of Olives there is a chapel with a picture-window view of Jerusalem commemorating where Jesus wept, the chapel of *Dominus flevit*. The mosaic on the front of the altar depicts a great hen with outspread wings under which are sheltering a mass of little yellow chicks. Around the mosaic are the lamenting words of Jesus: Jesus as the mother bird! There are links between such imagery and the iconography of Isis — see Felix Christ, *Jesus Sophia* (Zurich: Zwingli-Verlag, 1970) 139.

40. Gerhard von Rad, *Old Testament Theology*, trans. D. Stalker (New York: Harper & Row, 1965) 2:334.

41. For the first, see Jb 28:1–27; Sir 1: 6, 8; Bar 3:15–32; for the second, Prv 8:12; Wis 7:25f, 8:3f, 9:4, 9, 11.

42. Particular attention to the wisdom theme of eating and drinking is given by Adela Yarbro Collins, "New Testament Perspectives: The Gospel of John," *Journal for the Study of the Old Testament* 22 (1982) 47–53.

43. Raymond Collins, "The Search for Jesus: Reflections on the Fourth Gospel," *Laval Théologique et Philosophique* 34 (1978) 29–48.

44. The philosophical argument appears in Dunn, *Christology in the Making*, 214, and Reginald Fuller, *The Foundations of New Testament Christology* (New York: Scribner's, 1965) 76; the kerygmatic argument is offered by Brown, *The Gospel According to John I–XII*, 523; the gnostic argument by James Robinson, "Logoi Sophon: On the Gattung of Q," in *The Future of Our Religious Past*, 98.

45. Jean LaPorte, "Philo in the Tradition of Biblical Wisdom Literature," in *Aspects of Wisdom in Judaism and Early Christianity*, ed. Robert Wilkens (Notre Dame, Ind.: University of Notre Dame Press, 1975) 103–41.

46. *Fuga* 51–52. Cf. Richard Baer, *Philo's Use of the Categories Male and Female* (Leiden: Brill, 1970). In his index under "Female" the author lists the following entries synthesized from Philo's writings: destruction of the; as the fallible part of God; inferiority of the; neutralization of the; pejorative terminology about.

47. Joan Chamberlain Engelsman, *The Feminine Dimension of the Divine* (Philadelphia: Westminster, 1979) 74–120.

48. E. Schweizer, "Aufnahme und Korrektur jüdischer Sophiatheologie im Neuen Testament," in *Hören und Handeln: Festschrift für E. Wolf* (Munich: C. Kaiser, 1962) 333f.; F. Braun, "Saint Jean, La Sagesse et l'Histoire," in *Neotestamentica et Patristica* (Leiden: Brill, 1962) 123; Knox, *Paul and the Church of the Gentiles*, 84. Others who count the gender of Sophia as a factor include Brown, *The Gospel According to John I–XII*, 523; R. Barbour, "Creation, Wisdom and Christ," in *Creation, Christ and Culture*, ed. Richard McKinney (Edinburgh: T & T Clark, 1976) 38; and F. Dillistone, "Wisdom, Word and Spirit," *Interpretation* 2 (1948) 287.

49. Dunn, *Christology in the Making*, 212.

50. Origen, *De princ.* 2.6.2. For overviews of the use of Sophia in this period see H. Jaeger, "The Patristic Conception of Wisdom in the Light of Biblical and Rabbinical Research," in *Studia Patristica*, ed. F. Cross (Berlin: Akademie Verlag, 1961) 4:90–106; Robert Grant, "The Book of Wisdom at Alexandria," in *After the New Testament* (Philadelphia: Fortress, 1967) 70–82.

51. Engelsman, *Feminine Dimension of the Divine*, 147.

52. *Sapientia:* "Sed aliter mittitur ut sit cum homine; aliter missa est ut ipsa sit homo" (*De Trin* 4.20.27).

53. Louis Bouyer, *Seat of Wisdom*, trans. A. V. Littledale (New York: Pantheon Books, 1962); Susan Cady, Marian Ronan, Hal Taussig, *Sophia: The Future of Feminist Spirituality* (San Francisco: Harper & Row, 1986) 55–60.

54. For a good overview, see Virginia Ramey Mollenkott, *The Divine Feminine: Biblical Imagery of God as Female* (New York: Crossroad, 1984).

55. Trible, *God and the Rhetoric of Sexuality* (see chap. 3, n. 30) 33; see 31–59. Mayer Gruber, "The Motherhood of God in Second Isaiah," *Revue Biblique* 90 (1983) 351–59, argues against Trible that users of the Hebrew word for compassion, such as Jeremiah, were not necessarily conscious of its etymology. That may be so, but the point is that feminist biblical criticism *is* aware and its interpretation releases the word for a new use.

56. Elaine Pagels, "God the Father/God the Mother," in her *The Gnostic Gospels* (New York: Random House, 1981) 57–83.

57. Kari Elisabeth Børresen, "L'Usage patristique de métaphores féminines dans le discours sur Dieu," *Revue théologique de Louvain* 13 (1982) 205–20.

58. For Anselm's prayer, see heading of chap. 8 below; Julian of Norwich, *Showings* (see chap. 2, n. 44); Carolyn Walker Bynum, *Jesus as Mother: Studies in the Spirituality of the High Middle Ages* (Berkeley: University of California Press, 1982); and Eleanor McLaughlin, "Christ, My Mother: Feminine Naming and Metaphor in Medieval Spirituality," *Nashotah Review* 15 (1975) 228–48.

59. Jean Daniélou, "Le culte marial et le paganisme," in *Maria: Etudes sur la Sainte Vierge*, ed. D'Hubert du Manoir (Paris: Beauchesne et ses Fils, 1949) 159–81; Marina Warner, *Alone of All Her Sex: The Myth and Cult of the Virgin Mary* (New York: Knopf, 1976); Virgil Elizondo, "Our Lady of Guadalupe as a Cultural Symbol: The Power of the

Powerless," in *Liturgy and Cultural Religious Traditions* (*Concilium* 102), ed. Herman Schmidt and David Power (New York: Seabury, 1977) 25–33; Andrew Greeley, *The Mary Myth: On the Femininity of God* (New York: Seabury, 1977); Elisabeth Schüssler Fiorenza, "Feminist Spirituality, Christian Identity, and Catholic Vision," in *Womanspirit Rising*, 136–48; Boff, *The Maternal Face of God* (see chap. 3, n. 27); Elizabeth Johnson, "Mary and the Female Face of God," *TS* 50 (1989) 500–526.

Chapter 6 / Classical Theology

1. Henri de Lubac, *The Discovery of God*, trans. Alexander Dru (New York: P. J. Kenedy, 1960) 163.

2. Augustine, *Sermo* 52, c.6, n. 16 (*PL* 38.360). See discussion in Victor White, *God the Unknown* (New York: Harper, 1956).

3. Karl Rahner, "The Hiddenness of God," *TI* 16:238; so too William Hill, *Knowing the Unknown God* (New York: Philosophical Library, 1971).

4. Von Rad, *Old Testament Theology* (see chap. 5, n. 40) 1:203–19; Christian Link, "Das Bilderverbot als Kriterium des theologischen Redens von Gott," *Zeitschrift für Theologie und Kirche* 74 (1977) 58–85.

5. Hans Urs von Balthasar, "The Unknown God," in *The von Balthasar Reader*, ed. Medard Kehl and Werner Löser, trans. Robert Daly and Fred Lawrence (New York: Crossroad, 1982) 186; so too John Courtney Murray, *The Problem of God* (New Haven: Yale University Press, 1964) 5–16.

6. X. LeBachelet, "Dieu IV: Sa nature d'après les Pères," *Dictionnaire de Théologie Catholique* 4/1 (Paris: Letouzey et Ané, 1939) 1023–51.

7. For what follows, see Wolfhart Pannenberg, "The Appropriation of the Philosophical Concept of God as a Dogmatic Problem of Early Christian Theology," in *Basic Questions* (see chap. 1, n. 34) 2:156.

8. The analogy is von Balthasar's, "The Unknown God," 184.

9. *De Trin* 7.4,7.

10. Augustine, *Sermo* 52, c. 1, n. 16.

11. *De Trin* 8.8.12.

12. " ... inter Creatorem et creaturam non potest tanta similitudo notari, quin inter eos major sit dissimilitudo notanda" (*DS* 806; see J. Neuner and J. Dupuis, eds. *The Christian Faith: in the Doctrinal Documents of the Catholic Church* [New York: Alba House, 1981] 109).

13. *ST* I, q. 3, preface. David Burrell, *Knowing the Unknowable God: Ibn-Sina, Maimonides, Aquinas* (Notre Dame, Ind.: University of Notre Dame Press, 1986), vigorously demonstrates this point. By contrast, in his encyclopedia essay on God, Leo Scheffczyk skips from Augustine to Nicholas of Cusa in describing apophatic theology, omitting Aquinas altogether ("God," *Sacramentum Mundi* [New York: Herder & Herder, 1968] 2:382–87).

14. William Hill, *Knowing the Unknown God*, especially chap. 4; and his *The Three-Personed God* (Washington, D.C.: Catholic University of America Press, 1982) 62–69. See also Karl Rahner, "An Investigation of the Incomprehensibility of God in Thomas Aquinas," *TI* 16:244–54; M. D. Chenu, *Toward Understanding St. Thomas*, trans. A. M. Landry and D. Hughes (Chicago: Henry Regnery, 1964) 310–22; and Per Erik Persson, *Sacra Doctrina: Reason and Revelation in Aquinas*, trans. Ross MacKenzie (Philadelphia: Fortress, 1970), who writes: "The crucial importance of revelation in regard to the content of the *Summa* is also demonstrated by the fact that we do not find in Thomas any autonomous 'natural theology' that is independent of *revelatio*" (269).

15. Aquinas, *In Boeth. de trin.* 1, 2, ad 1.

16. Aquinas, *De potentia* 7, 5, ad 14.

17. Karl Rahner, "Justifying Faith in an Agnostic World," *TI* 21:130–36. See also William Hill, *The Search for the Absent God*, ed. Mary Catherine Hilkert (New York: Crossroad, 1992).

18. Hill, *Knowing the Unknown God*, iii, 138, 204, and passim.

19. Rahner, *Foundations* (see chap. 4, n. 8) 44–89; and his "The Concept of Mystery in Catholic Theology," *TI* 4:36–73.

20. Kasper, *The God of Jesus Christ* (see chap. 2, n. 11) 128.

21. Von Balthasar, "The Unknown God," *Reader*, 186.

22. Elie Wiesel, *Night*, trans. Stella Rodway (1960; repr., New York: Bantam Books, 1982); Arthur Cohen, *The Tremendum* (see chap. 2, n. 7); Gustavo Gutiérrez, *On Job: God-Talk and the Suffering of the Innocent*, trans. Matthew O'Connell (Maryknoll, N.Y.: Orbis, 1987).

23. *DS* 3016, in Neuner and Dupuis, 45–46 (*Dei Filius*, chap. 4).

24. Aquinas, *De Divinibus Nominibus* 1,2. For Aquinas's mature treatment of analogy, see *ST* I, q. 12–13. Complete list of texts is found in George Klubertanz, *St. Thomas Aquinas on Analogy: A Textual Analysis and Systematic Synthesis* (Chicago: M. C. Library, 1960). An enlightening interpretation of Aquinas in the light of Wittgenstein's linguistic notions of family resemblance, language games, and meaning as actual use is David Burrell, *Analogy and Philosophical Language* (New Haven: Yale University Press, 1975). See Nicholas Lash, "Ideology, Metaphor and Analogy," in *The Philosophical Frontiers of Christian Theology*, ed. Brian Hebblethwaite and Stewart Sutherland (Cambridge, Eng.: Cambridge University Press, 1982) 68–94, for a cogent explanation of the positive value of the negative knowing in analogy.

25. Moses Maimonides, *Guide for the Perplexed*, trans. M. Friedlander (New York: Dover, 1951) 87–88.

26. Nicholas Lash, "Continuity and Discontinuity in the Christian Understanding of God," *Irish Theological Quarterly* 44 (1977) 291–302.

27. See Gerhard Ebeling, "Luthers Reden von Gott," in *Der Gottesgedanke im Abendland*, ed. A. Schaefer (Stuttgart: W. Kohlhammer, 1964) 35–53; and Brian Gerrish, "To the Unknown God: Luther and Calvin on the Hiddenness of God," *JR* 53 (1973) 263–92. Karl Barth, *Church Dogmatics* vol. 1, pt. 1, *The Doctrine of the Word of God*, trans. G. T. Thomson (Edinburgh: T & T Clark, 1936; rep. 1963) x; Wolfhart Pannenberg, "Zur Bedeutung des Analogiegedankens bei Karl Barth," *Theologische Literaturzeitung* 78 (1953) 17–24; idem., "Analogy and Doxology," in *Basic Questions* (see chap. 1, n. 34) 1:211–38; and Elizabeth Johnson, "The Right Way to Speak about God? Pannenberg on Analogy," *TS* 43 (1982) 673–92.

28. Rahner, *Foundations*, 73.

29. Erich Przywara, *Analogia entis: Metaphysik, Ur-Struktur und All-Rhythmus* (Einsiedeln: Johannes-Verlag, 1962); see W. Norris Clarke, "Analogical Talk of God — An Affirmative Rejoinder," *Thomist* 40 (1976) 61–95.

30. Tracy, *The Analogical Imagination* (see chap. 3, n. 12).

31. The question of basic mentalities, or patterns of perceiving and relating, is a primary one in ecumenical dialogue. Paul Tillich was one of the first to make creative use of these distinctive world views, contrasting "Catholic substance," or the ecclesial, sacramental embodiment of God's presence, with the "Protestant principle," the rejection of any ecclesial reality which usurps the role of God as God (*Systematic Theology* [see chap. 2, n. 49] 1:37, 227, and 3:135, 245, and *passim*). For articulation of the Catholic critical principle, see Carl J. Peter, "Justification by Faith and the Need of Another Critical Principle," in *Justification by Faith: Lutherans and Catholics in Dialogue*, vol. 7, ed. George Anderson, et al. (Minneapolis: Augsburg, 1985) 304–15.

32. I appreciate the position of Frederick Ferré, "The Logic of Analogy," in *The Challenge of Religion*, ed. Peter Bertocci et al. (New York: Seabury, 1982) 104–113, who holds that even though analogy may not be any longer metaphysically credible, it still remains linguistically useful for speech about God.

33. De Lubac, *Discovery of God*, 124.

34. *SCG* 1, 31:4.

35. Ricoeur, "Naming God" (see chap. 4, n. 12) 222; B. W. Anderson, "God, names of," in *The Interpreter's Dictionary of the Bible*, ed. G. A. Buttrick et al. (Nashville, Tenn.: Abingdon, 1962) 2:407–17.

36. A. Marmorstein, *The Old Rabbinic Doctrine of God* (1927; repr, New York: KTAV, 1968) 17–147. A similar listing of Christian names of God during the same period is compiled by Hans-Werner Bartsch, "L'emploi du nom de Dieu dans le Christianisme primitif,"

in *L'analyse du langage théologique: le nom de Dieu*, ed. Enrico Castelli (Paris: Aubier, 1969) 185–200.

37. E. von Ivanka, "Le problème des 'noms de Dieu' et de l'ineffabilité divine selon le pseudo-Denys l'aréopagite," in Castelli, ed., *L'analyse*, 201–5.

38. John Mbiti, *Concepts of God in Africa* (New York: Praeger, 1970); see also Charles Nyamiti, "The African Sense of God's Motherhood in the Light of Christian Faith," *African Ecclesiastical Review* 23 (1981) 269–74.

39. *ST* I, q. 37, a. 1.

40. De Lubac, *Discovery of God*, 120–21.

Part 3 / Speaking about God from the World's History

1. For detailed criticism see Karl Rahner, "Observations on the Doctrine of God in Catholic Dogmatics," *TI* 9:127–44.

2. Joann Wolski Conn, ed., *Women's Spirituality: Resources for Christian Development* (New York: Paulist, 1986), especially the essay by Sandra Schneiders, "The Effects of Women's Experience on Their Spirituality," 31–48; Charlene Spretnak, ed., *The Politics of Women's Spirituality* (Garden City, N.Y.: Doubleday, 1982); Sally Purvis, "Christian Feminist Spirituality," in *Christian Spirituality III: Post-Reformation and Modern*, ed. Louis Dupré and Don Saliers (New York: Crossroad, 1989) 500–519; overview in Anne Carr, *Transforming Grace* (see chap. 1, n. 15) 201–14.

3. For example, Karl Rahner, *The Trinity*, trans. Joseph Donceel (New York: Herder & Herder, 1970); Jürgen Moltmann, *The Trinity and The Kingdom*, trans. Margaret Kohl (San Francisco: Harper & Row, 1981) 2–9, 178; James Mackey, *The Christian Experience of God as Trinity* (London: SCM Press, 1983) 42; Walter Kasper, *God of Jesus Christ* (see chap. 2, n. 11) 277. In classical terms this method entails giving priority to the trinitarian missions *ad extra* over the processions *ad intra*. It is a practical working out of the axiom that the economic Trinity is the immanent Trinity, and vice-versa.

Chapter 7 / Spirit-Sophia

1. From *Hildegaard of Bingen: Mystical Writings*, trans. Robert Carver, ed. Fiona Bowie and Oliver Davies (New York: Crossroad, 1990) 91–93.

2. The notion of experience, already pressed into service in chap. 4 to describe women's conversion, is notoriously difficult to clarify. I use the term with some trepidation to refer to the existential movement of human beings' interpretation of reality within their cultural tradition. See Rahner, *TI* 16 (*Experience of the Spirit: Source of Theology*).

3. Peter Hodgson, *God in History: Shapes of Freedom* (Nashville, Tenn.: Abingdon, 1989), chaps. 3 and 4.

4. Kasper, *God of Jesus Christ* (see chap. 2, n. 11) 202.

5. These images are suggested by Tertullian, *Adversus Praxeas* 8.

6. Hildegaard of Bingen, *Scivias* (see chap. 1, n. 12) 190 and passim. Here I render only the metaphors and not the full Hart and Bishop translation, which articulates the Spirit as "it." See Barbara Newman, *Sister of Wisdom: St. Hildegaard's Theology of the Feminine* (Berkeley: University of California Press, 1987).

7. Brian Gaybba, *The Spirit of Love* (London: Geoffrey Chapman, 1987), with extensive bibliography; and Kasper, *God of Jesus Christ*, 198–229. Primary patristic texts are presented handily in J. Patout Burns and Gerald Fagin, *The Holy Spirit* (Wilmington, Del.: Glazier, 1984).

8. *ST* I, q. 36, a. 1.

9. Barth, *Church Dogmatics* (see chap. 6, n. 27), "God in His Revelation," 339–83, and "The Eternal Spirit," 533–60.

10. Karl Adam, *The Spirit of Catholicism*, trans. Justin McCann (1923; repr., New York: Macmillan, 1955) 51.

11. Congar, *I Believe in the Holy Spirit* (see chap. 3, n. 17) 1:159–66.

12. Leo XIII, *Iucunda Semper* 5, in *The Papal Encyclicals: 1740-1981*, ed. Claudia Carlen (Wilmington, N.C.: McGrath, 1981) 2:356–57, emended toward inclusivity. For critical analysis, see Heribert Mühlen, *Una mystica persona: Die Kirche als das Mysterium*

der Identität des Heiligen Geistes in Christus und den Christen (Munich: Schöningh, 1968) 461–94.

13. Elsie Gibson, "Mary and the Protestant Mind," *Review for Religious* 24 (1965) 397.

14. In addition to Mühlen and Congar, see René Laurentin, "Esprit Saint et théologie mariale," *Nouvelle Revue Théologique* 89 (1967) 26–42.

15. Heribert Mühlen, "The Person of the Holy Spirit," in *The Holy Spirit and Power*, ed. Kilian McDonnell (Garden City, N.Y.: Doubleday, 1975) 12.

16. Kasper, *God of Jesus Christ*, 198, 223; John Macquarrie, *Principles of Christian Theology* (New York: Scribner's, 1966) 294; Georgia Harkness, *The Fellowship of the Holy Spirit* (Nashville, Tenn.: Abingdon, 1966) 11–12; Norman Pittenger, *The Holy Spirit* (Philadelphia: Pilgrim Press, 1974) 7–8; Congar, *I Believe in the Holy Spirit*, 3:6; Joseph Ratzinger, *Introduction to Christianity*, trans. J. R. Foster (New York: Herder & Herder, 1970) 256–57; Wolfhart Pannenberg, *The Apostles Creed: in the Light of Today's Questions*, trans. Margaret Kohl (Philadelphia: Westminster, 1972) 130; G. J. Sirks, "The Cinderella of Theology: The Doctrine of the Holy Spirit," *Harvard Theological Review* 50 (1957) 77–89.

17. Kilian McDonnell, "A Trinitarian Theology of the Holy Spirit," *TS* 46 (1985) 191.

18. Word count by Henry Van Dusen, *Spirit, Son and Father* (New York: Scribner's, 1958) 52. In the New Testament alone there are over 300 references to "Spirit." Of these, 220 speak simply of Spirit or the Spirit; over 90 use the nomenclature Holy Spirit (compared to only two uses of this term in the Hebrew Scriptures); 19 references are made to the Spirit of God, of the Lord, or of the Father; only 5 times does the phrase the Spirit of Christ appear.

19. McFague, *Models of God* (see chap. 1, n. 12) 169–71; 157–80.

20. Paula Gunn Allen, "Grandmother of the Sun: The Power of Woman in Native America," in *Weaving the Visions* (see chap. 1, n. 19) 22; from her *The Sacred Hoop: Recovering the Feminine in American Indian Traditions* (Boston: Beacon, 1986).

21. Moltmann, *God in Creation* (see chap. 4, n. 28) 14–15.

22. This note is sounded clearly by Gordon Kaufman, *Theology for a Nuclear Age* (Philadelphia: Westminster, 1985). It is the basis for Sallie McFague's choice of *Models of God* as mother, lover and friend in relation to the world as God's body.

23. Metaphors from the hymn *Veni Sancte Spiritus*, Sequence for the feast of Pentecost; perhaps written by Stephen Langton as the twelfth century turned into the thirteenth.

24. Leonardo Boff, *Trinity and Society*, trans. Paul Burns (Maryknoll, N.Y.: Orbis, 1988) 217. See also José Comblin, *The Holy Spirit and Liberation*, trans. Paul Burns (Maryknoll, N.Y.: Orbis, 1989). Similarly, seeking an example of the Spirit's renewing power in society, Georgia Harkness found it in the social movement against racism (*The Fellowship of the Holy Spirit*, 172–81).

25. *AH* 3.12.13.

26. For precise scriptural references to the points here summarized, see: birth, Mt 1:20 and Lk 1:35; baptism, Mk 1:9–11 and parallels; temptation, Mk 1:12–13; ministry, Lk 4:18–21 and Mt 12:28; cross, Heb 9:14; resurrection, Rom 1:4; the last Adam as a life-giving spirit, 1 Cor 15:45. For development of the relation between Jesus and the Spirit in Scripture, see James Dunn, *Jesus and the Spirit* (Philadelphia: Westminster, 1975); Kasper, *God of Jesus Christ*, 2C2–10; Yves Congar, *The Word and the Spirit*, trans. David Smith (San Francisco: Harper & Row, 1986).

27. For precise scriptural references to the following summary, see: Spirit poured out at Pentecost, Acts 2:1–42 and Jl 2:28–29; reminding, Jn 14:26; guiding into all truth, Jn 16:13; baptism, 1 Cor 12:13 and Gal 3:27–28; community charisms, 1 Cor 12; fellowship, 2 Cor 13:14; children of God, prayer, Rom 8:14–17; Spirit's fruits, Gal 5:22.

28. *De Trin* 5.11.12; 15.17.27; 15.18.32; and 15.19.33–37.

29. Hans Urs von Balthasar, "Der Heilige Geist als Liebe," in *Spiritus Creator* (Einsiedeln: Johannes Verlag, 1967) 106–22; the author goes on to resolve this dilemma by reflecting that God's love corresponds to the tripersonal essence, and hence has a trinitarian structure.

30. *ST* I, q. 20, a. 1; see 1 Jn 4:16.

31. *ST* I, q. 37, a. 1.

32. *ST* I, q. 36, a. 1.

33. *ST* I, q. 37, a. 1 and 2.

34. *ST* I, q. 38, a. 2. The classical use of gift as a name for the Spirit rests on numerous scriptural texts, which refer to "the gift of the Holy Spirit," meaning the gift that the Spirit is; see Acts 2:37–38; 10:44–46; 11:15–17.

35. Aquinas wrestles with this problem, finding a solution in the use of many analogies, each correcting the other (*ST* I, q. 42, a. 2).

36. Dante, *The Divine Comedy, Paradise*, trans. Dorothy Sayers and Barbara Reynolds (Harmondsworth, Eng.: Penguin Books, 1962), canto 33, lines 142–45. At the end of his vision of paradise Dante writes:

> High phantasy lost power and here broke off;
> Yet, as a wheel moves smoothly, free from jars,
> My will and my desire were turned by love,
> The love that moves the sun and the other stars.

37. *De Trin* 6.5.7.

38. Aquinas, *SCG* 4, chaps. 21 and 22, especially 22.2 and 22.3; also *ST* II-II, q. 23. See Walter Principe, "Affectivity and the Heart in Thomas Aquinas's Spirituality," in *Spiritualities of the Heart*, ed. Annice Callahan (New York: Paulist, 1990) 45–63.

39. McFague, *Models of God*, 157–67, and *Metaphorical Theology* (see chap. 1, n. 23) 177–92. Her analysis points out limitations that philosophy and anthropology have placed upon this model, as well as objections it may entail in the area of religious practice, while nevertheless she retrieves it in a good and usable manner.

40. Brian Wren, *What Language Shall I Borrow? God-Talk in Worship: A Male Response to Feminist Theology* (New York: Crossroad, 1989) 164.

41. Quoted in Isasi-Diaz, *Hispanic Women* (ch. 1, n. 21), 16.

42. Peter Hodgson, *God in History*, 108.

43. See chap. 12 below for further discussion.

44. Basil of Caesarea, *De Spiritu Sancto* 9 (ET: *On the Holy Spirit* [Crestwood, N.Y.: St. Vladimir's Seminary Press, 1980] 43).

Chapter 8 / Jesus-Sophia

1. "Prayer to St. Paul," *The Prayers and Meditations of St. Anselm*, trans. S. Benedicta Ward (New York: Penguin Books, 1973) 153–56; emended for inclusivity.

2. See implications in Piet Schoonenberg, "Spirit Christology and Logos Christology," *Bijdragen* 38 (1977) 350–75; Kasper, *Jesus the Christ* (see chap. 2, n. 13) 230–74; Congar, *I Believe in the Holy Spirit* (see chap. 3, n. 17) 3:165–73; and the analysis by Philip Rosato, "Spirit Christology: Ambiguity and Promise," *TS* 38 (1977) 423–49.

3. Balthasar, *Reader* (see chap. 6, n. 5) 178, speaks boldly of the "incarnational tendency of the Holy Spirit"; the Jewish roots of this notion are explored in Jacob Neusner, *The Incarnation of God: The Character of Divinity in Formative Judaism* (Philadelphia: Fortress, 1988).

4. A paradigmatic critique is made by Mary Daly, *Beyond God the Father* (see chap. 1, n. 9) 69–97; see Rita Nakashima Brock, "The Feminist Redemption of Christ," in *Christian Feminism* (see chap. 2, n. 39) 55–74; Rosemary Radford Ruether, "The Liberation of Christology from Patriarchy," *New Blackfriars* 66 (1985) 324–35; and summary analysis by Carr, *Transforming Grace* (see chap. 1, n. 15) 158–79.

5. For historical description, see Jaroslav Pelikan, *Jesus through the Centuries: His Place in the History of Culture* (New Haven: Yale University Press, 1985), chaps. 4 and 5.

6. *Faces of Jesus: Latin American Christologies*, ed. José Míguez-Bonino, trans. Robert Barr (Maryknoll, N.Y.: Orbis, 1984).

7. Ruether, *Sexism and God-Talk* (see chap. 2, n. 33) 117.

8. Congregation for the Doctrine of the Faith, "Declaration on the Question of the Admission of Women to the Ministerial Priesthood" (*Inter Insignores*), *Origins* 6/33 (3 Feb. 1977).

9. Ruether's question in *Sexism and God-Talk*, 116–38, and in her *To Change the World: Christology and Cultural Criticism* (New York: Crossroad, 1981) 45–56.

10. For this and the following model, see Carr, *Transforming Grace*, 117–33.

11. See Myra Marx Ferree and Beth Hess, eds., *Analyzing Gender: Perspectives from the Social Sciences* (Beverly Hills, Calif.: Sage, 1987); Iris Young, "The Ideal of Community and the Politics of Difference," *Social Theory and Practice* 12 (Spring 1986) 1–26; and Joan Scott, "Deconstructing Equality-Versus-Difference: Or, the Uses of Poststructuralist Theory for Feminism," *Feminist Studies* 14 (Spring 1988) 33–50.

12. Recall Schillebeeckx, *Christ* (see chap. 2, n. 37) 731–43.

13. Audre Lorde, *Sister Outsider* (Freedom, Calif.: Crossing Press, 1984) 111–12.

14. *De Trin* 4.20.27. Recall above, chap. 5.

15. See extended treatment of this theme by E. Schüssler Fiorenza, *In Memory of Her* (see chap. 2, n. 32) 118–59. I am indebted to this work for its incisive and lyrical presentation of Jesus-Sophia.

16. Happily, the books about these women are becoming legion. In addition to E. Schüssler Fiorenza's, *In Memory of Her*, see Elisabeth Meier Tetlow, *Women and Ministry in the New Testament* (Lanham, Md.: University Press of America, 1980); and Elisabeth Moltmann-Wendel, *The Women around Jesus*, trans. John Bowden (New York: Crossroad, 1986).

17. Moltmann-Wendel, *A Land Flowing with Milk and Honey* (see chap. 1, n. 19) 127–32.

18. Rita Nakashima Brock, *Journeys by Heart: A Christology of Erotic Power* (New York: Crossroad, 1988); Joanne Carlson Brown and Rebecca Parker, "For God So Loved the World?," in *Christianity, Patriarchy and Abuse: A Feminist Critique*, eds. Joanne Carlson Brown and Carole Bohn (New York: Pilgrim Press, 1989) 1–30; Mary Grey, *Feminism, Redemption and the Christian Tradition* (Mystic, Conn.: Twenty-Third Pub., 1990). See also Francis Schüssler Fiorenza, "Critical Social Theory and Christology: Toward an Understanding of Atonement and Redemption as Emancipatory Solidarity," *CTSAP* 30 (1975) 63–110; Schillebeeckx, *Jesus* (see chap. 5, n. 11) 294–319; and Leonardo Boff, *Passion of Christ, Passion of the World*, trans. Robert Barr (Maryknoll, N.Y.: Orbis, 1987).

19. "Final Document: Intercontinental Women's Conference," in *With Passion and Compassion* (see chap. 1, n. 20) 188.

20. Ruether, *Sexism and God-Talk*, 137.

21. Bernard Häring, *Free and Faithful in Christ* (New York: Crossroad, 1984) 139.

22. Elisabeth Schüssler Fiorenza, "Wisdom Mythology and the Christological Hymns of the New Testament," in *Aspects of Wisdom* (see chap. 5, n. 45) 17–41.

23. Schneiders, *Women and the Word* (see chap. 2, n. 57) 54. See the "feminist redemption of Christ" accomplished by emphasis on Christa-Community, in Brock, *Journeys by Heart*; and the symbolization of "Christ for the Body" envisioned by Susan Brooks Thistlethwaite, *Metaphors for the Contemporary Church* (New York: Pilgrim Press, 1983) 66–100. For women as the image of Christ, see above, chap. 4.

24. Vatican II, *Sacrosanctum Concilium* (Sacred Constitution on the Liturgy) 7.

25. Hans Urs von Balthasar, *A Theological Anthropology* (New York: Sheed and Ward, 1967) 267–68.

26. For historical background, see Alois Grillmeier, *Christ in Christian Tradition*, vol. 1, trans. John Bowden (Atlanta, Ga.: John Knox Press, 1975). In the course of this study a correlation between the christological controversies over the humanity of Jesus and the growing misogynism in early Christian centuries has strongly suggested itself: the inability to grant genuine humanity to Jesus in tandem with negating the genuine humanity of women, both as a function of men's dis-ease with the concreteness of their own humanity, possibly as a result of current forms of patriarchal asceticism.

27. The line of thought that I am following coheres with Karl Rahner's discussion, "On the Theology of the Incarnation," *TI* 4:105–20. Controversy surrounds the interpretation of this doctrine today; see John Hick, ed. *The Myth of God Incarnate* (London: SCM Press, 1976); Michael Green, ed., *The Truth of God Incarnate* (Grand Rapids, Mich.: Eerdmans, 1977); and Michael Goulder, ed., *Incarnation and Myth: the Debate Continued* (Grand Rapids, Mich.: Eerdmans, 1979).

28. Ruether, "Feminist Theology and Spirituality," in *Christian Feminism*, 21.

29. Patricia Wilson-Kastner, *Faith, Feminism and the Christ* (Philadelphia: Fortress, 1983) 90; Schneiders, *Women and the Word*, 55; see the latter for a fine discussion of the whole issue (50–67). The dispute over the ordination of women has pressed these arguments into service ever more stringently; see excellent discussion and bibliography in Carr, *Transforming Grace*, chaps. 2 and 3; and R. A. Norris, "The Ordination of Women and the 'Maleness' of Christ," *Anglican Theological Review — Supplement* 58 (1976) 69–80.

Chapter 9 / Mother-Sophia

1. Rebecca Jackson, nineteenth-century preacher; in Ruether, *Womanguides* (see chap. 5, n. 24) 18.

2. Augustine, *Sermo* 52, c.6, n. 16 (*PL* 38.360); a pivotal essay in this regard remains Karl Rahner, "The Concept of Mystery in Catholic Theology," *TI* 4: 36–73.

3. Adrienne Rich, *Of Woman Born: Motherhood as Experience and Institution* (New York: W. W. Norton, 1986 — tenth anniversary edition) 11.

4. John Paul I, *Osservatore Romano* (Eng. ed., 21 Sept. 1978) 2. See analysis by Hans Dietschy, "God Is Father and Mother," *Theology Digest* 30 (1982) 132–33, condensed from *Reformatio* 30 (1981) 425–32.

5. Catherine LaCugna, "Problems with a Trinitarian Reformulation," *Louvain Studies* 10 (1985) 337–38.

6. *ST* I, q. 33 a. 2.

7. Pagels, "God the Father/God the Mother" (see chap. 5, no. 56) 57–83. For the beginning of that struggle in biblical times, see E. Schüssler Fiorenza, *In Memory of Her* (chap. 2, n. 32) 243–315.

8. Aristotle, *Generation of Animals*, trans. A. L. Peck (Cambridge: Harvard University Press, 1943) 1:113; quoted in O'Faolain and Martines, eds., *Not In God's Image* (see chap. 2, n. 17) 119. For Aquinas's synthesis, see *ST* I, q. 92, q. 99; II-II, q. 26, a. 10; and III, supplement q. 64. Both Børresen, *Subordination and Equivalence* (see chap. 2, n. 18) and McLaughlin, "Equality of Souls" (see chap. 2, n. 18) provide incisive analyses of this position.

9. The thesis of Visser't Hooft, *The Fatherhood of God* (see chap. 3, n. 15).

10. Rich, *Of Woman Born*, 13. See also Joyce Treblicot, ed., *Mothering: Essays in Feminist Theory* (Totowa, N.J.: Rowman and Allanheld, 1984); Anne Carr and Elisabeth Schüssler Fiorenza, eds., *Motherhood: Experience, Institution, Theology* (*Concilium* 206) (Edinburgh: T & T Clark, 1989), with overview by Ursula Pfäfflin, "Mothers in a Patriarchal World: Experience and Feminist Theory," 15–22.

11. Luz Beatriz Arellano, "Women's Experience of God in Emerging Spirituality," ,*With Passion and Compassion* (see chap. 1, n. 20) 148.

12. Adrienne Rich, *On Lies, Secrets and Silence* (New York: W. W. Norton, 1979) 263–64.

13. Ursula King, "The Divine as Mother," in *Motherhood: Experience, Institution, Theology*, 135; see Margaret Hebblethwaite, *Motherhood and God* (London: Chapman, 1984), and the ensuing debate with Mary Pepper, "Finding God in Motherhood: Release or Trap?" *New Blackfriars* 65 (1984) 372–84.

14. McFague, *Models of God* (see chap. 1, n. 12) 102, quoting a phrase of Josef Pieper; this book, *Models of God*, contains the best systematic development of God as mother yet to appear (97–123).

15. Rebecca Chopp's observation, *The Power to Speak* (see chap. 1, n. 8) 123.

16. McFague, *Models of God*, 113.

17. *SCG* 1.93.

18. Arellano, *With Passion and Compassion*, 137.

19. John Simpson and Jana Bennett, *The Disappeared and the Mothers of the Plaza* (New York: St. Martin's Press, 1985).

20. Ma Frances Baard, in *Vukani Makhosikazi: South African Women Speak*, ed. Ingrid Oberg (London: Catholic Institute for International Relations, 1985) 122–23. *Vukani Makhosikazi* is Zulu for "Rise up, Women."

21. Sara Ruddick, "Remarks on the Sexual Politics of Reason," in *Women and Moral Theory* (see chap. 4, n. 15) 237–60.

22. From "Here I Stand," a poem by Boitumelo, in *Voices of Women* (New York: Women's International Resource Exchange, 1981).

23. The artist Meinrad Craighead expresses this vision in evocative paintings; see *The Mother's Songs* (see chap. 3, n. 1).

24. Gilligan, *In a Different Voice* (see chap. 4, n. 19); in debate with Lawrence Kohlberg, *The Psychology of Moral Development* (San Francisco: Harper & Row, 1984).

25. This is Gilligan's most recent perspective; see her essay "Moral Orientation and Moral Development," in *Women and Moral Theory* (see chap. 4, n. 15) 19–33. The essays in this book are focused on Gilligan's work and aim to develop it in multiple directions.

26. Juliana Casey, *Where Is God Now? Nuclear Terror, Feminism and the Search for God* (Kansas City, Mo: Sheed & Ward, 1987); John Haughey, ed., *The Faith that Does Justice* (New York: Paulist, 1977); Peter Henriot, Edward DeBerri, and Michael Schultheis, *Catholic Social Teaching, Our Best Kept Secret* (Maryknoll, N.Y.: Orbis, 1988); and Letty Russell, *Human Liberation in a Feminist Perspective* (see chap. 1, n. 28) are representative examples.

27. " ... the idea of 'oneself' as having absolute boundaries can no longer be sustained in pregnancy. 'I' am the 'other' and the 'other' is 'me'. ... In all recent research on pregnancy the dramatic interrelationship between fetus and mother is demonstrated and the use of any drugs, even an aspirin, can be detrimental. ... There is no human experience, not even coitus, as able as pregnancy to illustrate what is often obscured by our apparent separateness: we are essentially interrelated to one another" (Washbourn, "The Dynamics of Female Experience" [see chap. 4, n. 22], 93).

Chapter 10 / Triune God: Mystery of Relation

1. From the hymn "Who Is She?" Brian Wren, *What Language Shall I Borrow?* (see chap. 7, n. 40) 141–42.

2. Dialogue among world religions today makes it clear that the idea of Trinity is not exclusive to Christianity, although we are pursuing the Christian trajectory here. See Raimundo Panikkar, *Trinity and the Religious Experience of Mankind* (Maryknoll, N.Y.: Orbis, 1973); Ewert Cousins, "The Trinity and World Religions," *Journal of Ecumenical Studies* 7 (1970) 476–98; and Richard Viladesau, "The Trinity in Universal Revelation," *Philosophy and Theology* 4 (1990) 317–34.

3. Friedrich Schleiermacher, *The Christian Faith* (Edinburgh: T & T Clark, 1928), "The Divine Trinity," 738–51. See the excellent survey of nineteenth-century trinitarian thought and its persistence into twentieth-century attitudes by Claude Welch, *In This Name: The Doctrine of the Trinity in Contemporary Theology* (New York: Scribner's, 1952) 3–122.

4. Rahner, *The Trinity* (see Part III, n. 3) 9–21.

5. Hodgson, *God in History* (see chap. 7, n. 3) 94.

6. Rebecca Oxford-Carpenter, "Gender and the Trinity," *Theology Today* 41 (1984) 7–25, delineates six typical responses to the gender of the Trinity issue; Marjorie Suchocki, "The Unmale God: Reconsidering the Trinity" (see chap. 2, n. 45), proposes speech in terms of the justice-making functions of the Trinity; Gail Ramshaw Schmidt, "Naming the Trinity: Orthodoxy and Inclusivity," *Worship* 60 (1986) 491–98, presents the Abba-Servant-Paraclete option; Catherine LaCugna, "The Baptismal Formula, Feminist Objections, and Trinitarian Theology," *Journal of Ecumenical Studies* 26 (1989) 235–50, argues for retrieval of the nonoppressive meaning of God the Father. See further discussion by Patricia Wilson-Kastner, *Faith, Feminism and the Christ* (see chap. 8, n. 29), chap. 6.

7. For fine studies of the development of classic trinitarian doctrine in East and West, see J. N. D. Kelly, *Early Christian Doctrines* (San Francisco: Harper & Row, 1978) 109–37, 223–79; Jaroslav Pelikan, *The Emergence of the Catholic Tradition* (Chicago: University of Chicago Press, 1971) 172–225; Bernard Lonergan, *The Way to Nicea: The Dialectical Development of Trinitarian Theology* (Philadelphia: Westminster, 1977).

8. *De Trin* 5.6.7; see also 7.4.7.

9. Moltmann, *Trinity and the Kingdom* (see Part III, n. 3) 89, 126.

10. Kasper, *God of Jesus Christ* (see chap. 2, n. 11) 308–9.

11. *De Trin* 4.21.30.

12. "Let us never cease from thinking — what is this 'civilization' in which we find ourselves? What are these ceremonies and why should we take part in them? What are these professions and why should we make money out of them? Where in short is it leading us, the procession of the sons of educated men?" (Virginia Woolf, *Three Guineas* [New York: Harcourt, Brace, 1938] 36); Mary Daly, *Gyn/Ecology* (see chap. 2, n. 22) 37–42.

13. A plethora of recent works stress this rootedness of Trinity in the history of salvation, and trace its intellectual development in this light. See Hill, *Three-Personed God* (see chap. 6, n. 14); Robert Jenson, *The Triune Identity: God according to the Gospel* (Philadelphia: Fortress, 1982); Mackey, *Christian Experience of God as Trinity* (see Part III, n. 3); Kasper, *God of Jesus Christ*. The point is crystallized by Catherine LaCugna, "Reconceiving the Trinity as the Mystery of Salvation," *Scottish Journal of Theology* 38 (1985) 1–23; and Roger Haight, "The Point of Trinitarian Theology," *Toronto Journal of Theology* 4/2 (1988) 191–204.

14. Rahner, *The Trinity*, 48.

15. Pittenger, *The Holy Spirit* (see chap. 7, n. 16) 44.

16. The first of Piet Schoonenberg's three dozen theses in "Trinity — The Consummated Covenant: Theses on the Doctrine of the Trinitarian God," *Studies in Religion* 5/2 (1975–76) 111–16.

17. Rahner, *The Trinity*, 21–24, 82–103, and passim.

18. Edmund Hill, *The Mystery of the Trinity* (London: Chapman, 1985) 45–46, raises a problem regarding the term *immanent* in Rahner's axiom insofar as this word usually refers to the presence of God within the world. It would be more consistent with theological usage, he suggests, to say that the economic Trinity is the transcendent Trinity and vice-versa. He has a point. Given the widespread use of the axiom, however, we simply note that immanent in this case means immanent within God. See the explanation in Welch, *In This Name*, appendix A, 293–94.

19. Mackey, *Christian Experience of God as Trinity*, 295 n.155; see also Maurice Wiles, "Some Reflections on the Origins of the Doctrine of the Trinity," *Journal of Theological Studies* 8 (1957) 92–106.

20. LaCugna, "Reconceiving the Trinity," 13.

21. *ST* I, preface to q. 3. See above, chap. 6.

22. Gregory of Nazianzus, "Fifth Theological Oration" 8, in *Christology of the Later Fathers* (see chap. 1, n. 35) 198–99.

23. *De Trin* 15.24.45.

24. Ibid., 7.4.7.

25. Ibid., 5.9.10.

26. Hill, *Mystery of the Trinity*, 59–60.

27. Anselm, *Monologion* 78, in *Saint Anselm: Basic Writings* (see chap. 1, n. 12) 142.

28. *De Trin* 7.6.11.

29. Ibid., 8.2.3.

30. Hill, *Mystery of the Trinity*, 158.

31. *ST* I, q. 30, a. 3.; to the query whether the numerical terms denote something real in God, the answer is no.

32. *De Trin* 6.10.12. See *ST* I, q. 42, a. 4.

33. *De Trin* 15.2.2.

34. A plethora of these options are categorized, explained, and dialogued with in Hill, *Three-Personed God*, 83–237.

35. Barth, *Church Dogmatics* (see chap. 6, n. 27) 402; see whole section, "God's Three-in-Oneness," 400–440.

36. Rahner, *The Trinity*, 109; also his "Remarks on the Dogmatic Treatise *De Trinitate*," *TI* 4:77–102.

37. Moltmann, *Trinity and the Kingdom*, 171.

38. Moltmann, *The Crucified God* (see chap. 2, n. 13) 207.

39. Leonardo Boff, *Trinity and Society*, trans. Paul Burns (Maryknoll, N.Y.: Orbis, 1988) 9. For the same social conception cast in the categories of process thought and therefore with a stronger use of ontology, see Joseph Bracken, "The Holy Trinity as a Community of

Divine Persons," *Heythrop Journal* 15 (1974) 166–82, 257–70; and his *The Triune Symbol* (Lanham, Md.: University Press of America, 1985).

40. The key influential study on this point is that of Erik Peterson, "Der Monotheismus als politisches Problem," in *Theologische Traktate* (Munich: Kösel, 1951) 45–164. Yves Congar notes that this essay was originally written in 1935, the second year of the Nazi regime, and had political implications in its own right: "Classical Political Monotheism and the Trinity," in *God as Father?* (see chap. 2, n. 57), 35 n. 1. See *Monotheism*, ed. C. Geffré and J. P. Jossua (Edinburgh, T & T Clark, 1985), especially Giuseppe Ruggieri, "God and Power: A Political Function of Monotheism?" (16–27), and Christian Duquoc, "Monotheism and Unitary Ideology" (59–66).

41. Kasper, *God of Jesus Christ*, 307.

42. Moltmann, *Trinity and the Kingdom*, 191–222, and "The Motherly Father. Is Trinitarian Patripassianism Replacing Theological Patriarchalism?" in *God as Father?* 51–56.

43. These two models are not absolute opposites but distinct perspectives on profound mystery. In my view they belong to that phenomenon made famous by the physicist Niels Bohr in the dispute over whether light is made up of waves or particles. "A complete elucidation of one and the same object," he notes, "may require diverse points of view which defy a unique description." Both models should be used while the limitation of each is acknowledged; see his *Atomic Theory and the Description of Nature* (Cambridge, Eng.: Cambridge University Press, 1934) 96.

44. Macquarrie, *Principles of Christian Theology* (see chap. 7, n. 16) 174–85.

45. Kaufman, *The Theological Imagination* (see chap. 1, n. 3) 263–79.

46. McFague, *Models of God* (see chap. 1, n. 12).

47. Kasper, *God of Jesus Christ*, 308–9.

48. Heribert Mühlen, *Der heilige Geist als Person. In der Trinität bei der Inkarnation und im Gnadenbund: Ich, du, wir* (Münster: Verlag Aschendorff, 1967).

49. Tillich, *Systematic Theology* (see chap. 2, n. 49) 3:283–94.

50. Dorothy Sayers, *The Mind of the Maker* (London: Methuen, 1942).

51. Eberhard Jüngel, *God as the Mystery of the World: On the Foundation of the Theology of the Crucified One in the Dispute between Theism and Atheism*, trans. Darrell Guder (Grand Rapids, Mich.: Eerdmans, 1983).

52. Pittenger, *The Holy Spirit*, 122.

53. Letty Russell, *The Future of Partnership* (Philadelphia: Westminster, 1979) 25–43.

54. Gilkey, "God" (see chap. 2, n. 10) 88–113.

55. Lash, *Easter in Ordinary* (see chap. 4, n. 2), chaps. 14 and 16.

56. Hodgson, *God in History*, 93–112.

57. Panikkar, *Trinity and the Religious Experience of Mankind*.

58. Hildegaard of Bingen, *Illuminations*, commentary by Matthew Fox (Santa Fe, N.M.: Bear, 1985) 23.

59. *De Trin* 5.11.12; see also *ST* I, q. 36, a. 1; G. W. Lampe, *God as Spirit* (Oxford: Clarendon Press, 1977); Peter Hodgson, *God in History*, 93 ff.

60. *De Trin* 7.3.6.

61. Ibid., 7.1.2.

62. Ibid., 15.7.12.

63. Ibid., 15.17.28.

64. Julian of Norwich, *Showings* (see chap. 2, n. 44) 297.

65. In the sense of Alice Walker's *The Color Purple* (New York: Washington Square Press, 1982).

66. T. S. Eliot, "Burnt Norton," in *Four Quartets* (New York: Harcourt, Brace and World, 1971) 67.

67. *ST* I, q. 29, a. 4, and q. 30, a. 1.

68. *De Trin* 6.7.9.

69. Simone Weil, "Forms of the Implicit Love of God," in *Waiting for God* (see chap. 1, n. 12) 208.

70. Ruether, *New Woman, New Earth* (see chap. 2, n. 26) 26.

71. *De Trin* 7.1.2.

72. Ibid., 8.1.2.
73. Ibid., 9.1.1.
74. G. Lampe, *A Patristic Greek Lexicon* (Oxford: Clarendon Press, 1961) 1077–78; H. Liddell and R. Scott, *A Greek-English Lexicon*, rev. and ed. H. Jones and R. McKenzie (Oxford: Clarendon Press, 1968) 1393–94; Michael Schmaus, "Perichorese," *Lexikon für Theologie und Kirche* 8:274–76; and Brian Hebblethwaite, "Perichoresis — reflections on the doctrine of the Trinity," in his *The Incarnation: Collected Essays in Christology* (Cambridge, Eng.: Cambridge University Press, 1987) 11–20.
75. Hill, *The Mystery of the Trinity*, 117.
76. On this point see the interesting exchange between Yves Congar and Robert Kress reported in the latter's *The Church: Communion, Sacrament, Communication* (New York: Paulist, 1985) 15–22 and notes.
77. The Joffrey Ballet's repertoire includes a work entitled *Trinity*, having to do with the human Trinity of birth, copulation, and death. But when, after portraying human creativity, eroticism, and disintegration, the interracial cast of both genders melts off the darkening stage to the pounding rhythms of a requiem, leaving flickering candles in each one's place, another Trinity is evoked.
78. Kasper, *The God of Jesus Christ*, 296–97.
79. Carr, *Transforming Grace* (see chap. 1, n. 15) 156–57.

Chapter 11 / One Living God: SHE WHO IS

1. Sabbath Prayer, written by Naomi Janowitz and Maggie Wenig, in *Womanspirit Rising* (see chap. 1, n. 19) 176.
2. *ST* I, q. 13, a. 7.
3. Kasper, *God of Jesus Christ* (see chap. 2, n. 11) 306.
4. W. Norris Clarke, "A New Look at the Immutability of God," in *God Knowable and Unknowable*, ed. Robert Roth (New York: Fordham University Press, 1973) 45.
5. W. Norris Clarke, "Theism and Process Thought," *New Catholic Encyclopedia* 17:648.
6. *ST* I, q. 28, a. 1.
7. Anthony Kelly, "God: How Near a Relation?" *Thomist* 34 (1970) 191–229; William Hill, "Does the World Make a Difference to God?" *Thomist* 38 (1974) 146–64; John Wright, "Divine Knowledge and Human Freedom: The God Who Dialogues," *TS* 38 (1977) 450–77; David Burrell, *Aquinas: God and Action* (Notre Dame, Ind.: University of Notre Dame Press, 1979), especially 84–87; and Catherine LaCugna, "The Relational God: Aquinas and Beyond," *TS* 46 (1985), especially 655–56.
8. Keller, "Scoop up the Water" (see chap. 1, n. 27) 108.
9. *De Trin* 7.1.2.
10. Hill, *Three-Personed God* (see chap. 6, n. 14) 269.
11. *ST* I, q. 28, a. 2; see also q. 40, a. 1.
12. LaCugna, "The Relational God," 652.
13. *ST* I, q. 8, a. 1, 2, 3; *SCG* 3.66, par.7.
14. Karl Rahner, "On Recognizing the Importance of Thomas Aquinas," *TI* 13:11. This vision of God's immanent presence to the world has found new expression in the striking image of the world as God's body (McFague, *Models of God* [see chap. 1, n. 12] 69–78), or creation as the body of the Trinity (Boff, *Trinity and Society* [see chap. 10, n. 39] 230–31).
15. *ST* I, q. 8, a. 1.
16. *The Oxford Dictionary of the Christian Church*, ed. F. L. Cross and E. A. Livingstone (London: Oxford University Press, 1974) 1027. Charles Hartshorne prefers "neoclassical theism" to describe his position in process theology; see the classification of nine possible ideas of God and the created world in his "Pantheism and Panentheism," *The Encyclopedia of Religion*, ed. Mircea Eliade (New York and London: Macmillan and Collier Macmillan, 1987) 11:165–71. In his Gifford lectures John Macquarrie opts for "dialectical theism" lest his position be confused with pantheism. To argue his case he presents an illustrious ancestry for this alternative theology of God; theological forebears include Plotinus, Dionysius, Eriugena, Nicholas of Cusa, Leibniz, Hegel, Whitehead, and Heidegger

(Macquarrie, *In Search of Deity: An Essay in Dialectical Theism* [New York: Crossroad, 1985]).

17. Karl Rahner and Herbert Vorgrimler, *Theological Dictionary* (New York: Herder & Herder, 1965) 333–34. This notion is amplified in the study by Piet Schoonenberg, *The Christ: A Study of the God-Man Relationship in the Whole of Creation and in Jesus Christ*, trans. Della Couling (New York: Seabury, 1971).

18. Example in Piet Schoonenberg, "God as Person(al)," in *A Personal God?* (see chap. 2, n. 5) 89; Schoonenberg notes that the scholastic doctrine of participation and modern forms of panentheism are related.

19. Gershom Scholem, *Major Trends in Jewish Mysticism* (London: Thames and Hudson, 1955), especially chap. 7, "Isaac Luria and His School," 244–86.

20. Simone Weil, *First and Last Notebooks* (London: Oxford University Press, 1970) 120.

21. Hill, *Three-Personed God*, 76 n.53. See the illuminating essay from the Thomistic perspective by Joseph Donceel, "Second Thoughts on the Nature of God," *Thought* 46 (1971) 346–70, with drawings.

22. Moltmann, *God in Creation* (see chap. 4, n. 28) 88; see ibid., 86–93, and his *Trinity and the Kingdom* (see Part III, n. 3) 108–11.

23. Keller, "Scoop Up the Water," 111. This essay flags the need for a feminist revision of *kenōsis*, given the problem of women's internalization of the role of victim.

24. Moltmann, *God in Creation*, 88.

25. *ST* I, q. 3., a. 4. See the lucid discussion of medieval Islamic, Jewish, and Christian wisdom on this matter in David Burrell, *Knowing the Unknowable God: Ibn-Sina, Maimonides, Aquinas* (see chap. 6, n. 13).

26. Paul Tillich develops the notion of "metaphysical shock'; in his *Systematic Theology* (see chap. 2, n. 49) 1:163. This volume has extended discussion of the move from the philosophical notion of being to its theological use signifying God (1:163–289). Robert Scharlemann's, *The Being of God: Theology and the Experience of Truth* (New York: Seabury, 1981) is a superb study of the epistemological status of the ideas of God and being.

27. Macquarrie, *Principles of Christian Theology* (see chap. 7, n. 16) 98; and ibid., 97–105, for the example that follows.

28. *Periphyseon* 487B, as quoted by Macquarrie, *In Search of Deity*, 90.

29. Abraham Heschel, *God in Search of Man* (New York: Harper & Row, 1965) 121.

30. *ST* I, q. 3, a. 5. See Rahner, *Foundations* (see chap. 4, n. 8) 44–89, especially 61–65.

31. Daly, *Beyond God the Father* (see chap. 1, n. 9) 33–37.

32. LaCugna, "The Relational God," passim; see also Burrell, *Aquinas: God and Action*, 651 n.17 and passim.

33. Hill, *Three-Personed God*, 248.

34. Macquarrie, *Principles of Christian Theology*, 179–85.

35. Heschel, *God in Search of Man*, 160–61.

36. *TDOT* 5:500–521; *TDNT* 3:1058–81; Anderson, "God, names of," *The Interpreter's Dictionary of the Bible* (see chap. 6, n. 35) 2:407–17; and S. Goitein, "YHWH the Passionate: The Monotheistic Meaning and Origin of the Name YHWH," *Vetus Testamentum* 6 (1956) 1–9.

37. John Courtney Murray mounts a persuasive argument for this reading in *The Problem of God* (see chap. 6, n. 5) 5–25; so too does Martin Buber, *Eclipse of God* (see chap. 3, n. 4) 62.

38. For the history of how the name of historical promise became a metaphysical definition, see Kasper, *God of Jesus Christ*, 147–52.

39. *ST* I, q. 13, a. 11; also *SCG* I.22, par. 10. See explanation in E. Mascall, *He Who Is* (London: Longmans, 1943). The English translation "He who is" is standard.

40. *ST* I, q. 13, a. 11.

41. Johannes Baptist Metz, "Theology Today: New Crises and New Visions," *CTSAP* 40 (1985) 7.

Chapter 12 / Suffering God: Compassion Poured Out

1. Maya Angelou, "On Diverse Deviations," in *Just Give Me a Cool Drink of Water 'fore I Diiie* (New York: Random House, 1971) 19.

2. For historical overview, see J. K. Mozley, *The Impassible God: A Survey of Christian Thought* (Cambridge, Eng.: Cambridge University Press, 1926). A thoroughgoing contemporary argument for the position is mounted by Richard Creel, *Divine Impassibility: An Essay in Philosophical Theology* (Cambridge, Eng.: Cambridge University Press, 1986).

3. Moltmann, *The Crucified God* (see chap. 2, n. 13) 269.

4. Ludwig Ott, *Fundamentals of Catholic Dogma* (Cork, Ireland: Mercier Press, 1955) 46; see fuller description of the classical position by Jacques Maritain, *Saint Thomas and the Problem of Evil* (Milwaukee, Wis.: Marquette University Press, 1942).

5. Anselm, *Proslogion*, chap. 8, in *Saint Anselm: Basic Writings* (see chap. 1, n. 12) 13.

6. All religions of the world deal with this question; see John Bowker, *Problems of Suffering in Religions of the World* (Cambridge, Eng.: Cambridge University Press, 1970); and Edward Schillebeeckx's overview in *Christ* (see chap. 2, n. 37) 670–724.

7. Wendy Farley, *Tragic Vision and Divine Compassion: A Contemporary Theodicy* (Louisville, Ky.: Westminster/John Knox Press, 1990) 53–55.

8. Feodor Dostoevski, *The Brothers Karamazov*, trans. C. Garnett (New York: Modern Library, 1950), bk. 5, chap. 4; Elie Wiesel, *Night* (see chap. 6, n. 22); Toni Morrison, *Beloved* (New York: Penguin Books, 1988).

9. Reasons for this shift are analyzed by Marc Steen, "The Theme of the Suffering God: An Exploration," in *God and Human Suffering*, ed. Jan Lambrecht and Raymond Collins (Louvain: Peeters Press, 1990) 69–93; this volume contains a fine bibliography on the subject.

On the idea that the omnipotent God is an enemy of human freedom who must be killed or disobeyed for human maturity to transpire, see Wolfhart Pannenberg, *The Idea of God and Human Freedom*, trans. R. A. Wilson (Philadelphia: Westminster, 1973). Edward Farley proposes an intriguing alternative, namely, God as the founder of a people who covenants with them and through history builds up a cluster of images through which human life is shaped toward justice and peace ("God as Dominator and Image-Giver: Divine Sovereignty and the New Anthropology," *Journal of Ecumenical Studies* 6 [1969] 354–75).

10. Abraham Heschel, *The Prophets* (New York: Harper & Row, 1962), chaps. 12–18; see also Terence Fretheim, *The Suffering of God: An Old Testament Perspective* (Philadelphia: Fortress, 1984); and J. P. M. Walsh, *The Mighty from Their Thrones: Power in the Biblical Tradition* (Philadelphia: Fortress, 1987).

11. Hans Jonas, "The Concept of God after Auschwitz: A Jewish Voice," *JR* 67 (1987) 1–13.

12. This is compellingly argued by Arthur Cohen, *The Tremendum* (see chap. 2, n. 7).

13. Moltmann, *The Crucified God*, 246. See Warren McWilliams, *The Passion of God: Divine Suffering in Contemporary Protestant Theology* (Macon, Ga.: Mercer University Press, 1985), who presents the theology of Jürgen Moltmann, James Cone, Geddes MacGregor, Kazoh Kitamori, Daniel Day Williams, and Jung Young Lee.

14. Alfred North Whitehead, *Process and Reality: An Essay in Cosmology* (New York: Macmillan, 1929) 532. See Bernard Loomer, "Two Conceptions of Power," *Process Studies* 6 (1976) 5–32; Charles Hartshorne, *Omnipotence and Other Theological Mistakes* (Albany: State University of New York, 1984); and the critique of Hartshorne's proposal as well as Karl Barth's view by Sheila Greeve Devaney, *Divine Power* (Philadelphia: Fortress, 1986). Zeroing in specifically on the problem of evil is David Griffin, *God, Power and Evil: A Process Theodicy* (Philadelphia: Westminster, 1976), and his *Evil Revisited: Responses and Reconsiderations* (Albany: State University of New York Press, 1991); see also Marjorie Suchocki, *The End of Evil: Process Eschatology in Historical Context* (Albany: State University of New York Press, 1988).

15. Macquarrie, *In Search of Deity* (see chap. 11, n. 16).

16. *DS* 432, in Neuner and Dupuis, eds. (see chap. 6, n. 12) 162.

17. Hans Küng, *The Incarnation of God*, trans. J. R. Stephens (New York: Crossroad, 1987), excursus 2, "Can God Suffer?" 518–25. For similar arguments, see also Karl Rahner, "On the Theology of the Incarnation," *TI* 4:105–20; Hans Urs von Balthasar, *Love Alone: The Way of Revelation* (London: Burns & Oates, 1968); Jean Galot, "La réalité de la souffrance de Dieu," *Nouvelle Revue Théologique* 101 (1979) 224–45; and Waclaw Hryniewicz, "Le Dieu souffrant? Réflexions sur la notion chrétienne de Dieu," *Eglise et Théologie* 12 (1981) 333–56.

18. Sobrino, *Christology at the Crossroads* (see chap. 2, n. 13); Boff, *Passion of Christ, Passion of the World* (see chap. 8, n. 18).

19. Ronald Goetz, "The Rise of a New Orthodoxy," *Christian Century* 103/13 (16 April 1986) 385–89.

20. Soelle, *The Strength of the Weak* (see chap. 2, n. 57) 97. Sharon Welch argues that while divine omnipotence has the advantage that it functions to limit all earthly power, it paradoxically valorizes absolute power, which has dangerous political consequences: *Feminist Ethic of Risk* (see chap. 1, n. 22) 111–22. See the analysis of power in the classical model along with a proposed process-feminist model in Anna Case-Winters, *God's Power: Traditional Understandings and Contemporary Challenges* (Louisville, Ky.: Westminster/John Knox Press, 1990).

21. Phrases taken from Arthur McGill, *Suffering: A Test of Theological Method* (Philadelphia: Westminster, 1982) 61; Moltmann, *The Crucified God*, 205; and Gérard Rossé, *The Cry of Jesus on the Cross* (New York: Paulist, 1987), respectively. This tendency is epitomized in the title, though not all the content, of Bernard Lee, "The Helplessness of God: A Radical Re-appraisal of Divine Omnipotence," *Encounter* 38 (1977) 325–36.

22. Soelle, *Strength of the Weak*, 11–30, and Ernest Becker, *The Denial of Death* (New York: Free Press, 1973).

23. See Patricia Wismer, "For Women in Pain: A Feminist Theology of Suffering," paper presented at the Catholic Theological Society of America meeting, Atlanta 1991.

24. Mercy Oduyoye, "Birth," in *New Eyes for Reading* (see chap. 1, n. 20) 41.

25. Ibid., 42.

26. Rich, *Of Woman Born* (see chap. 9, n. 3) chaps. 6 and 7.

27. Phyllis Anderson, "Liberation in a Pastoral Perspective," *Word and World* 7 (1987) 70–77.

28. See account by Albertina Sisulu, in *Vukani Makhosikazi: South African Women Speak* (see chap. 9, n. 20) 233–37; and Anne Hope, ed., *Torch in the Night* (New York: Friendship Press and Washington, D.C.: Center of Concern, 1988) 71–72.

29. Newsletter, "Nuestra Voz: A Voice for Guatemalan Women," March 1990, I:1.

30. Something of the initiative of each of these women is revealed in the semi-humorous remark of former U.S. civil rights commissioner Mary Frances Berry: "If Rosa Parks had taken a poll before she sat down in the bus in Montgomery, she'd still be standing" (in Brian Lanker, *I Dream A World: Portraits of Black Women Who Changed America* [New York: Stewart, Tabori & Chang, 1989]).

31. Beverly Harrison, "The Power of Anger in the Work of Love," *Union Seminary Quarterly Review* 36 (1980–81, supplement) 49; rep. in *Making the Connections* (see chap. 4, n. 15).

32. Mary Daly, *Pure Lust: Elemental Feminist Philosophy* (Boston: Beacon, 1984) 375. Also Audre Lorde, "The Uses of Anger: Women Responding to Racism," 124–33, and "Eye to Eye: Women, Hatred, and Anger," 145–75, in *Sister Outsider* (see chap. 8, n. 13).

33. Barbara Summers, ed., in *I Dream a World*, editor's note, n.p.

34. Heschel, *The Prophets*, 284–85.

35. This argument is cogently made by Nel Noddings, *Women and Evil* (Berkeley: University of California Press, 1989).

36. Helen Kotze, "My heart cries out," in *Cry Justice!* ed. John de Gruchy (London: Collins, 1986) 112.

37. Analysis in Fretheim, *The Suffering of God*, 127–48; see also David Power, "When to Worship is to Lament," in his *Worship: Culture and Theology* (Washington, D.C.: Pastoral Press, 1990) 155–73.

38. In Tract. Megilla, *The Babylonian Talmud*, vol. 8 (Book of Esther), trans. and ed. Michael Rodkinson (New York: New Talmud Pub., 1899) 23; see also *Midrash Rabbah*, vol. 3 (Exodus), ed. H. Freedman (London: Soncino Press, 1939) 285.

39. Nehemia Polen, "Divine Weeping: Rabbi Kalonymos Shapiro's Theology of Catastrophe in the Warsaw Ghetto," *Modern Judaism* 7 (1987) 253–69; also Melvin Glatt, "God the Mourner — Israel's Companion in Tragedy," *Judaism* 28 (1979) 72–79. Dietrich Bonhoeffer captures a similar idea in his poem about Christian faith, where instead of going to God and asking for help in time of need, Christians engage in a different task:

> Men go to God when he is sore bestead,
> Find him poor and scorned, without shelter or bread,
> Whelmed under weight of the wicked, the weak, the dead:
> Christians stand by God in his hour of grieving.

"Christians and Unbelievers," in *Letters and Papers from Prison*, ed. Eberhard Bethge, trans. Reginald Fuller (New York: Macmillan, 1953) 225.

40. Simone Weil, "The Love of God and Affliction," in her *Waiting for God* (see chap. 1, n. 12) 117–36.

41. Phyllis Trible, *Texts of Terror* (Philadelphia: Fortress, 1984). See also James Crenshaw, *A Whirlpool of Torment* (Philadelphia: Fortress, 1984) for other texts where God is of no help.

42. Trible, *Texts of Terror*, 80–81.

43. Daly, "European Witchburnings: Purifying the Body of Christ," in *Gyn-Ecology* (see chap. 2, n. 22) 178–222, traces how these deaths were viewed and subsequently ignored by Western male historians. See the defamation of wise women in the influential handbook for clerical inquisitors written by Heinrich Kramer and James Sprenger, *Malleus Maleficarum* (or *Hammer Against Witches*), trans. with introductions, bibliography, and notes by Montague Summers (New York: Dover, 1971). H. R. Trevor-Roper, *The European Witch-Craze of the Sixteenth and Seventeenth Centuries and Other Essays* (New York: Harper Torchbooks, 1969), gives a historical overview.

44. Robin Morgan, from Chris Carol, "Hollowmas Liturgy," presented in Ruether, *Women-Church* (see chap. 1, n. 7) 225–26. On narrative remembrance as a salvific act in the face of suffering, and the future this opens up, see Metz, *Faith in History and Society* (see chap. 4, n. 11).

45. Cited in Luz Beatriz Arellano, "Women's Experience of God in Emerging Spirituality," in *With Passion and Compassion* (see chap. 1, n. 20) 139–40.

46. Gerald Vann, *The Pain of Christ, the Sorrow of God* (Oxford: Blackfriars, 1947) 59.

47. Fabella, "A Common Methodology for Diverse Christologies?" in *With Passion and Compassion*, 110.

48. Rosemary Radford Ruether, "Feminism and Jewish-Christian Dialogue," in *The Myth of Christian Uniqueness*, ed. John Hick and Paul Knitter (Maryknoll, N.Y.: Orbis, 1988) 147; also Thistlethwaite, "Jesus and Christa," in her *Sex, Race, and God* (see chap. 1, n. 22) 92–108.

49. Quoted in Jon Sobrino, "A Crucified People's Faith in the Son of God," in *Jesus, Son of God?* (*Concilium* 153), ed. E. Schillebeeckx and J. B. Metz (New York: Seabury, 1982) 25.

50. Wiesel, *Night*, 61: "Where is God?"

51. *ST* I, q. 20, a. 1.

52. William Hill, "Does Divine Love Entail Suffering in God?" in *God and Temporality*, ed. Bowman Clarke and Eugene Long (New York: Paragon House, 1984) 55–71; see the nuances introduced in his "The Historicity of God," *TS* 45 (1984) 320–33, where, by utilizing the distinction between divine nature and trinitarian persons, Hill acknowledges that "in some sense," though still immutable, God responds to human suffering and undergoes change relationally.

53. Boff, *Passion of Christ, Passion of the World*, 114.

54. Schweizer, *TDNT* 6:387–88. In this regard John Paul II writes that the Spirit, who personifies the suffering of God, enters "into human and cosmic suffering with a new outpouring of love, which will redeem the world" — his encyclical *Lord and Giver of*

Life (Dominum et Vivificantem) (Washington, D.C.: United States Catholic Conference, 1986), no. 39.

55. Bonhoeffer, *Letters and Papers from Prison*, 219–20: letter of 16 July 1944.

56. Joan Northam, "The Kingdom, the Power, and the Glory," *Expository Times* 99 (1988) 302.

57. Margaret Spufford, "The Reality of Suffering and the Love of God," *Theology* 88 (1985) 445.

58. Farley, *Tragic Vision*, 81. Again, "The discovery of the other who bears the consequences of my suffering and shares my condition is a powerful mode of personal communication and healing" (Daniel Day Williams, "Suffering and Being in Empirical Theology," in *The Future of Empirical Theology*, ed. Bernard Meland [Chicago: University of Chicago Press, 1969] 188).

59. King Lear on the heath to the blind Gloucester:

> *Lear:* O ho, are you there with me? No eyes in your head, nor no money in your purse? Your eyes are in a heavy case, your purse in a light, yet you see how this world goes.
>
> *Gloucester:* I see it feelingly.
>
> (King Lear, Act 4, sc. 6, lines 141–45)

60. *The Road to Damascus: Kairos and Conversion*, a document signed by Third World Christians (Washington, D.C.: Center for Concern, 1989), makes this crystal clear: one cannot ally oneself for profit with those who are killing poor people and, by attending Sunday Mass, still think of oneself as a Christian and follower of Christ.

61. Hodgson, *God in History* (see chap. 7, n. 3) 193; see Karl Rahner, "The Inexhaustible Transcendence of God and Our Concern for the Future," *TI* 20: 173–86.

62. Welch, *A Feminist Ethic of Risk*, 182, n.13, who points out that this usage was coined as early as 1924 by Mary Parker Follett; also Joanna Rogers Macy, *Despair and Personal Power in the Nuclear Age* (Philadelphia: New Society Publishers, 1983).

63. Brock, *Journeys by Heart*, 27–35 and passim; Audre Lorde, "Uses of the Erotic: The Erotic as Power," in *Sister Outsider*, 53–59.

64. McFague, *Models of God* (see chap. 1, n. 12) 85.

65. Welch, *A Feminist Ethic of Risk*, 167–72; see also Carter Heyward, *Our Passion for Justice: Images of Power, Sexuality, and Liberation* (New York: Pilgrim Press, 1984).

66. Farley, *Tragic Vision*, 86. Most of these thinkers take note of Paul Tillich, *Love, Power and Justice* (New York: Oxford University Press, 1960), who integrates these three elements as different expressions of being, each working to make the others effective. Power in particular is the force of being against nonbeing. His synthesis is highly suggestive even while it does not analyze how power works specifically within patriarchy.

67. Carr, *Transforming Grace* (see chap. 1, n. 15) 145. Also Elizabeth Janeway, *Powers of the Weak* (New York: Morrow Quill Paperbacks, 1981); and Joan Chittister, *Job's Daughters: Women and Power* (New York: Paulist, 1990).

68. The principles of nonviolent resistance are not weak. They call for vigorous action but not for killing. For one example of their effectiveness, see Philip McManus and Gerald Schlabach, eds., *Relentless Persistence: Nonviolent Action in Latin America* (Santa Cruz, Calif.: New Society Publishers, 1990).

Index of Authors

Adam, Karl, 129, 293n.10
Allen, Paula Gunn, 132, 294n.20
Angelou, Maya, 246, 303n.1
Anselm of Canterbury, 7, 28, 102,
151, 203, 248, 276n.12, 281n.30,
290n.58, 295n.1, 299n.27, 303n.5
Aquinas, Thomas, 6, 7, 24, 25, 35,
45, 46, 104, 109, 110, 113–115,
117, 121, 128, 142, 145, 173, 174,
181, 195, 216, 224, 226, 227, 229,
230, 234, 236, 239, 242, 276n.11,
280n.18–20, 282n.46, 283n.6,
283n.8, 283n.11, 291n.13, 291n.15–
16, 292n.24, 292n.34, 293n.39,
293n.8, 294n.30–31, 295n.32–35,
295n.38, 297n.6, 297n.8, 297n.17,
299n.21, 299n.31, 300n.67, 301n.2,
301n.6, 301n.11, 301n.13, 302n.25,
302n.30, 302n.39–40, 305n.51
Aristotle, 23, 24, 174, 297n.8
Athanasius, 108
Augustine of Hippo, 7, 99, 105, 108,
110, 141, 145, 195, 202, 204,
205, 212, 216, 219, 227, 276n.12,
291n.2, 291n.10–12, 294n.28,
295n.37, 296n.14, 297n.2, 298n.8,
298n.11, 299n.23–25, 299n.28–29,
299n.32–33, 300n.59–63, 300n.68,
300n.71, 301n.72–73, 301n.9

Bachiega, Mario, 51, 284n.24
von Balthasar, Hans Urs, 111, 141,
163, 291n.5, 291n.8, 292n.21,
294n.28, 295n.3, 296n.25, 304n.17
Barth, Karl, 116, 129, 205–7, 209,
292n.27, 293n.9, 299n.35, 303n.14
Basil of Caesarea, 108, 295n.44
Boff, Leonardo, 52, 207, 208, 209,
284n.27–28, 294n.24, 296n.18,
299n.39, 301n.14, 305n.53
Bonhoeffer, Dietrich, 266–67,
305n.39, 306n.55

Børresen, Kari Elisabeth, 280n.18,
290n.57
Braun, F., 98, 290n.48
Brock, Rita Nakashima, 270n.4,
295n.4, 296n.18, 296n.23, 306n.63
Brown, Raymond, 81, 95, 288n.10,
288n.16, 289n.38, 290n.44, 290n.48
Buber, Martin, 43–44, 75, 283n.4–5,
287n.36, 302n.37
Buckley, Michael, 279n.6
Burrell, David, 291n.13, 292n.24,
301n.7, 302n.25
Bynum, Caroline Walker, 283n.10,
290n.58

Calvin, John, 39, 282n.54
Camus, Albert, 248
Carr, Anne, 8, 21, 223, 270, 276n.15–
16, 278n.2, 279n.12, 279n.14,
281n.40, 282n.57, 283n.19,
286n.25, 295n.4, 296n.10, 297n.29,
297n.10, 301n.79, 306n.67
Chopp, Rebecca, 5, 32, 42, 276n.8,
280n.15, 281n.38, 285n.3, 297n.15
Christ, Carol, 38, 277n.19, 278n.23,
282n.52, 286n.14
Chrysostom, John, 110
Clarke, W. Norris, 225, 301n.4–5
Clement of Alexandria, 107
Cobb, John B., 51, 278n.27, 284n.25
Collins, Adela Yarbro, 287n.4,
289n.42
Collins, Mary, 13, 276n.5, 278n.30,
280n.23
Congar, Yves, 48, 51, 129–30,
283n.17, 284n.26, 288n.24,
293n.11, 294n.16, 295n.2, 300n.40,
301n.76
Conn, Joann Wolski, 293n.2
Conn, Walter, 281n.40
Craighead, Meinrad, 42, 283n.1,
298n.23

Index of Subjects

Abba, 48, 79–82, 193, 208
analogy, 113, 115–17, 120, 131, 142, 173
androcentrism, 23–25, 42, 44, 48–50, 69, 152–54, 157
anthropology, bipolar, unipolar, multipolar, 154–56
atheism, 19–20, 236–37, 250

baptism, effects of, 31, 72–75, 162
being
  analogy of, 114
  and God, 13, 45, 120, 206, 210, 228, 231, 233, 236, 238–40, 247, 251, 265
  feminist metaphors for, 236–37, 240, 242–44, 246, 273
  philosophical idea of, 114, 201, 209–10, 236–39, 247
  theological idea of, 118, 210, 231, 236–40, 242, 247
birth, in metaphor for God, 101, 171–72, 175, 179–80, 185, 255–56, 259

Christ
  Jesus, 3, 35, 71–73, 85, 140, 150–52, 161–62, 167, 180, 213, 234–35, 264
  whole community, 72–73, 161–62, 263–64
Christa, 74, 163, 264
Christology
  doctrine of, 35, 107, 151–54, 164–65, 167, 198
  problem of, 35, 71–72, 107–8, 151–54
conversion, 14, 29, 62–65, 67, 70, 75

disciples, women, 157–60
divine nature, a communion, 196, 207–8, 218, 220–23, 227–28, 273
dualism
  between God and world, 138, 147, 222, 224, 228, 230–31
  gender, 51–54, 70, 154–57, 174
  metaphysical, 69, 132, 225, 242
  within the self, 69, 132

ecology, 69, 136, 166, 183, 210
equality
  as feminist value, 31–32, 211, 223
  in trinitarian relations, 195–97, 211, 214–16, 218–22, 246, 273

father, as metaphor for God, 35–36, 47–48, 79, 81, 119, 153, 172–73, 175, 177, 193, 282n.57. *See also* Abba
feminist critique
  of impassibility, 69, 246–47, 249, 252–53, 267–68
  of non-relational God, 69, 140–41, 149, 225–27, 231, 233
  of omnipotence, 21, 252, 269–70
  of patriarchal God, 36–41, 112–13, 122–23, 149, 152, 252–53
  of patriarchal Trinity, 193, 196–97, 247–48
  of suffering God, 252–54, 267
feminist ethics, 67–69, 184–85, 259–60
feminist theology, 8–11, 17–22, 28–33, 36–42, 132–33, 184, 201, 252–53, 265